STAGES OF THOUGHT

STAGES OF THOUGHT

The Co-Evolution of Religious
Thought and Science

Michael Horace Barnes

OXFORD
UNIVERSITY PRESS

2000

OXFORD
UNIVERSITY PRESS

Oxford   New York
Athens   Auckland   Bangkok   Bogotá   Buenos Aires   Calcutta
Cape Town   Chennai   Dar es Salaam   Delhi   Florence   Hong Kong   Istanbul
Karachi   Kuala Lumpur   Madrid   Melbourne   Mexico City   Mumbai
Nairobi   Paris   São Paulo   Singapore   Taipei   Tokyo   Toronto   Warsaw

and associated companies in
Berlin   Ibadan

Copyright © 2000 by Michael Horace Barnes

Published by Oxford University Press, Inc.
198 Madison Avenue, New York, New York 10016

Oxford is a registered trademark of Oxford University Press

Library of Congress Cataloging-in-Publication Data
Barnes, Michael Horace.
    Stages of thought : the co-evolution of religious
thought and science / Michael H. Barnes.
      p.   cm.
    ISBN 0-19-513389-7
    1. Religion and science.   2. Religion and science—History.
I. Title.
BL240.2.B384   2000
291.1′75—dc21   99-23759

9   8   7   6   5   4   3   2   1

Printed in the United States of America
on acid-free paper

PREFACE

More than 20 years ago, when I first began to explore the ideas described here about long-term cultural cognitive development, half of the sources listed in the bibliography had not yet been written. So the research for this book was partly a process of reviewing older materials, but it was equally an ongoing process of keeping up with new materials. For a while, as postmodern relativism gained popularity, the scholarly currents were flowing against any attempts to identify large-scale cross-cultural similarities. "Thick descriptions" of individual cultures, one at a time, was the ideal. Nonetheless, even in these studies of individual cultures, it seemed to me that I could find similarities in the cognitive styles among otherwise quite different cultures. Fortunately for my peace of mind, books identifying cross-cultural patterns have been on the increase. I have drawn upon many of them in both the Introduction and Chapter 1.

Nonetheless, these years of research have given me a consciousness of my limitations for the task of this book, which is to describe human cognitive behavior across cultures and through human history. That is a lot for one person to cover. It is possible only by relying on numerous secondary sources, which in turn creates the risk of unwittingly accepting biased or distorted interpretations. I have tried to compensate for that risk by sampling many relevant primary sources, reading Mohist texts, the principal Upanishads, Bernard Silvester's cosmology, Newton's Scholia, and so on. But this is only sampling, and most in translation, another potential source of error. So I suspect that many a scholar will find it easy to point out errors and omissions in that scholar's area of expertise.

What I can best hope for from the scholarly experts in fields not my own is a willingness to try out the thesis offered here about cultural cognitive developments; to treat it as an interesting hypothesis worth exploring, to consider the evidence that makes the hypothesis at least plausible. Whatever survives such consideration might contribute significantly to our awareness of what is common to the human family, what we share in spite of our many differences, what kinds of development might be available to human societies everywhere, if those forms of development seem more advantageous than not.

ACKNOWLEDGMENTS

I have piled up many intellectual debts and many not so intellectual. Special credit should go to James Fowler's work. The analysis of individual faith development he provides in *Stages of Faith* has proved to be an excellent heuristic tool for cultural analysis also. Likewise, Robert Bellah's article "Religious Evolution" provided a succinct guide to interpreting the development of religions through time.

On a more personal level, I celebrate the years of argumentative friendship with Dennis Doyle. An expert on Bernard Lonergan, among other things, he made me hone my thoughts as we jogged or walked. He is not, however, to blame for what I think. A summer's work with Dennis and Byron Johnson gave me a chance to field-test Fowler's categories of faith development. It also gave me a taste of how enjoyable (and sometimes hilarious) social research can be with the right colleagues.

The University of Dayton has provided support in many ways, including summer grants and a convivial atmosphere. Chairpersons, from the now venerable Matt Kohmescher to Jim Heft and Tom Martin, have all been very good to work with. The current chairperson and good friend, Terry Tilley, provides continuing support and perceptive criticism. Thanks go also to the members of the DGDG, a long-standing, wine-sipping, scholarly discussion group, which has included Una Cadegan, Jack McGrath, Sandy Yocum Mize, Doyle, Heft, and Terry and Maureen Tilley. Some of these criticized parts of the manuscript, Gary Macy a chapter, Doyle most of it, Stephen Happel an early version, and Terry Tilley all of it. None of them is to blame either for the outcome.

Gratitude is due also to colleagues who have used my introductory text, *In the Presence of Mystery*, and have passed along to me their own thoughts about it or those of their students. It interprets religions through Bellah's evolutionary perspective, so it is a trial run of a sort on a major aspect of this present work. Rita Vasquez (Bowen) in particular— but also Mary Lou Baker Jones and Steve Ostovich—have provided very useful feedback, and in Rita's case, lessons on how to be a good teacher.

There are too many wonderful University of Dayton students to name, but some must be named anyway. Thanks to Jeff Rahl, scientist and friend, for his critical review of chapter 9. He will someday be writing his own defense of the scientific method. Thanks also to Eric Laurenson, artist-physicist at home with the mystical, who critiqued the whole manuscript from the viewpoint of a non-scholarly reader. A generation of student housemates have contributed much also. The Reilly-O'Keeffe connection and the Kevin Pahl road tours have proved especially endur- ing. I am grateful also for Don Wiebe's supportiveness.

It has been good to work with the professionals at Oxford University Press, from senior editor Cynthia Read and her assistants Nine Sherwin and Theo Calderara to the exceedingly careful production editor Lisa Stallings. And at home base, the University of Dayton, ongoing apprecia- tion is due for the daily support provided by administrative assistant Car- olyn Ludwig. Special thanks to Sarah Utaski, a cheerful master of pa- tience and exactitude, for her work on the bibliography and index, to Dan Smith, Carolyn, and Sarah for careful proofreading, and to Andrew Knight and Carol Farrell for their office aid. Final thanks to Kathryn Jane Kharas who suggested this whole wildly ambitious project many years ago, and to Carol Ann Heller, whose friendship has kept me going.

CONTENTS

STAGES OF THOUGHT

INTRODUCTION

This is a history of the human search for methods to determine which ideas about the world are true. More precisely, it is about the search for methods of determining factual truth about the world, not about what is sometimes called moral truth or aesthetic truth. Morals and aesthetics matter greatly, but they are not the main focus here. The focus is on the various methods religious thinkers and scientific inquirers have used to try to distinguish truth from error. The history of such attempts turns out to have a developmental pattern. This pattern puts current arguments about methods of knowledge in an intelligible and useful perspective.

Because I work in the field of religion and science, I have long been concerned with the truth-claims made by both religions and the sciences, as well as with the methods for judging whether those truth-claims are true. It was in this context, more than twenty years ago, that I was rereading some material by Piaget on cognitive development. At about the same time I first read Robert Bellah's essay "Religious Evolution." Though Bellah focused mostly on the content of religious beliefs, he also noted some differences in the methods or modes of thought in the different stages of religious development. Bellah's descriptions of the sequence of modes of thought in various religions, and in the cultures in which these religions flourished, matched fairly well with Piaget's categories of individual cognitive development. Rather naive at that point about the history of arguments in anthropology about cultural evolution, I started spending time in the library hunting down sources that might tell me more about this matchup.

There was relatively little available. I discovered Piaget himself had

3

occasionally ventured to compare individual and cultural development, but backed off from the topic. A few studies in anthropology offered some supportive evidence, but mostly indirectly. Talcott Parsons's *The Evolution of Societies* described a developmental pattern in cultural change that in turn was used by Niklas Luhmann in Germany.[1] Since Parsons and Bellah had once taught a course together on this, it was not surprising that their outlines were highly similar. James Peacock and A. Thomas Kirsch's *The Human Direction* nicely fleshed out the Parsons and Bellah theory with further illustrations.[2] But in general, Piagetian interpretations of cultural evolution were conspicuous by their absence. So I presented a small paper on this at the 1980 American Academy of Religion annual meeting, seeking leads to further sources. The reaction at the meeting was mild and unfruitful.

Still interested, I kept running across other theories of cultural development that were at least consistent with a Piagetian interpretation of history. The Soviet anthropologist Lev Vygotsky proposed that individual cognitive development might have its parallel in cultural development.[3] Vygotsky's student Alexander Luria agreed, emphasizing the importance of cultural invention to provide new cognitive tools. Luria and Vygotsky suggest that the logical and analytical thinking taught in formal schooling may not be a "natural" stage in individual development, as Piaget thought.[4] We humans may all share in a *capacity* to learn this cognitive style. But the many years of training required to become skillful in it implies it is not something to which we are naturally inclined, as we are, for example, to learn to speak a language. Whereas Piaget described mainly a growth of internal and innate capacities in interaction with the environment, Vygotsky gave more credit to the cultural context. Nonetheless, Vygotsky's description of the sequence of cognitive skills matches well enough with Piagetian descriptions of individual cognitive stages.

There are other theories of cultural development that fit well with Piagetian stages. Haydn White proposes a Piagetian reading of Western history, using literary tropes as guides.[5] Bernard Lonergan argues that over the centuries Christian theology went through three stages, from common sense to rational analysis to modern critical method. These nicely parallel the three final stages of Piagetian development.[6] In 1981 James Fowler published his *Stages of Faith*.[7] His summary of individual faith development includes a cognitive dimension that matches up well with Lonergan's historical analysis. His formulations are based not just on theories but also on extensive and carefully scored interviews. After some years of relative quiet on the topic, Fowler has recently interpreted pre-Enlightenment, Enlightenment, and post-Enlightenment thought styles as a sequence similar to his own Piagetian interpretation of individual development.[8] Richard H. Schlagel also uses Piaget to explicate the differences he sees between mythic thought and the kind of development represented by Parmenides' law of contradiction and Aristotle's formal logic. Schlagel speculates that the differences in thought styles in children, depending on their stage of development, might be true of humankind in general.[9] Kieran Egan has articulated a clear similarity between the stages of types of thought in school-age children and the development of thought styles in cultural history. He follows Vygotsky in arguing that later stages are much more dependent on culture than on innate tendencies.[10]

Most of these studies have a European focus, which raises the suspicion that the Piagetian developmental pattern is entirely a product of western European culture. But the Siberian tribespeople with whom Luria and Vygotsky worked had a culture with clearly non-European roots. Moreover, I was already finding evidence of a Piagetian pattern in non-Western cultures. Later chapters here will provide extensive references on this.

I continued to read anthropological literature in particular, as well as historical studies of moments of shift in thought styles in several cultures, including China and India, and prepared a more substantial paper for a Midwestern conference. At a "history of religions" section, I briefly presented aspects of the pattern as I then saw it, describing overall cultural evolution but with an emphasis on changes in cognitive skills or habits. Human beings are first of all language-using hominids. From our earliest life as *Homo sapiens*, we have used language to name and interpret and govern our life. Eventually, the neolithic agricultural revolution made it possible for thousands of people to live together in more complex societies. Beliefs about powerful gods appeared as the society of the numinous echoed the human society in which a few people of great power lorded it over many others.

Then in the fourth millennium BCE in Sumer (perhaps also in Egypt), literacy appeared. Other cultures inherited and improved upon Sumerian writing or invented their own. Literacy changes the human world by enabling people to encode and preserve ideas, to transmit them to far-away strangers, to leave them to later generations, to accumulate thoughts for comparison. In the sixth century BCE, give or take a couple hundred years either way, several major cultures took another step into reflectively explicit logic. In the classical eras of China, India, and Greece, a literate elite began to include those who explicitly tested the logical relations among their ideas, seeking an overall coherence. With this came also the idea of a single universal Whole, in the form of the cosmos, the Tao, Brahman, God, or other ultimate single principles. Intellectuals in these societies argued over the difference between the "real truth" and mere opinion or tradition.

Almost as soon as the desire for universal and reliable logical knowledge appeared, so did a form of skepticism. Our ideas are *our ideas*, said the skeptics, not eternal and perfect truth. Skeptics in China, India, and Greece pointed to the fallible character of human knowing. It was not until recent centuries, however, that European thinkers stumbled across a set of methods for applying some of this skepticism and getting reliable knowledge out of it. The classical search for logical and certain truth was then modified by the semiskeptical methods of modern science, which demands that every plausible theory be subjected to ongoing and publicly shared testing and application to see how well it really works in practice.

This outline seemed to me to be rather unexceptional. The history of religious thought in particular was clearly a history of development of the content of beliefs, their mode of expression, and the style of thought, from primitive uncritical stories about spirits and magic, to a more complex set of mythological narratives about great gods, to a later, more abstract belief in a single universal and unifying Ultimate, and perhaps then to a modern self-consciousness about all such beliefs as human interpretations. Other pieces of the picture had long been appearing in various scholarly sources, many of which will be reviewed and analyzed in these pages.

By this time the faces of those I was addressing at the Midwestern meeting were strangely still, even stony. I continued. There is a rough parallel, I claimed, between the Piagetian stages and the pattern of cultural development. According to Piaget, we begin as children by categorizing and lumping ideas together in small stories or narratives. As we get older, we take more care to distinguish between stories about Santa Claus and information we learn in school about Thailand or other strange places, to establish which is merely a story and which is true. By the age of twelve we begin to develop competence in formal logical analysis, leading to the great challenge of high school algebra and geometry. In adolescence we rejoice in the dogmatic certitudes we grasp with our intelligence, but as we get older and more experienced, we develop a somewhat skeptical caution about truth-claims, no matter how intelligent the argument. Language, literacy, logic, and a degree of reflexive skepticism emerge roughly in that order in the life of individuals and cultures. This comparison is inexact and incomplete, too brief to be clear yet. Not all individuals follow the same path of development, and cultures ride bumpy roads as they move along. It will take the contents of several chapters to describe the parallels in cultural and individual development more accurately. But this is approximately the outline I presented to the Midwest meeting.

The reaction this time was anything but mild. It was my first clear experience with postmodern political correctness. One of the listeners offered this succinct criticism: "For shame, Michael!" Other listeners gave more precise objections: Any theory of cultural development nominates some types of culture for the role of the less developed and others for the more developed. If cultural development is supposed to parallel individual development, then the cultures called less developed are being compared to children. This is a dangerous continuation of colonialist attitudes that have caused much suffering. Moreover, a theory of cultural development based on Piaget uses the standards of Western science to judge cognitive development. A theory that has arisen in one's own culture, Piaget's in this case, is given the privilege of judging the other cultures. This is another instance of "Western hegemonic discourse." More about these objections will appear in later chapters.

As the chapters to follow will argue, however, there is a lot of evidence that cultures do develop certain thought styles or cognitive methods in an identifiable, albeit sometimes uneven, sequence. Nonetheless, the objections should make us hesitate. Are there good grounds for developing another theory of cultural development, no matter how much evidence, when this runs the risk of arrogant and harmful error? We human beings obviously differ from each other in important ways. We live in specific societies, and each society may have its own values and practices and beliefs, and each such set of values and practices and beliefs may deserve a hearing on its own terms. Each of us also differs individually from others in our own society. Learning to accept "otherness" and to respect the "other," as we say now, is healthy and constructive.

A major reason to learn to accept and respect the other, however, is that beneath all our differences, we also share a common humanness. We should be concerned to discover everything that might allow us to understand each other better, including any patterns of development that may influence both individuals and cultures. Out of this we may find a few more things that bind us together in our common humanness.[11] We all learn to communicate through complex languages. We construct meanings and process information with the same kind of brain. We all interpret reality through stories.[12] We are all born able to learn to write. If there are a few basic thought styles that are fairly natural to humans, or if there are culturally created useful thought styles for which people in general have some aptitude, this is well worth attending to, because it tells us what we already share, or it tells us what we can teach one another, or it helps to make sense of our differences so that we can appreciate those differences with greater sympathy.

Interaction among cultures might be made smoother through greater understanding of similarities and differences in cognitive style. Some cultures are similar to one another in that they rely on certain Piagetian cognitive styles more than other cultures. Both Japanese and Americans use logically structured approaches to major aspects of life, and tradition-oriented chauvinism toward other aspects. Both the Confucian tradition and the Marxist theory in China are alike as attempts to structure society as a whole, but different in their approach to the value of tradition as an authority. Within any single culture, different cognitive styles coexist. They can illuminate human relations within a culture to recognize patterns in such differences, so we can deal with them deliberately and intelligently. There is very much still to be learned about us humans. If the picture of cognitive styles to be drawn here is at all accurate, we should address it, not avoid it. Until we humans stop causing one another great pain, we need to keep learning about ourselves, including patterns in how we think.

The charges of renewed colonialism should still be taken quite seriously. For one thing, they warn us against simplistic notions of "primitive" or premodern ways of life. In childhood we form our first images of paleolithic culture or the hunter-gatherer forms of life. Comic books and bad movies portray Stone Age people as semihuman, and current foraging cultures as menacing savages. Anthropologists, by contrast, learn from their prolonged stays among primitive people that once the language barrier is overcome, once the odd food and ritual become normal, the people turn out to be surprisingly like small-town neighbors. The people are as intelligent as humans in general; they share in laughter and anger and tears; they apply traditional construction techniques intelligently; they find ways to head off a fight; they learn how to brew some sort of beer and have a good party now and then.[13] Yet for all that, they are still "primitive" in various ways. As foragers, they must normally live in relatively small groups and move from encampment to encampment as they exhaust local resources. They do not have the option of city life, for better or for worse. Limited in technology, they must live intimately with the discomfort of fleas, lice, mosquitoes, and biting flies, with diseases that kill half the children before the age of ten. Lacking literacy, they do not have the option of tracking their own history over many hundreds of years to reflect on the many major changes of that history, or to choose what to reappropriate from the past. Many aspects of their lives are bound by limitations that they themselves are happy to overcome, with the help of steel axes, outboard motors, penicillin, and books for their children. It is not colonialism to observe all this.

The Plausibility of a Parallel between Individual and Cultural Development

A simpler objection to the idea of a parallel between cultural and individual development is to point to the sheer improbability of it. Piaget described stages of cognitive (and moral) development from infancy to adulthood. His theory of development is concerned mainly with children. But every culture is dominated by adults, not children. These adults have already had their own full history of cognitive development. Adult humans everywhere share in the same basic human genetic inheritance, including the same innate intelligence. Perhaps, as Jared Diamond argues, indigenous people may be more intelligent than others. The natives of New Guinea, a people typically categorized as primitive, have often suffered severe malnutrition, which might well hurt brain development. But this kind of harm occurs to brains, not to genes. Such periods might also be the time when harsh conditions "select" the brightest to survive, producing greater innate intelligence. Certainly the children of New Guinea grow up today to pilot great commercial aircraft and use computers well.[14] Diamond may or may not be correct about the innate intellectual superiority of natives of New Guinea. But the general point remains: strong innate human intelligence is everywhere evident in the world. Differences among cultures in cognitive style are learned differences.

It therefore seems difficult to make sense of a claim that differences in cognitive style among cultures are parallel to differences in individual cognitive development. It is easy to suspect that such parallels appear only to a Western mind biased in favor of habits of thought familiar in the Western industrialized nations. It would help alleviate suspicion of bias if it were at least initially plausible that something so odd as a parallel between individual cognitive development and the sequence of cognitive styles in culture could occur.

In fact there is a fairly simple explanation of how this parallel could occur. It has two main components. The first is that an easier style or method of thought is mastered more quickly and thoroughly than difficult ones. The second is that, as both Vygotsky and Egan have argued, at least some of the more difficult thought that humans engage in does not come naturally, as we say, but requires a cultural context which has first created or adopted new and more difficult cognitive techniques, and which then schools and rewards people for learning to use this more difficult kind of thought.

The cognitive tasks a young child can master are simpler than those that an adolescent can master, which in turn are simpler than those only a young adult can master. The same sequence of tasks seems to appear in the history of a culture's development. Cultures first learn the easier skills; the harder ones take longer to master. This is especially true because the harder ones often require first the creation of cognitive technology, like writing or formal logic, and then also require the creation of social institutions, such as years of formal schooling or tutoring, to train some people to become adept in the use of this cognitive technology.

Through our own long years of formal schooling we have become used to many difficult cognitive tools. Because we no longer recognize the subtlety of methods to which we have become accustomed, we are tempted to think, mistakenly, that the people of any culture could readily use those methods if they wanted. Then we conclude that to announce the absence of certain methods in a culture is somehow to insult the people of that culture, as though they had to be of limited intelligence not to do what we take for granted. Once again, it is not a lack of intelligence that limits primitive or other people in their cognitive methods; it is instead the particular history of this or that group which made it unnecessary to develop or adopt those methods. A primitive community will find little need to invent or learn long division, for example. In China it took centuries to develop the classics to which Confucius appealed, and more centuries to develop traditions of analyzing those classics. In India centuries of orally transmitted ritual songs preceded the written Vedas and then the major Upanishads and their philosophical reflections. In Egypt centuries of use built up a body of geometric practices, which Greek thinkers could then formalize into a system.

Cognitive Developments as Progress

Confucian classics and Vedic commentaries and formal geometry represent progress *if* one values such things. Whether such values are valid is not easy to address briefly. A person who places high value on relative simplicity and closeness to nature may judge that it is regressive rather than progressive to move from simple counting to higher math, or from traditional kin relations to Confucian social order. But the pattern of development may well exist, whether any of us find it valuable or not. The chapters that follow will attempt to establish what in fact has occurred in history in the development of several cultures. I value those developments, as it happens. But if I am wrong on the *value* of what has occurred, I still may be correct on what in *fact* has occurred. That can be judged at least partly on the basis of the information and argument in this book.

The long-term cultural process of the development of thought styles does not appear inevitable, although in retrospect one can understand why it could occur as it has. It is not a lockstep pattern of progress, but has its ups and downs. In individual development, a child grows from infancy through adulthood in stages that are quite consistent, one after another in a rather predictable path. Adulthood never precedes early adolescence. But a culture can gain and then lose skills in certain cognitive techniques. The Early Middle Ages in the western Mediterranean area, and the collapse of the Harrapan culture in the Indus River valley much earlier, are instances.[15] The actual history of major cultures of the world nonetheless manifests a strikingly similar pattern of development of cognitive skills and techniques, a pattern that echoes the path of individual cognitive development. The long uphill struggle of culture, however winding and strange the paths, has in several cases moved from the use of language, to literacy, to formalized logic, and even to an awkward reflexivity. That is what this book will explore.

A source of further complexity in perceiving specific stages of culture is that we do not leave our past behind, either individually or culturally. It is likely to be all muddled together in any individual. The earliest humans alive seem to have believed in many spirit beings. The spirits are still popular, as ancestors or ghosts, as visitors through channeling or séances (or as UFO pilots). The gods have not left us either. In some places like India they are explicitly reverenced as gods; in others they have been replaced by great angels or demons or godlike saints. Various classical theologies also remain vibrant in many religious traditions; they still engage in systematic analyses of the nature of the Ultimate and how one may relate to it. Much reflexive thought in the West has been atheistic, at least since Nietzsche. But there are also current reflexive theologies that take much of their religious heritage as tradition worth accepting and reinterpreting. In order to see each of the different thought styles as it emerged, the following chapters will sift carefully through the history of some major world cultures.

Religious Thought and Science

Since the eighteenth century there have been various theories of cultural development, often under the name of cultural evolution. Auguste Comte's nineteenth-century theory is a well-known instance.[16] According to Comte, the infancy of human culture was "theological." Primitive people worshipped invisible beings whose actions explained events in the world. The adolescence of human culture was the classical era of ancient philosophy. People learned to think logically and construct systematic theories of why things are as they are. Modern "positive" (empirical) science represents the maturity of culture. People have learned that only the interplay of theory with extensive evidence will provide reliable truth. Comte believed that each stage of culture builds upon what preceded it rather than replaces it. Any society except the most primitive is likely to be cumulatively layered. Comte thought that most people in his time continued in the "theological" mode of thought, even while many of the more learned perpetuated the theorizing of the philosophical mode; a few, like Comte, had made the leap forward into empirical science.

More nuanced versions of Comte's thesis have appeared in works by Donald Wiebe and by Stewart Guthrie. Wiebe reviews the shift in ancient Greece from mythological thought to philosophical-scientific, and argues that this is a shift away from religion to rationality.[17] Guthrie identifies religious belief as a form of anthropomorphizing to which we are genetically inclined, regardless of how irrational it now may often be, and which we can now recognize as such and, perhaps, leave behind.[18]

There is much to criticize in Comtean theories, particularly the supposed primitiveness of all religious thought. I will argue that the Comteans are partly correct: there has indeed been a somewhat patterned development of modes of thought through stages of cultural development. Comte was not correct, however, in restricting religious thought to the "infancy" of culture. Religious thought developed right along with overall cultural development. There is a "linguistic" form of religious thought, as Comte recognized, expressed in folktales of nonliterate people, in the form of animism and early polytheism. There is also the "literate" religious thought of the great polytheisms with their elaborate mythologies. Comte restricts "theological" thought to these linguistic and early literary forms. Contrary to Comte, however, there is also "logical" religious thought in the form of philosophical religiousness. Vedantic philosophy is clearly religious; so are Stoic philosophy, Philo's Hellenistic Judaism, and many other formally theologized ways to relate to the ultimate single order of things envisaged by the classical religions. A chapter will be devoted to this point.

The relatively recent arrival of the more reflexive method of public empirical testing that we call modern science has been a major challenge to traditional religion, whether in linguistic and literate or logical form or all three. Religious thinkers have developed various responses. Many speaking from within a religious commitment have decided to exempt religion from scientific rationality. They assert that religion and science are so distinctively different that religion sacrifices its soul when it submits to the demands of scientific rationality. Some versions of this exemptive strategy are severely traditionalist or "fundamentalist," formulated by Jews and Christians and Muslims who insist on the primacy of divine revelation over any human critical abilities.[19] There are more sophisticated versions of exemptive strategies. Friedrich Schleiermacher's nineteenth-century defense of a liberal Protestant religion identified it entirely with inner feeling or intuition, insisting that it was in no way derived from philosophical or rational analysis.[20] Mircea Eliade placed the foundation of religion in a unique experience of the Sacred, one that was intrinsically nonrational, as Rudolph Otto had said before him.[21] The Jesuit Michael Buckley, whose theological analyses are highly rational, provides a detailed historical argument that religion made an enormous mistake when it tried to ground itself in Enlightenment scientific rationality.[22] George Lindbeck proposes that religious beliefs be interpreted as cultural-linguistic unifiers and guides, not as objective and universally valid truth-claims.[23] Perhaps the extreme nonrationalist version of religion is Norman Malcolm's. He insists that religious faith is "groundless," certainly not dependent on rationality and evidence.[24]

While there are valid aspects to some of these interpretations, it is dangerous to loosen the ties of religion to the rational. In the extreme this runs the risk of Jonestown, Guiana, and Waco, Texas. It runs the milder risk of sustaining belief in medically unreliable healing methods or in "scientific creationism," or in organizing one's entire life to await the imminent end of the world. The historical analysis in the chapters that follow will try to show ways in which the use of rationality in religion has proved to be valuable.

Moreover, scientific rationality has had unavoidable affects on religion. Buckley, Otto, and Schleiermacher accept what were once serious changes in religious belief, changes made in order to conform to scientific standards that their culture developed. None of these three people, to use obvious examples, retains the old beliefs that illness and insanity are caused by demons or that the sun orbits the Earth. The "reflexive" character of modern science has also induced religious thinkers to produce several modern forms of theological method. These include the theologies called liberal, neo-orthodox, existential, correlational, and, most recently, postliberal. The last chapter will discuss this effect of science on religious thought.

Relativism and Truth

Serious values are at stake in the search for patterns of cognitive development in history. The first is the value of searching for general truths about human habits, tendencies, and potentials. Postmodern thought has taken up cultural relativism with glee and dedication, to the point where human commonalities are ignored. In the short run, this is driven by a desire to teach respect for every "other" we encounter. But in the long run, covering over our common humanness subverts efforts to promote respect for every person everywhere just because each person is human. Also at stake is the general value of truth-seeking. Deeply postmodern thinkers may view this goal as a remnant of outmoded Enlightenment thinking. Truth is contextual, they say. There is no objective and universally valid set of truth-claims, and no objective and universally valid method for establishing the validity of truth-claims. Each community is a form of life with its own language game. Each community, including each religious community, can only do its best to be truthful by the standards of that community, even if those who belong to other communities, such as the scientific community, reject those standards. Religions do not have to allow the scientific community to determine religious beliefs or influence the method of knowing used by religious people. So says postmodern thought.

But the success of the method of science runs contrary to this postmodern strategy to keep religion safe from science. The success of science is limited. It is not just that science does not know everything, though that is certainly true. The method of science is limited to evaluating truth-claims about how things are in the universe. The scientific method is useless for determining what basic values it ought to follow in selecting projects to pursue or in applying the results of its efforts. If by "science" we mean not the application of scientific method but instead all the activities of various communities of scientists, then "science" can be a dreadful failure at making such decisions. Only philosophy or theology or wisdom can determine what use to make of the method of science. But the method remains quite powerful for its limited goal of adjudicating truth-claims about how things are in the world. Religion does not serve either itself or humankind well by seeking to evade the effectiveness of science in truth-seeking. Some theologians have recognized that and have produced theological methods that allows religion and science to live cooperatively together. But there is a story to be told before we get to those theologians. They are at the current end of a long, long process of the evolution of cognitive methods in religious thought and science.

1

CULTURE AND COGNITION

The previous chapter provided a quick introduction to the general thesis of this book about cultural evolution.[1] This chapter will describe that thesis in more detail. This is partly to provide a clearer framework for the historical chapters, which make up the bulk of this work. It is partly to provide background for understanding and evaluating the material in the following chapter, which is an analysis of major criticisms relevant to the thesis.

Forms of Cultural Development

All cultures change over time, of course. The word "development" is meant to imply that some changes form a identifiable sequential pattern.[2] In spite of ongoing criticism of theories of cultural development during the twentieth century, many excellent studies continued to appear with data and analysis in support of such development.

There are sequential stages of economic development, from hunting-gathering, to horticulture or pastoral life, to full-scale agriculture, and then to commercial-industrial forms of subsistence. There are stages of social order, from "acephalous" tribal life, to hierarchically ordered class societies with authoritarian leaders, to groups with the concept and practices of citizenship. Such patterns are clear enough. From a survey of numerous cross-cultural studies, David Levinson and Martin Malone provide a list of seven measures of cultural complexity that have been validated as reliable measures of socioeconomic-political-cognitive patterns of development.[3] This material offers measurable criteria of various kinds

15

and shows a consistent and empirically clear pattern of change in cultures that fit well with the synthesis of cultural and individual development theories that will be offered here.

There is likewise a pattern of cultural development in cognitive styles, though the evidence for this is scattered among a number of different kinds of studies. The impact of literacy as a particular cognitive tool has been examined by Jack Goody, Walter Ong, and others, we will discuss in as chapter 4. The axial age transition to universalist and formally systematic thought in several cultures has been the object of various studies. One such transition, from Homeric to classical Greek culture, has been analyzed from multiple perspectives. An occasional book has focused on other specific moments of cognitive change in a culture, such as the shift from early to late medieval thought in Europe, as in Don LePan's 1989 study, *The Cognitive Revolution in Western Culture*. Other books mentioned in the introduction cover larger patterns in cognitive development, such as Merlin Donald's *The Origins of the Modern Mind*, which begins with chimpanzees, and Kieran Egan's analysis of the sequence of modes of thought as background for his recommendations for changes in educational practices today.[4] Ernest Gellner's description of the intellectual aspect of human development in his *Plough, Sword, and Book* fits snugly with the Piagetian-style outline to be provided here.[5] Scattered as they are over many aspects of cultural cognitive development, these works add up to rich resources on the topic. We will examine these sources in the course of the book.

There are many studies on stages of religious belief, from animism to polytheism to universalism, or from local to national to universalist beliefs. Robert Bellah, sharing some language with Talcott Parsons, identifies primitive, archaic, historic, early modern, and modern stages of religion.[6] Parsons shares Emile Durkheim's interest in seeing how religions justify and uphold the social order. Parsons is relatively silent about modern religion inasmuch as various secular ideologies have partly come to replace this public function of religion. Bellah, however, identifies, at least very briefly, a modern form of religious thought. For simplicity I will speak of only four stages of religious thought, accepting Bellah's suggestion that his "early modern" stage is a time of transition, not necessarily a distinct stage in itself. The names for these stages here will be primitive, archaic, classical (rather than "historic"), and modern. The developmental history of religious thought styles, mainly in the West but also in China and India, echoes larger shifts in cognitive methods. Finally, there are numerous histories of science and the scientific method. Some focus on "Western" culture by beginning with ancient Babylon and Egypt. Others, such as Joseph Needham's great history of Chinese science, include other cultures of the world. We will examine these and many other sources as we proceed.

A General Thesis

The general thesis of this book has two major aspects. The first is that cultural development has often included the development of new and more complex styles of thinking and expression that affect religion, science, and other locales of thought. The second is that some of these developments echo the pattern of individual cognitive development as described by Jean Piaget. This general thesis can be articulated more fully in the following seven points.

1. There are different fundamental styles of thinking, different cognitive techniques, each recognizable in the way it manifests itself in daily work, in religious beliefs and thought forms, in scientific approaches, in philosophical reasoning, and in other cognitive activities.
2. The more difficult of these styles of thinking will appear only later in any individual's development because of a need for experience, training, and continuing brain maturation.[7]
3. Piaget's description of the sequence of development of major cognitive skills is a fairly accurate guide to the basic styles of thinking that people learn as they develop.
4. A culture may maintain a simpler, easier style of thought as its dominant style for many centuries or even millennia, even if some individuals go beyond the culture's general achievement. (The simplest style may function as the common denominator of general social communication, among children and adults, the learned and unlearned, the very bright and the mentally slow.)
5. Though people everywhere share in the same basic human intelligence, some cultures have discovered cognitive tools to promote more complex and difficult cognitive styles, and to educate an increasing number of people in their use.
6. The most difficult cognitive styles are skills mastered in any culture only by a relative few (for whatever reasons) who nonetheless have significant impact on the general nature of the culture.
7. The actual history of religious thought in major cultures exhibits a sequence of development of thought styles suggested by the prior six points, a development in which science has shared.

This general pattern of development of religious thought as part of larger cultural development does not exclude moments of individual creative thought. In the 14th century BCE, Amenhotep IV of Egypt renamed himself Ikhnaton and proclaimed the lone supremacy of the sun god, Aton. Were he not the pharaoh, his rejection of traditional gods in favor of his god Aton would have been ignored as simple foolishness, or condemned as dangerous. In either case we might never have heard of this strange approach to monotheism long before clear monotheism appeared in other places in the world. In every culture there have undoubtedly been many innovators whose ideas and methods of thought galloped far in front of others of their times. But if the culture does not have the language and social structure publicly to support ideas of a new level of complexity or sophistication, then the thinking of the innovators will likely go unnoticed, be rejected, or revised into simplicity.

The pattern of cultural development identified here would not be so evident were there not a prior theory, that of Piaget, to guide the empirical search. A theory influences the selection and interpretation of evidence, and may distort the resulting conclusions. Caution is appropriate. The evidence that the pattern exists should be strong. The evidence will also be more plausible if there is some reasonable explanation why that pattern should exist. I am offering here a rather simple explanation: easier forms of thought precede more difficult forms of thought in both individual and cultural development. It remains possible, however, to identify a pattern accurately, without being able to explain why that pattern exists. Newton was rather certain about the pattern of attraction between physical bodies; he did not have a very good explanation of why that pattern should be as it is. The attempts made here to explain why the pattern of cognitive development exists may be wrong, partly or entirely. Even so, that may leave the fact of the pattern still there, still supported (or not) by the same evidence (or lack of it). The chapters in this book represent an attempt to marshal a great deal of evidence for the existence of the pattern of development.

By the end of this book these categories and their interrelations should be clear. For the moment, however, we can provide an initial account of three main points, to serve as a guide in reading the subsequent chapters. The first point is Piaget's theory of individual cognitive development. The second is a description of cultural development that focuses primarily on cognitive changes, in both religion and science, rather than economic or political or social changes. The third is a summary of the changes in religious and scientific thought that are part of both individual and cultural development. This chapter will give a general description of these three components. (The next chapter will address some major criticisms of them.)

A Piagetian Description of Stages
of Cognitive Development

History is complex and uneven. It is always a bit artificial to interpret it according to some large-scale pattern. The story of "cognitive history" forms a pattern only in a very large-scale and rough sense. To call it a "Piagetian" pattern is also to apply a rough label. Piaget's work focused on a number of very specific cognitive tasks associated with scientific rationality, including perspective-taking, recognizing the sameness of quantities in different shapes, doing certain mathematical operations, and so forth. The pattern to be described here is much more general, roughly matching summary outlines that Piaget has given of the results of his work.

It is important to distinguish between Piaget's description of the general differences in cognitive skills that children exhibit at different ages, and Piaget's attempt to account for those differences. Piaget proposes a theory about hidden mental structures that account for the observable cognitive skills.[8] While the observable skills can be described fairly reliably, the hidden mental structures behind those skills are more difficult to identify. Those who attack his theory about inner mental structures have nonetheless usually found his descriptions of stages of observable skills to be basically accurate. The next chapter will offer evidence that although Piaget's work has been surpassed by that of a new generation of developmental and educational psychologists, they have surpassed him in a way that leaves his general outline a useful heuristic guide to perceiving patterns in the development of individual thought styles.[9] His general outline of cognitive development also works quite well as a perspective from which to interpret large-scale shifts in the process of cultural change in cognitive method.[10]

Processes as complex as human thought might well be broken into many different categories or types or styles. Histories of development also take many forms. Perhaps twenty different schemata could be devised, each of them equally somewhat artificial. But in fact, it is a Piagetian pattern that appears and reappears in various studies, sometimes deliberately and sometimes not. As the introduction noted, Fowler and Egan explicitly drew upon Piaget as one of their major sources. James Fowler's Piaget-inspired descriptions of faith development provide insightful and tested guidance for interpreting modes of religious thought.[11] Fowler interprets "faith" rather broadly, with the result that his descriptions of stages of faith are also highly illuminating descriptions of general stages of modes of thought. Egan proposes his own terms to describe Piagetian stages (though he gives credit also to Vygotsky): Mythic, Romantic, Philosophical, and Ironic.[12] Lawrence Kohlberg's theory of the development of moral reasoning is heavily indebted to Piaget (and to Hobhouse).[13] Robert Kegan's description of Traditionalism, Modernism, and Post-Modernism as three types of current thought styles reflects his knowledge of Piaget and Kohlberg, perhaps, but is supported also by his own long work in cognitive development.[14] Haydn White's outline of stages of literary styles in Western history applies Piaget to long-term cultural development.[15]

Other portraits of stages of cognitive development from some who are not Piagetians, at least not explicitly, lend further credence to Piaget's descriptions. Karen Kitchener divides thought styles into "cognition," "metacognition," and "epistemic cognition" in a way that fits well with the difference among concrete operational, early formal operational, and late formal operational thought according to Piagetian studies.[16] Bernard Lonergan's analysis of major stages in the history of Christian thought, from the commonsense approach of the first Christians to the theoretical theologians of classical Christianity to contemporary religious thought sometimes guided by modern method, also parallels a Piagetian outline quite nicely.[17] Even William Perry's investigation of the stages of thought styles among undergraduates during their four years at Harvard bears a clear resemblance to aspects of Piaget's thought.[18] Students moved from an early formal operational confidence in reason to produce certitude, to a later formal operational acceptance of the conditional nature of knowledge. C. Daniel Batson and W. Larry Ventis describe three different styles of religiousness based on Gordon Alport's division between intrinsic and extrinsic motivation and their own concept of "quest." These styles fit fairly nicely, albeit unintentionally, with Fowler's Piagetian descriptions.[19]

Piaget's Stages

Between the ages of two and seven a child achieves what Piaget called "preoperational" thought. It is a kind of thinking whereby a child learns facts about the world and how to deal with the world, but with some particular limitations. The child is not adept at recognizing the difference between fantasy and reality. What a child thinks or imagines, seems quite real. To mentally see something vividly is to know it as true. It is a period when a child may have an invisible friend, when Santa Claus is as real as a distant relative, and when the difference between a lie and a mistake is hard to recognize. Concrete facts and small stories, few of them longer or more complex than the story of "Little Red Riding Hood," are the means by which preoperational thought grasps reality.

The criteria of truth are not explicit. What seems self-evidently correct *is* correct. The child depends on voices of authority, who teach both implicitly by language use and by explicit and specific instructions about the world. But language and instructions can be subverted by beliefs that have already taken up residence in the mind, or by vivid and appealing new ideas. We know from daily experience that this happens with adults as well as with children.

This "preoperational" thinking includes a kind of "magical" thinking.[20] It assumes that whatever one encounters can be understood by its symbolic similarity or attachment to whatever one already knows. The Mekranoti of the Amazon basin use a leaf with a sharp stingerlike thorn on it as an antidote for scorpion sting, even though it is not noticeably effective.[21] Because the walnut looks like a brain, perhaps there are brain qualities in the walnut which can be used in some way that current adult thought in the West would call "magical." We will see forms of "natural magic" along these lines in antiquity and in the Renaissance. Chapter 3 will discuss the presence of such thought in human life, beginning with primitive cultures.

What we first achieve as children is not completely lost to us later. The adult uses skills first learned in childhood, albeit usually with more ease and sophistication. Piaget claimed that once people have gained certain cognitive skills, they do not lose them; in that sense there is no regression. In daily life, however, people may use earlier and simpler skills rather than operate through later and more complex modes of thought. In that sense there can be daily "regressions."[22]

The next major stage in cognitive development, the concrete operational style of thought, usually appears about the age of seven. Sometime early in this period most children become more clearly aware of the difference between thought and reality. Santa Claus turns out to be a fiction; invisible friends have disappeared, and the child will even deny that she or he could ever have believed in something so silly as that.[23] The child learns that inner thoughts are truly private, separate from the public reality that we can all see; the child now knows that parents do not know whatever he or she is thinking.

The concrete operational stage is that of the bookkeeper.[24] The child learns about reality as a set of items and as a range of categories into which items can be placed, even in cross-indexed ways. The ten-year-old who collects baseball cards, remembers countless pieces of data from each, and can sort the cards in various ways is a good instance of well-developed concrete operational thought. Concrete operational thought interprets reality in concrete images and narratives. Not philosophical abstractions but hard facts and specific stories are the forms for ideas about reality. This kind of thought eventually includes skill at keeping track of longer and more complex stories. It is the ten-year-old, for example, who is first able to understand that different chapters in the same novel form one continuous and complex story (provided, of course, a child is raised in a culture that tells such long and well-integrated stories).

Concrete operational thinking is "commonsense" thinking, as Lonergan labels it. As in ordinary usage, a commonsensical person is "realistic," learning practical facts of life. Magical thinking does not disappear, at least not entirely. Adults use a mixture of styles of thought. People do not always care much about consistency in their thinking.[25] As with preoperational thought, a person's social context stands as the most powerful authority about what is to be taken as the truth, though firsthand experience also counts. The commonsense style of thought can be very successful. It is how most of us operate on an everyday basis.

Formal operational thought is the next Pigetian stage, beginning usually by about age twelve. It shows itself in an ability to contemplate hypothetical structures of reality, and to check out these ideas mentally for their internal coherence and for their consistency or lack of it with ordinary reality. This is the stage of "theory," in Lonergan's usage, if theorizing does not mean merely devising answers to ad hoc questions, but instead means reflecting systematically on all the interrelations among data in order to mentally devise and test some basic explanatory scheme or theory that will tie it all together in a new way, to devise alternative theories for the same data, and then to test the various alternatives against other data and other seemingly well-supported theories, to arrive at a logically sound conclusion that is consistent with the evidence. It is skill at understanding sentences like the previous one.[26]

Formal operational thought values explicitly systematic logic. It applies careful analysis and comparisons to avoid inconsistency of ideas and evidence. Logical thought can be done best when the culture provides an explicit and formal system of logic. This is a "metacognition," to use Kitchener's word, in that it thinks about thinking in order to make that thought consistent and coherent.[27] This skill normally requires training and practice. It carries no guarantee that a person will use it well or consistently. Logical analysis is now available to criticize any inconsistencies in the stories or ideas that once seemed easy to believe, or the ideas and values that once had the weight of authority and tradition behind them. Theoretical thought can be subversive of tradition. It becomes its own authority, as it were.

Logical analysis seems to give a kind of certitude. As formal operational thought solidifies, it may tend to a self-confident dogmatism, relying on the logical and hypothesis-forming workings of the mind to arrive at clear and correct truths.[28] "The adolescent goes through a phase of attributing unlimited power to her or his own thoughts."[29] Chapters 5 through 8 will describe the impact of this mode of thought on religion and science in more than one culture.

Later and more experienced formal operational thought goes beyond dogmatic rationalism to become conditional thought.[30] Like early formal operational thought, it constructs logically coherent systems of thought and rejects ideas that lack logical internal consistency. It will doubt ideas that conflict with other ideas which have proved reliable. But late formal operational thought also builds on the experience of error. Theories that once appeared unassailable in their theoretical "rightness" and their good fit with the evidence have later turned out to be false according to further evidence or better reflection. How to think, how to know what is true, how to judge what should be relied on as though it were the truth, becomes more of a problem. The full flowering of the capacity for formal operational thought includes a recognition of the limits of theory and the need to compare theory with reality in an ongoing way.[31] Theories are recognized to be models and images that must be constantly and carefully checked against all relevant experiences to test their ongoing adequacy. Lonergan calls this "method." It is Kitchener's "epistemic cognition." The particular skill of this stage can be summed up as critical reflection and testing, an ongoing testing of our vivid impressions (preoperational tendency) or empirical observations and stories (concrete thought) as well as theories (formal thought). Its first powerful and extensive manifestation in history is in modern science, though it influences some modern theologies as well. Chapters 9 and 10 will explore this style of thought.

Stages of Cognitive Styles in Culture

There have been numerous theories of cultural evolution, from as long ago as Lucretius in the first century BCE.[32] Anne R. J. Turgot (1727–1781) made a more recent and influential effort to analyze cultural development. He proposed that "The general process of the growth and development of societies is a natural process, comparable to the process of growth of the individual from infancy to adulthood, or that of the plant from seed to flower."[33] He highlighted the place of modes of thought in development, granting to all races equal intelligence but attributing differences in thought styles to the education provided by each culture.[34] Turgot influenced figures of the Scottish Enlightenment (in the same time period). As part of a continuing adjustment to the discovery of the "savage" tribes of the Americas, they outlined the pattern as one of progress, from hunting-and-gathering culture to pastoralists, then to agriculturalists, to commercial empires, and finally to the crowning achievement, which was the incipient scientific-technological culture of the eighteenth century.[35] This outline in turn influenced the many nineteenth-century theories of cultural evolution.

We now have the benefit of countless additional studies in paleontology and cultural anthropology to enable us to make some generally safe statements about cultural development. Two million years or so ago, our hominid ancestors survived because their genes programmed them sufficiently well that they could carry on with limited need for complex learning, communication, and reflection.[36] By twenty thousand years ago the first great crossing had already occurred. The earliest forms of culture were well in place. Tools, clothing, humanly constructed shelters, fire for cooking and warmth, formal burial, cave drawings, and bone carvings to mark phases of the moon give evidence of the human mind at work. Most important, language had replaced genetic programming as the most powerful source of guidance. A genuinely human culture now existed. The earliest fully human culture can be labeled "linguistic."[37]

(There are signs that Neanderthals also possessed human intelligence. The physiology of their larynx and brain impressions on their skulls indicate they may have been capable of complex speech, though perhaps not as capable as our Cro-Magnon ancestors.)

Primitive Culture

Archaeology tells us many things about the daily life of the first humans.[38] Current hunting-gathering societies provide us with other clues. Today primitive hunting-gathering cultures are egalitarian, without hereditary rulers, though often some individual, through strength of personality or skill at shamanic practices, may fill the role of leader. In various places hunting and gathering came to be supplemented by animal herding or by small-garden horticulture, which can have significant impact on the overall culture.

Primitive cultures are oral cultures.[39] They portray reality as a collection of people, things, and events, sometimes organized into multiple categories with many or most things in their correct place, though the boundaries of the categories are sometimes vague.[40] Tradition and commonsense observation dictate what is true. It is the tradition of the group, its language categories and beliefs, that forms the commonsense knowledge of the people and tells them what they are observing.

Primitive religion, if the name "religion" is appropriate,[41] consists of beliefs and practices concerned with invisible beings and powers, which we now usually call spirits and magic. Primitive peoples believe in many spirits but they do not worship them. They deal with them as with parent figures or as difficult neighbors one must learn to get along with, but not as beings requiring formal worship. Whether belief in magic counts as religion at all has long been argued.[42] Nonetheless, it is safe to say that belief in spirits and magic is at least a kind of prereligion. Belief in spirits in particular is a basis for the later belief in other, much larger invisible living beings who can influence lives, the gods. Chapter 3 will elaborate on this early form of religiousness.

Whether primitive human thought has any relation to scientific thinking is disputed.[43] On the one hand, it is possible to divide primitive from modern culture precisely by insisting on the difference between mythical superstition and rational science, as has so often been done. On the other hand, every science must begin with information and categorizing. Even the most primitive society collects data about its world in order to stay alive and functioning. Even the most primitive society can be exceedingly skilled in analyzing specific pieces of information, such as the age, condition, and amount of droppings of an animal worth hunting, or in constructing a hypothesis about fish in a river and testing that hypothesis by fishing methods. We will return to the topic of primitive "science" in chapter 3, especially in relation to Robin Horton's comparison of primitive beliefs to science.

Archaic Culture

About ten thousand years ago the invention and increased application of large-scale agricultural methods gradually produced a new kind of culture, which we can call "archaic," following Parsons and Bellah. Farming led to concentrations of settled populations in villages and cities. Major irrigation projects in Mesopotamia, Egypt, the Indus valley, and along the Mekong River and the Yellow River in China led to highly organized "hydraulic empires," as Karl Wittfogel called them, and a great growth in commerce.[44] Eventually literacy was born, including bureaucratic record-keeping as well as organized compilations of myths into lengthy hymns or poems. Information and stories could now grow more complex. The cognitive skills needed by a bureaucracy or priesthood became important enough to require a system of formal education.[45]

Here there is clearly religion: the formal worship of the gods in temples dedicated to such worship. The official and full-time priesthood now offers sacrifices and reads omens. Where there were once spirits alone, now there are also gods, spirits of enormous power, lording it over the spirits and humans alike, as kings rule erratically over their kingdoms. As a culture develops inner social, political, and economic organization, so also the realm of the invisible beings develops a hierarchical system of power. In many places the practical information of archaic culture is already on its way toward a more formal science. The astronomical observations of the Babylonians to serve astrological purposes, the measuring techniques of the Egyptians to settle land disputes after the annual floods, and the irrigation techniques in various parts of the world, represent more complex use of information and cognitive methods. Chapter 4 will discuss this.

Classical or "Axial" Culture

Primitive culture and archaic culture are similar in much of their thought styles except for the effects of literacy. Both tend to rely on tradition. Magical thinking is commonplace in both, as it is also in contemporary cultures. Literacy, however, was prelude to another radical shift in methods of thinking, which appeared about twenty-five hundred years ago in the era labeled the "axial age" by the philosopher Karl Jaspers.[46] It is the age of the great "classical" civilizations. The notion of a single and ultimate unity to all reality arose in China, India, Persia, Judea, and Greece. In Greece, China, and India, philosophers (who were sometimes also what we would call both theologians and scientists) self-consciously sought the overall structure of all things at once. They moved from reliance on tradition and commonsense observation to reliance on systematically logical explanatory theories of universal scope.[47]

Breaking with both tradition and common sense in varying degrees, these philosophers looked behind the obvious in order to find all-embracing hidden patterns. They speculated on causes that were not only hidden to the eye, as were the traditional magical powers and spirits and gods, but were also the universal structures or forces that accounted for all the individual happenings of the universe. They demanded that these structures and forces all fit together in a logically coherent unity. If any one idea contradicted another, then one of them had to be wrong. By this radical norm a person could criticize both common sense and tradition, including the myths by which people had long interpreted their lives.

The thoroughgoing use of this criterion of logical coherence constituted the revolution from archaic to classical (or "axial") consciousness. Theoretical thought came to outweigh common sense in the formal reflections of the intellectual elite. We can presume that individuals in all cultures, including primitive ones, have thought logically in some ways. Each human attempt to devise an explanation for some event is an exercise in logic, at least on a small scale. But it was in the great classical cultures that the search for an ultimate, logically coherent structure behind the everyday universe first became a publicly shared and encouraged mode of thought, handed on by explicit and often formalized training, among at least a few people.

The theoretical speculations of the classical age were ambitious. The ancient Greek philosopher Parmenides found perfect logical unity by denying the reality of all change, an idea with its parallels in later Indian thought. Plato searched for the eternal and perfect essences of all things, as did the Taoists in China. In the fourth century BCE Aristotle developed a full formal logic, even as the "logician" Hui Shih in China sought to formalize the rules of thinking. Mo-tzu (470–ca.391 BCE) and the Mohists also analyzed the rational standards to be applied to science and to religious beliefs, though the Mohists may have been more "modern" than classical because of their emphasis on empirical evidence and theories as models.[48]

Theorizing far outran the evidence available. But out of this search for overall logical explanatory coherence came reflections on the universal demands of justice, or on the ultimate nature of truth and truthfulness, or on pure ideals of government and public morals, and much else that cultures still cherish. Out of these speculations came the beginnings of a new form of science. Aristotle studied biological differences, formulated theories of why the sea is salty, and analyzed the movement of the stars, all through a comparison of various theoretical possibilities in relation to available evidence. Among the ancient Greek physicians many were "dogmatists," guided by philosophical theories of basic elements of the universe; others were "empiricals," basing their judgments not on theory alone but also on actual experiment.

A great shift in religious thought was part of the axial change. In the sixth century BCE the great universalist religions appear. In China traditional notions of yin and yang provided the background for belief in a universal and ultimate Tao. Notions of the transmigration of souls and of divine power in India produced belief in the Ultimate named Brahman or Atman while logically systematic reflections were transforming traditional polytheism into classical forms of religion, in some cases subordinating the gods to a higher Reality or even ignoring the gods.[49] It is in the parts of the Rig Veda that were written most recently, probably no earlier than 800 BCE, that there is speculation about the ultimate transcendent reality.[50] By the time of the Babylonian Exile the Judean god, Yahweh, became the Creator God of the universe. The Greeks proposed candidates for supreme divinity, in the form of Plato's One, or the Stoics' Logos, or Aristotle's Unmoved Mover.

Empirical-Critical Culture

Within the last few centuries there has been a fourth revolution in the style of thinking, one still developing. To the criterion of logical consistency has been added a new emphasis on ongoing and public empirical testing, of subjecting every theory, no matter how logically appealing, to open-ended testing against the evidence. This is the modern "empirical-critical" method in science. A defining aspect of empirical-critical thought has been the conviction that neither commonsense observation and tradition nor logical explanatory theorizing is entirely reliable, that we must continuously engage in a public empirical testing of even our own favorite truth-claims, even at the expense of our own biases and special interests in making those claims. This constitutes a self-reflecting (or "reflexive") awareness that knowledge is conditional and tentative; that every interpretation of reality, no matter how wonderfully coherent or consistent with the apparent evidence, is the product of human thinking; that it is an interpretation and not the simple truth, one interpretation among a range of possibilities. This idea is at least as old as the skeptics of ancient Greece and India, but in modern scientific culture it has been accepted widely as an integral and constructive part of a rational search for truth.

While the classical or axial revolution appeared in what we now call philosophy and theology and science all in one, the current revolution has been most evident specifically in the growth of science. This revolution is not quite what the early scientists were preparing themselves for. In fact, to many of the early scientists the empirical-critical approach appeared to be a skepticism that was opposed to their great project of discovering the real truth about the universe. But science has an ironic nature. While it has been extremely successful in discovering things about this universe that had long eluded the most insistent questionings of humankind, at the same time its continuing successes have been dependent on a willingness to doubt all observations and theories, to leave them open to further testing by any critic, to treat them as models for interpreting reality rather than as simple truth. Science, ironically, knows more by doubting more.

Religious thought has also been affected by the rise of the empirical-critical method, though the response of religion is varied. The last chapter will examine a number of these responses, from the existential leap of faith to the redefinition of religion as emotive-expressive or cultural-linguistic. As the cognitive style of the culture has shifted, some religious thought has incorporated much of that shift (though other contemporary religious thought defines itself precisely as a rejection of both modern rationalism and skepticism).

Some have argued that scientific rationality is a Western creation, not a universally valid approach to truth. This account is too narrow. Other cultures, particularly those of India and China, have rich traditions of rational analysis dating from the same era as that of ancient Greece. Each of those cultures, moreover, has also had its own school of skeptical philosophers whose approach to truth was quite similar to that of contemporary Western empirical-critical science. It was western Europeans who stumbled upon ways to make the general empirical-critical approach surprisingly effective, in the form of modern science. But that does not make this approach valid only in the West. In spite of the foreign origin of the specific sciences imported into China, India, and elsewhere in the last few centuries, this style of thought already existed in the indigenous traditions and in the intellectual capabilities of the people, as we will see in later chapters.

The Evolution of Religious Thought

Many voices have opposed the idea that religion evolves. Nineteenth-century opposition was sometimes rooted in atheism. As the introduction noted, Comte reduced religion to a superstitious stage in the evolution of types of thinking. Feuerbach, Marx, Freud, and others likewise relegated religion to the status of mistaken belief in invisible beings like spirits and gods. Now that we know better, they said, we can dismiss such beliefs as the changeless superstition of the ignorant. A few defenders of religion today argue that we cannot rule out the existence of such beings.[51] Those few could agree that religion does not evolve, but has remained basically the same since at least the days of animism and polytheism. Others argue more subtly (see Shweder's argument in the next chapter) that such beliefs are rationally legitimate within the boundaries of other cultures' norms for belief.[52] But the most frequent religious response today is to accept the judgment that animism and polytheism are indeed mistaken in the way they interpret and express basic religious experience. Classical theology argues rationally in favor of belief in a single Ultimate. Liberal theology proposes that anthropomorphic beliefs should be replaced, ideally, by a sophisticated sense of a Universal Being or Whole or Holy Mystery.

Other positions are harder to classify. Mircea Eliade rejects the idea of religious evolution. He insists that religion has a changeless nature as an experience of the sacred. For the most part, he sees the process of changes in religious history as a finding and losing and finding again of the basic religious experience, insights, and values. On the other hand, he is open to the possibility of an evolution of the forms of expression of this experience. The original experience of the sacred, he even says, "prepared the way for systematic thought."[53]

Fortunately, we do not have to take a position on whether it is only modes of religious thought or religion itself that has been evolving. The focus of this book is on the history only of cognitive methods or styles. We will examine the major shifts in modes of thought from primitive to modern times in the West, and to a lesser degree in Chinese and Indian history. Religious thought, not all aspects of religiousness, is the focus of attention. Whether religious thought is at the heart or near the periphery of religiousness is a question that can be argued outside of the pages of this book. An examination of the actual history of religious thought, however, can provide information to help carry those arguments forward.

Three Major Aspects of
Religious Thought

What the chapters in this book will try to show is that religious thought, along with science, has developed roughly through four major forms or styles, highly suggestive of Piagetian stages. Three aspects of religious thought help to identify major types: the mode of expression, the content, and the cognitive style.

The earliest *mode of expression* is the relatively simple folktale of primitive culture, in which various origin stories and other lore interpret reality and life for people, along with a good collection of commonsense information about the world. Literacy produces a later mode of expression. Some religious stories become much more complex, in the form of long mythic narratives, and religious beliefs are often more clearly distinct from everyday information. The third mode of expression of religious thought appears in the axial age era, in China, India, and the West. Folktales and mythic narratives remain popular but are now in competition or cooperation with a more abstract and universalizing form of thought. The fourth mode of expression of religious thought is a highly self-conscious symbolic awareness that has resulted from the self-critical awareness of modern philosophy and science.

The changes in *content* can be sketched quickly by a return to Bellah's outline. There are four general types of religious beliefs (or "symbol systems"). The first is animism, belief in spirit beings of relatively human size and power. The second is polytheism, belief in spirit beings of such great power that they require worship. The third is a universalizing belief in some single Ultimate Being or Condition or Power. The fourth is a hard-to-name, self-aware form of belief that treats all beliefs as human symbolic representations of whatever is taken to be the ultimate or basic Reality. The first three of these stages can also be characterized as tribal, national, and universal.[54] There is no easy name for the fourth stage; much depends on whether one stresses contemporary pluralism in religion or instead looks for some universal human experience. For now I will call it the "reflexive" stage.

The modes of expression and the content of belief correlate highly with four *cognitive styles,* in the Piagetian sense that will be explained in the next section of this chapter. Primitive animist cultures rely mainly on a style of thought in religion that can be called *folktale-magical* and has analogies with preoperational thought, though it includes concrete operational thinking. Archaic polytheistic cultures retain primitive style of thought, but literacy creates an overlay of *literate-mythical* thought. Literacy makes people more adept at concrete operational skills of categorizing and comparing ideas, more apt to construct long, coherently organized narratives. Classical universalist cultures are those which add some degree of *systematic-theoretical* thought, the early formal operational thought of Piaget. "Critical culture" is a name to identify the peculiar additional method of modern science that I will call the *empirical-critical.* In Piagetian terms this is late formal operational thought. This thought style has led many contemporary theologians to adopt a more symbolic or existentialist approach. The last chapter will describe several such theologies.

The Cognitive Styles in Contemporary Society

Even in contemporary industrial societies a person may live a life guided mostly by the kind of thought that characterized primitive and archaic civilization. It is the "bookkeeping" style of thought—collections of ideas assembled and used without explicit concern to test for overall logical coherence among them all or to be critically aware of the conditional nature of the evidence and the interpretation they represent. On a day-to-day basis we are all mostly preaxial—that is, pretheoretical and pre-critical, relying primarily on tradition and commonsense observations with a little ad hoc logic applied as needed.

The preoperational style of thought is common enough today. Wild beliefs in a disconnected jumble of ideas are evident in supermarket tabloids like the *Weekly World News*, with its tales of UFO aliens and Tibetan secrets for raising the dead to life. The New Age movement promotes many odd beliefs—in ESP, plant consciousness, or mood-altering crystals—odd enough for psychologists to refer to them as magical thinking.[55] Whether "magical" is the best label or not, there is a tendency here to believe things that appeal to the imagination regardless of lack of any rational support. Those whose thought is most "magical" are just barely formal operational, as it were, passing tests for the kind of early formal operational thought used by fourteen-year-olds but failing more difficult tests. Many adults give uncritical credence to all sorts of beliefs about demonic possession, about ancient visitors from outer space, or about voices from the past speaking through living "channels." These adults may have very good memories for recounting information from many sources, yet show little critical ability to distinguish between a reliable source and an unreliable one. Many are good at imagining a worthwhile story for their lives but are not very good at taking a rationally objective survey of their own situation and habits and goals, and putting it in the larger context of hypothetical alternatives open to them.

Concrete operational thought is the ordinary mode of thought for most of us most of the time. So it is not surprising that it appears today also in explicitly religious forms. Robert Wuthnow describes religious fundamentalism as part of "folk piety," and his description matches quite well, if unintentionally, with the concrete operational style of thought. Folk piety is based on personal experience rather than formal arguments. It is composed of relatively discrete sayings, a set of independent parts gathered but not organized into a coherent unity. It is "a symbol system comprised of a relatively large number of elements, but with a low number of definite relations among pairs of elements." It is focused on solidarity groups and its oral tradition.[56] This is the style of thought that dominates by default in archaic cultures. It is also fairly normal human thinking.[57]

Our culture, however, has also taught most people how to use at least a little of the axial-age type of systematic and logical thought on some occasions. High school geometry is an instance of this. So is any attempt to invent and choose among alternative forms for a yearlong budget, figuring in taxes and retirement savings and insurance costs and future schooling for the kids with contingency plans for emergencies, all in relation to long-term goals and perhaps even religious or philosophical interpretations of life, in order to bring some overall coherence to it all.

When a person does employ large-scale formal operational analyses, explicitly rethinking even the basic structures of the person's life or of the universe, the person can do this because prior generations have demonstrated that this mode of thought is available if a person works at it, and because those prior generations have developed cognitive techniques for such thought. Prior generations practiced how to review previous laws, beliefs, theories of nature, or whatever; then to look for large-scale ways of reinterpreting them; and then to test these large-scale interpretations for inner coherence. They have handed on organized methods of logic, pro-and-con styles of argumentation, structured outlines for interrelating ideas. People learn these techniques through schooling, both formal and informal.

In spite of such education, however, these methods of classical consciousness are difficult and are used only occasionally or only by a relative few.[58] Systematically logical theorizing has its impact by being gradually imported into the underlying structures of the culture, its government and ethical codes and ideals, not by being the common daily practice. Our ideal of equal and universal justice under a government of laws, for example, is an ideal people respect in theory but have a hard time living up to. People often respect such ideals because they receive them as tradition and treat them as common sense, rather than because they derive them logically from their own coherently systematic reflections, say, on the nature of the person as a social being in history, or as a child of God who is part of a cosmic Providential plan.

The same is true with the modern empirical-critical cognitive style that has resulted from reflections on the methods of science. We can presume that from primitive times people did a bit of what science does.[59] They asked questions about things, formulated theories to account for things, and then checked up on whether the theories are really true, often remaining only partly convinced by evidence. The difference between primitive and modern culture is not that people today are the first to have discovered the possibility of formulating theories and testing them. Modern scientific culture has taken two additional steps. It explicitly recognizes the need to formulate theories much less haphazardly than is the custom in primitive and archaic cultures; and it does the testing much more rigorously and publicly than in classical cultures. Modern scientific culture has formalized an everyday human process into a self-conscious method. In practice not even the best-trained scientist follows a neat pattern of observation and theorizing and testing. The path of discovery is convoluted, crisscrossing itself through many blind alleys along the way. But the general method of science is eventually to organize the experiences of the journey into data (observations), theories, and tests in order to be able to check more clearly how reliable the conclusions are so far. This general method is no longer just an incidental and unschooled approach of this person or that; it is now the formal ideal behind complex techniques for determining what is probably true.

Once again, if many people today employ the method of science well, it is *not* because they are more intelligent than other people. The people of even the most primitive society share in the same general human intelligence. It is the tools and training that different cultures provide that determine which cognitive skills a given group of people will have available to them. (Chapter 8 will return to the method of science, addressing manifold issues raised by current philosophy and sociology and history of science.)

2

ADDRESSING THE CRITICS

As the introduction indicated, theories of cultural evolution in general face hostile criticism, and Piagetian categories only seem to make things worse. The historical evidence in the next chapters is the main response to such criticism. Whether there is indeed a pattern of development of styles of thought across cultures in religion and science can best be decided by looking at the relevant evidence. But a quick examination of some major criticisms may at least remove obstacles to an open consideration of that evidence. Criticisms can be divided into three main categories: criticism of theories of cultural evolution, criticism of Piaget's ideas, and criticism of Piagetian theories of cultural evolution. This chapter will describe and respond briefly to all three.

Criticisms of Theories of Cultural Evolution

We can start with Franz Boas. He and his students led the fight in the early part of the twentieth century against theories of cultural evolution. His first target was racism. He vigorously rejected claims that the peoples of Europe had a natural superiority which accounted for their particular achievements. He attacked claims that other cultures were inferior to European ones precisely because of inherited racial differences.[1] He pointed to the achievements of many cultures over five thousand years of history, including the long period when Islamic culture was far more advanced than that of the semibarbaric northern Europeans.[2] Boas further argued against lockstep and highly precise explanatory theories of cultural evolution—especially theories that attended to a specific element of culture, such as economics, and tried to explain everything else in terms of that element.[3]

Even Boas, however, supports aspects of a general theory of cultural evolution. In contradiction to present-day cultural relativists, he offers standards for judging other cultures' level of advancement. First is intellectual achievement, an increase of rational forms and of knowledge. Second is an increase in "playful techniques," including art. Third, both of these are made possible by new techniques for survival and the production of food (*general* economic advance) that allow for more leisure time and greater ability to survive variations in living conditions.[4] Although Boas expresses doubt that moral development could be used as a standard of advancement because of the great amount of subjective judgment concerning moral values, he praises the extension of a ban on murder from one's immediate kin, to larger social groups, to all the people of one's nation, and, ideally, to all people everywhere. Boas speaks of this as though it is an obvious example of cultural progress.[5] He theorizes that this depends in turn on the accumulation and use of better techniques for thinking:

> In the history of civilization, reasoning becomes more and more logical, not because each individual carries out his thought in a more logical manner, but because the traditional material which is handed down to each individual has been thought out and worked out more thoroughly and more carefully. . . . The number of thinkers who try to free themselves from the fetters of tradition increases as civilization advances.[6]

Thus even an early enemy of racist and imperialist approaches to anthropology could support the argument in the following chapters that there has been a pattern of development of cognitive styles in various cultures.

The ambiguities in Boas's own position have their echoes in current anthropology. Many anthropologists reject Eurocentric and deterministic progressivism, yet promote more sanitized theories.[7] They are often suspended between two contrary approaches to interpretations of culture. One approach is to seek the maximum of science, as John D. Y. Peel puts it, by looking for necessary universals.[8] These are characteristics that are universally shared by all cultures and that are necessary for the survival or functioning of any culture. Caring for children is one; finding food is another; using language is a third.[9] There may be relatively few such necessary universals, but to identify any widespread patterns of behavior that are at least quite important in the functioning and survival of the group brings us closer to a scientific understanding.[10] Opposed to this are interpretations that "accept history," as Peel says. That is, they strive for a clear and deep description of the specifics of any given society in its location in time and space. They do not look for patterns common to other societies or seek to discover what is necessary or highly important for people in any culture.

Peel proposes that the intersection of these two basic approaches produces five modes of comparative method, five different expectations in the analysis of culture. These are (1) to uncover an ideal, universal history; (2) to track a branching, concrete history of societies; (3) to ignore history entirely and study only one culture or society at a time; (4) to do regional studies that show the development of changes within a certain cultural area; and (5) to study precisely the histories of societies-in-change rather than societies at some frozen moment in their history.[11] My approach includes aspects of both (2) and (5), but claims also to identify some parallels among the developmental histories of some major cultures in their modes of thought in religion and in science.[12]

Ernest Gellner takes a similar approach, looking for major parallels in cultural developments. He rejects theories that propose some ideal universal history, whether arising from genetic factors or, especially, from any teleological impulse toward higher stages. He insists that if later stages build on earlier ones, this is not to say that the later ones are bound to happen; there is no necessity for a culture to develop at all, and regression is always possible.[13] Yet he thinks he sees significant historical patterns of development. The title of his book, *Plough, Sword, and Book*, identifies three major developmental variables: means of production, forms of political control, and modes of cognition.[14] Gellner tracks these three variables as they develop together through major stages of cultural transformation.[15] In his analysis of cognitive development, he argues roughly in favor of an outline of history similar to what I am proposing. First, the arrival of literacy and "the disembodied word" made it possible for meaning to live on, even in the absence of the one who articulated the meaning.[16] Then the axial age provided unified world pictures.[17] Finally, recent centuries have seen the "the dethronement of the concept" and the elevation of critical scientific method to place of dominance.[18]

Gellner's analysis is highly compatible with a Piagetian interpretation of cultural development. A Piagetian approach can make greater sense of the major cognitive shifts in cultural development that he describes, from language to literacy to logic to reflexively critical thought.

There are works by opponents of some specific theories of cultural evolution that nonetheless provide good support for the particular description of cultural development offered here. Tim Ingold's extensive review, analysis, and criticism of nineteenth- and twentieth-century theories of cultural evolution leaves intact the more general descriptions of increased social complexity that accompany changes in the means of subsistence. He agrees that new and more complex forms may appear in a culture in addition to older and simpler forms, even of styles of thought.[19] Stephen Sanderson is an anti-progressivist, arguing that social change is not the same as progress.[20] Earlier forms of society are as good for their people as later forms, he says. But he does support the common description of a pattern of cultural development, from the Neolithic revolution to major feudal civilizations to capitalism.[21] The list of current anthropological explorations of cultural evolution could be extended. (The notes contain further references for those interested.) It should at least be clear that there is no consensus among anthropologists against all theories of cultural evolution or development.

One of the most striking aspects of even antievolutionary writing is that it often unwittingly ends up giving support, indirectly and even directly, to some sort of general evolutionary account of cultural development. Though it can be tedious to run through a number of examples, it is important to show how frequently the language that anthropologists and others use is misleading. In particular, one can often read of primitive people who use "systematic" or "theoretical" thought, whose stories are said to be quite sophisticated or as complex in their own way as those of literate or postaxial societies. But time after time, a close reading of the sources making these claims reveals something other than what the complimentary language implies.

Ruth Finnegan, for example, flatly rejects evolutionary interpretations of primitive life, insisting that the literary and artistic genius evident in the oral literature she has studied merits full respect. Yet to illustrate her point she describes the transformation of the Genesis story of Adam and Eve, learned from missionaries, into a less elegantly organized folktale with a simplification of some of the more complex elements.[22] It may be true that oral literature merits great respect, even while it is also true that literacy provides significant additional advantages for telling and passing on stories.

Anthropologists often use language about primitive culture that implies more than their own descriptions indicate. Ronald and Catherine Berndt, for example, speak of the "mythic cycle" of stories told by various Aboriginal groups in Australia, thereby suggesting to the reader a collection of stories as well organized, perhaps, as the late Teutonic myths. But the stories cited by the Berndts are simpler and less organized than this. The story of the odd adventures of one animal in primal time ("dream time") precedes a story of a certain water well and two primal humans, with no connection between the stories, and so on for many stories. The "cycle" is more like a string with beans and shells and beads of many different colors.[23]

Bruce Chatwin claimed another kind of order for the Aboriginal "songlines," stories sung in certain sequences. Each story contains descriptions of pieces of the landscape. Each sequence of stories forms a map, Chatwin claimed, guiding a traveler from landmark to landmark, to reach the journey's goal.[24] The pieces of the map are thus encoded in a form that can be memorized. But as Chatwin recounts the stories, it is difficult to see their role in mapping. The story of the lizard who ate some dingo pups at the middle bore hill, for example, sounds like a typical folktale with no apparent "mapping" element.[25] (Chatwin also seems to have felt free to shift between fact and fiction in his works, without warning to the reader.)

Edwin Hutchins spends an entire book analyzing the legal argumentation used by Trobriand Islanders in land disputes in order to show that these people have highly sophisticated thought processes. But the specifics he provides in the book are repeated instances of very concrete and immediate thought, perhaps impressive for memory of details of who controlled what pieces of land at what time in the past, and for "chunking" together many specifics into a simpler assertion. Hutchins does not present any of this as instances of logically systematized law or critical reflection. In fact, he reveals some of the limitation of the Trobrianders' thought style by agreeing with Bronislaw Malinowski's earlier judgment, that the logic the Trobrianders use is partly hidden from them.[26] Hutchins says explicitly that their own "code" (their language) is "referentially transparent" to them—they use it without a conscious distance from it as a tool they are employing.[27]

Similarly, Christopher Vecsey describes Iroquois legends as "metaphysical groundwork" for a set of "complementary dualisms." Again the language masks what Vecsey's actual description shows: that the Iroquois themselves are not aware they are doing anything more than telling stories about how things came to be as they are.[28] Impressed with what he sees as hidden structures, unnoticed functions, or implicit meanings of the stories, Vecsey is using modern literate categories to interpret the Iroquois stories in a way the Iroquois themselves traditionally did not do.

Aletta Biersack tries to establish that the Paiela, a West African people with whom she lived and whom she studied, do have that elusive cognitive skill—the alternative logic, the logic of primitive thought that is a true logic and not an inferior form of developed Western logic. But in fact while claiming to have identified this logic, Biersack provides good evidence for the contrary. Arguing that "the Paiela are conversant with a number of principles associated with pattern and information . . . ," what she actually shows is that the Paiela are not consciously aware of such principles. They do their counting through concrete practices of using different body parts. They have various shortcuts, such as the equivalent of adding two hands to get ten instead of counting each finger. Such shortcuts can be made sense of by fairly sophisticated modern analyses. But the Paiela do not make such analyses; they just have concrete practices. It is Biersack who interprets the Paiela practice through modern categories.[29]

Claude Lévi-Strauss claims that the mind of the primitive is "totalizing," that it tries to subdue all pieces of reality by fitting them within proper categories. Yet when he describes, for example, a Native American story about how buffaloes became edible, the story is quite disconnected from other stories and categories of these people. They do not seem to do very well at this "totalizing." It is Lévi-Strauss who has to interpret that this is what they are doing even though they do not know it.[30] Similarly Evans-Pritchard tried to offer a strong defense of the knowledge of a Nilotic people, the Azande, on the basis of the practical usefulness of their knowledge. But he then also noted that "The Azande cannot analyze his doctrines as I have done for him."[31]

Robin Horton, whose work we will see more of in chapter 3, cites some specific instances of what he takes to be an implicit sophistication in primitive thought styles. To illustrate, he cites Meyer Fortes's work on West African beliefs in multiple souls.[32] Each person has more than one soul, more than one inner self, as it were. One soul takes care of sickness and health, of life and death; another is the center of the personality traits that make a person able to be a member of the tribal group; another relates a person to the ancestors; and so on. Horton agrees with Fortes that this constitutes a "theoretical" scheme for interpreting the different ways in which a person relates to the world and to others. In fact, Horton graces this belief with the label of "a simple but typical operation of abstraction and analysis."[33] The language can be misleading, however. In spite of the claims about abstraction and analysis and theorizing that Fortes and Horton make, their examples are consistently instances of what seems to be concrete operational thought. The function of these beliefs in multiple inner spirits is indeed to do "theoretical" duty. But the beliefs accomplish this not in a systematic-theoretical style; they do it by reifying the relations of the person to the world and to others, turning those relations into souls, without being aware of the "theoretical" function of these souls. This is concrete operational thought.

The difference of thought styles is evident in that Fortes and Horton can use formal operational thought to analyze the theoretical function of preliterate thought, whereas the preliterate people cannot do the same even for themselves, much less for another culture and language. For Fortes to describe their belief in souls as "theoretical" is to apply a word from a cognitively more advanced culture. Preliterate people do not explicitly recognize what abstraction and analysis are, are not able consciously to discuss whether their beliefs indeed represent abstraction and analysis.[34] Their thought is similar to modern science, Horton argues, because the full method of science does include fact claims or beliefs that help to explain things. True enough. But the full method of science also includes explicit formulation of alternative hypotheses and a self-consciously critical perspective that seeks evidence as tests of the fact claims and hypotheses. As Horton and Fortes describe the beliefs of primitive peoples, the beliefs are taken as the simple truth, known through common sense and tradition. What Horton has to say about the thought of primitive people is quite valuable, as we will see in the next chapter. But his language must be read with care.

Finally, though this list of instances is already a bit long, some mention has to be given to Mircea Eliade, because of his great influence among many students of primitive religion. Eliade claimed that primitive people are able to "construct theory" and to have a "pragmatic ontology," "a collection of truths fitting coherently into a system or theory," constituting a "transcendent model." He selects these words quite deliberately, "so as to demonstrate the aspect of theory in 'primitive' religion which is so often missed." He adds that all this is "totally different from our modern style, with its roots in the speculation of the Greeks."[35] A careful reading of the evidence that Eliade then provides, however, is that words such as "theory," "ontology," and "system" refer to a kind of thought which is relatively simpler and more concrete than that of any of the great traditions, not just Western-Greek but also those of India and China. This different style of theoretical or systematic thought seems to have neither theory nor system. The primitives of whom he speaks are not aware that they have a "transcendent model"; they only know that they do the rituals they are supposed to and as they are supposed to. Eliade tends to gather rituals and stories and symbols into general cross-cultural categories, an approach that makes it difficult to recognize the discord between his sweeping claims and the specific beliefs of which he speaks. Once in a while he dwells long enough on a single group's stories to allow the reader to get a clearer idea of whether there is indeed theory, system, or transcendent models in primitive thought. When he summarizes the basic stories of the Australian Bagadjimbiri, for example, he simply lines up in sequence various rather disconnected primal actions and events that contributed various rules and facts to the mixture of life as it now exists.[36]

Criticisms of Piaget's Theory

Once again historical evidence must count most heavily in determining what styles of thought have emerged in cultural histories. Yet it would certainly cast suspicion on a Piagetian interpretation of that evidence if Piaget's theories were discredited. Fortunately, a review of criticisms of his theory will show that the stories of his theory's demise have been greatly exaggerated.

Much of Piaget's theorizing was devoted to attempts to explain *why* certain changes in cognition occurred, to speculate on what must be going on inside the mind to produce the changes in behavior that he observed. I will not claim to know much about the inner processes of cognition. My general proposal is rather simple: to show that the major shifts in thought styles that Piaget observed provide an excellent map of the sequence of major shifts in thought styles in the history of several major cultures of the world. My explanation of the sequence of those cultural shifts is also much simpler than the explanations that Piaget sought concerning individual development. I propose only that thought styles which appear earlier in individual or cultural development are easier, and that later ones are more difficult and depend upon various cognitive tools not available in every culture. There is undoubtedly more going on in both individual and cultural development than that simple proposal. But it is wiser to keep the focus on the actual history of cultural developments rather than get enmeshed in speculative details.

Even my modest goal appears threatened, however, by critics of Piaget. Marjorie and Michael Rutter, for example, baldly declare: "Clearly, Piaget's idea that all cognition develops through four successive stages, with each stage characterized by the emergence of qualitatively distinct structures, has to be rejected."[37] Similarly, Alison Gopnik and Andrew Meltzoff proclaim: "In the wake of the collapse of Piagetian theory, cognitive development has been a bit of a mess."[38] They say later that "More recent research requires that we abandon both Piaget's empirical claims and his theoretical conclusions."[39] Not even Piaget's general empirical descriptions of cognitive development remain trustworthy, it seems.[40]

The Rutters provide a clue to the actual state of Piagetian theory, however, when they go on to explain that what they mean by their sweeping rejection is only that the Piagetian stages are neither so discrete nor so discontinuous, nor are they so invariant, as Piaget's way of speaking often implies. So they backpedal a bit: Piaget's general description "is not entirely wrong."[41] The same pattern recurs throughout various criticisms. First there is a seemingly flat rejection of major specific aspects of Piaget's theory, with Piaget's claims perhaps exaggerated a bit to make the criticisms clearer. Then there are sufficient qualifying statements to indicate that Piaget's rough outline of cognitive development is nonetheless still valid.

We can follow Robbie Case, a leading neo-Piagetian, as he summarizes criticisms of Piaget's ideas under three headings.[42] The first criticism is that Piaget failed to see how much the skills achieved at a certain age were already present in simpler form at an earlier age. Piaget's language about development sometimes seems to imply a clean discontinuity between two discrete stages, as though there were a sudden leap to an entirely new level of understanding. But recent extensive research supports a case for greater continuity of development. Later skills can be found in simpler form at an earlier age. An example is the skill of perspective-taking. A three-year-old sitting in front of a toy house cannot describe how the house looks to someone sitting at the side of it. A seven-year-old can do this. The seven-year-old has moved to a new and more difficult cognitive stage. On the other hand, a one-year-old child can follow the gaze of an adult as though to see what has captured the adult's interest. Perhaps this is a very early and simple form of perspective-taking, one that slowly improves over the years.[43]

A second criticism listed by Case is closely related to the first. Critics claim that Piaget was wrong in seeing the transition from one stage to another as a general, overall transformation of thought style, with the various types of skills all developing together. Piaget had noted "decalages," instances where a child who had moved to a new stage of cognitive development nonetheless lagged on one specific skill or, on the other hand, had leaped forward on one skill but not others. There is enough research, the critics say, to show that there is more "decalage" than Piaget normally took into account, more individual differences concerning the pace at which different skills develop.[44] Critics argue that this diminishes the probability there is an overall reconfiguration of the child's format of thought at specific steps in the developmental process.

These first two criticisms described by Case turn out to be far less than fatal to Piaget's general description. Susan Carey, for example, argues that Piaget's theory of "structural transformation," a transformation of the format of the mind as the person moves from one stage to another, could perhaps be accounted for as an ongoing accumulation of many different skills that continuously improve through experience and training. Carey organizes her case by identifying four kinds of cognitive tasks. First, children learn more techniques for thinking about thinking and language through daily interaction with adults, who tell them to think about such things, and give examples of how to do this. Second, children become familiar with foundational concepts such as causality, concepts through which many other connections or relations can be recognized. Third, children learn specific tools like literacy, mathematical notation, and list-making. Fourth, they gain domain-specific knowledge, whether about raising beets or fixing the car or reading a book. As all four types of skills interact, the child gradually accumulates the complex of abilities that constitutes adult thinking.[45]

Nevertheless, Carey ends up declaring that the general Piagetian description of stages of cognitive development is correct. She says that though development is an accumulation of various skills, it is no longer "merely" one of accumulation. Gaining all these types of skills is a complex and interactive process that occurs in stages over many years. Carey differs from Piaget mainly in the account of how and why this developmental process occurs.In brief, even in the hands of one of its critics, once again the Piagetian theory about stages in the development of cognitive skills proves clearly viable as a description of major steps along a developmental path.

Modularity theories offer a further explanation of the decalages Piaget noted. Jerry Fodor proposed in a 1983 book that we have different kinds of input systems, in the sense that one network in the brain—a "module," in Fodor's language—is innately prepared to recognize different natural objects in the environment, another to respond to or engage in social acts, another to manipulate objects as tools, and (in humans) another for language. Fodor also argued for a kind of "central processor" module that can integrate these inputs and respond to them. Howard Gardner agreed with Fodor on the mind's modularity, but argued against the existence of a central processor.[46] Gardner appealed to the evidence of child prodigies, who show great competence in one kind of thought but not in others, and to the effect of localized brain damage that impairs one or two aspects of mental activity but not others.

The theory of brain modularity has held up fairly well. Stephen Mithen provides extensive evidence from archaeology to show distinct mental modules for natural history (keeping track of objects and patterns in the environment), sociality (grooming, status, sex), technology (tool construction and use), and language.[47] But Mithen argues also for a "general intelligence" that connects and coordinates the other modules, which he compares partly to Dan Sperber's idea of "a module of metarepresentation" facilitated by the language module.[48]

Let us presume that the modularity of the mind is fairly well established. What this implies for the validity of Piaget's general descriptions of the main stages of cognitive development is another matter. In different people, different modules may well develop at a different rate, and different cultures may provide rather thoroughgoing training in one mental skill but not another. But Gardner's reference to rare child prodigies reminds us that enormous differences in different mental skills in the same person are not the rule. Most people are able to learn tool use, natural history, social practices, and language to an adequate level of competence *and*, moreover, to continue to develop such skills over the years of infancy, childhood, and adolescence.[49]

Finally, Robbie Case and Wolfgang Edelstein report on a generation of studies which show that decalages turn out not to be such a problem as some of the anti-Piagetians claim.[50] They divide studies of cognitive growth into two groups (with a division less neat than I am giving here). One group of studies identifies "local task knowledge," which may vary with context and with the individual. These are the decalages, the presence of which makes development appear to be a much more piecemeal process than Piaget's clear stages. The other group consists of the clear "cross-task correlations," which show a high degree of coherent stage development at certain periods in a child's life.[51] Overall thought processes demonstrate a new general level of competence.

The degree to which our minds are modular and to which they also have something like a general intelligence will continue to be argued by neuropsychologists and others. In the end, the relevant question for us here is only whether Piaget's description of major points along the developmental path is a generally accurate one. Once more, even those critical of Piaget's theory do not dispute this.

The third major type of criticism of Piaget listed by Case is that Piaget overemphasized the degree to which the cognitive development of the child is the individual achievement of a creative and active learner. Critics claim that Piaget understated the dependence of the child on society and culture for advancing in cognitive skills, and that he exaggerated the autonomous impulse to learn and develop new modes of thought, following its own inwardly directed path more than absorbing whatever skills the culture happened to teach.[52] The critics say that social factors contribute much more significantly to the development of cognitive skills than Piaget acknowledged. This charge is valid in its own way. Piaget's interest was not in what the child learns from the social environment. His interest was in how the child develops innate abilities to think about and deal with the environment. (In fairness, though, Piaget himself sometimes stressed the important part that society has to play.[53]) But this criticism addresses the causes of development, not whether the development pattern occurs.

Ironically, a recent critic of Piaget's theory claims that Piaget did not go far enough in focusing on the inner processes of the child. Annette Karmiloff-Smith first agrees with the general idea of modularity, that cognitive development is built upon many phases of growth in different skills rather than upon a few major large "stages." She attributes the different rates of development in different skills to the modular construction and operation of the brain, as more recent neurophysiology reveals. Like Fodor and Mithen, she attributes various cognitive skills to specific innate tendencies, such as those for language or for face recognition. But she wants to go beyond modularity, as she puts it. Neither Piaget nor Fodor seems, to her, to get to the really interesting specific inner activities of the child's mind. So in spite of several anti-Piagetian comments, in the end Karmiloff-Smith does not dispute the general Piagetian outline of observable development of cognitive skills. She simply wants to learn in much greater detail the inner processes of the mind, particularly of infants.[54] In any case, it is not of great importance for the description of cultural development to resolve the issue of general intelligence versus modularity, or to determine the many highly specific inner processes of individual development.

The plausibility of cognitive development stages is further supported by neurological studies. Case appeals to evidence concerning advances in the myelinization of neural cells that aids in brain cell function and takes place at certain points in life: one month, four months, one to two years, three to four years, ten years, and eighteen to twenty-five years.[55] In an important longitudinal study, R. W. Thatcher, R. A. Walker, and S. Guidice used EEG analysis to map the brain activity of 577 children from two months of age to early adulthood. They found growth spurts in brain development that nicely preceded the times of major cognitive development as described by Piaget.[56]

In all of this, critics show more support for the general Piagetian developmental sequence than is at first evident. Deeply involved in trying to move further in understanding cognitive processes and development, the critics are often most highly aware of the ways in which they differ from Piaget, rather than of the ways in which they take much of his work for granted as a convenient but limited background for their own work. In the end, current critiques of Piagetian theory pose no obstacle to using Piaget's general description of cognitive development as a guide to interpreting a pattern of cultural development. Piaget's description of stages helps to *categorize* thought styles more clearly. His theory also helps to recognize the particular *sequence* in which stages of thought appear in cultural history. In cultures as in individuals, the easier modes of thought appear first and continue to be used even when more difficult modes of thought are added. People tend to use easier modes of thought when they can; but some cultures have built up means to teach people to use more difficult modes and reward them for this.

Piaget's many works are still somewhat deficient as a guide to cultural development in one important way: they might be taken to imply that cognitive development is mainly an individual matter, not strongly affected by culture. Let me repeat once again, it is not differences in native intelligence that determine what styles of thought will predominate in this or that culture. In any society adults teach children and other adults certain cognitive skills that have been developed over some generations. If certain cognitive tools are missing—literacy is one that makes an obvious difference, for example—then the mode of thought in a society will be more limited than need be.

The Critiques by Richard Shweder

We have examined criticisms of theories of cultural evolution and criticisms of the thought of Piaget. There are also criticisms precisely of Piagetian theories of cultural evolution. Richard A. Shweder is the most prominent and dogged of such critics. To deal with his objections is to respond to most of the relevant criticisms.

Shweder objects to what he calls simplistic two-stage developmental theories of culture, which compare the poor superstitious savage against the scientifically rational modern person.[57] He indicts both Gellner and Piaget, for example, for portraying premodern people in general as living in "a dark age of intellectual confusion."[58] He then declares firmly in favor of cultural relativism.[59] Although reality may be the same objectively, he says, different cultures see it differently and have different criteria for determining which interpretations of reality should be accepted as correct.[60] Thus, by the standards of Europe a few centuries ago there were indeed witches, including self-confessed ones. Thus Nubian-Islamic belief in jinns is strong enough to produce effects as though of real jinns. Those in our culture who deny spirits, ghosts, gods, and witches are engaged in what Shweder calls a Nietzschean protopositivist empiricism, which proclaims that only seeing is believing.[61] He defends the right of other cultures to believe a variety of things that most modern anthropologists, using Western standards of rationality, would say are illusions or fictions. He says that he is defending the right of other cultures to have their own standards of "rationality."

As with the hidden rationality of primitive people mentioned earlier, unfortunately, Shweder does not say just what those standards are. He cites native beliefs in "wandering or reincarnating souls, witchcraft and sorcery, spirit possession and exorcism, pollution and purity, illness and health, karma and sin, gods and their goddesses, and so on."[62] Anthropologists claim that such native ideas are mistaken, that by such beliefs the natives are imposing a set of false beliefs on the world. The anthropologists err, says Shweder. The native is "adamant" that these ideas are "not simply creations or phantasms of the mind, but rather conceptions of reality that illuminate experience and take us beyond ourselves to reality."[63]

Shweder's point is that the natives take these beliefs to be literally true. He is correct in that, of course, but this sidesteps the issue of whether outsiders can use modern rational standards to question the accuracy of such beliefs. While Shweder lauds the power of these beliefs to "illuminate experience" or "take us beyond ourselves to reality," this is language that primitive peoples do not use. Shweder is reading his own modern understanding of religious beliefs into the natives' speech. (At one point he even seems to defend the truth of these beliefs. He notes that witches in Scotland, Russia, and other places confessed to similar acts and habits: a pact with the devil, night flights, the black Sabbath. He asks rhetorically whether delusions could all turn out similar accidentally.[64] This makes sense only as an argument that belief in pacts with demons and Sabbath flights are not delusions.)

Shweder repeats, and exaggerates a bit, some standard criticisms of Piaget's conclusions. He argues that Piaget is wrong in his notion of stages of cognitive development, because children exhibit simple levels of supposedly adult thinking,[65] and adults exhibit supposedly childish modes of thought.[66]

> What the evidence shows is that by clever manipulation of task content, an experimenter can demonstrate either the absense [sic] of logical thinking in an adult or the presense [sic] of logical thinking in a three year old! So what's all this talk of habitual pre-operational thinking?[67]

Shweder does not entirely reject the *categories* devised by Piaget to describe different styles of thought. Shweder's argument is that these different styles do not occur in neat sequence, in the development of either individuals or cultures. When he compares a child's thought with an adult's, or the contemporary thought styles of the Oriya in India with those of contemporary North Americans, he does not object to using Piagetian descriptions, as long as there are no implications of a general pattern of cultural evolution.[68] He prefers, though, to speak of "frames" of thought rather than "stages."

Shweder proposes that it is "frame-switching" rather than progressive development that accounts for differences in thought styles, particularly among different cultures. Any individual may have a variety of frames of thought, regardless of age. Different cultures prefer different frames of thought. Early forms are not replaced by later ones, especially in "nonrational domains of knowledge" such as kinship systems, ideas about friendship, understanding dreams.[69] If people of contemporary industrialized societies were measured by the norm of cognitive skills, it would turn out that they generally are somewhat primitive, he says.[70] Adults everywhere tend to use local and content-specific ideas, a kind of concrete operational thought, rather than abstractly general concepts. The differences evident in a given culture as well as among cultures may be due, once more, to "frame-switching" to fit different contexts. Adults able to use different modes of thought switch from one to the other as needed.[71]

Shweder is correct in saying that different cultures teach different ways of thinking, and correct that adults may use thought styles that children also use. He is correct also that adults may switch among different frames of thought. He is probably not assuming, however, that young children, like adults, are capable of intermediate algebra and advanced auto repair. In fact, he notes in passing that children will use simpler forms of any frame than an adult might.[72] His strongest claim would seem to be only that some skills which appear well developed in adults are rooted in simpler mental processes that first appear in children. Shweder does not claim that the three-year-old is capable of the clever manipulation used by the experimenter. Even though the child may have some early form of a skill that will undergo much greater development, there is a significant difference in cognitive abilities between the child and the adult. The adult experimenter, trained in psychology, is able to take a metacognitive perspective on the task and analyze it precisely as a cognitive task. The adult is then able to take the task apart, identify simpler elements in it, in order to create a simple form of the task for the child. Shweder misses the crucial point that in some cultures there are fewer frames of thought available to adults than in others.

In spite of all this, mild testimony to the reality of cultural evolution, especially in cognitive techniques, comes from Shweder himself. In a debate between Shweder and Christopher Hallpike about the use of preoperational thought by primitive people, Shweder acknowledged the reality of cognitive evolution in a limited sense:

> [Hallpike] limits his thesis to the issue of explicit knowledge. If that is all that Hallpike wants to claim—that individuals and cultures differ in the extent to which they reflect on what they know and explicitly formulate it, and that those who get schooling are better at self-reflection—there would be little to quarrel about. Such a modified thesis has nothing to say about the type of intellectual operations available to a people and it is consistent with the findings of cognitive development research. The modified thesis merely asserts that there is a difference between implicit and explicit understanding of principle and that some cultures are more rationalized, although not necessarily more rational, than others. Self-consciousness about thinking probably is a useful cross-cultural and developmental variable; not everyone has good verbal access to their own available intellectual processes or operational skills.[73]

Here Shweder agrees that the developmental theories are correct about stages of techniques in bringing to *explicit* awareness certain kinds of reasoning. He just claims not to find this very significant. The whole set of formal operational cognitive techniques that Karen Kitchener calls "metacognition"—the ability to reflect on reflections, to think about thinking—leaves Shweder relatively unimpressed.[74] He is more impressed with a hidden rationality in primitive thought. He extends the word "rational" to include "nonrationalized" processes. Even when trying hard to defend the cognitive style of primitive people, Shweder thus again acknowledges that they do not show themselves able to reflect on their own thought processes the way Shweder and others can. Rationality is "there" only in the form of implicit "principle." Calling it "rational" may be legitimate, in that there is a commonsense sort of logic in the thinking even of children. But it is not the formalized awareness of logical structure in language and thought that appears in some cultures during the axial age.

Shweder agrees with critics who say Piaget treats the propensity for cognitive development as so strong that a child needs only the ongoing ordinary experiences of life for this development to occur. We have much more to learn from culture than Piaget acknowledges, says Shweder.[75] He cites many ways in which individuals actually do not achieve cognitive development on their own, especially formal operational styles of thought.[76] The simple thought forms of a child may remain the standard thought forms of adults, unless their society trains them in more complex forms of thought. As we have already seen, this conclusion is quite consistent with the notion of a cultural evolution of cognitive styles. (Kieran

Egan, Shweder, and I would all agree that Vygotsky is more accurate here, by stressing the role that culture plays.)

Perhaps one of the most significant statements by Shweder in favor of a theory of cultural cognitive evolution, albeit indirectly and apparently unintentionally, is made as part of his argument that modern people are poor at formal operational thought.[77] He cites a 1965 study to examine how well college students could correlate material, in this case between cloud-seeding and rainfall.[78] When the information was presented bit by bit in sequence, the students did very poorly at determining whether there was a significant correlation between the seeding and rainfall. But when the information was summed up in a 2 × 2 table, a much greater number of the students were able to reason through the problem and come up with a valid answer. Shweder cites this as evidence that people can have the capacity to think in certain ways but be unable to use that capacity well without certain cognitive tools such as a 2 × 2 contingency table, a tool that he calls "certainly a formal operational instrument." This is an excellent example of what constitutes cultural cognitive evolution: the development of new cognitive tools and a process of educating people in their use. Tools like literacy, list-making, memory techniques, rules of rhetoric, categories for analyzing drama, 2 × 2 tables, musical notation, and so forth have to be developed. The development of such tools has taken thousands of years. The tools must in turn be taught to each new generation, so methods of teaching complex cognitive tools also have evolved over centuries.

It finally comes down to the empirical issue of whether there are observable patterns of development in different cultures, along lines described by Piaget for individual cognitive development. Shweder says this has not happened. He says that in various cultures today there are many cognitive styles, from the supposedly primitive to the supposedly modern. But this evades the question of whether, looking back historically, it is possible to identify when each of those cognitive styles first seems to have appeared in history in some clear and explicit and effective form. The way to discover whether there is a patterned sequence of the appearance of cognitive skills is to review the relevant historical record.

Shweder does not directly address the evidence available from a variety of sources on the lack of formal operational thought among primitives. He gives short shrift to studies on the difference between nonliterate and literate modes of thought, and to studies on the axial age shift. In his arguments, his major examples are based on the Oriya of India, whom he has studied, and who exhibit a variety of styles of thought, shifting mental frameworks as needed. This is not surprising in a society where literacy and a long legacy of religious philosophy provide experiences relevant to the skills required for many different modes of thought, from preoperational to formal operational. Shweder's analysis makes no mention of many explicitly Piagetian cross-cultural studies. Some were cited in chapter I (see note 3). Pierre Dasen and Alastair Heron give a full review of a great variety of studies done of primitives to test Piaget's theory of cognitive development.[79] There are yet other surveys of primitive thought styles, by Richard Lee and Irven DeVore, Gavin Seagrim and Robin Lendon,[80] and John W. Berry.[81] For all of these the Piagetian framework holds up well, save only that formal operational thought is notable by its absence in nonliterate cultures.[82]

On Judging Other Cultures

Learning about other cultures places us inevitably in the position of using our own cultural categories. In a book that Shweder coedited, Robert A. LeVine, writing on the Gusii of Kenya, describes their many beliefs in magic and spirits and their lack of any clear division among religious, mental, and medical matters. He notes in particular that the Gusii do not talk about inner feelings and motives. They focus instead on external behavior, including even their own.[83] LeVine then warns against imposing Western categories such as "primitive" to interpret the Gusii way of thinking. But, unavoidably, he has already used Western categories. It is not the Gusii who notice there is no mention of internal states of mind; it is not the Gusii who notice there are no distinctions among religious, mental, and medical matters. These are all judgments made by a University of Chicago professor.

The best we can probably do, if we are to get beyond our own culture's borders at all, is to acknowledge the problem, then proceed first to try to get the facts right about various cultures. Arguments over how to evaluate those facts can come later. It is not always easy, certainly, to disentangle judgments of fact from judgments of value. Every culture raises its people to attach certain values to certain facts, sometimes in ways the people are not fully aware of. But enough historical material will be reviewed in these pages to give the reader a good chance to identify and challenge valuations disguised as facts.

Use of a Piagetian model for describing cultural evolution can suggest that cognitive development is the single best standard to use in gauging the overall progress of a culture, as though thinking techniques are the major measure of a culture, leaving little room for appreciation of moral, aesthetic, social, and emotional factors. It is good to be wary of thinking that the cognitive history of any society is the whole story or the only important part of the story. Nonetheless, no one should be surprised to find that in human affairs, modes of thought do have a major impact.

Each style of thought has value. The value of preoperational thought is that it is imaginative and creative. Concrete operational thought is very good at tracking all the specifics of life that a person needs to learn to get along, especially since so much of life does not fit neatly into any grand systematic program, and thus can only be memorized bit by bit if a person is to manage it well. These two kinds of thought, each in its own way, are also a good basis for social cohesion. Each values the traditions of the group; each expects people to respect the rules of the group; each promotes loyalty among the group against outside threats. Any contemporary adult using predominantly concrete operational thought can live a mature, wise, productive, humane, and enjoyable life, as a good worker, parent, neighbor, and citizen. An adult can become an expert in a field of work or study, a leader in promoting certain ideas or lifestyles, without much formal operational skill. The basic cognitive strategies that we all learn by the age of twelve are ordinarily quite sufficient to live our lives. Adults rely on these strategies because they are effective for most of life's purposes.

Formal operational thought nonetheless has its advantages, which the chapter on classical thought will delineate more thoroughly. It is also a more difficult style of thought, one that seems to remain latent in any person without schooling in it, except perhaps the rare genius. Where it appears, formal operational thought is nonetheless a very *useful addition* to a culture.

We should acknowledge rather than cover up the fact that there are differences in cognitive skills among both people and cultures, some of which are indeed superior achievements in at least some sense. Some students in school find it far easier than their peers to master certain types of thinking skills. Many people find it far easier to succeed in business or public relations, often more so than the academic achievers. Other people do a much better job at maintaining a happy family context, between the spouses, between the parents and children, and among a variety of relatives and neighbors. Others exhibit artistic sensibilities and skills that enrich everyone's lives. Yet others are gifted in athletics or strength, or in keeping track of minutiae in housekeeping and bookkeeping. Above all, some show an aptitude for moral courage and compassion.

It is perhaps the impact of formal schooling that makes us conscious of and sensitive about differences in cognitive skills. The effect of praise and neglect by teachers, the frequent judgments passed on us and recorded in grade sheets, combine to instill in us a delicacy about any public evaluation of intellectual skills. We are not so delicate concerning artistry, family-building talents, and so forth. We should not seek to avoid the issue of differences in cognitive skills, but should strive to make efforts to put those skills in the larger context of the many other human skills worth developing and praising. We need standards of excellence that give direction to our efforts to develop these skills. This is easy to do in athletics and the arts. We need to have standards in family-building that can guide the new generation of parents. We need to do much more concerning moral values. We also need to maintain intellectual standards of excellence.

The review of the history of the development of cognitive skills, from easier to more difficult, will be a review of the intellectual possibilities open to any society eventually if its members choose. A good description of how those abilities appear sequentially in history will provide an extra framework for estimating the relative value of those abilities. I place a high value on all of the major styles of thought, from magical to mythical to logical to critical-symbolic. Each contributes much to life. In my opinion, the society that has all of them available is the society that is best off. Others may see things differently in any of several ways. But the evaluation can proceed better if we understand more of what we have to evaluate. I hope this book can contribute to that understanding.

3

COGNITIVE STYLES IN PRIMITIVE CULTURES

Primitive Religious Thought

We can begin the study of primitive thought with a look at primitive religion.[1] As we will see later in this chapter, it may be said also to be a primitive form of science. There are many complications in describing religion in primitive culture. What counts as "religious" has been in dispute. So has the extent to which religion is cognitive or "intellectual," and therefore can legitimately be studied as a mode of thought at all. Finally, we will have to consider the evidence for interpreting primitive religious thought through Piagetian categories.

As chapter 1 noted, there are three aspects to religious thought: (1) the beliefs, (2) the mode of expression of the beliefs, and (3) the style of thought that lies behind the mode of expression and beliefs. These three are closely knit in practice, but can be distinguished. This chapter will struggle through various issues in order to arrive at the following conclusions. First, the religious *beliefs* of egalitarian foraging cultures include belief in spirits and magic, treated by primitive people as significant but fairly commonplace beings and powers. It is the type of religious belief that Edward B. Tylor called "animism." Belief in gods, "polytheism," apparently begins to develop only as the culture develops clear social class structure. When chiefs come to rule among people, then gods also rule in the spirit world. Second, these beliefs are *expressed* in folktales of relative brevity rather than in the long narratives that appear in cultures with literacy, and rather than in the abstract systematizations that appear in postaxial societies. Third, the *style of thought* of primitive culture, and thus also of its religion, is a mixture of preoperational and concrete operational thought. On the basis of the evidence available, it is difficult to be more precise about the Piagetian style of thought characteristic of primitive societies, whether simple foraging ones or more complex ones. The most significant aspect is the apparent absence of formal operational thought from all preliterate cultures, in spite of many rather sophisticated attempts by anthropologists to discover or evoke such thought. Formal operational thought is difficult to find, if it is found at all, until the axial age, after which its presence is quite clear in more than one major culture.

Because the point is a sensitive one, it is worth repeating yet again that the people of primitive cultures are as fully endowed with natural human intelligence as the people of any culture. The search to identify aspects of primitive religious thought that are most characteristically primitive is a search for cultural factors, not genetic or "racial" differences. It is a search to discover the ways in which primitive cultures teach people how to apply their human intelligence to the tasks of life. There is little doubt that different cultures teach people different ways of thinking. The issue is whether some differences in thought styles reflect a general human developmental sequence from easier to more difficult modes of thought, a sequence that appears in both cultural and individual development, in particular along Piagetian lines.

A second point worth repeating is that modern people and primitive people *share* beliefs, modes of expression, and styles of thought. Many people in industrial societies believe in spirits, at least in the form of souls, angels, and devils; they tell brief stories from tradition or from personal experience; and they use concrete operational thought and preoperational thought as their normal daily style of thought. If we continue to assume, as we should, that the people of modern cultures are no more intelligent than primitive people, it is not surprising that modern people will continue to use the same cognitive methods as their primitive kinfolk. Because of this, primitive thought will not always seem especially primitive. Cultural development has not eliminated earlier and more basic thought styles; instead, it has added more difficult thought styles to the overall mixture of cognitive techniques available in a culture. Modern people have available to them cognitive tools that primitive cultures do not seem to offer their people.

A number of difficulties stand in the way of a clear picture of primitive culture. A first difficulty is that we often have no way of knowing whether a given hunting-gathering society is carrying on traditions that go back only a hundred years or many thousands of years, whether that society has been influenced significantly by outsiders from a more complex society, or whether the society is newly primitive after a "fall" from a more complex state.[2] Amazonian tribes, for example, may look to us as though they have been primitive as long as they have existed. Yet there is archaeological evidence of more complex agriculturally based life in the Amazon delta and other places, a culture that apparently collapsed around the time of the coming of Europeans and the diseases that then spread throughout the New World.[3] Perhaps the ancestors of current Amazonian primitive societies possessed a more complex set of cognitive methods. If so, it is all the more striking that the hunting-gathering life-style now should lack that extra complexity, as though certain cognitive techniques will be abandoned if there is not a complex social arrangement to sustain their use.

Science fiction scenarios describe lost civilizations with advanced skills. Perhaps there were some primordial cultures, now entirely lost to our view, that had developed sophisticated cultural forms including formal operational techniques: a coded marking system to represent language, a schooling system to teach the marking system, a set of words and techniques for thinking about language construction and about logical forms of thought, a set of techniques for teaching people how to learn these techniques. We have no evidence, however, that there were such lost civilizations. If there were, we would then have to wonder what historical sequence of development led to the acquisition of such techniques. The only alternative is to suppose that somehow the human race was born like Athena, already in full possession of an entire range of difficult skills that nonetheless require extensive educational processes to be passed on to the next generation. Who educated the first generation? Where did they learn their skills? We must either have a theory of cultural development or else invoke the gods or God (or aliens from outer space, though we would then have to ask how they developed to the point of being able to visit and educate us humans).

We could more modestly speculate that perhaps the general level of cognitive skills among Old Stone Age people was a little higher than that of many of the primitive people today. The cave art at Lascaux and Chauvet, and the notched bone calendars of Paleolithic Europe, suggest cultures that might have developed significant cognitive techniques in other areas. Perhaps contemporary hunter-gatherer cultures are poorer and more limited in various ways than early Cro-Magnon culture. Perhaps the relatively few hunter-gatherer cultures that exist today, unlike the first human societies, live poorly on marginal land because more technologically and economically advanced groups have taken over the most favorable locations for human life. If this is so, then contemporary primitive cultures do not represent early human life accurately.

Nonetheless, there are in existence today a number of cultures whose dominant cognitive styles are of the simpler sort that can be mastered by most ten-year-old children. This indicates that a human culture can function fairly well, even with quite simple cognitive habits and techniques. We can also compare the cognitive styles of hunting-gathering groups with those of other preliterate peoples whose means of subsistence includes gardening or herding practices, and whose social structures are more complex, to see whether the lack of literacy in all of these is accompanied by certain styles of thought. This provides a baseline. We can then identify the history of changes in modes of cognition that follow upon literacy, then of the further changes that follow upon the appearance in a culture of explicit forms of "metacognition" and "epistemic" cognition.

A second difficulty in interpreting primitive cultures is that many studies of primitive peoples were carried out by anthropologists who had limited expertise at recognizing and describing different cognitive styles. Barbara Rogoff, for example, notes a misapplication of Piagetian tests. When Piaget asked children about "conservation" of an amount of water poured from one vessel into another, he carefully elicited the children's reasoning behind their conclusions. Some cross-cultural researchers, claims Rogoff, sought only to know whether the children got the correct result, thereby overlooking important information as to how the child arrived at the conclusion.[4] (We should note, however, that after her critical review of the Piagetian cross-cultural studies, Rogoff concludes that the evidence for cultural developmental differences along Piagetian lines is quite good.)

The list of exaggerated claims about the "metaphysics" or "systematic theorizing" of primitive people cited in the previous chapter also illustrates anthropologists' lack of familiarity with cognitive theories. The antievolutionist and antiuniversalist stance of twentieth-century anthropology contributed to this. Each culture was to be studied on its own, not analyzed according to categories that transcended a society and compared one society with others. An anthropologist needed to study only the cognitive style of the people he or she was trying to understand. A comparative approach, on the other hand, requires that one become familiar with a full range of basic possible thought styles. We should pay most attention to the efforts of anthropologists who are well trained in cognitive studies in general as well as in attempts to adapt various cognitive tests to particular primitive cultures.

A related third difficulty in studying the thought of primitive cultures is using cognitive tests developed in Europe, and applying those tests to cultures that are quite different. The content, format, criteria, and style of social interaction involved in using the tests could easily confound any results. Daniel Wagner and Harold Stevenson, for example, note that when Australian Aborigine children were examined by outsiders, the children often seemed slow to arrive at concrete operational thought, but did not appear slow when examined by people of their own ethnic or language group.[5] Those who share the same language, idiom, examples, and stories can evoke a more complex response from children. Fortunately, as we will see, some anthropologists have become accustomed to acknowledging the problem and compensating for it.

A fourth difficulty is distinguishing between the common overt verbal behavior of a people and the kind of thought processes behind that behavior. We cannot uncritically suppose that people who publicly use only simple forms of categorizing, numbering, giving instructions, or offering explanations necessarily possess only those simple forms of thought. Perhaps rather sophisticated individual thinkers in primitive cultures mask the level of sophistication of their thought by following everyday speech conventions that are adapted to communicate with the least sophisticated people in the society.[6] If the societies in which these hidden geniuses live show no evidence of such sophisticated thought, the best we can conclude is that the geniuses by themselves do not have much impact on those societies' public thought styles. If such geniuses are common enough, that would be all the more evidence that it takes long cultural development before their presence can be identified.

A fifth difficulty is determining where to place the lines to distinguish one form of culture from another. To track cultural changes, we could combine ideas from Talcott Parsons and Robert Bellah, for example, to produce six classifications: classless primitive foragers; early class societies with hereditary chiefs or kings; preaxial literate civilizations; postaxial civilizations; early modern neoclassical culture; and modern critical-empirical culture. Studies of "primitive" thought have often lumped together the first two of these categories, egalitarian foraging peoples and early preliterate but multiclass societies. For simplicity, this chapter will do the same. There are occasionally reasons to distinguish between truly primitive peoples and more developed herding and/or complex horticultural societies. But unless otherwise indicated, this chapter will treat as "primitive" all societies that are both noncivilized (do not live in cities) and nonliterate.

Because of all these difficulties the description of primitive thought in this chapter will be restrained and tentative. The main purpose is not to establish with simple exactness how primitive people think, though we will see some interesting attempts at this, especially those of Robert Horton and Christopher Hallpike. The main purpose is to establish a roughly accurate baseline for comparing stages of culture. That will be a picture of the general thought styles which primitive cultures exhibit, according to some of the most extensive and careful analyses available. The advances in methods of thought represented by the literacy of early civilization, then by axial age systematically logical reflection, and finally by recent critical-empirical testing, will stand out more clearly by observing as best we can how primitive people speak and seem to think.

A reminder of differences among thought styles can be of use in reading what follows. In Piagetian descriptions the differences are roughly the following. Preoperational thought collects bits and pieces of information without organizing them into large or complex categories. Concrete operational thought organizes ideas into larger and more complex categories, showing an ability to cross-index ideas or things in consistent ways. Formal operational thought is able to devise hypothetical alternative ways of explaining the categories, and of testing those explanations for logical coherence with each other and with evidence. Later formal operational thought treats any systematically or logically derived conclusions with greater awareness of their conditional nature.

These four styles of thought include what could be called increased ability in "reality discrimination." A preoperational style of thought is least critical about the truth-value of pleasing or appealing ideas. Even though it will often accept the word of someone who seems to be authoritatively in the know, the lines between reality and fiction are nonetheless rather blurred. A concrete operational style of thought is more concerned to discriminate between truth and fiction, though in practice it may be little better at achieving this goal. Where the preoperational habit will be to believe whatever feels right, the concrete operational will rely more on firsthand evidence and on the authority of those whom the group treats as the leaders or the wisest or the official holders of tradition and truth. Formal operational thought adds one more criterion, that of overall logical consistency among ideas and of ideas with the evidence. This places authority in the hands of the thinking individual. Late formal operational thought does the same, though with a bit more humility, as it were; with more critical awareness of the difficulties of establishing what is true or not true.

The Religion of Egalitarian Foraging People

Foraging cultures are normally most primitive in social organization. The land provides limited food for hunters and gatherers. This requires low population density. Foragers thus typically live in small groups, in which everyone is familiar to everyone else. This in turn produces egalitarian societies. The word "egalitarian" is a bit misleading. A few people will possess greater social influence than others. An excellent hunter, a person whose shamanistic skills are thought especially good, an elder with extensive practical experience, will each be more than simply "equal" to the others in the group. Many groups also grant higher status to men than to women, a common enough lack of equality in these and other societies. Anthropologists speak of such groups as egalitarian nonetheless, because of the absence of a hereditary class system. The child of any mother and father has equal status with other children of the same sex and age.[7]

There is good evidence that egalitarian foraging cultures have the simplest beliefs of the sort that are usually called "religious." Dean Sheils's study of the correlations between mode of subsistence and religious belief indicates a fairly consistent pattern.[8] The less the social differentiation within the society, the less likely is a belief in any genuinely godlike beings. Foraging peoples believe only in everyday, small-scale magic and in human-sized spirit beings. The spirit beings that inhabit the primitive world are of many kinds. They can include the primordial beings, often theriomorphic (animal-shaped) like the Raven or Hyena or Bear, that account for the present state of the world. The spirits can also include significant clan ancestors of recent times, animal spirits, spirits of certain objects and places, and the spirits of the dead in general. These spirit beings exist side by side without any explicit hierarchical ordering among them, a jumbled collection of invisible beings to deal with and tell stories about.

Many of the beliefs of foraging peoples are not contained in folktales or myths; they are just pieces of information about their world. Pascal Boyer, for example, cites the beliefs of a Cameroon people, the Fang, about the spirits of the dead. At first the spirit is called a *bekong*, a malevolent spirit that wanders around with others who have died recently. These spirits cause a lot of trouble for people. But when the formal funeral is finally held, a few months after death, the *bekong* becomes an ancestor who now individually aids and protects people. This information that the Fang possess about spirits is not stated as coherently as this paragraph presents it. Boyer was able to summarize Fang belief in this way out of bits and pieces of information. "The propositions above," says Boyer of his description of Fang beliefs, "typically emerge from people's statements about *bekong*; they do not constitute an integrated system. The ideas are vague for the Fang themselves."[9]

When beliefs do find expression in folktales ("myths"), they are brief, often elliptical, omitting pieces of information needed for clarity or completeness unless one is already familiar with the story. The stories are unconnected except perhaps by having the same characters in more than one story. The "trickster" stories of various cultures, for example, will feature the same primordial being like the Raven or Hyena, engaged in behavior that is strange even to the storytellers. The collection of stories reflects the overall composition of the primitive universe—a loose collection of facts and places and rules and powers and beings, visible and invisible—with no large-scale organizing elements.[10] I call these stories folktales rather than myths, to distinguish them from the epic myths of later literate archaic cultures.[11]

The beliefs change somewhat in cultures large and complex enough to have "chiefs" or kings. These are "advanced primitive" cultures in Parson's categories, usually based on horticulture or herding as their means of subsistence, or perhaps living off bounteous seaside resources.

Such hierarchically ordered tribes may add a few spirit beings of larger-than-human power, large enough in power to deserve the name "gods."[12] In the early part of this century Fr. Wilhelm Schmidt challenged the claim that egalitarian foraging people do not have gods.[13] Andrew Lang had suggested that even the most primitive people had a belief in a high god—a supreme god among others, often a god who had created the whole world.[14] Such a belief implies a degree of hierarchical order in the universe. Schmidt gathered what appeared to be massive evidence in support of this high god thesis. For him this was a sign of a primordial monotheism, an idea that fit nicely with the official Catholic belief at that time that the whole human race was descended from a single first pair of parents who had known God.[15] For others today this notion of a universal belief in a high god is evidence that primitive peoples are not so terribly primitive after all.

Schmidt's evidence is no longer convincing. He overlooked differences between egalitarian foraging cultures and hierarchically organized herding or horticultural ones. While advanced primitive cultures, those that have a hereditary ruler and a ruling class, often have a belief in a high god of sorts, this generally is not true of egalitarian foraging people. The Semai of the Malay peninsula were purported to hold the thunder god as a high god. Robert Dentan demolished this with his retelling of a bawdy and rather disrespectful story of how Thunder got his voice.[16] Thunder turns out to be a human-sized spirit being from primal times. In the 1930s Father Gusinde discovered that the Tierra del Fuegans, questioned rather often about their beliefs for the previous one hundred years, had believed all along in a high god that no outsider had been told about before. Why? Because no one had asked, was the reason the tribesperson gave.[17] It is equally possible that an individual Fuegan informant decided that if anthropologists or priests were interested in the idea of a high god, it was worth providing them with an instance, even if the informant had to make it up on the basis of information derived from generations of missionaries.[18]

Jonathan Z. Smith argues that this is what happened in the case of the high god Io of the Maori of New Zealand. A single informant, acquainted with Christian beliefs (and after a century of previous inquiry by interested Westerners), was the sole source, says Smith, for the claims about this instance of belief in a high god.[19] Michael Gelfand provides an odd kind of confirmation of doubts about the high god theory. He supports the frequent claim that African religions have a creator god, albeit an indifferent and far-removed deity, a god that is irrelevant to daily life.[20] But in the appendix of his book, surveying the beliefs of many tribal cultures in Africa, Gelfand lists a number of them without any such high god at all. Similarly, in their review of aspects of traditional societies, Alice and Irvin Child end with a claim that foraging societies have a high god more often than more complex societies do. They do not provide evidence for this. They do, however, provide over two hundred pages of specific information about "traditional" beliefs, both primitive and early archaic, almost none of them related to any high gods even as they tell it. The exceptions are a secondary reference to E. E. Evans-Pritchard's mention of a word that may mean high god or spirit power in general, and to a Navajo belief in "gods."[21]

Based on his experiences in the Niger delta (1914–1916), Amaury Talbot describes local tribes as advanced primitive, with explicit class differentiations. But he calls their religion animism, a collection of beliefs in spirits, magic, sorcery, and taboos without any high gods.[22] Talbot also noted that the various tribal groups of Nigeria and neighboring countries had long been exposed to the influence of Christian missionaries, before that of Islamic traders, and possibly even of ancient Egyptian culture. Any belief in a high god may derive from such outside influence. When John Middleton describes the Lugbara of Uganda, for example, he writes as though they had always had a belief in a high god. But he finally notes that there have long been Christian, and before that Muslim, influences on the Lugbara.[23] This creator high god could easily be a belief tacked onto tradition under outside influence.

Guy Swanson devised a statistical approach to the question of high gods. George Murdoch had estimated that anthropologists had studied about thirty-five hundred different non-Western preindustrial societies. Murdoch divided these into fifty areas of the world, and in each area further classified the societies according to their level of social complexity. This included such factors as the means of subsistence, the number of people living in one band or tribe or other social unit, the number of "sovereign groups" present in a society (i.e., familial, political, religious groupings with some clear differentiation among themselves). Murdoch selected 556 different societies, that together cover all 50 areas, as a sampling. Swanson drew up a protocol for interpreting the religious beliefs and practices of societies, including whether there were any high gods. He then randomly selected 50 societies out of the 556. With the aid of a group of graduate students trained in the protocol, these fifty societies were categorized according to the factors Murdoch had used. The ratings on these factors were then compared with the kinds of beliefs in spirits and/or gods present in the societies. Though there were exceptions, the general pattern was clear. The simpler foraging societies in which there was no distinct political class or organization lacked belief in a high god; those societies which had a hereditary political class, and in which the political leadership was a "sovereign group," were by far most likely to have a high god.[24] In sum, there are now enough cross-cultural data to establish that generally a high god appears only in advanced primitive and archaic cultures, where there is a differentiation of classes.

Real human life, of course, is always much messier than neat, ideal-type categorizations. The Native Americans of what is now the western

Canadian and Alaskan coastal areas were foragers, but nonetheless had a multiclass social structure. The wealth of food from the sea supported a high population density with two or three distinct classes (if slaves are included as a lowest class). On the other hand, Phillip Guddemi reports that a tribal group in Papua New Guinea, the Sawiyano, which has taken up horticulture in the last few centuries, has nonetheless retained characteristics of social organization and religious belief that are more usually associated with hunter-gatherers (foragers). The reason may simply be that the Sawiyano are surrounded by hunter-gatherers, whose influence helps hold the Sawiyano to their own original hunter-gatherer cultural style.[25] The reverse of this situation partly holds for the Nuer of the southern Sudan. They are a herding society like their neighbors, the Dinka. Like their neighbors they seem to have a high god, whom the Nuer call Kwoth. But unlike their neighbors they are a classless society. The Dinka have two major classes for the males, the priests (closer to diviners and shamans in our usual categories) and the warriors. Bruce Lincoln estimates that the Nuer were a clan or subtribe of the Dinka in the not-too-distant past, and have similar religious beliefs about a hierarchy of spirit beings, beliefs that have been maintained by tradition and by continued contact with the Dinka, even though the Nuer no longer have the class hierarchy that is usual among those who believe in a class hierarchy among the spirits.[26] To make it all even more confusing, it is not clear whether Kwoth is a god, strictly speaking, or is just a name for what we might call the supernatural in general. Furthermore, there is a strong possibility that all these tribal groups have had some contact with Islamic ideas about a supreme God, ideas that may have influenced tribal thought to some extent. (Another nearby Nilotic group, the Shilluk, has a divine king like the Egyptian pharaoh. Perhaps ancient Egyptian culture made its influence felt this far up the Nile.[27])

This initial description and comparison of characteristics, beliefs, and thought style of primitive religion is already complex. As was mentioned, other issues are also in dispute. A first is whether primitive people are religious at all. A second is whether primitive religion, if it exists, is "intellectual," its beliefs constituting answers to questions about causes of things. A third, finally addressing the issue of primitive religious thought, is whether the intellectual dimension of primitive religion, if any, can legitimately be characterized according to Piagetian categories. These three questions will be taken up one at a time in the following sections.

Problems in Defining
Primitive Religion

The problems begin with the fact that primitive people are not aware of having "religion" in our modern sense of the word, as a set of beliefs and practices clearly distinct from other aspects of life that are considered unreligious. Primitive people are aware of spirit beings and invisible powers that shamans and sorcerers can manipulate; they are aware of moments of transition in the life of a person or of the whole tribal group that must be ritualized in certain traditional ways; they have a sense that some objects or places or rites have a special quality. But they do not define these as distinctly "religious."

Emile Durkheim, to the contrary, claimed that primitive people were conscious of a sharp division between the sacred and the profane such as is common in modern culture. "The sacred and the profane have always and everywhere been conceived by the human mind as two distinct classes, as two worlds between which there is nothing in common."[28] Mircea Eliade happily echoed this, proclaiming that for primitive people the sacred is "a wholly different order" from the profane.[29] Eliade praises Rudolph Otto's rather sophisticated Western interpretation as a good guide to the sacred.[30] Here the sacred or "holy" is encountered in an experience of an awesome and fascinating mystery.[31]

The reality is more ambiguous, however. There may be quite a bit more of Hegel and Schleiermacher in this description of the holy than there is of primitive experience. Otto is the product of a Western heritage quite different from primitive culture. A similar suspicion arises when Joachim Wach makes sense of the category of the sacred by using the fairly modern ideas of William James and Paul Tillich.[32] Äka Hultkrantz claims there is a clear difference in primal religion between the sacred and the ordinary, but he then qualifies his claim by saying that the sacred nonetheless blends into the everyday; it is just the more awesome or unusual aspects of the everyday. Then Hultkrantz adds that for Native Americans all of nature is sacred, so that there is no merely profane reality.[33] Peter Worsley is more emphatic that the distinction between the sacred and the profane is artificial when applied to primitive thought. In his study of Melanesian cargo cults he cites instances to show that the ancestors' spirits are called up like extra hands to help out in work; that strange "powers" are just unusual, neither specifically sacred or profane; that the name for magic is simply the name for work.[34] Similarly, when speaking of the "divinities" (spirits) of the Dinka, Douglas Lienhardt asserts flatly that the distinction between the natural and the supernatural is foreign to the Dinka.[35] In a discussion of traditional *kami* reverence in Japan, Alfred Bloom declares that the whole cosmos is so thoroughly permeated by the "spiritual" presence of the *kami* that the division between divine and profane existence is hard to draw.[36]

The weakness of the distinction between sacred and everyday appears also in the use of supposedly sacred objects. The "bull-roarer" is part of Australian Aboriginal life, a "sacred" source of a strange sound. To the boys undergoing initiation into adulthood the bull-roarer is revealed to be two ordinary pieces of wood swung around on a thong until its vibrations make a loud, deep sound.[37] A continent away, in the Venezuelan forest, the Yanomamö snort the hallucinogenic *ebene*, which puts a person in touch with various spirits in rocks and trees. The spirits are invited to enter the man's chest (women do not use *ebene*) and fill him with their power. They can make the person a bit crazy, so other Yanomamö may hide all weapons from their *ebene*-intoxicated comrade. This contact with spirits can be done rather casually, even daily, as a person chooses. Shamans do this to get help from spirits or to contact them in order to drive spirits from a sick person. But this matter-of-fact practice seems more like practical medicine (or a "trip," to use 1960s jargon) to the Yanomamö than a sacred activity.[38] On yet another continent, the Mbuti pygmies of the Zaire rain forest sometimes disappear among the trees to sound a sacred voice. Colin Turnbull, who lived among them, was disappointed to discover in one case that the voice was made by using a piece of drainage pipe like a tuba. The pygmies made the noise more in a spirit of having fun than of religious awe.[39] None of this is as clearly and distinctly "religious" as we might like, if we are to discuss the nature of primitive religion clearly.

Even if we grant some validity to the distinction between sacred and profane, the difficulties are not over. There are challenges to the claim that primitive beliefs and practices are really religious at all. Edward Tylor observes that many Europeans were reluctant to classify primitive dealings with spirits and magic as religion. Typical of Tylor's position is his response to the claim by J. D. Lang (one that Lucien Lévy-Bruhl seems to echo) that the Aborigines of Australia have no true religion. As Tylor presents Lang's ideas: "The aborigines of Australia have no idea of a supreme divinity, creator, and judge, no object of worship, no idol, temple, or sacrifice, but that 'in short they have nothing whatever of the character of religion, or of religious observance, to distinguish them from the beasts that perish.'"[40] Tylor responds by citing evidence from Lang's same work about the small offerings that the Aborigines leave for a particular spirit being named Budyah, and about the sacrifice of young girls at times to "propitiate some evil divinity."[41]

This argument is largely a matter of definition. Europeans accustomed to worship of gods or God were reluctant to label as "religious" the various ways primitive peoples have dealt with invisible beings and powers. Primitive people approach the spirits more as neighbors—some irritable, some helpful, some of more influence than others—all of them having the normal human desire to receive attention or gifts. Even a sacrificial offering may turn out to be less "religious" than a European may wish. The Childs cite an instance of a Tanzanian tribesman killing and offering a bull to his dead wife, to ask her to stop bringing him misfortune in retaliation for the harm he did her while she was alive.[42] This is a bribe, as it were, rather than an act of reverence, much less worship.

Tylor deals with all this by offering a broad definition of religion. While it may be true that at some very long-ago time in human prehistory there may have been an absence of religion, current primitive beliefs in and dealings with spirits should be called religious. Rather than artificially exclude primitive beliefs from the domain of religion, says Tylor, the "minimum definition of Religion" should be any "belief in Spiritual Beings."[43]

Lucien Lévy-Bruhl also weighed in for this fight.[44] In his still famous comments on primitive thought, he seems to imply in places that the acts by which primitive people deal with ancestral and other spirits may be sacred acts, but not quite religious acts.[45] An example is his longer analysis in *Primitive Mythologies*, about folktales of the natives of Australia and New Guinea.[46] In the course of noting the difference between the primal times and historical time, which for the natives covers only about five generations, Lévy-Bruhl comments on native practices. The ancestors who died only a few generations ago can affect current happenings, so offerings and sacrifices must be made to them. Not so with the primal ancestors, whose activity is done.[47] Lévy-Bruhl then says this about the tribal ceremonies in honor of primal ancestors:

[These ceremonies] bring about a sense of participation and intimate communion with the beings. They are thus equivalent to religious rituals, though it is true they take a form unlike the religious ceremonies we are accustomed to, and are not addressed to what we would consider as gods.[48]

In the course of three pages Lévy-Bruhl thus describes (1) what he calls a prereligious set of rituals of participation with the primal ancestors and (2) offerings and sacrifices to beings who are not gods but are more immediate ancestors, and alludes (3) to a third kind of religious ceremony that is addressed to gods, and therefore is a type of ceremony missing from Aboriginal practices. This third is what he identifies as what his European readers might consider true religious ceremonies. He does not further explain what he means by this.

Lévy-Bruhl's ambiguous analyses remind us that disputes about categories can go on and on with no resolution. We can at least categorize the beliefs and practices of primitive people relating to invisible beings and powers as "protoreligion." They are the beliefs that we almost unthinkingly call religious because later forms of religion also include belief in the invisible realm as one of power and activity relevant to human life. When we find twenty-five thousand-year-old burial sites in which useful objects like obsidian knives are buried with the body, we are tempted to conclude not only that this implies some belief in a life after death for a person's spirit but also that this can be called an instance of primordial religious belief. I will call primitive animism by the name of "religion" in order to acknowledge the continuity between belief in the spirits of foraging cultures and belief in the more powerful spirit beings we call "gods" to whom sacrifice is offered. They differ in their size and nature, but all of them are invisible, conscious beings able to have some influence on human life.

Primitive Religion as Intellectual

Edward B. Tylor's interpretation of religion has been called "intellectualist" because he thought of primitive religion as a set of beliefs used to make sense of reality in the same way that people do today. Tylor claimed there has been a progressive development of better habits of observation and reasoning.[49] Like people of today, primitive people reasoned by analogy and by an association of ideas; they used trial and error; they just failed to have methods to test their beliefs well.[50]

Lévy-Bruhl intended to rebut Tylor's claim that primitive people, like people of any culture, arrive at their beliefs by seeking the causes of events.[51] He argued that primitive people used a "prelogical" style of thought. He rejected Tylor's supposition that the intellectual quest of individuals for causes was the source of belief in spirits. Lévy-Bruhl sought to replace this supposition with the Durkheimian notion of "collective representations." People like Tylor mistakenly assumed, says Lévy-Bruhl, that the beliefs of the primitives "exist in individual minds similar to their own."[52] But belief in spirits and their activity does not arise from individual thought; it is, rather, the collective heritage of the group.

> Being collective, they force themselves upon the individual; that is, they are to him an article of faith, not the product of his reason. And since the collective representations, as a rule, predominate most where the races are least advanced, the mind of the "primitive" has hardly any room for such questions as "how" or "why." The ensemble of collective representations which master him and excite in him an intensity of feeling which we cannot even imagine, is hardly compatible with that disinterested contemplation of a matter which a purely intellectual desire to probe into its cause would demand.[53]

There are a number of obvious problems with Lévy-Bruhl's response. His description of how collective representations are handed on to individuals as articles of faith is certainly correct for most people in any culture. But these articles of faith may nonetheless be accepted as explanations, as descriptions of the causes of events, and thus are "intellectual" in that sense. It is at least plausible to suppose that these articles of faith are maintained among a people precisely because their intellectual function of offering explanation is valued. Furthermore, Lévy-Bruhl evades the issue of where the collective representations first arose. It does not seem far-fetched to suppose that if they function as descriptions of causes, as they certainly seem to, that they originally arose as explanations offered by one or more individuals for certain events. To call this into question, Lévy-Bruhl has to demean the intelligence of primitive people, allowing them no room for "how" and "why" questions. He also has portrayed the "intellectual" approach as "disinterested." We can recognize, however, that a deeply interested and emotionally involved person may have greater motive to question the "how" and "why" of things. On the whole, Tylor comes off far better than Lévy-Bruhl.[54]

Tylor's ideas and Lévy-Bruhl's response sound like old and outdated arguments.[55] Not so. Some current theorists insist that religion is most basically not about beliefs but about symbolic expression of inner experience, feeling, or orientation. Dewi Phillips, as the introduction noted, proposes that religious beliefs are descriptions of the state of the feelings of the religious persons, not truth-claims.[56] He cites Tylor's claim about a dying mother who breathes into the face of her newborn in order to transfer life to it.[57] Phillips says that this is not a mistaken belief because it is not a belief at all. It is a gesture from a dying mother, an expression of feeling. He says more generally that people who make religious fact-claims are "closer to superstition."[58] On the face of it, this is an instance of someone interpreting the religious beliefs of others according to the person's own notion of the nature of "true" religion. It would be bizarrely contrary to all evidence to claim that primitive people do not think of these beliefs as true but rather as symbolic expressions of their emotional states. Tylor, Lévy-Bruhl, and many others provide compendia of primitive people's countless beliefs in spirits and their activity. Phillips and others are imposing their own belief concerning the true nature of religion upon primitive people.[59] If the natives only knew better, Phillips implies, they would recognize that they should not treat their own beliefs, whether individual or collective, as true. They should instead treat their beliefs as symbols of their inner concerns and emotions and attachments.[60] To simplify things, let us just say that the nature of "true" religion—or the "true" nature of religion—can be argued elsewhere than here. The relevant point is that except for a few people, those who believe in spirits, gods, God, and other invisible beings generally take their own beliefs to be factually true, not just emotional expressions.

Lévy-Bruhl's analysis of "prelogical" thought, however, still poses the possibility that the beliefs of primitive people might be part of a style of thought that is quite different from what we are accustomed to, and therefore might not be subject to Piagetian categories. The beliefs of people who take their beliefs to be factually true might yet be beliefs that differ in some significant respect from beliefs as we know them, not just in content but in mode of thought. Thus primitive religion may indeed be "intellectualist" or at least "cognitive" in some sense of the word, contrary to the claims of Phillips and others, and still be distinct enough in thought style not to fit within Piagetian categories at all.

The word "prelogical" unfortunately distracts from the major characteristics of the kind of thought that Lévy-Bruhl perceived in the many reports he read on primitive culture. He himself regretted the word eventually and said he wanted to speak of "mystical participatory thought."[61] In his earlier work, *How Natives Think*, Lévy-Bruhl here and there provides what seem to be descriptions of major characteristics of the mystical mode of thought in general. First, it is emotional, laden with fear or hope, and not coolly objective.[62] Second, it looks to "imperceptible forces" that are nonetheless real.[63] Third, it is "participatory" thought, through which the native has an identity with various beings and forces.[64]

Though Lévy-Bruhl is trying very hard to identify some strange native mode of thinking, his examples repeatedly point merely to belief in supernatural beings or in magic. He finds this irrational, an acceptance of contradictions that the logical (Western) mind would reject. For the most part, then, Lévy-Bruhl is not actually identifying some mysterious thought style. He is just expressing astonishment that the natives are anthropomorphic supernaturalists—people who believe in invisible spirits (and magic) as causes of events—instead of scientific naturalists like modern Europeans as he sees them.[65]

Robin Horton's analyses of primitive religious thought show that belief in spirits is not as far from science as Lévy-Bruhl and other scholars claim. On the basis of his own years of anthropological study in Africa, Horton tries to show that various beliefs of primitive (nonliterate) cultures in many spirit beings and in magic are not radically different from the ideas of modern science.[66] Behind the specific beliefs of primitive animists and modern scientists is a common human enterprise—to make sense of experience by formulating explanations that are based on analogies with other experiences. Horton is thus supporting an "intellectualist" notion of religion in its preliterate form. He describes parallels, as he sees them, between primitive thought and that of modern science.

First of all, the theories of science are ordinarily analogies drawn from other aspects of experience. The planetary model of the atom, and descriptions of how genes "try" to reproduce themselves as though they were consciously goal-directed, are instances of explanatory models used by science that are drawn from other ideas or experiences people have. Similarly, when primitive people explain events as the result of spirits, they are formulating theories by analogy with their own experience of themselves as conscious agents who cause events to happen.[67]

Second, scientific theories omit some aspect of the original analogue. To explain the actions of gas by analogy with a room full of tiny balls bouncing off each other is useful only as long as some attributes of the balls—size, color, surface texture—are omitted. So also with the spirits and gods, who are like people but with some attributes omitted, such as physical solidness.[68] Third, science often modifies its original theory to fit new evidence. Horton cites ways primitive thought does this to account for odd behavior by the spirits.[69]

Finally, Horton argues, the modern scientist tends to do the same as the primitive person when an inherited belief or theory is questioned, which is to cling to a traditional belief regardless of any lack of evidence, perhaps even regardless of contrary evidence. In spite of the scientific ideal of open-mindedness, even the scientist will tend to reinterpret contrary evidence in such a way as to preserve the theory. The scientific method requires attention to testing and evidence, but the scientists involved may nonetheless be rather traditionalist.[70]

Horton can compare primitive thought to science in some ways because the full method of science does include fact-claims or beliefs that help to explain things. It also includes the use of models and analogies and some reflection on evidence. In fact, human thought in general—religious and scientific, primitive and modern—will include these aspects of thought. But the full method of modern science also includes aspects missing from primitive thought as Horton himself describes it. The roots of science are certainly here. But both religious thought and science together have a long developmental path ahead of them.

Hallpike on Primitive Modes of Thought

Horton makes a good case for the continuity thesis: that primitive thought is not entirely different from the thought of contemporary people. Both primitive and modern people seek to make sense of reality by formulating ideas about the causes of things and events, and then apply those ideas in daily life. The question is, then, whether the way in which primitive people do this reflects a cognitive style that fits within Piagetian categories, and whether primitive cultures lack cognitive skills present in later literate and other cultures. A study that stands out for the thoroughness with which it attends to the style of primitive thought is Christopher Hallpike's book *The Foundations of Primitive Thought*. His project is to describe in detail a wide range of anthropological studies of the cognitive styles of various nonliterate tribal peoples. Hallpike's conclusion is that primitive (nonliterate) cultures manifest a high degree of preoperational practices in word and probably, therefore, also in thought. This is all the more evident in the absence of cognitive skills that some people in modern cultures use quite freely. These are skills in classification, number and measurement, conservation of quantity, categories of space and time, ideas about causality, and methods for distinguishing between inner ideas and outer reality. It is worth a look at Hallpike's case. He attends to many specific characteristics of preoperational thought, and no one has explored the relation of primitive thought style to Piagetian categories more thoroughly than he. A summary of his major points and evidence will provide an excellent sense of the kind of relevant evidence available.

Hallpike's analysis operates on three levels: the descriptive, the comparative, and the explanatory. Most of the book is a description of many aspects of how primitive peoples seem to think, a description based on numerous direct anthropological studies, both formal and informal, of the way in which primitive people argue with each other, teach their children, describe events, handle skepticism, respond to Western tests of intelligence or mental skills, and so on. Hallpike also provides a careful comparison of the results of all these studies with specific aspects of Piaget's analysis of the kinds of thought styles used by children as they mature, a comparison which results in the conclusion that there is a high amount of preoperational thinking among primitive people. Finally, Hallpike adds some explanatory considerations about why this preoperational style should be so evident, considerations that stress the effects of what the life situation, including both cultural tradition and environment, promotes and inhibits.

Like many of his predecessors, Hallpike is concerned with general patterns of thought—"collective representations"—rather than with the accomplishments of a few unique individuals. He wants to determine what the common and public mode of thought is among primitive people, using Piagetian categories to classify the thought style. Different people in any society will appropriate the collective representations in different ways. His question is whether those ways in primitive cultures encompass the full range of the modes thought Piaget describes, including those of formal operational thought.[71] If not, his supposition will be that the social and physical environment has not pushed the society into the development of the more complex modes of thought.[72]

Studies of children in different cultures provide more evidence that we humans everywhere at least partly share a similar cognitive history.[73] Children of comparable age in "West Africa, Aden, Iran, Hong Kong, and Geneva give almost identical answers" to Piagetian problems.[74] If the children of all societies use the same mode of thought at some point in their development, then the adults of all societies also have this mode of thought as part of their own personal history. It should not be surprising if adults everywhere, including primitive societies, continue to use these modes of thought.

Hallpike also makes a point especially relevant to the analysis of primitive religious thought. Durkheim, Frazer, Lévy-Bruhl, and others treat supernaturalist beliefs in spirits, magic, or gods as oddities that separate modern people from primitives and make the latter hard to understand. Hallpike bluntly calls this "largely nonsense."[75] Supernatural beliefs are part of every society. The real problem with understanding primitive thought is that it is "inarticulate," enclosed in ritual and custom but not explicated verbally.[76] It is *how* people hold their supernatural beliefs that is at issue. It is, for example, the difference in how the same Christian beliefs may be held by "an Irish peasant and a Jesuit theologian."[77] There can be a difference in thought style about the same content.

A large amount of work by others stands behind the first level of Hallpike's analysis, describing how primitive people think. Michael Cole and associates, for example, spent a number of years working with the Kpelle of Liberia, both with those in a traditional tribal setting and those exposed to some degree of formal Western-style education.[78] Cole worked carefully to eliminate cultural bias in the methods used to study how the Kpelle thought, changing investigative techniques, using the stories of the Kpelle rather than Western ones, experimenting with different kinds of problems. Those without formal schooling were not able to verbalize their methods of rice farming or to express the pros and cons of why they grew rice on dry hills rather than on the low-lying wetlands. Those with schooling, however, could articulate both methods and reasons fairly well. The Kpelle found it easy to fit this schooled way of thinking with their old way. The new way merely extended the cognitive skills of the Kpelle.[79] A change in cultural context here determined what styles of thought and expression were available, in a set of circumstances that illustrates a developmental pattern.

Hallpike carefully and thoroughly examines the results of many such studies of primitive cultures. There is typically a lack of both large-scale generalizations and logical ordering of ideas.[80] Education is by demonstration: "do it like this."[81] (As is often the case, Bernard Lonergan provides good language to name this style of thought: "doing the truth," as opposed to later stages of "saying the truth" and "understanding the truth."[82]) The tellers of traditional stories cannot articulate the theme or moral of the stories; they can only retell the specifics. In telling of their own experiences, the speakers seem unable to edit the experiences to select the salient moments but instead repeat events chronologically, including aspects irrelevant to the main point of the story.[83] There is a decided inability to derive logical conclusions, as in the famous logical problems that Alexander Luria put to Siberian preliterate people. Luria asked some Siberian tribespeople to consider this problem: In the North all the bears are white. Someone went to the North and saw a bear there. What color was the bear? Time after time the tribespeople answered that only someone who had been there could actually say. The response by all but one of them (the exception had formal schooling) was a steadfast refusal to consider the logical implication that the bear was white. Hallpike does not therefore argue that tribespeople are mentally incapable of abstract logic, but that their experience of life has taught them to rely on concrete experience and not on anything else. Yet the outcome is the same—people so unfamiliar with even simple forms of abstract logical argument as to be unable or unwilling to use it even when guided toward it by insistent questioning.[84]

In each of several chapters Hallpike reviews different aspects of thought. The fifth chapter analyzes classification abilities. Among the studies he reviews, he notes his own firsthand study of the Tauade of New Guinea.[85] As an anthropologist Hallpike was able to construct classifications of people according to tribe, clan, and family. Few things are more important to primitive people than kinship relations. They determine whom they can marry; who their allies and enemies are; what obligations and taboos they must observe. The Tauade, however, could not give him this information directly. What they could do was to list who their parents were and who their parents' major relatives were. As is usually the case, the anthropologist, Hallpike in this instance, had to construct the actual kinship lines piece by piece. (We saw the same situation in the first chapter, with Evans-Pritchard among the Azande and Hutchins among the Trobrianders.)

Hallpike borrows a nice analogy from modern culture to illustrate the limitation of primitive discourse. The game Twenty Questions begins with someone who has mentally selected the item that the others are to guess by a series of twenty questions. This person starts the game by announcing that the item is either "animal, vegetable, or mineral." With this as a start, fourteen-year-old children in our culture are able to construct at least a crude strategy of moving from very general categories (Is it alive?) to more narrow ones (Is it a famous person?) to yet more narrow ones (Is it a politician?) until the item turns out to be Margaret Thatcher. Most eight-year-olds, however, are not able to use such a strategy, and will blurt out questions at random. But even fourteen-year-olds need to learn and practice such games to develop skill at logical strategies. Games such as Twenty Questions, along with many similar experiences in school, teach children to be able to engage in this early and simple formal operational game. This kind of training is missing from preliterate cultures.[86]

Hallpike continues to build his case. The sixth chapter is on number and measurement, illustrating his claim that primitive cultures do not have language or practices that show explicit awareness of numbers as logical classes (lumping fives or eights or tens into functional units for quicker counting).[87] The seventh chapter analyzes the understanding of spatial relations. Hallpike identifies an almost exclusive reliance on sheer memory of concrete places and paths rather than a use of a mental framework of coordinates.[88] The same chapter analyzes primitive ways of dealing with time to show a common lack of prestructured abstract frameworks.[89]

The ninth chapter focuses on "conceptual realism." Preoperational thought is rather poor at distinguishing between ideas that are vivid and appealing and ideas that are true. It is not just a failure to have learned which ideas are probably true and which are not. It is a limited ability to recognize the significance of the distinction. What is plain and vivid to the mind must therefore be true; "truth" has no other clear meaning. This includes the contents of dreams (or visions).[90] It is accompanied by a belief that names identify the true nature of things, that names are "natural" rather than arbitrary social conventions. To manipulate a word may also be to manipulate the reality, a kind of "magical" thinking, though also a kind of "science" of how things work.[91] All of this in turn is part of a mode of thought that is not clearly aware of thought as a distinct inner process which produces ideas, dreams, words, and emotions. Hallpike gives numerous examples of each of these among primitive people.[92] As chapter 1 of this volume noted, this is highly characteristic of preoperational thought.

This leads in turn to the topic of causality in Hallpike's tenth chapter, particularly about the nature of chance or accidents. Primitive people tend to overgeneralize the notion of causality by attributing every significant event to some single specific cause. The loss of a fish, too many bee stings when robbing a hive, the death of a child or a middle-aged person—all must have some specific identifiable cause, whether it be a malicious spirit or an enemy using sorcery or the violation of a taboo. It is a sign of intelligence, of course, to look for causes rather than to assume that things can occur with no cause whatsoever. But primitive culture does not push people very far toward evaluating probabilities or the plausibility of various ideas about what the specific causes of this or that effect might be.[93]

There is much more in Hallpike's book. He bases his conclusions on a large amount of anthropological work by others, as well as on his own studies among the Konso of Ethiopia and the Tauade of Papua New Guinea.[94] He provides a great deal of evidence that there is a strikingly large amount of preoperational thought among primitive people and that there is no clear sign of any formal operational thought.

Challenges to Hallpike

Hallpike's study does not stand unchallenged. Among the many who reviewed Hallpike's book, most of them favorably, two are quite critical, Richard Shweder and T. O. Beidelman.[95] Gustav Jahoda also devotes a few pages to criticism of Hallpike, as does Brian Morris.[96] Collectively, so do Marshall Segall, Pierre Dasen, John Berry, and Ype Poortinga.[97] The criticisms are sometimes misdirected, attacking positions Hallpike does not take or exaggerated versions of what Hallpike says.[98] It is difficult to read some of the criticisms without getting the feeling that there are two different books by Hallpike with the same title, one of them making a carefully nuanced and detailed case that there is a large amount of preoperational thought in evidence among primitive (nonliterate) people, the other making simplistic and absolute assertions without adducing much evidence to define their meaning. The critics read this second book; I read the first.

A first charge is that Hallpike says primitive people are locked rigidly into an almost exclusively preoperational style of thought.[99] This does not adequately represent the many qualifications Hallpike makes regarding his findings. He does claim that primitive society has no collective representations on the level of formal operational thought.[100] But through his many chapters he offers careful analysis, not just assertions, showing pros and cons concerning possibilities, offering the evidence and references to the reader for further consideration.

A second charge is that Hallpike overlooks the degree to which modern people use the same supposedly preoperational and concrete operational thought he finds among primitives.[101] Yet Hallpike explicitly and repeatedly notes that adults in modern cultures often think the way primitive people do.[102] A third charge is that Hallpike thinks of all creativity and imagination as a regression to a simpler level of thought.[103] In fact Hallpike disagrees with Piaget's tendency to see preoperational thought as only fantasy. Hallpike takes a more positive view of such thought as providing "creative and imaginative representations of the relations between man and the world about him, in the same manner as a perceptive novel."[104] Such spontaneously imaginative thought can exist, however, without the additional cognitive tools for analyzing the thought, its symbolic function, its relative success at this function, its power to evoke certain emotional responses, and so forth. As Hallpike puts it, the symbols function "at the sublinguistic level."

A rather odd charge initiated by Shweder and repeated by Morris is laid against Hallpike's interesting but passing observation concerning the level of public discourse in a primitive society. One could expect that there would be as many very bright individuals in a primitive society as in a modern one. One could guess that perhaps some individuals might even show formal operational skills in spite of the general level of exchange among the people, just as happens in a modern society. Among other thoughts Hallpike had on this was the observation that if only 50 percent of the people were good at concrete operational thought in a society where preoperational thought was the only alternative, then in only one out of every four two-person conversations would both people be able to converse intelligibly on the level of concrete operational thought. Hallpike was not asserting that this percentage is the case. He was only noting a lowest common denominator tendency in public communication among people. This factor, along with others, might account for why it would be difficult for any society to learn to use more complex cognitive skills, might account for why the collective representations of a society tend to remain at the simplest level required in that particular context for survival and decent functioning of the group.[105]

Shweder transforms this observation into a claim that Hallpike proposes a major "rule" which governs societal communication. Shweder then attempts to show that no such rule holds by using evidence from modern society, where people shift back and forth between styles of thought, even to the point where 90 percent of a group of college students performed at a preoperational level on a task.[106] While this study and Shweder's conclusion may be valid about students in a modern society, it establishes that preoperational thought is indeed common to humans everywhere, making it all the more plausible that primitive people also might rely heavily on it. Shweder does not address the further question of how much concrete operational thought is present among primitive people, and whether formal operational thought is exhibited at all.

The criticisms by Segall et al. seem inconsistent. On the one hand, they cite Cole and Scribner's unease with cultural development theories, because such theories interpret differences as "deficit" or even "retardation." The authors say it would be a mistake to use the absence of certain *concrete* operational skills on some specific tasks to judge that the people of some cultures think more like children in Western societies. They explicitly criticize Hallpike for this. On the other hand, the authors then come up with their conclusions about cognition and cultural development, conclusions that suggest a rough Piagetian model: "The empirical results allow us to opt for an intermediate solution, a simultaneous universality of hierarchical sequences and cultural variation in the timing of development." Clearly they do accept Piagetian developmental (hierarchical) sequences in cultures in general. They just want to stress that the whole life context of any group of people may make them better or worse on certain specific cognitive tasks.[107] They describe this position as intermediate between Piagetian orthodoxy and a complete cultural relativism. It is dubious that Piagetian orthodoxy truly claims that culture and experience have no significant effect on cognitive development. But in any case, given their conclusions about the importance of training in certain cognitive skills and the reality of hierachical stages, Segall and colleagues should have little objection to Hallpike's work.

Beidelman offers an interesting criticism of Hallpike that opens doors to other aspects of human development. He accuses Hallpike of failing to consider aesthetics and ethics, suggesting that a good study of these aspects of primitive thought would undercut the "evolutionist view of human thinking" that Beidelman finds in Hallpike.[108] Perhaps this is so. There is, however, an extensive list of studies of ethical reasoning based on Lawrence Kohlberg's theory, studies that have produced results quite compatible with Hallpike's estimate of primitive cognitive styles.[109] Much depends here on what aesthetic and moral standards a person thinks are the relevant ones to apply in estimating the relative state of development of a society. There is enough to do in these pages on the cognitive styles in culture, religion, and science, without also considering morality and aesthetics.

Even the critics are not entirely negative. Some at times give support to aspects of Hallpike's thesis, as just noted, support all the more to be acknowledged because it is not given readily. Morris says Hallpike is correct that the classifications used by primitive people are pragmatic, not theoretical, and "are not conceptualized into logical hierarchies.[110] He then faults Hallpike for not paying enough attention to "empirical taxonomies," as though Hallpike would find more cognitive sophistication there were he to look. In fact the fifth chapter in *Foundations* is quite thorough on this.[111] Jahoda also gives some support to Hallpike. He notes that even shamans who reflect on reasons not to overhunt a territory are nonetheless not "abstract philosophers," that they usually just follow "myth" rather than analyze what would be wisest to do.[112] In response to Hallpike's claims that primitive people do not analyze their own thought, Jahoda's response is not to claim that they do, but only that modern people often do not do this either, a point with which Hallpike agrees.[113]

Our own conclusions based on Hallpike's survey can be relatively modest. First, that both preoperational thought and concrete operational thought are present and influential in primitive society. Second, that both modes of thought should be present is to be expected, inasmuch as they clearly exist also in more complex societies. Third, these modes of thought stand out in primitive culture by default, inasmuch as there is no clear formal operational thought to overshadow or inhibit or compete with them. The descriptions that Hallpike provides are enough to establish what many other anthropologists have documented: that preliterate people habitually manifest thought styles which would fit well into the Piagetian categories of preoperational or concrete operational thought, with much more preoperational thought than we might otherwise expect, had not Hallpike pointed out its strong presence in primitive societies and in our own. It is from this baseline that we can move on to the impact of later cognitive developments in religion and science, and in life in general.

Conclusion

This has been a prolonged tour through the realm of the analysts and critics of ideas about primitive culture. In the end there is nothing about primitive thought in this summary that is truly new. Primitive people must have realistic empirical knowledge about their world in order to survive. This is not yet science, even though the human ability to make fairly good judgments about the facts before us are essential to science.

Preoperational thought is common, as it is in more complex cultures also. Concrete operational thought takes care of empirical knowledge for primitive people quite well, as it does for most of us today most of the time. Except for the use of Piaget's categories to get extra perspective on the mode of thought, most descriptions of primitive religion already picture it fairly accurately as a rather standard animism. Primitive cultures in general transmit their beliefs through relatively simple folktales. Primitive people do not have the linguistic tools or habits of analyzing their own stories that the anthropologists do. Simple as this description is, it stands battered by many interpretations of primitive thought, and by frequent attacks on anything that suggests primitive cultures are in some sense less developed than—well, than more developed cultures. The most basic point of this chapter is that in comparison with primitive cultures, other cultures have additional modes of thought at their disposal, for better or for worse, including modes of religious thought and the aspects of thought that will develop into science as we now have it.

4

ARCHAIC THOUGHT,
PRELITERATE AND LITERATE

This might be called the chapter on the "in-between cultures." Primitive cultures differ greatly in their thought style from axial-age classical cultures. Many who have argued over the nature of primitive religion seek like, Lucien Lévy-Bruhl, to identify two major modes of thought, the participatory and the rational in his case, or, like Jack Goody, speak of "the great divide." The actual history of development is more complicated than this contrast between two types of culture, however. So this chapter will deal with two "in-between" stages of culture, as it were; the early and late archaic stages that lie between primitive foraging cultures and literate classical cultures. Each stage of archaic culture is the result of a major revolution in human affairs. The first follows the Neolithic agricultural revolution; the second, the revolution of literacy.

A Preview

The invention of agriculture allowed large numbers of people to live permanently in one place, near their fields. Cities were born. Agriculture supported more extensive trade among cities, creating a larger world in the minds of the inhabitants. In the cities greater class and role differentiation appeared. As the human social world developed more differentiated roles and relations among people, the same happened in the realm of spirit beings. Some of them took on the power and prestige of gods. This was a change in the content of beliefs. We can call this preliterate polytheistic city culture "early archaic."

When literacy appeared after about 3000 BCE, it had an even more powerful impact on the cognitive style of cultures. Primitive people express their sense of reality through relatively short folktales and songs. Preliterate archaic culture continued this practice with brief mythic tales, worship formulas, and hymns of praise. Literacy made it possible, or at least much easier, to replace these shorter formulations with longer and more complexly plotted grand myths. Some of the older folktale elements appeared within the larger epic or saga, now placed in the context of a long sequence of events with a beginning, middle, and end. This was a change in the mode of expression. We can call literate polytheistic cultures "late archaic." Such cultures existed in Egypt, Mesopotamia, the Indus valley, and China's great river valleys, many centuries prior to the appearance of classic cultures with explicit formal operational thought styles.

The steps leading from primitive to archaic to classical culture in various places in the world have been more irregular and unclear than this simple outline indicates. This is partly because the process is not a lockstep progression that all cultures smoothly follow.[1] It is partly also because some potentially relevant studies of thought styles have not been carried out. Many descriptions of the evolution of societies have elaborated on fairly precise stages of economic or political or social development. Studies of differences of *thought style*, however, tend to focus on a single "great divide," as it has been called, between primitive and classical or even primitive and modern. The development of modes of thought in non-Greek cultures, especially, needs much more attention.[2]

Archaic Cultures and
the Great Gods

About ten thousand years ago in the fertile crescent that stretches from Palestine to Mesopotamia, some societies intensified earlier practices of planting and harvesting grain. Within a few thousand years large-scale agriculture was present in Egypt, Mesopotamia, the Indus valley, and river valleys in China. Irrigation and other farming methods supported thousands of people; cities appeared; soon small empires also. Long before 3000 BCE, Mesopotamian cities vied for dominance over broader territory. By 3000 BCE the upper Nile and the delta area of Egypt were combined into one kingdom. In the Indus valley the influence of the cities of Harappa and Mohenjo-Daro was widespread from around 2500 BCE. The legendary Emperor Yu initiated the Xia dynasty in China sometime around 2200 BCE.

Literacy developed in Sumer by 3000 BCE and around the same time in Egypt, then in the rest of the ancient Near East, later still in the Indus valley, and finally in China. The religious beliefs in the preliterate centuries exist now mainly as remnants within the written records available, and through linguistic traces.[3] This makes it difficult to know precisely what the preliterate beliefs and practices were like.[4] The polytheism of ancient texts is not necessarily the same as the polytheism of the periods that preceded written texts.[5] The gradual elevation of some spirits to local godly power and then to cosmic power is an important aspect of the whole story of the evolution of religious belief, but the dividing line between local and cosmic gods is obscure. The evidence is strong, for example, that the proto–Indo-Europeans offered sacrifices of cattle and horses to a sky god. But it does not tell us how big the sky was in the minds of these worshipers, how great the power of the sky god, and how wide his realm.[6] Celtic carvings appear to refer to over four hundred gods scattered around Europe in various locales. If these are human-sized invisible beings with some limited ability to benefit or harm people, we should probably call them "spirits." If they are larger than ordinary powers, with the larger jurisdiction that a great Celtic chief might have, then the word "god" is more appropriate. The widely worshiped sky god of the Celts seems large enough in power to qualify. But there are other invisible beings of uncertain size or power.[7]

The appearance of gods does not by itself represent a change in the basic style of thought. The written record of religious beliefs seems most often to be built out of what had been preliterate bits and pieces—various hymns or different folktales about origins. The world in which the early gods lived was still a world described in brief, relatively unconnected stories.[8] It was still a concrete operational world, inasmuch as a person needed only to remember the specific hymns, rituals, and stories, each in its own time and place. We have no direct evidence to say more than this, but we should suppose that preliterate people relied daily on preoperational thought, like people everywhere in all cultures, including our own.

The Impact of Literacy

Denise Schmandt-Besserat traces the origins of literacy to about 3800 BCE in Sumer with a token system used in commerce.[9] Thousands of tokens have been found, in certain specific shapes: cones, spheres, disks, cylinders, and tetrahedrons. Some are plain; others have surface markings. Each seems to stand for certain types of articles. Cones and spheres represent grain; cylinders represent animals. The surface markings that appear on later tokens seem to represent more specific qualities or quantities. After hundreds of years of the use, from around 3200 BCE tokens were placed in spherical clay "envelopes" with markings impressed on the outside to indicate what tokens were contained within the envelope. (Many envelopes were covered with elaborate artwork.) Someone apparently soon figured out that the impressed markings could substitute entirely for the tokens: a circular mark indicates spherical tokens; wedge marks stand for cones. By about 3100 BCE clay tablets with impressed markings largely replaced the impressed envelopes and their tokens. A bit later pictographs appeared on clay tablets: a boar's head, for example. The pictographs were simplified into formalized markings made by a stylus. By 2900 BCE the Sumerians were using a cuneiform script. Literacy was born. Schmandt-Besserat describes the process as one of increasing abstraction. The original tokens were abstract representations of quantities of grain or oil or cattle. Then the impressed markings on clay envelopes represented the tokens within the envelope.

The Sumerians may have set the example of literacy for the world, with the exception of the Mayans and possibly the Chinese.[10] In the third millennium BCE there was perhaps as much contact between the Sumerian cities of Mesopotamia and the Indus valley cities of Mohenjo-Daro and Harappa as there was with Egypt. At least there are as many archaeological signs of objects traded with one as with the other.[11] There are fragments of an early pictographic writing from Harappan culture prior to 2000 BCE, a set of glyphs that some think were inspired by and partly derived from Sumerian glyphs. (This form of writing died out when the Harappan culture fell. The roots of modern Indic writing, showing Semitic influence, did not appear until perhaps as recently as the sixth century BCE.)[12] In China oracle bones with inscriptions signal the beginning of literacy, around 1700 BCE.[13]

Walter Ong[14] and Jack Goody (once with Ian Watt)[15] have been two of the strongest voices proclaiming the power of literacy to transform culture by changing not only communication techniques but also mental habits. Literacy is a means to record what previously could only be said or shown by gesture. It adds a text-to-reader mode of transmission of ideas to the previous speaker-to-listener mode. On first glance literacy does not seem to change the basic human operation of transmitting ideas from person to person. But Ong and Goody show otherwise. Their claims are not always easy to substantiate, but they are usually theoretically plausible and rest on pertinent illustrations as evidence, especially Goody's many examples from anthropology.

In an oral society there are no fully private ways to record or retrieve information; it takes at least two people in face-to-face contact. There are no manuals of instructions on how to do things.[16] No one can look things up; one must find a person who has the desired information. Instruction normally depends on example rather than verbalization. In a purely oral culture, details of the past must necessarily be lost; even in cultures that promote extensive memorization, as of Hindu ritual formulas or of family lineages by the griots of some West African groups, other events or discoveries or practices or ideas from the past will be lost and must be reinvented. The content of written works must finally exceed the capacity of even the greatest memory. Brahmins perform impressive feats of memory, storing up the words of the Vedas for all the rituals they must perform. Yet all the many Vedic rituals and hymns could be contained in a volume or two on an ancient library's shelf, alongside hundreds of other volumes.

Other aspects of orality are less obvious. Because orality relies on formulas as a memory aid, every event may be shaped to fit a formula.[17] Purely oral stories thus tend to have "flat," stereotyped characters.[18] By contrast, literacy has created greater richness of description and flexibility of expression, which lead to greater richness and variety of interpretation.[19]

Oral societies can change the past and then honestly enough deny they have done so. Goody cites the example of a story of the Gonja of northern Ghana. Jakpa, the founder of the people, long ago arrived with his seven sons. Each of the sons originated a line of the seven tribal chiefs of the Gonja. At least so the story was recorded by the British in some detail at the turn of the twentieth century. Before long, one of the tribes had been absorbed into a neighboring people; another was dissolved by the British. Sixty years later the Gonja told the British that there had been only five sons, and insisted that is what their story had always said.[20] The function of many such stories, of course, is social rather than historical. The stories legitimize a current social order rather than present accurate history. But the Gonja, like other nonliterate people, do not acknowledge this. They insist on the historical accuracy of the story. Theories about sociological functions of folktales or myths are a step beyond their level of discourse (as is any reference to a "level of discourse").[21]

Literacy can engender a degree of skepticism about knowledge from the past. Even where orality preserves some of the past in genealogy, story, and myth, these are changeable, collapsible, bit by bit. Literacy preserves the past more exactly through endless documents: histories, letters, deeds, contracts, branching genealogies.[22] New ideas then stand in clear contrast to old ones preserved in writing. This produces a degree of skepticism about at least some old ideas. That in turn can create a more general skepticism about received wisdom or tradition. Such skepticism is not much in evidence in archaic cultures. Tradition carries enormous weight.[23] Yet it may have been a long history of literacy that eventually led to the critical skepticisms which appeared in the classical era of the axial age.

Literacy produces a greater awareness of language as a tool. A writer must be more self-consciously aware of how she or he is using language. Because oral communication is face-to-face, it has the advantage of allowing people spontaneously to tailor their words to the occasion and to the listener, omitting anything a given listener can be presumed to know. Literate communication requires words that fit many potential readers, some of whom are far away in time or space and whose background knowledge is not always known. Where orality allows one to point, literacy demands careful verbal naming and grammatical placing. So literacy comes to require clearer and more explicit articulation of ideas and their relations.[24] The literate telling of a long story, as in a written epic myth or a novel, is a highly self-conscious way of organizing a complex flow of events.[25] Language itself becomes an object of study.

Literacy demands further tools for handling a vast volume of information. It eventually produces such volumes of knowledge that no one can master it all.[26] External storage systems perform the work of memory.[27] Techniques for filing knowledge, for sorting it, for regaining access to it, become as important as the knowledge itself. Hence knowledge-handling processes become valuable skills, and some people must become adept at treating knowledge as an objective collection of information and ideas. Formal schooling develops to train people not only to read and write but also to handle the information-management systems for filing and retrieving records.[28]

Literacy promotes more complex and inclusive levels of abstraction. Every common noun in any language is already an abstraction, of course: the word "dog" is an abstraction from the reality of many concrete individual animals with similar characteristics.[29] Literacy makes it possible to develop much more complex classificatory categories through which many items are gathered into subclasses, which in turn can be put in a single class, which can then be related to a yet more inclusive class. Biological categorization of species in genera, genera in families, families in orders, and so forth is an example.[30] A dog is a canine is a mammal is a vertebrate. Each higher category is more abstract—farther from the many concrete specifics—than the subcategories it contains. A greater amount of abstraction enters standard language use, to function alongside other cognitive tools.[31] More important, the various levels of abstraction can be complexly organized into a *coherent system*, preparing the way for a full, formal operational style of thought.

Literacy promotes greater privatization of thought. The face-to-face communication of orality demands a greater degree of give-and-take between speakers and listeners. Oral communication can always be questioned immediately, challenged, changed. Written communication allows a person to develop an entire line of thought in privacy and deliver it in absentia, on a take-it-or-leave it basis. This encourages the privatization of thought and allows the individual to objectify her or his own life experiences more thoroughly, without interruption.[32] The diary is a prime example of this.[33] Goody and Watt argue that this privatization also influences the sense of self. A person gains a particular sense of self through direct interaction with others, either a social self in accommodative interchange with others or a private self permitted an extended, one-sided presentation of a person's seemingly self-sufficient opinion.

Literacy clearly has great effects. A culture that adds literacy to its means of communication is different from one that does not. In the history of humankind, thirty to forty thousand years passed without literacy. When it arrived and secured a place in a culture, that culture had developed or "evolved" beyond at least one of the limits of the cognitive methods of its preceding stage. To judge that this development constitutes progress and not merely change requires a further evaluation. Most of us will find it easy to assume that literacy is a positive development, as do Ong and Goody. Yet even a person who perceives the effects of literacy as at least partly harmful confirms some of the conclusions of Ong and Goody.

Donald Topping complains of the effect on Pacific Island children of going to school to learn reading and writing.[34] He describes the world of school literacy as one of "analysis and segmentation." Knowledge of the world is broken up into pieces so that the pieces can then be rearranged in patterns of linear reasoning. This is frustrating to many of the students, Topping says, because it is opposed to their everyday "holistic" mode of thought that perceives their world in a nonsegmented way, as a whole system.

Topping's description, however, also shows that what Topping calls a "whole system" is not something that the Islanders are aware of either as a whole or as a system, unless they have been schooled to think in this literate and reflexive way about the things they name with their language use. He thus confirms the conclusions of Ong and Goody by complaining that they are correct. Literacy teaches analysis and linear reasoning. Literacy leads the students to analyze even their own tribal life and thereby alienates them from tradition.[35] Literacy forces the individual into a new personal identity somewhat distinct from that of the tribe, through the use of reasoning, through interaction with written words instead of with individuals.[36]

Out of ancient Mesopotamia and Egypt came complex mathematics and geometry and celestial records, innovations that also depend on literacy. Before 2500 BCE the Sumerians had drawn up multiplication tables for determining the area of fields or estimating the volume of a pile of bricks.[37] The Egyptians needed to time the arrival of the late summer flood, and as far back as 2700 BCE had recorded the discovery that when Sirius rose at dawn, the floods would come two days later.[38] Out of a belief in the sacred powers of the stars to influence lives, the Babylonians kept track of the stars' movements in some detail, producing the information that would later allow Thales of Miletus to secure his reputation by predicting a solar eclipse.[39] Late archaic cultures also experienced a shift in morality, away from the traditional customs of preliterate people, which are accepted as simply the way of the ancestors, to a codified law, based on decrees of the gods.

Ong, Goody and Watt, and others tend to write sweepingly of the effects of literacy, as though literacy quickly and simply produces the effects they describe. But they would acknowledge that not all of the effects were immediate. Literacy spread from Sumer by the third millennium BCE. Yet in Athens, that most literate of cultures, in the fourth century BCE, Plato was suspicious of relying on literacy. Aristotle was the first we know of to make extensive use of prior written records in his own works. Texts were expensive. Major libraries were not commonplace. Hundreds of years of literacy preceded the axial-age shift of the sixth century BCE. The major point has been made, however: literacy is not merely the addition of an information storage system. It has had a major impact on social relations, self-awareness, and levels of abstraction. Literacy may well be credited, as Goody does, as the human invention that led to the "great divide" between primitive and modern modes of thought. But if Goody is correct, it is because literacy made possible the subsequent great intellectual shift of the axial age, which will be described in the next chapter.

Against the "Great Divide" Theory

The "great divide" theory of Goody and others represents a belief in cultural development. Brian Street, an opponent of theories of cultural development, tests such theories for us again by his attacks on Goody's thesis. Many of Street's ideas are variations on objections to theories of cultural evolution of the kind seen in the previous chapter. But Street speaks for many. Richard Shweder, for example, would cheer him on. So it is useful to examine what he says.[40]

Ong and Goody have an "autonomous model" of how literacy works, says Street. This model treats literacy as a neutral tool that is bound to have the same effects anywhere it is applied. It treats literacy as intrinsically supportive of open, rational, critically self-aware modes of thought. Thus literacy is supposedly autonomous of any culture-specific or ideological bias. Street here challenges Ong and Goody on the same grounds that others oppose evolutionary theories of culture. Both the general theories of cultural development and the particular theories of the effects of literacy, Street complains, falsely use the criteria of one culture to judge another culture. Invoking the work of a variety of anthropologists, Street simultaneously attacks the "autonomous" model and the "great divide" theory. Here are his challenges, somewhat abbreviated, some of them overlapping a bit:[41]

1. Where the "autonomous" model suggests a lack of full rationality among the nonliterate, E. E. Evans-Pritchard and others have pointed to a hidden logic in orality.

2. Orality and literacy are in fact mixed in all literate societies; one cannot neatly separate two types of cultures.
3. There are literacies, not just literacy; Japanese, Chinese, ancient Egyptian, and other literacies need to be treated distinctly.
4. The whole debate over rationality is biased from the first by the values of Western post-Enlightenment culture.
5. There is no way to measure logic across cultures, using the scientific methods of one culture to evaluate different methods in different cultures.
6. The standards of "objectivity" and "neutrality" in particular are neither objective nor neutral: They are values specific to Western post-Enlightenment culture.
7. There is no autonomous meaning in texts, as literary deconstruction has shown.
8. Literacy can be known only in concrete social contexts, which are already burdened by various political and ideological forms.
9. The practice of literacy is always in the context of a certain stratified kind of social order and control.
10. Thus the qualities of thought and practice that are inherent in literacy are really part of some society's conventions and values.

Street's conclusion: Literacy must be understood not as autonomous but as ideological—always bringing with it certain cultural presuppositions, methods, and values. The "autonomous" model of the nature and effects of literacy falsely portrays the nonliterate as "primitive" and nonrational.

Some of Street's claims were addressed in chapter 3. As to challenge 1, about a hidden logic, we have heard from a number of anthropologists who defend the primitives against a charge of having a less developed cognitive style, but who nonetheless acknowledge that primitive people lack explicit, systematic understanding of such major aspects of their own lives as their kinship relations. On challenge 2, we can indeed recognize a mixture of orality and literacy in all literate cultures, just as there is a mixture of concrete and formal operational thought. The issue, however, is whether literacy is entirely missing in some cultures and whether this absence of literacy makes a difference in modes of expression and thought styles in those cultures.

Street's other complaints have their own rather heavy ideological burden. He writes mostly as though he is convinced that in principle there can be no such thing as modes of thought which human beings in general can share because they are human. He writes as though no significant aspect of human thought could have general currency among people everywhere. He presents this at times as a philosophical position, based on the kind of reflection philosophers have enjoyed since Pyrrho developed his principles of skepticism back in the fourth century BCE, or since Descartes, Malebranche, Berkeley, Hume, and Kant reflected on the limits of knowledge. Now it is Wittgenstein, or the Frankfurt School and

Habermas, or Quine and Sellars and Rorty, or the historians of science like Kuhn, Feyerabend, and Shapin and Schaffer, who assert or imply a cultural relativity of all human knowing.[42] Street agrees.

There is a persuasive rationale for this ideology, a rationale that Street repeats in his own version: Human knowledge develops slowly, over generations. Each generation invents certain names and thereby categorizes aspects of reality in certain culturally determined ways. There are also value judgments embedded in every language; and different cultures value different things in different ways. All people bring with them the images, values, and presuppositions of their own social context and their own personal background and interests. Thus there is no objective and neutral foundational truth that can be used as the reference to test other truths or from which to deduce further truth. The social determination of knowledge and of methods of knowing is so strong and pervasive that it is useless to seek general cross-cultural truth. It is therefore also invalid to judge other cultures' methods and practices by any standards but their own.

Chapter 9 will engage in a lengthy philosophical analysis of the possibility of some important degree of objectivity and universality to certain truth-claims. As we noted earlier, however, it should not be surprising from the first if the single species *Homo sapiens* had common ways of dealing with reality, such as using sight and touch and hearing as sources of evidence, such as using at least a basic human logic about the connection between how antelope have acted in the past and how they might be expected to act today, such as the efficacy of a spear or a cooking pot.[43] It takes an ideology of cognitive relativism to ignore the many common aspects to human knowing.

Street's objections are so sweeping as to call into question the possibility of writing valid history. Historians try to rely on evidence. History does include a great deal of interpretation, with all the possible ideological bias this might imply. Yet if it is possible to write history at all, it should also be possible to write a history of patterns of cognitive changes. Street and others provide theoretical arguments against the possibility of such a history. But whatever we can point to as actual fact is clearly possible, regardless of a priori arguments to the contrary. The arguments should be on *whether in fact* we can identify specific cross-cultural patterns of human knowing in history, and whether there is some developmental sequence to those patterns. The evidence and analyses in this book are intended to provide such a case: that a common form of cognitive evolution has in fact occurred in major cultures around the world.

Ironically, Street gives some indirect support for what he otherwise wishes to deny. He notes that people in industrial societies are often not very rational. Using this to argue against cultural evolution, he supposes some universality of scientific reasoning:

The anthropological evidence, then, suggests that there is scientific and non-scientific thought in all societies and within all individuals. Observers have simply failed to remark the scientific nature of much of the thinking of so-called "primitive" people and have perhaps over-stated the "scientific" nature of thinking in their own societies.[44]

We can agree with Street here by agreeing also with Robin Horton, as we did in chapter 3, that there is some continuity of primitive thought with some aspects of current science—to seek causes, to rely on evidence, to use a basic (if largely implicit) logic. We can also agree that people in industrial cultures often think as primitive people do. The issue, to repeat, is whether there are some *additional* thought styles that later stages of culture use and that preliterate cultures lack.

Street addresses this by noting modes of abstraction and categorizing. He rejects the claim of Greenfield about the Kpelle of Liberia: that they lack "the classificatory and analytic isolating functions of language."[45] In rebuttal Street notes that every common noun isolates and categorizes phenomena. By this Street is again identifying a cognitive universal, something shared by all societies. He is correct, of course. But Street leaves untouched Greenfield's actual point, based on the work of Michael Cole and others cited in chapter 3: that there are levels of self-awareness and explicitness in the use of language beyond merely categorizing, and that the unschooled Kpelle show little sign of these additional modes of thought, which are employed by literate Kpelle as well as the literate of various other cultures. (Street himself has already accepted the equiva-lent of this by accepting Evans-Pritchard's idea that the logic of primi-tives is hidden from them.)

Part of Street's analysis is based on studies of current modes of literacy and language use among differently educated youths.[46] Street cites the work done in New York by William Labov (1973) on the street language of "negro youth." According to Street, Labov argued that the language of the street has its own legitimate logic and complex grammar.[47] Street sums up Labov's conclusion about street language: "[It] turned out to have all of the qualities generally *associated* [my emphasis] with logical thought—facility with complex propositions, meaningful sequence, rule recognition, syllogistic reasoning, etc." Street continues: "The adult or child who uses these [language] rules must have formed *at some level of psychological organization* [emphasis added] clear concepts of 'tense mark-ers,' 'verb phrase,' 'rule ordering,' 'sentence imbedding,' 'pronoun' and many other grammatical categories which are essential parts of any logi-cal system."

Street is properly impressed, perhaps, with the extraordinary sophisti-cation of human language. But what he describes is the language facility that a ten-year-old child can achieve. The "level of psychological organi-zation" is a nonconscious level for most people in any culture. When

Street speaks of "clear concepts" of tense markers, he manifests a reflexive awareness, a "metacognition" of language, that is not found among primitive people nor among many people in modern cultures. It seems to have required literacy to produce (1) a reflex awareness of language, (2) new categories of grammar and logic for use in all this reflective activity, and (3) an awareness of the self as one who must reflect on language. Even many college students, who ordinarily make fairly good use of tense markers and so forth, are only barely aware that this is what they are doing. They have learned a language from the time they were two years old. They learned how to speak a language by listening and by trial and error (and in accord with an innate grammar, if Noam Chomsky is correct). They were schooled in grammatical forms such as the use of "tense markers," but often forget this rather abstract way of analyzing language.

Of the claims that Street rejects, some may indeed go a bit too far. By simplifying the "great divide" into only two categories, primitive and modern, Goody and others may attribute a bit too much to literacy alone as the cause of great cognitive change. Goody also says that literacy aids the shift from little communities to complex cultures, whereas it may be the other way around. The development of the complex irrigation-based commercial society of Sumer may have driven the development of literacy.[48] Goody says that literacy distinguishes myth from history. In fact, some great epic myths are the products of literate culture that do not yet strive for nonmythical history.[49] Literacy made nonmythic history possible eventually, but another cultural development was required for this. That is the axial-age shift which will be described in chapter 5.

Literacy and Religious Thought: The Epic Myth

A major effect of literacy was to lengthen and complexify the stories that could be told about the gods. Oral cultures tell of the world in relatively brief "folktale" stories; there are no long and complex epic myths in exclusively oral cultures.[50] It is not a significant change just to extend the length of a story. It is a significant change, however, to interrelate many parts of a longer story in a single complex plot. Oral cultures sum up the world in bits and pieces.[51] Literacy produced works in which there is for the first time a beginning, a middle, and an end of long sequences of stories.[52] The Gilgamesh Epic,[53] the Homeric tales, and ancient Chinese epics[54] all have within them individual tales that may once have been told separately without much concern for chronology or logical interrelations, like the many trickster tales of North America or Africa, or like the string of tales about certain ancestral heroes among many Australian Aborigines. But writing down such tales makes the question of temporal sequence clearer. The adventures of Gilgamesh and his friend Enkidu had to take place in a sequence after the taming of the wild Enkidu and before his death. The search by Gilgamesh for immortality had to follow his bereavement over Enkidu's death and be a result of it. Each complex part of the story builds logically upon another complex part.

In some cases epic myths have been attributed to strictly oral cultures or contexts. Milman Perry's investigation of Yugoslav oral epics and the poets who recited them gave him and his student Albert Lord reason to suspect that epic poetry was strictly oral.[55] But Perry's son, and eventually Lord, also acknowledged that the Yugoslav and the Homeric epics were influenced by the literate worlds in which they were produced.[56] Similarly, the Norse mythological cycle and the Icelandic sagas, once proclaimed to be products of orality alone, are the result of literacy working on originally more disjointed oral traditions.[57]

Even these literate tellings of stories are somewhat ragged, not so well organized as post-axial literature would be. The longest of all the early literate stories, perhaps, is the *Mahabharata*, a collection of stories and wisdom. The great battle that is its central event is prefaced and surrounded by multiple stories. Joan Puhvel describes it as a repository of para-Vedic material, including the "Visnuite minibible," the *Bhagavad Gita*.[58] Similarly, the *Ramayana*, the stories of Homer, the epic of Gilgamesh, and the Jahwist narrative in Genesis include old stories placed within a new and larger narrative framework.[59]

The easiest hypothesis to explain the bumpy ride one gets moving through these early epics is that habits of careful consistency were not part of the standards of preaxial literacy. Rational consistency is a cognitive goal and habit that took centuries to develop. To the contrary, Joseph Russo ascribes the logical inconsistencies he finds in Homer not to a lack of certain cognitive habits, but to the "situation of high affective energy or mood" that outweighs "the more cerebral power of the analytical or logical."[60] Yet there is little sign of the analytical or logical in archaic cultures, even literate ones. At the same time the emotionally charged dramas of postaxial-age Athens are more internally consistent. We can conclude that the epic myths of archaic culture are a development toward greater complexity of narrative, but not yet as complex and coherent as the systematic analyses produced in axial-age cultures, or even as carefully constructed as the drama and poetry and oratory of those later times.

Toward the Axial Age

The universe of primitive foraging people is relatively small. Even the wide-ranging Aborigines of Australia lived in a smaller world than, say, the early archaic Chinese or late archaic Mesopotamians or Egyptians.

The spirits of foraging people are no larger than most neighbors or have a scope of power limited to a piece of the sky or an event like thunder. The early gods of Polynesian or Celtic culture were often barely more than spirit-sized. The universe of literate late archaic cultures was much larger. The sun god could rule over the entire Earth in Egypt, usually with many other gods playing various roles. The great Marduk, god of Babylon, could accept the power of fifty earlier gods in return for his defeat of Ti'amat, albeit with many other important gods still to be served by human offerings. The postaxial-age search for a single ultimate Reality is prefigured even more strongly in Akhenaton's elevation of his sun god to supremacy. Unlike Amon or Marduk or Zeus, Aton is not a high god reigning among many gods. By Akhenaton's decree Aton is the only god to be worshiped. Perhaps Zarathustra also conceived of Ahura Mazda as a kind of single ultimate God, confronting the Satanic Father of Lies but assured of absolute victory in the end. If so, and if Zarathustra lived at the end of the second millennium BCE, as some argue, this was a step toward the kind of monotheism that was sustained only after the axial age.

From the troubled times between the Old and Middle Kingdoms of ancient Egypt, about 2000 BCE, comes the meditative piece entitled by James Pritchard "A Dispute over Suicide".[61] It deals with inner thoughts by describing a dialogue that an Egyptian man has, not with himself but with his soul, over whether he should commit suicide.[62] The soul is opposed to the idea, but the man lines up his arguments poetically in neat order, like a scribe making a list, until the soul is convinced that death will be better than life.

The individual has an explicit presence in this meditation on suicide. The argument of a man with his soul is the story of an individual as such, contemplating his personal conditions of life. There is similar early interest in the individual in segments of the Egyptian Book of the Dead (roughly from the late second millennium BCE) that contain long lists of offenses which the person who has died may claim to have avoided, and thereby appeal to the gods for a happy afterlife on the basis of individual innocence. In the Babylonian story of Gilgamesh the king, his great friend Enkidu reflects on the sadness of life, cursing his fate at the hand of the goddess; and Gilgamesh meditates on the fact of death and the limitations of life. This is relatively sophisticated thought, more complexly explicit in its statement and analysis of life's conditions and of emotional responses to them than primitive or even early archaic tales are likely to contain.[63] In the axial age an even more sophisticated thought would flourish.

Literacy is artificial. Orality, like concrete operational thinking, is natural. It took many centuries for writing to become an obvious means of communication in the great literate archaic cultures. Belief in a single ultimate Reality is also, perhaps, artificial. On the face of it the universe does not look as though it were under the influence of a single ultimate Power. Order exists amid disorder. The seasons roll around regularly, but with unexpected drought or flood. Either the supreme power is erratic like a god, an anthropomorphic being who changes his or her mind, or there is no single supreme power at all, only a mélange of gods in somewhat unpredictable interaction. It was bold for thinkers in Greece, India, China, Persia, and Palestine to claim that in spite of the disorderly complexities of life and nature there is a single Being or Force or Law that rules everything at once. This was a new belief; it was a new *kind* of belief; it accompanied a new style of thought that emerged in the axial age. It is the topic of chapter 5.

5

THE AXIAL AGE AND THE
CLASSICAL STYLE OF THOUGHT

Striking changes appeared in intellectual life in and around the sixth century BCE in China, India, and Greece, and elsewhere. Karl Jaspers called this the "axial age" to characterize it as the time when several major human cultures shifted on their axes to point in a new direction. The label may wrongly connote an abandonment of an old direction in order to take up a new one. In fact, the new classical style of thought was *added* on top of the existing primitive and archaic-literate styles. This addition transformed the cultures in several significant ways, yet the old styles continued on, and not merely as a remnant. The primitive and archaic styles of thought continue as a significant part of electronic cultures today.[1] To describe the axial transformation, this chapter will again review three aspects of cognitive style—content of belief, mode of expression, and style of thought—in classical China, India, and Greece. First, a few general statements about classical thought will provide guidelines for interpreting the specific descriptions of these cultures.

In all three cultures there was a search for the single Ultimate Reality in terms of which it would be possible to make sense of everything else. No merely supreme god among lesser gods would do. Only a Reality that transcends the gods and all else could satisfy the searchers. In China it was the formless and incomprehensible Tao, in India the Brahman beyond categories or the incomprehensible Atman, in Greece the "One" of Plato and eventually of Philo Judaeus and then of Christians. Other philosophers would seek out a less fully Ultimate Reality. The Stoics, for example, gave reverence to the divine Logos, the ultimate and universally influential principle of rational order in the universe.

Implied in this search for a single Ultimate is universalism, the belief that there is one basic truth or set of interrelated truths about all things. This included belief in a unity and reliability in the patterns of nature, a belief that undergirds what we now think of as science, and initiated a new stage in the history of science. Classical cultures did not create science from scratch. Studies of nature's events and patterns were part of literate archaic societies. Astronomy, mathematics, geometry, medicine, natural history all have roots in practices and observances that preceded classical times. But belief in an ultimate unity to nature and the Power that lies behind nature took science to a new level. A later section will discuss this further.

The belief in a single Ultimate and a universal order to all things sometimes also included a severe perfectionism. This appears most clearly in religious theories of salvation. Primitive people usually hope for only a good life here and now, though a few of them believe that their current life will continue after death, perhaps in a new place over the mountains or beyond the horizon of the ocean. Archaic people could sometimes expect a pleasant life after death. A few favored mortals might live with the gods. Most expected a dreary afterlife at best. But classical people, at least in India and Greece, disdained any mere continuation of life. Platonists expected a perfect spiritual life beyond the changeable forms we know on earth. Christianity adopted this idea in the form of belief in a spiritual bliss in heaven. Buddhists sought a total detachment from all worldly things in order to achieve the state of nirvana. Hindus hoped to achieve utter release into the oceanic Self or Atman. Robert Bellah characterizes this as "world-rejection." The origin of this rejection of the world lies, I suspect, in the vision of perfect order and values that the classical mind articulated. The highly imperfect order of ordinary life becomes painfully visible by contrast with the mind's ideal order. Classical perfectionism can thus lead to world-rejection.

In Greece, as in India and China, discursive analysis became the mode of expression for the rational arguments of philosophers (including those we might now call theologians and scientists). The humanlike gods had required narratives to tell of their deeds. The universal order of things could best be described by a measured explication of highly abstract concepts and relations among the concepts. The Ultimate required philosophical or theological or scientific essays in place of the concrete images of traditional folktales and archaic myths.

(This does not imply that all narrative can be classified as a primitive or archaic mode of expression.[2] Primitive and archaic thought is one sort of narrative thought: naive and literalist. After the axial age most people continued to tell their old stories and created new ones. But after the axial age at least some people took a more reflexive position on narratives, using them with a critical awareness of narrative as a particular genre among others. Plato is an early instance of this; he saw the value in using some narratives to educate. Thus, while he thought some old myths should be rejected because they represented bad values (the gods fighting among themselves out of lust, envy, and power hunger), other myths should be retained, refashioned, or created in order to educate. Aristotle analyzed the nature and function of forms of drama. Modern literary analysis has moved toward an even stronger appreciation of the power and validity of narrative forms of expression and thought, but has done this from an even more sophisticated perspective than that of axial thought.)

Because the world is a *uni*-verse, all things somehow fit together in one grand scheme. To discover this scheme, a person must be able to check all human ideas about life and the universe to see whether they fit together. This is a very difficult task. It requires great care in keeping track of concepts and their interrelations. Thinkers in the classical cultures began to analyze how to analyze; they struggled toward a formal logic and towards explicit criteria of truth.

In a sense, classical cultures merely extended the normal practice of daily informal logic. The basic logic by which we all live says that when two of our ideas about reality conflict with one another, something is wrong. Two primitive hunters discussing the freshness of antelope tracks are doing so to arrive at a "logical" conclusion about whether the antelope is likely still to be near. But in the axial age informal logic was raised to a much more formal level. The axial age is the beginning of the full formal practice of systematic analysis, weighing the pros and cons of a case, checking them against the evidence to see that they fit the evidence, and checking them against each other to see how logically they may fit together.

This is the thought style that Piaget categorizes as formal operational thought, which he associates with scientific rationality. Bernard Lonergan refers to it as "theory," a concern to understand the logical coherence of ideas. Karen Kitchener calls it metacognition, the practice of examining one's own ideas for their coherence and validity. It is a rationalist style of thought because it relies on the criterion of "fit," of how well ideas fit with evidence and how well ideas fit coherently with each other. It assumes that there must be, or at least should be, some reliable coherence among all facts and ideas. This is an assumption of intelligibility, as we will see at greater length in a later chapter.

This assumption of intelligibility implied in the criterion of "fit" gives a person a place to stand intellectually for judging tradition. It allows a person to ask whether specific pieces of hallowed information really fit together with other pieces of information and with what the person takes to be good evidence. This further allows a person to question beliefs that are inconsistent with other ideas or with strong evidence. History makes it clear that traditional beliefs indeed met serious challenge from axial-age thought.

Any society anywhere may have individuals who challenge traditional beliefs and practices, but in general, primitive societies accept tradition as truth. An important criterion for "truth" in such societies is that-which-has-been-known. This criterion resides alongside the everyday criterion of evidence. What people see and touch and taste is true. But for all the things a person cannot see and touch and taste, it is tradition that must be relied on, for knowledge about spirits, about what places have bad power (magic, taboo), about omens. When literacy arrives, the comparisons between new knowledge and old may corrode this trust in tradition somewhat, as chapter 4 noted. Yet the authority of tradition still is enormous, perhaps partly by default. How else is a person to learn important truths? In classical cultures, tradition remains powerful. But the classical use of systematic analysis and formal logic provides a counterbalance to tradition and may sometimes contradict it. The general effect of this style of thought is what we now call "demythologization," a process we will see more of in chapter 6.

Once again, we can pause to remind ourselves that all groups of people everywhere are born with equal innate capacities to think in formal operational ways, though there are differences among individuals in any society. In postaxial cultures, some people have learned to use formal operational thought when their culture educates them in tools for such thought. These are tools such as learning to define words carefully and consistently, to sort out pieces of information in different groupings, to list pros and cons of evidence, to review the evidence and groupings to see which produce more coherent schemata, to articulate explanatory hypotheses and test them for consistency with other beliefs and with evidence, and so forth.[3]

These tools are cultural products, not self-evident practices. They are cultural products that did not appear until after many thousands of years of human history. They are cultural products that have had enormous impact on the societies that educate their young in the use of these tools. The axial-age achievement is all the more marvelous in that three major centers of civilization came to share in most of it within a few centuries. Apparently the human mind had been capable of such thought all along. But like literacy, it took some while for the relevant techniques to be developed for human use. This chapter will give more examples of various cognitive skills or techniques (I use the words interchangeably here) that are part of the classical style of thought. We will look at beliefs, modes of expression, and cognitive style in India, China, and Greece.

These three cultures remained quite distinct from each other. Greece may have pursued issues of logic further than the other two. India achieved a greater unanimity on the metaphysical structures of existence than the other two, through a fairly common belief in samsara, karma, and dharma. China kept more archaic habits of thought than the other two.[4] Yet all three manifested a new interest in universalizing thought, in seeking an Ultimate, in analyzing language use. All three found it necessary to employ a more analytical or systematic mode of expression. All three, in other words, developed or borrowed ways to use more of the innate human capacity for formal operational thought.

Classical Culture in India

By the sixth century BCE many schools of thought in India, religious and philosophical, exhibited the major characteristics of classical thought. Belief in the gods and spirits and magic began to be overshadowed by belief in a single Ultimate of some sort, in terms of which it was possible to explain the universe as a whole. Belief in certain universal aspects of life, such as karma, complemented belief in the Ultimate. A world-rejecting perfectionism appeared. The narrative style of thought continued in full force, but a more abstract and systematic set of reflections appeared for the first time. Within a few centuries there was more than one school of formal logic.[5] There was even a skeptical movement, the significance of which will be discussed later.

It is tempting to speculate on the cause of the great change in thought styles in India. Percival Spear describes the sixth century BCE as a time of great "unrest and ferment," both material and social.[6] Materially the Indo-Aryan tribes were shifting from pastoral to agricultural life, and the limited tribal groups were becoming large territorial kingdoms. The merchant (Vaisya) caste became more important as trade increased, and may have resented the supposed superiority of the Brahmins and the ruling caste (Kshatriya). Socially the Aryans and non-Aryans were still undergoing a difficult process of accommodation as the caste system continued to develop and different religious and language groups encountered one another. It was this context that produced "a religious and intellectual ferment comparable with that of contemporary Greece."[7]

Whatever the reasons, during these centuries there appeared a highly influential universalizing and logical thought. This can be seen in the history of the Vedic literature.[8] These sacred texts have their origin in hymns and other religious materials that go back perhaps as far as 1500 BCE, the time of the beginning of the Aryan invasion of India.[9] As we have them now, the Vedas contain a mixture of types of beliefs. Sarvepalli Radhakrishnan and Charles Moore, in fact, discern a three-step evolution of beliefs in the Vedas concerning the gods or God. They claim that the polytheistic hymns are the earliest material in the Vedas, followed by monotheistic ideas, and then by monism in the most recent material.[10]

The four Vedas are largely archaic in content and form. Barbara Stoler Miller gives a good sense of the form of the Vedas by translating the word "Veda" as "Sacred Lore."[11] They are indeed collections of lore, of hymns and rituals from preaxial times. They are mostly polytheistic,

concerned with ritual appeasement of the gods and with the manipulation of various kinds of sacred or magical power. The hymns are not
integrated with each other.[12] The *Rig Veda* contains over one thousand
ancient hymns to a great variety of gods.[13] Hymn after hymn begins with
words like these: "I will extol the most heroic Indra" or "I glorify Agni" or
"I will proclaim the mighty deeds of Vishnu."[14] This praise accompanies
sacrificial ritual. The *Sama Veda* is composed mostly of rearrangements
or expansions of hymns in the Rig Veda. The *Yajur Veda* contains instructions on the proper performance of ritual. The *Atharva Veda* is full of
magical incantations that Wendy D. O'Flaherty calls "ancient folk material."[15] The general tone of the Vedas is concrete and mythological, says
A. L. Herman, a thought style that reminds him of ordinary unreflective
thought today.[16] The major attribute of the gods is not moral rectitude
but sheer power.[17] The material and form of the Vedas are thus generally
typical of archaic culture.[18]

In the parts of the *Rig Veda* written most recently, however, *perhaps*
as early as 800 BCE, speculation about the origin of the universe suggests
a new mode of thought that reflects upon the problem of establishing the
single unity behind all diversity, the single source of all multiplicity. The
most famous such section is *Rig Veda*, book X, chapter 129, verses 1–7,
beginning:

> Then was not non-existent nor existent:
> > there was no realm of air, no sky beyond it.
> What covered it, and where? and what gave shelter?
> > Was water there, unfathomed depth of water?
> Death was not then, nor was there aught immortal:
> > no sign was there, the day's and night's divider.
> The one thing, breathless, breathed by its own nature:
> > apart from it was nothing whatsoever.[19]

Equally difficult lines follow, attributing the creation of everything to the
"one thing": the creation first of the universe and then of the gods.

These ideas have a history. The axial age is not one of utterly new
ideas without foundation in anything earlier. A. L. Herman speculates,
for example, that earlier ideas about Varuna in book VIII of the *Rig Veda*,
had suggested a greatness of the Divinity that approximates a belief in
omnipotence and omniscience. Nonetheless, there is also a striking difference in axial-age expressions about an Ultimate. Herman is arguing what
he thinks the older Varuna hymn text *implies*, not what it actually says.[20]
The lines quoted above take religious thought into a new stage.

The shift from polytheism toward belief in a single Ultimate becomes
fully clear and steady in the Upanishads, some also written *perhaps* as
early as 800 BCE. These are often referred to as commentaries on the
Vedas, but in fact they comment mostly on the few lines in the Vedas

that show an incipient monotheism or monism. In those known as "the principal Upanishads," about ten in number, there is a clear monotheistic belief in a single supreme personal Being and a few lines that suggest belief in a Reality that transcends even personness.[21] The Kena Upanishad, II, 3–4, for example, describes the Ultimate that is Brahman or Atman in these words (which the *Tao Te Ching* later echoed):

> It is conceived of by him by whom It is not conceived of.
> He by whom It is conceived of, knows It not.
> It is not understood by those who [say they] understand It.
> It is understood by those who [say they] understand It not.[22]

Similarly, the Katha Upanishad has this description of the steps toward the infinite Person (Perusa), which is identified with Brahman:

> Higher than the senses are the objects of sense.
> Higher than the objects of sense is the mind;
> And higher than the mind is the intellect (*buddhi*).
> Higher than the intellect is the Great Self (Atman).
> Higher than the Great is the Unmanifest (*avyakta*).
> Higher than the Unmanifest is the Person.
> Higher than the Person there is nothing at all.
> That is the goal. That is the highest course.[23]

The Upanishads teach the path toward *moksha*, release from the cycle of reincarnation. They teach a person how to find release from individual self in order to be merged into the Supreme Self (Atman) that is also Brahman. This is both philosophical and religious. It is philosophical in that it offers rather orderly analyses of the structure of the universe and human life; it is religious in that it teaches a person how to meditate upon truth and live correctly, so as to come closer to salvation, which is ultimate release into oneness with Atman.

Other religious schools flourished at this time, exploring the relatively new doctrines of samsara (the cycle of rebirth) and karma (the cosmic moral structure that determines the condition into which one is reborn). *Samkhya* is the axial-period movement that is credited with the first development of formal logic and methods of knowing.[24] The word *samkhya* means "enumeration" or "calculation." The movement is called this because it enumerates the basic principles of the universe and of knowledge. The classic formulation once existed in the text *Samkhyakarika*, attributed to Isvarakrshna.[25] Isvarakrshna had an explicit and abstract theory of causation: Every effect preexists in its cause; out of nothing comes nothing, so all that occurs is a change in preexisting reality. He also delineated the three sources of reliable knowledge: tradition or the instruction of the sages, evidence or perception, and logic or inference (of which three major types exist). Because the most basic aspects of reality are imperceptible, tradition and logic are most important in these matters.[26]

In the axial age the *Carvaka* school, from about 600 BCE, went to the contrary extreme of denying everything except the material world as known empirically.[27] Like the *Samkhya* school, *carvaka* analyzed the nature of all reality and of the means by which we know reality, but did so in order to arrive at a skepticism about the gods, about future life, and about inference.[28] Like the other two non-Vedic systems, Buddhism and Jainism, it did not rely on Vedic or other "tradition." Thus perception alone remained as the source of reliable knowledge. But even perception is limited. In the *Tattvopaplavisimha*, a seventh-century CE *carvaka* text (there is a scarcity of earlier original materials), Jayarasi attacks the possibility of making valid inferences on the basis of sense experience: "The knowledge of an invariable relation [between universals and perceptions] cannot be established. . . . Nor is it possible to conceive of such a relation subsisting between a universal and a particular object because of the indemonstrability . . . of universals."[29] Similar skepticism appeared in China and Greece, so it is worth repeating this idea by quoting Moore and Radhakrishnan as they summarize *carvaka* materialism: "The materialists deny the validity of inference, as inference depends on universal connections, and perceived data, which are particulars, do not warrant belief in universal connections."[30] This quasi-Humean position is doubly significant. It first of all demonstrates a concern for methods of knowing, for what Kitchener called "metacognition." Second, it recognizes, if only to reject, the implicit assumption behind the use of logical inference as a means to understand the real world: that the real world has universal connections, that there are causal or other patterns so pervasive and reliable that from particular instances one may validly infer something about the universal structure of things.

The richness of speculation in India from the sixth century BCE and later is extraordinary. The six so-called orthodox and three heterodox schools represent a wide range of positions, some rather abstract, about the reality (or unreality) of the universe, about its most basic structural aspects, and about the problem of knowing what is true. Both the *Nyaya Sutra* and the *Vaisesika Sutra*, from around the second century BCE, contain material on formal logic.[31] The ninth-century CE work of Shankara is famous as an example of highly abstract thought that produced a theoretically sophisticated systematic theology.[32] In cognitive style the philosophers of India have been quite adept at formal operational theorizing.

One result of religious speculation in India was a classic form of individualism. Each person is an individual self endlessly reincarnated until the self achieves *moksha*, understood as dissolution in the infinite ocean that is Atman, ultimate and absolute unchanging Self. Each self has complete individual responsibility. The person's acts determine the person's karma, the burden of guilt or merit that determines the person's next state of life and the person's proximity to *moksha*. This individualism is bound to a strong responsibility to accept one's given place in society. The major duty to be fulfilled to earn good karma is the duty of one's place in the caste structure. A willing and devoted attention to one's social duties is an essential part of the moral obligations a person must individually fulfill.

Most of the classical schools of thought in India ultimately reject life in this world. The Buddhist searches for nirvana, and the Hindu desires release from the cycle of rebirth in favor of dissolution into the eternally changeless Atman. Both seek release from a world that is so intrinsically flawed as to be no source of lasting hope of any kind. Similar ideas arose later in the West, a sign perhaps of how the theoretical mind can devise such formally beautiful ideals that the limitations of the concretely real world appear increasingly burdensome and painful.

Even as philosophical religiousness flourished, most people in India nonetheless continued to live by polytheism. Sometime between the second century BCE and the second century CE, after the appearance of the universalizing classical mode of thought, two collections of stories appeared, the *Ramayana* and the *Bhagavad-Gita*. Just as the abstractions of Hellenic thought do not satisfy most people in the West, so also in India the concrete stories of these two narratives won the hearts and minds of most.[33] The teaching of the *Bhagavad-Gita* is similar to that in the Upanishads, but the form of a story about the warrior Arjuna and his charioteer, who is Krishna, an avatar (incarnation) of the great god Vishnu. Personal devotion to Krishna as helper and friend is much more appealing to the imagination than abstract formulations of truth. Similarly the story of the *Ramayana* delineates basic truths of karma and dharma, but through the story of another incarnation of Vishnu, this time as prince Rama.

Both tales are typically mythical in that they are history-like narratives of significant deeds by gods and demons. Both also, however, gather together in one place an enormous amount of traditional material about the origin of things, the nature of human life, the basic structure of the cosmos, and how everything led up to the major events of the narratives. It is as though the two myth tellers wanted to contend with the new broad-scope cosmic theorizing of the more philosophical schools by offering narratives as big and complex as any philosophical work. For most people of India, these two narratives remain far more popular than any of the more philosophical forms of religiousness.[34] The philosophically minded today enjoy the *sattva marga*, the way of intellectual meditation; but most people of India find their consolation in *bhakti marga*, the way of devotion to a god or gods, a more concrete or commonsense form of religiousness. It has been true of India, as of everywhere else, that the use of formal operational thought in philosophy, science, and religion is not the ordinary way of people. The achievement of the classical age, in

India as elsewhere, was to add a new dimension of thought to the overall currents of the culture, not to eliminate the old.

Classical Culture in China

As in India, the origins of China's classic era lay in a time of troubles. The Chou dynasty had ruled much of northern China since defeating the Shang in the twelfth century BCE. The last two centuries of this dynastic era are called the Warring States period, to indicate that for nearly two hundred years (403–221 BCE are the usual dates given) there was no strong central rule. Perhaps here and in India the unrest and turmoil prodded certain people to search for fundamental principles that could guide the government and all of society into a renewed peaceful order. Perhaps the chaos of the times also made more people ready to listen to new ideas. Whatever the reason, the period from the fifth to second century BCE was a time of great innovation in thought: in content of belief, in mode of expression, and in methods of thought. About two or three centuries after the traditional dates assigned to the Upanishads in India, the classical mode of thought appeared in China. After many centuries of myth and magic, some Chinese thinkers sought the Ultimate, the foundational power or principle of all else. Further, out of a need of one school to make the case that it was more correct than another, explicit methods of analysis and argumentation appeared. This was the time of the classics of Taoism, of early generations of Confucianism, of the Sophists, the Mohists, and the Logicians.

Myths had long preceded the more formal thought of the axial age. The earliest collection of myths is "Questions of Heaven," which Anne Birrell calls "the most valuable document in Chinese mythography,"[35] even though it is only 186 verses. The nominal author is Ch'u Yuan. The "Questions of Heaven" is the third part or "chapter" of *Songs of Ch'u*, from the fourth century BCE. In the origin stories there is no first creator of things. Instead there is originally just light and dark, yin and yang, and nine layers of sky. Under a sky dome is a square earth held up by pillars. (Birrell suspects Egyptian influence here, and perhaps Akkadian.[36]) A larger collection of myths comes from the Han dynasty. *The Classics of Mountains and Seas* is made up of chapters written partly in the early Han (ca. second century BCE) and partly in the later Han times (ca. first century CE, perhaps). Throughout the stories the standard mythic events and heroes explain the origins of farming and fire, tell of metamorphoses and virgin births, and dream of immortality. There was no Homer or Hesiod in China at this time, no one who decided to shape the myths into a larger, coherent narrative. "Early Chinese myths existed as an amorphous, untidy congeries of archaic expression."[37] We have collections of brief stories, folktale myths, as it were, because of their relative brevity and their lack of logical connection with each other.

From among the mythic tales a classic form of thought eventually emerged. It was a typically long process, from polytheism to universalism. Thirteenth-century BCE oracle bones of the Shang period indicate belief in various spirits of nature, including a high God, Shang-Ti. The Chinese paid special attention to the ancestors, including ancient kings.[38] Where the Aryans, like most peoples, had worshiped mainly gods of storm or mountain or natural elements like fire, the Chinese focused on ancestors, especially long dead and legendary emperors.[39] Some of the emperors may have once been nature spirits, but generally they had once been men, like other ancestors, and then had become gods, as it were, objects of reverence and worship.[40] These ancestors continued to play a "narrative" role, as Benjamin Schwartz puts it, in the lives of their clans.[41] That is to say, there was a continuing but variable or irregular interaction between the significant ancestors and the living.

The high god Shang-Ti was the source of authority for the Shang emperor. The Chou, who conquered and replaced the Shang as the dominant dynasty in northern China in the eleventh or twelfth century BCE and later, identified their own high god T'ien with the Ti of the Shang. When the Chou made this identification, they broke the link of the high god with a specific dynasty and laid the foundation for the notion that Heaven would grant legitimacy to any dynasty that functioned well for the people. This in turn gave to Heaven or Ti a greater degree of transcendence than was the case when Ti was simply the high god of a particular people.

In retrospect, we could anticipate that Heaven might eventually become a supreme and metaphysical Personal Ultimate analogous to the God of Western religions. But the development of religious beliefs in China followed a different path. Taoism emphasized the impersonal forces of nature, and looked behind or beneath them, as it were, to discover the Ultimate Way (Tao) of things. Confucian thought repeated the belief in conformity to the Will of Heaven, or more exactly to the Tao of Heaven, but without treating Heaven as a personal God with whom the ruler and people must have good relations.[42] The Sophists and Mohists took yet other positions, in which neither gods nor a God plays a central role.

Confucius (551–479 BCE) insisted that in prior times the great dynasties had incorporated both the basic principles (*tao*) of ordered life and the specific norms of behavior (*li*), which together constitute that ordered life.[43] His major concern was to describe the character of the superior man whose actions would create the proper way of government, family, and life in general. There are lines in the *Analects* (the sayings of Confucius) that describe Confucius as a person concerned with good relations with the ancestors or with Heaven as a god to whom one may pray (3:

12–13), brief words that could as easily be part of an archaic polytheism with little sense of a single and universal Ultimate. The experts differ on the degree to which the *Analects* represent a high point of archaic thought or the beginning of axial-age thought.[44] To find clear signs of axial-age thought, whether in belief in an Ultimate or in other aspects, we have to go beyond the *Analects*.[45]

In the next few centuries in China, from the fourth BCE through the third CE, many other sets of beliefs remained more archaic than classic. Many contain no search for an Ultimate. Many skip systematic inquiry into how and why there are universal patterns. Most ignore attempts to analyze how to analyze, how to think logically.[46] In this period old myths were collected, without attempts to integrate them into a larger systematic whole. Benjamin Schwartz concludes from this that even though Chinese thought in the axial age reached "the image of an all embracing and inclusive order," China did not become so rationalistic or transcendentalist as other axial cultures.[47]

But China nonetheless also had some striking forms of the new axial-age or classic style of thought: its search for a single Ultimate, its universalizing, and its development of formal logic.[48] Taoism is a major instance of the first two of these. The Taoism that arose in the fifth or fourth century BCE reflects a much older set of beliefs in certain patterns in nature, especially the Yang and Yin pairs of contraries: hot and cold, wet and dry, male and female, and so forth. Taoism sought the ultimate Way (Tao) that gives rise to the two contraries in the three aspects of reality—earth, heaven, and the living beings in between.[49] Perhaps the contents of the *Tao Te Ching* (The Book of the Power of the Way) came from around the time of Confucius, in accordance with legends about its supposed author, Lao Tzu. The form we have, however, is from the fourth century BCE. By this time there are clearer statements suggesting a universal Ultimate Reality so far beyond the limits of ordinary things that it is ineffable. (The number after each set of verses indicates from which of the eighty-one "stanzas" of the *Tao Te Ching* the verse is taken.)

> The Tao that can be told of is not the eternal Tao;
> The name that can be named is not the eternal name.
> The Nameless is the origin of Heaven and Earth;
> The Named is the mother of all things. (1)

> Tao produced the One.
> The One produced the two.
> The two produced the three.
> And the three produced the ten thousand things.
> The ten thousand things carry the yin and embrace the
>   yang, and through the blending of the material force they
>   achieve harmony. (42)

He who knows [the Tao] does not speak.
He who speaks does not know. (56)

A century after the probable assemblage of the *Tao Te Ching*, a broad Yin Yang School attempted to work out a whole cosmology, with a description of the basic stuff of the world and of the process by which it has come to be the world as it now is. Around the third century BCE this school took one of the ancient classics revered by Confucius, the *I Ching* or *Book of Changes*, and expanded upon it with ten "wings" or commentaries. The wings include the claim that there is a single Great Ultimate out of which the basic yin and yang arose, from which came two pairs of lesser yin and yang.[50] Both Joseph Needham and James Thrower compare this Yin Yang School (as a form of Taoism) to the "scientific naturalism" of Lucretius.[51] Thrower in fact calls it a "pantheistic naturalism" that replaced mythological views.[52]

There were other signs of a classic style of thought. The first great challenge to Confucian thought, in the fifth to third centuries BCE, was not Taoism but Mohism; and the strongest aspect of the challenge was Mohism's universalist morality. Confucius proposed a morality modeled on good family structure. Primary devotion was due the head of the family, then to others according to their place in the family scheme. Primary civil devotion was due the emperor. Mohism preached a more universal and egalitarian love of everyone, including the stranger.[53] "The way of universal love and mutual benefit" is an alternative name for Mohism. The Mohist Sung Hsing, who flourished around 300 BCE, tried to counter the archaic code of honor. Insults may be disgraceful socially, he said, but not morally. The truly moral person refuses to fight when insulted. There are universal moral standards superior to the social requirements of one's time and place. "An individual's valuation of self can be wholly independent of others' approval or disapproval."[54]

The competition between Confucian and Mohist thought, as well as among these and other positions, spurred the development of modes of careful argument.[55] A few lines hint at the overall style of *The Mo Tzu*, the work reporting the words of Mo Tzu: "How do we know that Heaven loves all the people in the world? Because it enlightens them all. How do we know that it enlightens them all? Because it possesses them all. How do we know that it possesses them all? Because it feeds them all." The chapter continues, analyzing who receives misfortune and who receives good fortune and why, the major aspects of a good character that is deserving of good fortune, and so on. In its form it is an orderly essay, not a mythic narrative.[56]

A later chapter attacks fatalism and declares that this doctrine must be examined. Here, significantly, Mo Tzu is described as laying down three standards for determining what is true or not, similar to the standards laid down by Isvarakrshna in India. The first standard is to test an idea against the sayings of the ancient wise rulers. The second is to test an idea against the evidence as seen by people in general. The third to is test an idea by its consequences. Mo Tzu then goes on to show that fatalism fails the tests of these standards.[57] Like classical thinkers in other cultures, Mo Tzu is concerned to elaborate (universalist) criteria of truth.

China's ancient schools of thought were perhaps never as concerned with formal logic as those of the ancient Greeks. Yet there is one fourth-century BCE group of Chinese thinkers who have been labeled the Logicians, Hui Shih the most noted of them. His writings show him to be not so much a logician as an analyst of the problems of language.[58] "When the sun is at noon it is setting." True enough; at one second past noon the sun is going down rather than coming up, yet it is not "setting" in the usual sense of being near the horizon. "The South has no limit and yet has a limit." True enough; there is no clear line dividing south from north because south is relative to where one is, yet south is not north.[59] Similarly, Hui Shih elaborates on the relation of a thing and its attributes through a famous difficult analysis of naming a white horse. "Is it correct to say that a white horse is not a horse?" the analysis begins. "It is correct," is the response. "Why?" Hui Shih provides an answer worthy of Zeno and his Paradoxes, worthy also of the most fervid contemporary deconstructionists of language.[60] To condense two pages of Hui Shih into a pair of sentences: If a yellow horse is different from a white horse, then a yellow horse is different from *a* horse—that is, from the white horse. But if a yellow horse can be different from a horse, so can a white horse be different from a horse.

All in all, there seems to be something of a consensus among scholars that the Chinese remained less interested in the metaphysics that so entranced thinkers in India and Greece, and did less also to develop an explicit logic. Yet the schools of late Chou and early Han times, from the fifth to the first century BCE, show a search for a single Ultimate as well as for universal principles of nature and human life. They show a meta-cognitive awareness that how we use language determines how we think. Thus China had an axial shift of its own. Through the ensuing centuries Buddhist thought and neo-Confucian philosophy used the cognitive tools of philosophical analysis. The formal operational style of thought has had a home in China as elsewhere.

About the same time, texts attributed to Chuang Tzu (or Zhuangzi) took a somewhat skeptical attitude. Paul Kjellberg and Philip Ivanhoe compare these writings to the summary of Greek skepticism produced by Sextus Empiricus in Western antiquity. Kjellberg notes that it is usual to interpret each of these writings as responses to specific schools, to the Stoics by Sextus and to the Neo-mohists by the Zhuangzi. But they have something in common also. "Their basic arguments take on an epistemology so widespread as to be almost universal."[61] Skepticism thus appears in China as it did in India and also in Hellenic thought about the same time.

This review of ancient Chinese thought certainly is quite incomplete. There are other schools and thinkers besides those mentioned here. These brief paragraphs are inadequate to do justice even to the thinkers and schools that are mentioned. But enough has been said to indicate that China, like India, did indeed take part in an axial-age addition of new and influential ideas, and that the beliefs, modes of expression, and forms of thought represent an addition of belief in an Ultimate and in universal patterns of nature; of rationally reflective essays to the modes of expression; of a concern for the uses of language and standards of evidence or argument; of the application of the standard of "fit" (i.e., of how well ideas and evidence fit together). These are characteristics of formal operational or "theoretical" or metacognitive thought. A third significant place where this axial shift occurred is, of course, ancient Greece.

Ancient Greece

Ancient Greek society went through the typical stages of development. There are signs of a primitive form of culture in the background of its history. In times too early to be called pre-Homeric, the people living in Greek territory did not deal with gods but with spirits. They did not worship or offer gifts to the spirits but simply tried to drive them away to prevent them from causing trouble.[62] We have clear evidence for belief in the gods in the Homeric period, an archaic stage of culture with at least local kings and a ruling class. Even in this later time, the thought seems to be of the kind that Christopher Hallpike might legitimately identify as concrete operational or even preoperational. It is thought resting on sensory images and myth-pictures, in John Finley's words.[63]

It was a time when people did not have the language or thought habits for identifying their own feelings and inner thoughts very well as their own; they thought of them as placed in the person by a god. The many instances of this way of speaking provided Julian Jaynes with evidence for an unusual theory. He claims that in archaic Greek culture, one half of the bicameral human mind spoke to the other half. Thoughts were perceived by one half as coming not from the other half but from outside the person entirely. So the archaic Greeks spoke constantly of thoughts being placed in their minds by the gods.[64] Jaynes is probably mistaken in his claim that brain functioning itself changed in this way. He may simply be identifying a preliterate thought style in which a clear sense of inner self is absent, as both Hallpike and Alexander Luria noted.[65]

Homeric times were typically preliterate in their measure of personal worth. Individual human beings as such had no rights in Homer.[66] External factors such as wealth and power, and especially heroism, counted.[67] Using guile to achieve success was an admirable skill. The highest goal in life was to earn high esteem through heroic accomplishments, especially as a warrior. It was a shame culture rather than a guilt culture, says Eric R. Dodds, borrowing the language from Ruth Benedict.[68] Losing face could be more unbearable than death; but whatever a crafty person could get away with without loss of public respect was fine. There were no universal standards of justice or truth against which a person could measure self-worth. To Homer not even the gods were what we would call morally admirable.[69] They had power and could do what they wanted; they were also extremely touchy about their honor (i.e., their external and public standing rather than their inner worth).[70] These ideas are typical of an archaic culture. They are also fairly typical of concrete operational thinking and "pre-conventional" moral thought in adults, in Lawrence Kohlberg's categories.

Homeric culture gave way to a more complex culture built upon the economic growth of Greek city-states, both on the mainland and in colonies such as the Ionian cities. The relatively high degree of variety and flexibility in social patterns may have been as important as the new wealth in its effects on the culture.[71] The interplay of Babylonian and Egyptian and Greek culture, with Persian influence soon to be added, and even perhaps ideas from India; the lack of an entrenched ruling class in the new colonies; the ability of a person to leave one city-state and travel to another, with different rules; the shift in wealth and power because of the new commerce—all these opened the way for innovation.[72] Moreover, the eventual end of political diversity and openness with the downfall of the city-states was soon followed by an end both to new ideas and even to the full theoretical strength of the old ideas.[73]

Whatever the causes may have been, a change took place. Archaic thought styles, whether preliterate or literate, continued. Mythical narratives of the interventions of the gods in human lives maintained their popularity among most people. But a new kind of thought, and a new set of cognitive techniques and premises, were developing. These would inject new standards and ideas into the culture of the times, and these standards and ideas would dominate the intellectual world and affect even the popular world of ancient classical times, from the fourth century BCE to the second century CE. This was classical thought, the universalizing systematic-theoretical cognitive style that formal operational thought makes possible. With it came new notions of moral standards and of individuality. With it science entered a new stage, and religious thought changed to keep up with it.

The story of pre-Socratic philosophy is too well known to repeat much of it. Thales, Anaximines and Anaximander, Pythagoras, Heracleitus, Parmenides, Leucippus, and Democritus constitute an honor roll of philosophers who explored ideas about the basic stuff of which all things are made and the basic processes by which all things take place. They replaced the poems of Homer and Hesiod with prose reflections and analysis. They sought to determine how to distinguish truth from mere opinion, and how to make language clear for the sake of rational argument. They did what thinkers of India and China were doing in approximately the same centuries or shortly before or after. Methods of logical, and eventually scientific, analysis have been developed most thoroughly in Western cultures, but this is not a peculiarly Western mode of thought.

By the time of Aristotle, formal operational thought had developed very well indeed. Soon Atomists, Epicureans, Stoics, and Platonists competed to have their theories of the universe accepted. As in China and India, some philosophers worked out criteria of clear and valid thought. They theorized about theorizing. The mind in love with theory seeks order, regularity, predictability. As Aristotle would say, there is no science (*episteme*) (i.e., no real knowledge) of the individual instance. It is knowledge of the universal that constitutes the fullest knowledge.[74] That which is permanently and reliably true, especially that which is true of everything that happens, is the basis for all other true ideas. This is incontrovertible in one sense. The unpredictable in the extreme is something like what an infant first knows, one image after the other with little reliable connection among them. Reliable knowledge begins when conservation begins—when the child knows that the pillow which was there a moment ago must still exist even though it is no longer visible. All knowledge beyond raw sense impression has some element of this basic supposition of permanence, of continued existence.

As we come to discover that some things are more lasting than others, it is the lasting that provides the reference to be able to understand other things. The tree with its root deep in the ground provides the reason why the new leaves appear every year. The rotation of the Earth provides the reason why specific stars rise at different times of the year. The continuing presence of gravity explains why each and every thing falls to the ground. When the ancient Greeks began to look for the basic stuff out of which all was made and for the basic principles of order according to which all things happen, they necessarily had to look to whatever is most regular, most reliable, most unchangingly true in order to move closer and closer to reliable explanations of things. This insistence on intelligibility through permanence is an extension of the primitive human insistence that things make sense, that events have causes which explain why the events happened as they did. The atomist Leucippus is credited with saying, "Nothing happens at random; everything happens out of reason and by necessity."[75] Moreover, where primitive (and concrete operational) thought will settle for loose collections of explanatory stories, classical (and formal operational) thought also seeks to explain the collections by identifying their underlying coherence, their "fit" with each other in relation to something more general or more basic.[76] The logical consistency among our ideas of the permanent and wide-reaching aspects of reality partly determines the plausibility of those ideas.

The new philosophy in ancient Greece also accompanied or created a new moral sense. Philosophers elaborated universal ethical norms that in theory could be applied impersonally to everyone.[77] The discussions by Socrates and Plato of the nature of the good and of justice and of virtue, Aristotle's idea of the virtuous person, the Stoic description of a natural law ethics are all instances of this. Plato's Meno provides an example of the contrast between archaic morality and the new classical type. When asked to describe what true excellence or virtue (*arete*) is in a person, Meno at first praises a person who fits with the ordinary (and archaic) moral sensibility of his time, one who achieves success for self and friends, ideally also doing damage to their enemies. Socrates then begins to push Meno to acknowledge a more universal and objective sense of justice, which should be applied to any person equally.[78]

In the Hellenic philosophies from the time of Plato and Aristotle, ethics was based on the nature of the human person, and the person in relation to the universe. This provided a norm that transcended merely local customs and laws. Through rational analysis, it was argued, a person could arrive at a true understanding of human nature, and from this derive the specific ideas of how a person ought ideally to act.[79] Different schools had different ideas of human nature. Plato and Aristotle defined the person primarily as a social being, a citizen. The Epicureans followed their atomistic materialism to its logical ethical outcome: that the good of the person is material good—physical pleasure (though this includes psychic peace).[80] Stoics agreed that pleasure is the good, but defined it as harmony with the divine Logos.[81] In all these there is a universal standard based on the general nature of the human person in relation to the overall nature of the entire universe.

It is also clear from this that the individual could now define self by relation to the new general standard of human nature. It would no longer be necessary, though it would remain the normal way, to define self by ethnic identity, local allegiance, or family ties. As Dodds puts it, "For the first time in Greek history it mattered little where a man had been born or what his ancestry was."[82] The principle was in place to override the normal human pattern of giving preference to relatives, of establishing personal worth by social class, of the bigotry that sees some people as a group intrinsically superior to other groups. An individual of whatever race, city, or family would be able, in theory, to take pride in being one who lived up to the universally valid objective standards of moral excellence. In practice, humankind has never succeeded very well in following this ideal, but the ideal provides a standard in comparison with which the normal way can be recognized as not adequate. The ideal is a major achievement of the universalizing tendency of classical thought. The Stoic, the Mohist, and the Hindu can all appeal to universal standards of moral order.

It is tempting to speculate on why formal operational thought found homes in the three cultures just described. Perhaps the typically formal operational aspects of thought appeared first in India and then spread elsewhere. The usual dates given for late Vedic materials and the principal Upanishads suggest this. Perhaps literacy had prepared the way for this thought style in many cultures, awaiting only that social moment when one culture would first light the fuse for itself and others Or perhaps formal operational thought emerged independently in different cultures for some as yet unidentified reason. Whatever the case, it is clear that people of different cultures can enthusiastically employ formal operational thought and become adept at it. It is also clear, however, that many centuries of human development passed before the axial age. The widespread use of well-developed formal operational thought apparently requires special resources or circumstances.

The quick survey in this chapter of the axial periods of India, China, and Greece is not the whole story of the axial age. Zoroastrian ideas developed in the direction of a monotheism, an ethical idealism, and an apocalyptic semirejection of the world.[83] So did Hebrew thought, particularly from the time of the Babylonian exile.[84] A fascinating historical story of development awaits a fuller telling. We have seen enough, however, to lay a basis for focusing more on the development of religious and scientific thought in the axial age in the West, in chapter 6.

6

PHILOSOPHY, RELIGION, AND SCIENCE IN WESTERN ANTIQUITY

Chapter 5 described the addition of postaxial, formal operational thought to the overall cultural mix in India, China, and Greece. This added "metacognition" to "cognition" in Kitchener's categories, "theory" to "common sense" in Lonergan's language. Where once only preoperational and concrete operational styles of thought were clearly evident and influential, suddenly, within a few centuries, formal operational thought was both clearly evident and quite influential among the cognitive elite. Where traditional stories and rules and information once ruled alone, formally systematic thinkers granted themselves the right to reinterpret the universe as a whole and to criticize traditional ideas in the name of rationality. The traditional ethics of honor and status now had to compete with the new ethics of universal norms. A notion of the individual defined through universalist theories of human nature and value competed with the older idea of identity through family or other relatively parochial group. The effect of this new mode of thought is apparent in religious thought as well as in philosophy and science.

From this chapter forward, the focus will be mainly on developments in Western culture. Primitive animism is a worldwide reality, from prehistoric to contemporary times. Archaic polytheism is likewise part of the history of many cultures around the world. The axial shift, the addition of the full formal operational style of thought, appeared in three (and more) major cultural contexts. The style of thought continued to develop in many cultures. There are medieval Confucian and Vedic religious philosophies, for example, just as there is a medieval era of philosophy in Europe, partly mediated by Islamic thinkers (and Jewish thinkers in Islamic countries). But in European-centered culture, science eventually developed a late formal operational style of thought. This development is unusual enough to require special attention to the history of scientific and religious thought from Hellenistic to modern European times. For most of those centuries, classical (formal operational) thought maintained its prestige, though not always great influence.

Religion in an
Intelligible Universe

The introduction described the conclusions of Auguste Comte in the early nineteenth century, and of Donald Wiebe and Stewart Guthrie more recently, that the classical axial age was a shift from religion to non-religion because it was a shift from prerational, anthropomorphic interpretations of the world to rational, naturalistic interpretations. The general Comtean thesis is that the human race had its mental childhood when it believed in invisible beings such as spirits and gods. The human race had its cognitive adolescence, so to speak, when it moved to the rational thought of philosophy in classical times. The human race began to achieve its intellectual maturity when it developed empirical or "positive" science.

The Comtean theory supposes that the use of philosophical rational standards erodes religious belief. This is only partly accurate. Axial-age rationality erodes traditional beliefs in unpredictable interventions by invisible beings. It promotes belief in a reliable natural order without such interventions. The new rationality thereby called many older religious traditions into question. Yet the history of classical philosophy reveals that rational philosophic thought can also be religious. Rational analysis may change religious thought by changing religion's content, mode of expression, and method to more theoretical forms; but religion interpreted through formal operational thinking can remain religion, even as it becomes more philosophical and scientific. (This has significant implications for understanding religious thought in our own times, a topic of a later chapter.)

It is not possible to draw neat distinctions among the philosophy, theology, and science of classical thought. The Upanishads are all three at once; so are some axial-age writings of China. The same is true of ancient Greek thought. Heracleitus's philosophical theory of the cosmos, for example, was an attempt at what today are considered scientific questions: the origin and processes of the universe as we see it. Heracleitus's thought is also a theology, seeking the divine fire that gives energy to the universe. Aristotle's philosophy was some of the very best science of his time. It also included a theory of the divine Unmoved Mover as the final explanation for the ongoing activity of all things. Stoic materialism placed a divine Logos at the heart of the cosmos. We will see more instances below of intimate unity among what we would normally call philosophical, scientific, and religious thought.

Axial-age thought sought to create a unified body of knowledge. It supposed that there is a set of universal and fully reliable causes that constitute the single universe. This implied that unusual or surprising events are just as much products of the overall pattern of orderly causes as are commonplace events. Axial-age thought tended to reduce every strange event to an unforeseen conjunction of fully reliable patterns of nature. It is a tendency that can be seen clearly in various ancient Greek philosophies, as a later section of this chapter will explore.

The issue is again the intelligibility of things. The great new supposition of axial-age thought was that deep down, reality is fully *intelligible* (with the exception of the single Ultimate in terms of which everything else is explained). This means that beneath the surface confusion and disorder, behind the seemingly unpredictable and incoherent sequence of things and events in the world, there is a deeper set of utterly reliable forces or laws or truths. These most basic truths account for everything else. Ancient philosophers-theologians-scientists in Greece, India, and China looked and hoped for such basic intelligibility. Whatever the reason for their optimism, they jumped into the task with confidence.

It is difficult to see how one could establish a priori that the universe is in fact highly intelligible. The axial-age search for an all-encompassing rational scheme of things might have turned out to be unrealistic. Rational theorizing may be very satisfying to a logical mind, a mind in love with the theoretical systematizing that formal operational skills allow a person to engage in. It may be highly desirable to such a mind to have a world in which there is a clear and ultimate coherence to things. But it is something else to assume that the universe will indeed satisfy this rather ambitious mental desire. Perhaps the universe is in fact too erratic. Perhaps there are too many randomly acting forces.

After the fact, from the viewpoint of the discoveries of modern science, we can recognize that only a highly reliable set of natural laws could produce a universe stable and long-lasting enough to provide the context for stellar evolution, the formation of planetary systems, and the evolution of life over billions of years. If nature were not extremely regular and reliable, we could not be here to think about it. But twenty-five hundred years ago, this would have been just one more speculative system of ideas among others, without adequate evidence to judge how true it might be.

The belief which most strongly suggested a degree of irrationality and unpredictability to events was the common religious belief that there are many invisible, conscious agents at work in the world, spirits and gods with freedom to have an effect on the course of events. After all, a major source of surprises in history are the actions of human beings, themselves free agents. By their thought and choices they are able to manipulate nature and make it do "unnatural" things. Humans dam rivers to create lakes, form metal into shapes that cut and pierce, pump air through bellows to artificially increase a fire's heat. If we visible, thinking, and choosing beings can do such strange things with our limited knowledge, the ancients could ask, why is it not possible that there are invisible beings who can do the same? The air is not visible and yet moves the trees; the breath of life in a person is not visible, yet without it a person dies.

If there are invisible beings who can act in nature and history in the way humans can, then many events will not be intelligible, except as the acts of humanlike persons whose motives can only be guessed at or learned through oracles and signs. If there is a high god of enormous power who intervenes in nature and history, then the explanation for even great events or patterns may be the secret will or choices of this god. This is an "intelligibility" of sorts, but one opaque to the human mind. The human ability to discover reliable and regular patterns that explain things, will be frustrated at that point. Rational inquiry will bump up against the blank wall of the unpredictable whim of invisible beings, of spirits, gods, or a God, unless these beings are themselves bound by laws of nature to behave in a fully reliable way (like Spinoza's God).

We can ask whether the axial-age thinkers, the ones who enthusiastically adopted the formal operational methods of thought, had adequate evidence to abandon belief in the intervention of the gods or spirits as explanations of events around them. The predictability of the movement of the heavenly bodies, so precise as to allow the prediction of eclipses, suggested that these heavenly beings were natural objects, not gods. Galen argued that epilepsy, the divine madness, was natural and not caused by spirits or gods. Epicurus said it would be contrary to divine bliss for the gods to get involved in events of history. The evidence of the skies was clear enough, and confirmed by predictions of eclipses. But how did Galen and Epicurus know they were correct? They obviously believed reality to be rationally intelligible. But we can ask what grounds they had for this belief.

The basic question can be asked in an awkward but revealing way: Are there reasonable grounds for believing that the universe is thoroughly reasonable? Given the evidence of disorder, unpredictability, confusion, and discord in this universe, it might be most reasonable for a person to conclude that the universe is at best only partly intelligible. It may be reasonable to reject the theory that reality is rational. The desire of the rational mind for overall intelligibility may be doomed to frustration.

The distinction between a fully intelligible universe, and a partly intelligible universe whose parts and patterns do not all connect coherently with each other, is a major dividing line between archaic religion and classical religion. Most religion in history has remained archaic at best, down to contemporary times, though there is often a classical element within the same tradition. The word "Taoism" applies both to "popular" Taoism, which attends mainly to the spirits, demons, and ancestors, and to "philosophical" Taoism, which seeks unity with the deepest patterns and truth of the cosmos. *Bhakti marga*, the path of devotion to the gods as major aids in life's journey, expects the gods to be able to intervene to bend the iron law of karma on behalf of their devotees. *Bhakti marga* is far more popular than Advaita Vedanta, which looks beyond the gods and reduces everything that is real to the Ultimate Brahma. Both mingle in the Hindu tradition. Trust in the aid of the saints or the gifts of the Holy Spirit constitutes the everyday religion of many Christians, even while the far fewer learned theologians speak of God as Infinite Mystery (Karl Rahner) or the God Beyond God (Paul Tillich). Everyday concrete operational thought works quite well for life in general. It fits well with the disorderly appearance of the world, more so than formal operational theories of a deep and full coherence to all things. It should not be surprising that most people are quite comfortable with a concrete operational style in religion, even if this is not so rationally coherent as a formal operational theology or philosophy. Nonetheless, where the Comteans like Wiebe and Guthrie separate religious beliefs from rational thought, we can instead identify both concrete operational and formal operational styles as religious, albeit in different ways.

Some Classical Rational
Religious Thought

One type of theory of the universe is materialism. Most ancient materialisms were not religious. In India, for example, the *Carvaka* school, one of the three "heterodox" movements of the axial-age, argued for an atheistic materialism. All that exists is part of the material universe, composed of the four elements: earth, air, fire, and water.[1] This school likewise argued against belief in rebirth and karma, orthodox beliefs of Hindu tradition which suppose that there is something like a soul or spiritual aspect of the self that can survive the death of the material body. *Carvaka* denied both. It is simply unreligious. It fits the Comtean scheme, wherein philosophical reflection rejects and replaces religious thought.

In ancient Greece, Epicurean atomism played a similar role, though with a minor religious aspect. Leucippus and Democritus had developed the idea that everything is composed of extremely small and indivisible particles moving in empty space: atoms in the void. Epicurus adopted this as his basic science. All things are combinations of atoms. How and where and when they combine is partly a matter of some basic and changeless characteristics of atoms. This is Epicurus's equivalent of what we would call laws of nature. It constitutes the element of "necessity" in the universe. How the atoms combine, however, is also partly a matter of happenstance. When and where the atoms falling through the void manage to swerve this way or that is not predetermined. Thus chance joins necessity as the two basic forces affecting the events of the universe. This constitutes a rather complete basic description of the stuff (atoms), context (the void), and the forces (chance and necessity) that together explain everything else. Even minds, whether human minds or divine, are products of this material stuff, context, and forces. The gods live in everlasting repose, wise enough not to do anything except accept their blessed state. Prayers and sacrifice to them are useless.[2] Belief that the gods intervened in human affairs was insulting to the gods, Epicurus claimed. Belief that there was a life after death for humans was incorrect. It was important to reject both of these beliefs explicitly because they were sources of pain in life.[3] Fear of the gods and fear of what happens after death were two of the major obstacles to the life of mental peace that was the goal of Epicurus's philosophy.

Epicurus did believe in invisible beings worthy of being called gods. In fact, their quiet repose, their unendingly calm state of soul, should be a model to people on how their own lives should be lived. Yet he offered a highly reasoned justification for not worshiping them, for not making offerings to them. Whether this philosophy should be called religious is uncertain. The gods are really not all that important.

The Stoics, on the other hand, were simultaneously materialists and religious. In this philosophy, the entire universe is material, including any mental and divine elements in it. The ultimate divinity is simply the most refined and noble aspect of material reality. The Stoics argued for the continuity of matter, in opposition to Epicurus's theory of indivisible particles flowing in empty space. Most important, the Stoics rejected chance. They argued that the universe exhibits immensely rational order, not unplanned or purposeless chance. From sun and moon, to rocks and seas, to plants and then to animals, the universe has a hierarchical structure that serves the highest form of life, which is human life. Evidently the order of the universe has to represent some cosmic Force of rationality. The Stoics normally called this immanent Force Logos, though at times they labeled it Zeus. This was the active mental element of the universe, of which human minds are also an instance. The Stoics said that earlier mythology had mistakenly presented this supreme power in the universe as an anthropomorphic god. This was an intellectually less mature way of understanding things, corrected by Stoic philosophy. The Stoics thus agreed with the Epicureans that neither Zeus nor any other god intervenes in the events of history and nature. But they proposed reverence for the divine principle of rational order that dwells in all the universe and in which humans participate as rational beings.[4]

Among some Stoics, belief in the thoroughly rational order of nature reached a kind of fatalism, a belief that every event is the outcome of prior causes, which in turn flow from their causes, in a perfectly rational sequence. Cicero (106–43 BCE) presents a "middle Stoic" version of his former teacher, Posidonius (d. ca. 51 BCE), which was repeated centuries later by Pierre-Simon LaPlace in different words:

> Since all things happen by fate, if there were a man whose mind could discern the inner connections of all causes, then surely he would never be mistaken in any prediction he might make. For he who knows the causes of future events necessarily knows what every future event will be. . . . Things which are to be do not suddenly spring into existence, but the evolution of time is like the unwinding of a cable; it creates nothing new but only unfolds each event in its order.[5]

Yet even this fatalism participates in the general religious character of Stoic philosophy. Its context is a reverential awe of the divine Logos; it provides a confirmation of a moral law inherent in the universe.

Epicurean and Stoic "materialism" stands out by contrast with Platonic spiritualism. For Socrates and Plato it is the intellectual mind of a person that is nonmaterial. Plato has Socrates show this in different ways. One is to raise the question of the *Meno*, of how the mind can recognize truths when it sees them. The answer is that the intellect in each person must have preexisted the current life state and have become familiar with the basic natures of things in that preexistence. Another way is by the series of contrasts that Socrates presents in the *Phaedo*. The body is corruptible, the mind is not corruptible. The body is like a servant or slave; the mind is like a ruler. Clearly the mind belongs to a realm different from the corruptible and confusing one of physical existence. Its true happiness lies in escaping the prison of the body, avoiding future bodily reincarnation, and dwelling with the gods in the spiritual realm of the Forms. Plato's search for the spiritual self is similar in a number of ways to the Hindu search for the deepest self in a person, the reality that survives the death of the body and can be reborn into a new bodily state. Plato uses dialectic analysis to guide this search, however, not appeals to seers or to tradition.

Aristotle must be mentioned here also, if only out of respect for this great thinker. Even as arguments among Stoics, Epicureans, and Platonists heated up, Aristotle's philosophy-science-theology was already the most extensive, in part because he had reviewed his predecessors' various opinions and arguments and responded to them, building upon their work by accepting some aspects (Empedocles' four basic elements of earth, air, fire, and water) and rejecting others (the changeless universe of Parmenides), in part perhaps simply because of his great genius and attention to extensive and varied information. From multiple details of the structures of living and dead organisms to the ultimate causes of everything, to the basic categories and tools for analyzing organisms and causes, Aristotle examined it. Whether doing what we would call zoology, physics, astrophysics, psychology, ethics and political theory, theology, or logic, even literary analysis, he applied techniques of careful method, of sequential analyses of parts, of comparison of alternative hypotheses and the evidence available to confirm or reject hypotheses. His thought was highly structured, though not just "linear," as some current critics have it. It was structured in many interlocking considerations from smallest part up to ultimate causes.[6] It was all highly rational but also highly "holistic," to use another current term, in that in his enterprise the connection of anything to everything else as much as possible was always part of the project. He did not resolve all that he took up. It was neither a static system nor a closed system. He continued to explore how different theories might fit with the evidence and how different cognitive tools might fit with different kinds of evidence and theories.[7] But the systematic and logical approach is clear.

In the next few centuries Plato's thought turned out to appeal to more people than Aristotle's, though some aspects of Aristotle were adopted by other philosophical schools.[8] Middle Platonism absorbed some aspects of Stoic thought but retained the belief in a spiritual soul. The third-century CE Neoplatonism of Plotinus affirmed the reality not only of individual souls but also of the world Soul. Plotinus's universe has its primal source in the ineffable One, from whose overflowing fullness the supreme Nous or Intelligence emanates; and from this Nous a cosmic Psyche or Soul emanates. Contained, as it were, in the Nous are the forms or essences of things. Contained in the cosmic Soul is the power of all life in the universe, from which emanate the many individual spiritual souls, whether of godlike heavenly beings or humans. The human person is a soul who comes closest to her or his own true nature and bliss by seeking a spiritual return to its ultimate source, a mystical union with the divine One.

Many of these cosmological or metaphysical worldviews are clearly religious. Epicurus recommended imitating the noble calm of the gods. Stoics urged a reverential conformity to the rational order of the universe, as well as an appreciation of the person as a manifestation of the Logos within all things. Plato recommended escape from this physical world after death to live with the gods in intellectual joy. Plotinus took his readers all the way to blissful unity with the Ultimate One. In all of these forms of religious thought, divine intervention is absent. Beneath the seeming confusion and complexity of the universe is a cosmic structure, in which humans have their place and in which some lesser gods or a single ultimate divinity is worth imitation, reverence, or intimate contact.

Middle Platonist and Neoplatonist thought, however, accepted ideas that sound odd to us. They promoted ideas about migrating souls and magical powers that are now part of New Age religions. Neoplatonic magic was based on the double idea that (1) the individual soul has power to influence events in the physical world, and (2) the individual soul has some contact with soul reality in general in the cosmos. This sounds rather mystical and even superstitious to us, and indeed it probably represents a decline in intellectual standards. But there was a reasoned basis for it in Platonic philosophy and its dualistic assumption that the soul and body are two distinct kinds of realities. The soul, by definition, is not a material agent bound by material limitations of time and space. Yet the soul can affect the body. Spirit energy is harnessed every day to perform physical feats such as walking and talking. Just how the soul is able to do this was unknown to Plato and Plotinus.[9] But it was clear from daily activity that the soul indeed could do it. Soul power could by its nature have great effect on material objects, a kind of "natural magic."

The goal of "natural magic" is to get in touch with hidden lines of power in the universe, to become harmonized with invisible cosmic forces, to learn how to adjust one's inner thoughts and feelings to affect external material and spiritual realities, perhaps to learn some semisecret techniques for doing all this as a kind of technology of the invisible.[10] The Neoplatonists were hoping that they might discover enough about the mechanics, as it were, of invisible forces to manipulate them successfully. Today television works because we have learned to manipulate the patterns of the usually invisible force we call electromagnetism. It seemed rational enough in the second century CE to believe that weather, life, disease were the products of invisible forces. To want to understand how they worked in order to control them is part of the scientific impulse. Platonism (and hermetic magic) achieved renewed popularity in Europe in the sixteenth and seventeenth centuries, as one form of the new attempts at scientific thought.

The Neoplatonist vitalistic model of the universe seemed to many in antiquity to provide a reasonable account of the wonderful goal-directedness of the seed that grows into a tree, of the newborn animal that easily grows into its proper behavior as an adult of its species, and of the human person's ability to contemplate the nature and values of things. These life activities seemed to require life forces at work in and through the universe. This provided a reasoned basis for a general vitalist model to interpret nature. (Renaissance Neoplatonism, German idealism, and other romanticisms agreed, as a later chapter will recount.) Stoic philosophy had attributed this to the Logos and the rational principles "planted" in the world by the Logos. (The Stoics, however, had by now abandoned their early attempts to turn this into a complete physics, and restricted themselves mainly to ethics but also to logic.)

The point of reviewing the various philosophies of the ancient Western world here is to ask about the relation of rationality and religious thought, in particular about formal operational thought in religion.

"Natural magic" sounds somewhat irrational today to any but New Age enthusiasts. Epicurus's belief in gods and Stoic belief in the divine Logos of which human minds are a part both seem far from standard science and reason today. Yet these were not just "beliefs." They were often reasoned conclusions, argued out analytically, with evidence and analysis given to show how alternative views were inadequate. Aristotle's extensive work on method is well known, as in his *Posterior Analytics*. But he was not alone in his concerns.

Epicurus, for example, discusses methods of knowing, to show how to arrive at reasonable conclusions. He proposes three major sources of true knowledge: sense perception, inference, and clear vision. The most important of these is immediate sense perception. Epicurus analyzes circumstances under which sense perception may mislead a person, and recommends testing the mental images against new instances of the kind of experience in question. The second and third methods are for "imperceptibles." Some of them can be inferred to exist even though they cannot be directly sensed. These are the atoms themselves, for example, whose existence can be inferred by the mind on the basis of other knowledge. The other kind of imperceptibles is the gods. We know they exist by "clear vision."[11]

Epicurus's "clear vision" supposes that when our minds are struck by an idea strongly and clearly and consistently, that idea must be similar to a sensory impression, a product of minute particles emanating from an outside object and impinging upon the senses or, in this case, the inner mind.[12] This fits well with Epicurus's basic theory of knowledge, his attempt at an understanding of how the mind and senses get their information about reality. This was his science of knowledge. In this case it establishes the existence of the gods. The last criterion, of clear vision, does not strike us as valid today, partly because we have much more information about the composition and processes of the universe. Yet Epicurus was offering a coherently reasoned analysis. Though we think he was wrong in his conclusion about the existence of the gods, he was rational in his mode of argument.

Skepticism

Traditional archaic polytheism with its strongly concrete operational thought style was not the only alternative to the new cosmological philosophies. The first major alternative was a reasoned skepticism. We have already seen that some kind of formal skepticism is a cultural concomitant, it seems, of theoretical thinking. In the axial-age in China, India, and Greece, as the various philosophical schools first developed, almost from the first there were those who gave reasons why we can never really know for sure what is true. Skepticism in ancient Greece developed in opposition to the somewhat dogmatic certitude that early Stoics and Epicureans claimed for their thought.[13]

Of the ancient philosophical Greek texts, the most "modern" (or post-modern) is the *Outlines of Skepticism* by Sextus Empiricus.[14] This third-century CE work summarizes various forms of a tradition tracing itself back to Pyrrho, whose goal was to cure people of dogmatism so that they might thereby achieve a certain peaceful detachment. Pyrrho seems to have written nothing himself.[15] But leaders of the Academy, Plato's school, took up the cause. The *Outlines* indirectly tells the story of the development of various school), distinguishing the interpretation of Arcesilaus (d. ca. 242 BCE) and his Middle Academy from that of Carneades (d. ca. 129 BCE) and his New Academy, and so on.[16] But the *Outlines* is mainly a careful summary and analysis of skeptical arguments as to why no one can really know what is true or not, nor what is good or not, and therefore should employ a suspension (*epoche*) of all judgment. Early skeptics developed ten "modes" or basic arguments for a skeptical stance. Later skeptics incorporated much of this and added some ideas to produce a shorter list of five modes or even just two. Aenesidemus developed a third and somewhat different set of eight modes to refute explanations based on causality.[17] Each of these three sets of modes foreshadows late twentieth-century arguments about the possibility of reliable knowledge, including scientific knowledge.

The ten early modes are divided by Sextus Empiricus into three main types: those about the person as the knower, those about the object known, and those about the relation between the knower and the known. Among the first type is the first mode, based on differences among animals. Dogs hear things humans cannot; hawks see things humans cannot. So human senses are too limited to judge things accurately. The second mode is based on differences among humans. One person can hear what another cannot; one person judges a substance to taste good, whereas to another person it tastes bad. The third is based on disagreement among the senses. Perfume smells good and tastes bad. The modes continue, showing that the same person may judge things differently at different times under different conditions, that different cultures hold to different truths and values, and so on. These ten modes together foreshadow current cultural relativism as well as the theory of the social construction of knowledge.

In the five later modes, Sextus Empiricus presents what today would be called an antifoundationalist position. Every judgment relies on premises that themselves must first be judged to be true on the basis of other premises, and so on ad infinitum. Moreover, there is a reciprocity among truth-claims. One truth-claim is plausible because it agrees with another, which is plausible because it agrees with the first.[18] Sextus Empiricus here is close to the idea now common in philosophy of knowledge, that every concept and truth-claim takes its meaning, as well as its claim to validity, from its relation to other concepts and truth-claims in a network (or "language game") of meanings.

In the third set, Aenesidemus's eight modes to overthrow causal arguments, the issue of verification appears in a form both ancient and modern: How does one ever show that the hypothesis which the evidence seems to confirm is the *only* hypothesis that could account for that evidence? There especially could be some hidden causes at work about which we can know nothing.[19] Finally, all arguments about evidence and hypotheses and plausibility appeal to standards of evidence, logic, reasonableness. There is no way of establishing the validity of the standards without appeal to some further standards about what constitutes valid standards, and so on ad infinitum again.[20] Once again Sextus Empiricus gives a preview of a twentieth-century antifoundationalism. The three collections of "modes" together add up to something like contemporary postmodern thought, which is built upon beliefs such as the social construction of knowledge, cultural relativism, limits of verifiability and falsifiability, the interdependence of concepts and truth-claims, antifoundationalism, and the value- and theory-laden character of knowledge. Chapter 9 will return to these topics in a discussion of the nature of modern arguments about the nature of knowledge.

But in addition to these truly skeptical arguments, there are also moments in the *Outlines* that suggest a method to achieve highly reliable judgments about reality. Carneades proposed to live by probability (*pithanon*). His New Academy made distinctions among degrees of plausibility. A coiled rope in a dark room might be a rope or a snake. Either is a plausible judgment at first. But one can inspect or scrutinize with degrees of care. A second look may show that it is a rope. A further inspection of color, texture, flexibility, and its lack of motion all add up. One can then consider whether there are contrary indications of any kind to "distract" one from the judgment that it is a rope. The New Academy, says Sextus Empiricus, gives probable assent to appearances that are (1) plausible, (2) scrutinized, and (3) "undistractable."[21]

This is not far from science today, which seeks plausible accounts of things, scrutinizes them by public, long-term testing, and seeks to rule out all alternative accounts (all "distractions").[22] As Sextus Empiricus presents the case for judgments of probability, his approach is not thorough enough to be science; it does not look for an overall unity of all ideas and evidence as an ongoing test of the reasonableness (probability) of the truth-claims. So it remains skeptical about knowing very much about reality. More important, it does not seek to advance knowledge through a deliberate application of method. The skeptic, as one who does not have much hope of achieving great knowledge, would have little incentive to work out such a method. Yet the method of modern science is prefigured in this approach of the New Academy. This approach, like that of modern science, fits with descriptions of late formal operational thought, and perhaps also with what Lonergan called "method."[23] We will see more on that in a later chapter. In antiquity, skepticism did not try to do more than to counteract the dogmatic orientation of other positions. It offered not science but peace of mind through *ataraxia*, an uncaring or detachment worthy of a Buddhist.

The Decline of Classical Rationality

It apparently is not easy for a culture to maintain a high degree of formal operational thought, just as it is not easy for an individual to maintain deliberate clarity and logic in thinking, especially in a large-scale systematic way with careful, self-conscious concern for clear and logical method. The millennium in Western culture from roughly the fifth-century BCE Athens to the fifth century CE Roman Empire was a time when the classical style of thought first flourished, maintained a strong hold for a time, but finally began to fade. It eventually ceded its authority to a newly strong archaic style. We can mark the change by noticing three aspects of the formal operational cognitive style that appeared in classical antiquity in the West:

1. Trust in the systematically coherent intelligibility of reality
2. Training in an explicit method of determining what is true
3. Interest in increasing accurate knowledge.

Various personal and social characteristics tend to accompany these three intellectual aspects of classical thought. Classical writings define the individual person as an instance of a universal human nature and in relation to the cosmic whole; they define social relations or ethics through universal principles; and they measure a person's self-worth by reference to seemingly objective and universally valid moral standards. When classical thought had an intellectual rebirth at the end of the early Middle Ages, these personal and social elements were part of it.

In the centuries of the decline of the Roman Empire, these aspects of classical thought came to be overshadowed by a concrete operational style of thought that is apparent in a steady increase of the following:

1. Belief in an unpredictable world of divine interventions; a world best described by a myth-style narrative plot rather than systematic analyses
2. Reliance on authority and tradition as the major means for determining truth
3. A sense of the inevitability of ignorance.

In this return toward a more archaic style there are also personal and social elements. The self is defined primarily as a member of a family or clan or tribe; society is organized through allegiance to a leader; and external honor and status are valued more than interior uprightness.

There are divergent views about when the decline began. Giovanni Reale castigates those who attribute to Plato and Aristotle the whole of post-Socratic accomplishment, as though original philosophy and science ended with them. Reale emphasizes the great contributions of others in the subsequent Hellenistic age.[24] According to one historian, an informed person in the second century BCE would have predicted the coming of a "perfect Age of Reason."[25] Furthermore, philosophy continued to be an important element of Hellenistic and Roman culture. Science flourished as late as the second century CE in the reigns of Hadrian, Antoninus Pius, and Marcus Aurelius up to the time of the plague.

Yet the signs of decline appear early to Robert Grant. Many of the achievements to which Reale points, says Grant, were mainly in wisdom and ethics, not in scientific philosophy.[26] Grant argues that by the first century CE the age of classical philosophy and science had passed.[27] The theoretical approach retained a good reputation among philosophers in spite of criticisms by the skeptics. In practice, though, an archaic style of thought slowly came to prevail, one that relied more on storytelling, some of the stories quite wondrous, than on the systematic logic and critical analysis of theoretical thinking. Grant sees signs of the decline in the increase of belief in mystery cults, mysticism, and magicians. He describes the new way of thought in a way that matches exactly the tendency of archaic commonsense thought to work with knowledge in smaller and unconnected pieces: "The general principles of Aristotle had been forgotten, and descriptive science had developed a taste for anecdote."[28]

Others agree with Grant. From after the time of Theophrastus, the successor to Aristotle as head of the school of Peripatetics in Athens, up to the early third century BCE, there were few new scientific or philosophical ideas, complains Edward Hussey.[29] The irrational returned in the form of belief in astrology, in occult powers in various natural objects, and in wonder-workers. Geoffrey Lloyd offers a similar summary: Hippocrates had argued that epilepsy was natural, not produced by gods, and philosophers had articulated belief in the causal regularity of natural processes. Such ideas were now being transformed into more mystical interpretations about cosmic magic and sympathies.[30] The mystery cults were rising in response to and in competition with the rational philosophies.[31]

Not much new knowledge was produced in late antiquity. Knowledge passed on from earlier times was often simplified and distorted. Even in the third to first centuries BCE, Eratosthenes and Posidonius produced predigested popularizations in the form of encyclopedias of philosophical-scientific knowledge. Roman writers later used these, as in Pliny's *Natu-*

ral History.[32] Pliny tried to discriminate between trustworthy and un-trustworthy sources, but produced a compendium of information and misinformation, such as reports on one-eyed or dog-headed people, all showing much more fascination with facts than attempting to explain why the facts were as they were. Where philosophers had engaged exten-sively in systematic and logical analyses of evidence, the major sources of knowledge now were memory substitutes, compilations of information. Where critical analyses of logical plausibility and evidence had once ruled, now it was mainly a matter of sorting through traditional authori-ties.[33]

There is disagreement on the causes of the decline. Eric Dodds sees it beginning as far back as the end of the Peloponnesian War, when out of the stress of war and then anger at defeat, Athenians turned against the new thinkers and the difficulty of their achievements.[34] In fact, he sees the end of the "great age of intellectual discovery" as a sign of fear of freedom, fear of the need to determine things by thought and choice rather than by tradition.[35] Lloyd sees the problem simply in the end of particular circumstances that promoted the use of rational thought. The Hellenistic and later Roman worlds were not like the golden age of Ath-ens, when free speech and democratic openness not only allowed new thought to flourish but also required skill in rational argument in the political forum.[36]

An important further obstacle to the perdurance of rationality was the inability of the philosophers to determine which of their basic world-views, if any, might be correct. No one philosophy could show itself sim-ply superior to the others. And all the philosophies were subject to the critique of skepticism. In retrospect we can surmise that well-developed habits and techniques for empirical testing might have been of major help.[37] The various philosophical theories of knowledge placed limited emphasis on empirical investigations. Aristotle had said that firsthand experience is the source of our basic knowledge about the nature of things, but he did not appreciate the role of ongoing empirical investiga-tion to test the supposed knowledge of the nature of things and also to test the theories or deductions based on that knowledge.[38] With logical clarity Aristotle could show that stacking up empirical evidence could never finally prove a case but only make it probable.[39] He was looking for a stronger basis of truth than this.

Had there been great successes in developing effectively useful scien-tific ideas, the lack of certitude might not have counted for much. If effective cures or better chemistry for making dyes or other practical re-sults had been achieved, empirical inquiry might have earned high re-pute even if its conclusions were technically only "probable," as the skep-tics could point out. Even today the average person is not bothered by a lack of philosophical clarity on how we do science, or by a lack of certitude as to the conclusions of science, as long as science delivers. But the striking successes of modern science were lacking in Hellenistic times. There were few instruments to help in measuring and verifying; there was a lack of interest, perhaps, in doing the dirty fieldwork; there were not very good mathematical notation and methods for doing complex and precise calculations. Whatever the reasons may have been, during the apex of ancient philosophy, theory construction ruled over experimentation. But theory turned out not to be enough. Frances Yates sums up much about these times in describing the origins of the Neoplatonist hermetic tradition, supposedly revealed truths about the hidden patterns of force in the universe:

> The world of the second century was weary of Greek dialectics which seemed to lead to no certain results. Platonists, Stoics, Epicureans could only repeat the theories of their various schools without making any further advances, and the tenets of the schools were boiled down in text-book form, in manuals which formed the basis of philosophical instruction in the Empire.[40]

While the philosophers speculated and theorized, belief in magic and the intervention of the gods continued as a major force in the ancient Mediterranean culture. Even in the era of greatest philosophizing, theory did not replace commonsense and fantastical imagination, but lay over it, absorbing some of it into a more rational system but leaving much of it to flourish as it always had. As the light of philosophy and science dimmed, the continuing glow of the magical and mystical and marvelous attracted more attention.

Grant and Hussey overlook the rational element in Neoplatonism as a philosophical system, but they are accurate in much of their criticism. Though Neoplatonism absorbed the philosophical efforts of early Platonists, Stoics, and Aristotelians, it lacked the logical rigor, the thoroughgoing analyses that Aristotle or others would have demanded. Mixed into the coherent structure of the Neoplatonic universe were various gods and occult powers whose existence was asserted, not explained. Neoplatonism was based as much on popular credulity as on the empirical investigations and carefully logical analysis of earlier philosophy.[41] Plotinus (205–270 CE) accepted without objection the commonsense knowledge that said one could read portents in the stars and produce true love through magical spells.[42] The popular Hermetic literature of these times, attributed to the ancient revelations in Egypt by Thrice-Great Hermes as the Egyptian god Thoth, supported the use of magic and mysticism in myriad ad hoc ways, based on the authority of revered or divine ancients.[43]

Rational Philosophy in Early
Christian Thought

Even as the philosophical heritage of Greece was stagnating, the newly born Christian church was working with what that heritage had to offer.[44] The results were mixed. Christianity was born in newly credulous times and participated in that intellectual atmosphere. Christians believed in their own forms of divine actions in history; they rejected much of the philosophical tradition but also absorbed enough to reinterpret in philosophical language many of their own beliefs about the nature of God or about Jesus as Son of God.

The influence of Hellenic thought is evident in the works of Philo of Alexandria, known to Christians as Philo Judaeus. Philo provided the foundation for major elements in later Christian theology.[45] Like the Stoics, Philo said that the divine governance of the world was by way of the laws of nature, the patterns of causal necessity. But he added that God is also able to infringe upon those laws and perform miracles for God's own good purpose. God has this power because, contrary to Hellenic belief in the everlasting existence of the material universe, God had created even the universe itself. Contrary also to the Hellenic belief that God was the highest part of the universe, Philo insisted that God was quite distinct from the universe. God was not part of nature but was supernatural. In comparison with God, even the most powerful gods or demons were merely "natural," in the sense of being part of the created order of things. If this broke the boundaries of human understanding, it was necessary to remember that God was beyond human understanding as the unnameable, unspeakable, incomprehensible Creator.

Christianity had a complex mixture of ideas from rather early in its history. Like most people of the times, Christians believed in magic, even if they attributed it only to evil powers. A. A. Barn notes that Christians had a special reason: "All the Christian theologians believed in the existence of magical acts; not to do so would mean disbelieving the stories of the Old and New Testaments, from that of the witch of Endor to that of Simon Magus."[46] Part of the same milieu was belief in prophecies. Thus when Justin Martyr tried to show that the Christian faith was not only noble and of ancient lineage but also such that a rational person should believe in it, part of his evidence was the prophecies of a Christ figure which the Christians discerned in the Hebrew Scriptures.[47] This is evidence of a sort that would not have been accepted in the philosophical atmosphere of earlier times and was not accepted by philosophers of his own time.[48]

Many of the philosophers respected the monotheism of Judaism and Christianity for its good sense to recognize a single ultimate divine principle. But the God of most Jews and Christians was a bit too anthropomorphic for the philosophical temperament, precisely because this God did not embody regularity and reliability. "To the Greek mind, God embodied the principle of universal, immutable order, self-contained and without any desire: he is in need of nothing. The image of a God as a moral personality, choosing some people over others and active in history—an all-powerful busybody—insulted the Greek sense of harmony."[49]

Minucius Felix, a Christian apologist (d. ca. 250 CE?), represented in his dialogue *Octavius* the (Stoic) philosophers' objections to the Christian God as a meddler who destroys the reliable order of nature:

> What monstrous absurdities these Christians invent about this God of theirs . . . that he searches diligently into the ways and deeds of all men, yea even their words and hidden thoughts, hurrying to and fro, ubiquitously; they make him out a troublesome, restless, shameless and interfering being, who has a hand in everything that is done, interlopes at every turn. . . . Further, they threaten the whole world and the universe and its stars with destruction by fire, as though the eternal order of nature established by laws divine could be put to confusion, or as though the bonds of all the elements could be broken, the framework of heaven be split in twain, and the containing and surrounding mass be brought down in ruin."[50]

In response to these charges Minucius Felix offered rational arguments. He omitted from his defense many of the beliefs that were most peculiarly Christian, such as the Incarnation, in order to focus on ideas familiar to philosophers, especially concerning divine creation and rule of the universe. While he wanted to present a philosophically reasoned case, his Christianity demanded that he also accept supernatural intervention in history and nature. His final answer to the objections of the philosophers was that all unbelievers deserved the fires of hell.[51]

Some Christians, nonetheless, felt a need to be as rational as the standards of the times required. A basic Christian response, borrowed from Philo, was to emphasize the superiority of their God over all things as Creator of the entire universe, rather than as just a divine principle within the cosmic order of things. Thus, while Origen (ca. 185–ca. 254 CE) agreed with Celsus and Stoics in general that God does not act *contrary* to nature, he followed Philo to argue that God goes *beyond* nature. As the omnipotent creator of everything, God is truly *super*natural and can do what nature does not have the power to do.[52] The God who made nature is not bound by any laws of nature. If nothing that exists has any existence apart from God's creative and sustaining power, then certainly everything is under God's authority.

Philosophers responded by challenging the idea of omnipotence as self-contradictory. Even the ultimate Divinity must be bound by the rules of rationality—by the need not to be self-contradictory. "If he is omnipotent, can he reverse the past, or make the truth be false, or annihilate himself?"[53] Still at stake are the reliable intelligibility of nature and the ability of the human mind to grasp that intelligibility. Unfortunately for the philosophers, they still did not have a body of empirical science of proven success as evidence that their approach was the more correct. They had to rely on theoretical arguments about what a Divine Power would or should do, or on paradoxical arguments about the lack of coherence of a concept of an omnipotence that could not destroy itself. Rationally inclined Christians like Origen could offer their own theoretical counterarguments.

Many Christians were happy simply to abandon the path of systematic rational analysis. They agreed with Tertullian there was a great distance between Athens and Jerusalem.[54] This is normal for people of any time, perhaps. But some of these Christians were also intellectual leaders. Irenaeus, the second-century bishop whose writings had great influence, borrowed arguments from skeptics against philosophical knowledge. He cited the ignorance of "physicists" about the home of migrating birds, the storehouse of hail and snow, why the moon waxes and wanes, differences among fluids, metals, and stones, and the origin of the Nile. While we may speculate, only God has the answers. "On all these points we may indeed say a great deal while we search into their causes, but God alone who made them can declare the truth regarding them."[55] Scripture teaches us all we need to know in this world; in the next life God will teach us the rest.[56]

Even while Irenaeus sided with skeptics against other philosophers, he made a case for Christian belief in a way far less rationally systematic than even that of the skeptics. Irenaeus reasoned, as it were, only to replace reason with the authority of scripture. He claimed that God must have acted to preserve the original meaning of the Hebrew scriptures in the translation into Greek made by the seventy Jewish sages (the Septuagint).[57] Similarly, Lactantius (ca. 240–320) met the challenge of rationality by lowering the standards of what is reasonable. He argued that if animals can conceive by the wind, as he claims everyone knows, "why is the spirit-conception of Jesus remarkable?"[58] Hilary of Poitiers, Gregory of Nyssa, and John Chrysostom later asserted the importance of miracles as events that are evidence of divine activity precisely because miracles exceed both the power of nature and the human power to understand.[59] An archaic style of thought, little concerned with the overall rational coherence of reality and relying on the authority of religious tradition, replaced at least partly the classical standards of rational reflection as the primary source of truth.

Even those Christians who strove for greater rationality might emphasize its limitations. In the late second century CE, Clement of Alexandria, living and thinking in a philosophical center and trying to offer a reasonable defense and interpretation of Christianity, nonetheless defended faith in the place of reason. The Greek philosophers, he noted, think of faith as futile and barbarous.[60] Clement calls it a voluntary preconception, an assent of piety, that in the end is as reasonable as any first principle: "Should one say that knowledge is founded on demonstration by a process of reasoning, let him hear that first principles are incapable of demonstration. . . . Hence it is that the first cause of the universe can be apprehended by faith alone."[61] Clement used the reasoning of Aristotle to discredit reasoning, as Irenaeus had used the skeptics. Clement in fact [mis] quotes Isaiah 7:9, as Augustine did after him: "Unless you believe, neither shall you understand."[62]

Where rational analysis and systematization had once ruled, piecemeal allegorical interpretation began to dominate as the means to interpret and understand nature. The *Physiologus*, a late fourth-century work of animal lore by an unknown author, was very influential. Augustine liked it, and it continued to be popular in early medieval times. But it was highly allegorical, attending to the habits of animals in order to learn moral lessons rather than to understand nature. It begins, for example, with a description of the lion that masks its tracks from the hunter by whisking its tail over them as it walks, just as Jesus masked his divinity from unbelievers.[63] The problem with this pious use of natural history is that it was wrong about the actual behavior of lions. "That such a book could flourish to such an extent is a clear indication of the extent to which zoology had declined. . . . By the end of the fourth century Christian instruction in natural science, like natural science itself, was practically dead," declares Edward Grant.[64]

Grant seems to put much of the blame on Christianity for the general decline of philosophy and science, of formal operational rationality.[65] But it is difficult to single out early Christianity for special blame for the decline of reason. Stagnation had set in before the appearance of Christianity. The general consciousness of the times no longer grasped the significance and value of the cognitive style of the classic philosophers. Theory was dying; imaginative common sense was reasserting its ongoing presence, now free from the overburden of logical systematization and critical questioning. Christianity did not cause this.[66] Christians sometimes tried to translate some of the more mythical stories in their tradition into a more rationally coherent form.[67] From Clement (and the earlier Philo) to Augustine the tendency to allegorize passages of Scripture was often a means to get beyond the narrative simplicity and scientific inadequacy of stories about six days of creation, for example.[68] But Christianity's belief in miracles, and its relative disinterest in physics and the more rigorous standards of rationality, are part of the general decay of cognitive standards of the time. Christianity and credulity grew together.[69]

7

THE DECLINE AND RECOVERY
OF CLASSICAL RATIONALITY
IN THE WEST

Near the end of chapter 6, two short lists set forth differences between aspects of the classical formal operational thought style and the always-present concrete operational style that predominated in the early Middle Ages by default. We will see specific instances of those points.[1] But in religious thought the issue that most directly indicates a tension between concrete operational and formal operational thought is that of miracles. From Augustine through Aquinas and on into the sixteenth and seventeenth centuries, this was a troublesome topic, as it still is today for many religious people.

Miracles in an Orderly World

The fewer the miracles, the great the intelligibility of the world. For a religion which believes that an Intelligent Being designed and created the universe, the maximum number of miracles compatible with a fully orderly natural world is one. That is the single ongoing miracle of creation which produces and sustains a world that operates entirely by inbuilt natural ("secondary") causes. If there is even one more intervention into the orderly processes of nature by a divine power that is distinct from nature, to that precise extent the universe is less intelligible. To repeat an idea from chapter 6, however: It is not possible to establish a priori that the universe is fully intelligible. Only if atheism could first establish its own claim to be true, could anyone be rationally sure that there are no supernatural interventions. Yet the struggles over this issue in the centuries from Augustine to early modern science were mostly among different kinds of religious believers, not between atheists and believers.

Augustine

In the centuries from late antiquity to early modern science, Augustine's approach to miracles carried great authority. (Galileo quotes Augustine when he wants to defend his own Copernicanism.) But Augustine had a difficult time making up his mind on how to deal with them. He knew they must occur. The biblical stories of miracles, especially the incarnation and resurrection of Jesus, but also various miracles performed by Jesus, had God's authority behind them. Moreover, in spite of some occasional caution about miracle claims in his own time, he recognized miracles associated with the shrines of martyrs as an important part of true Christian faith. He ended up with as many as four different theories about miracles, theories that others would use in the centuries to follow.

To understand the first theory of miracles, imagine that there is no reliable order of natural ("secondary") causes, but that God is the always-present direct ("primary") cause of everything. The sun rises each day because God is constantly and *directly* compelling it to rise and set (or compelling the Earth to keep turning on its axis). The grass grows each day because God is always *directly* making that growth happen. God is directly making it rain occasionally, directly guiding particles of water to absorb minerals from the earth, directly guiding the roots of the grass to absorb those particles, and so forth. In such a universe every event is a kind of miracle in the sense of a direct act by God.[2] In this sort of universe, however, the everyday, ongoing billions of direct acts of God are not called *miracula* because they do not evoke wonder, because they are not marvels. It is only the unusual direct acts of God that are *miracula*. Augustine speaks in several places as though God operates in this way. Here is one of the most famous passages to this effect:

> While man plants and waters, who draws up the moisture through the roots of the vine except God who gives the growth? But when water was changed into wine with unaccustomed swiftness at the Lord's command the divine power was revealed, as even fools acknowledge.[3]

In general it is God who makes it rain, who makes plants flower, who gives life to infants in the womb. But when the rain is sudden, when the plants flower unexpectedly, when the gift of life is to one who has just died, then people call it miraculous (wondrous, marvelous) because these forms of God's action are unexpected. In these ideas of Augustine the distinction between the ordinary and extraordinary events in nature blurs; all of them are God's direct work.[4]

In other places Augustine speaks of miracles quite differently, in a way that would please any Stoic. These miracles are events resulting from sequences of natural causes, sequences that God had planned and planted in seminal form at the beginning of creation, to blossom forth for the edification of observers at a later date. While such wondrous events startle people, they are nonetheless the result of sequences of causes and effect that God from the very beginning had made part of nature's own (secondary) causality.[5] If this were the only way Augustine spoke of miracles, it would involve only the one primordial miracle of a carefully planned creation.

Between the first and second ways of defining miracles is a carefully reasoned third way, which allows God to plan an orderly universe and also to intervene in it. Here the word "miracle" has its more modern sense, of specific and direct divine intervention in the order of natural secondary causality to accomplish what the natural order could not have accomplished on its own without such intervention. One of Augustine's examples of such a miracle is the changing of a rod into a serpent.[6] Augustine's partial concession to a Stoic-style rationality is to say with Origen that even such miracles are not truly *contrary* to nature but only in excess of what nature alone can do. In his *De Genesi ad Litteram* (On the Literal Meaning of Genesis) he explains further the basic idea:[7]

> God, however, did not place all causes in the original creation but kept some in his own will. . . . Nevertheless those which he kept in his own will cannot be contrary to those which he predetermined by His own will; for God's will cannot contradict itself. He established them, therefore, in such a way that they would contain the possibility, not the necessity, of causing the effect which would proceed from them.[8]

Later in life, in *The City of God*,[9] Augustine similarly argues that it is not contrary to nature for nature to act contrary to its usual patterns. The immutable heavens themselves have shown change, as when the planet Venus once altered color, according to reliable observers. So it is not impossible that God, who created all natures according to his own pleasure from the first, would "change these natures of his own creation into whatever he pleases, and thus spread abroad a multitude of those marvels which are called monsters, portents, prodigies, phenomena." Augustine in effect argues that nature was made flexible by God, slack enough in its order to contain many possibilities that nonetheless exceed nature's own normal causal laws. (Aquinas later proposed this same model of nature in his account of how God can perform miracles.)

A fourth category of miracles includes those wonders performed not by God's genuinely supernatural power, power truly above and beyond the limits of nature, but by what later would be called "preternatural" power, a nondivine spiritual power alongside nature's regular order but nonetheless part of creation.[10] These miracles are the work of souls, angels, or the gods (Augustine thinks of them as demons) acting upon matter.[11] Even humans can do wondrous things, as in the case of vestal virgins who carried water in a sieve without spilling any.[12]

This fourth category, as well as the earlier mention of monsters and portents, alerts a contemporary reader to a great contrast between Augustine's conclusion and what would best fit with a thoroughgoing search for rational intelligibility. Augustine invokes the idea of a divine Agent whose actions and purposes and plans are not knowable to humans. The search for intelligibility must therefore end at this point. Augustine is quite explicit about this: The skeptics say about Christian miracles, "If you wish us to believe these things, satisfy our reason about each one of them." Augustine replies: "We should confess we could not, because the final comprehension of man cannot master these and such-like wonders of God's workings."[13]

Augustine's defense of miracles places many of the events of nature and history beyond human inquiry, in the free and unpredictable choices of invisible beings, especially God. Like others of his time, Augustine is not being unreasonable in his model of the universe. He lacked adequate evidence to make him suppose that there were no such invisible active beings. Various philosophical models of the universe included this possibility, including the fairly well accepted Neoplatonist model.

But reasonable as his model of the universe might be for his time and context, the effect of Augustine's thought was nonetheless to subordinate rational inquiry to a silent or prayerful humility and ignorance. Augustine did not find it important to include knowledge of the physical world in his systematic understanding of things. Like Irenaeus, he was willing to leave aside knowledge of "physics":

> Wherefore, when it is asked what we ought to believe in matters of religion, the answer is not to be sought in the exploration of the nature of things, after the manner of those whom the Greeks call "physicists." Nor should we be dismayed if Christians are ignorant about the property and the number of the basic elements of nature, or about the motion, order, and deviations of the stars, the map of the heavens, the kinds and nature of animals, plants, stones, springs, rivers, and mountains; about the divisions of space and time, about the signs of impending storms, and the myriad other things which these "physicists" have come to understand or think they have. For even these men, gifted with such superior insight, with their ardor in study and their abundant leisure, exploring some of these matters by human conjecture and others through historical inquiry, have not yet learned everything there is to know. For that matter, many of the things they are so proud to have discovered are more often matters of opinion than of verified knowledge.[14]

Augustine's observations about the limits of science or physics are legitimate. The claims of the physicists, especially then, were often conjecture or opinion, and even just plain wrong. And Augustine is speaking not about a general human need for knowledge but about the need specifically in religion for knowledge of the universe. In a work of his mature years, *The Literal Meaning of Genesis*, Augustine goes to impressive lengths to consider a vast range of scientific information and relate it to the creation narrative in Genesis.[15] But where the philosophical physicists were still eager to affirm the rational intelligibility of all of nature, Augustine was content to let much of it slip by.[16]

The Early Middle Ages

The decline of standards of rationality in the West was steep, though not into total darkness.[17] Christianity had absorbed as much of the classical culture, perhaps, as the times could sustain. The ideal of learning would still produce a Boethius (ca. 475–525) or an Isidore of Seville (ca. 560–636). The monastic preservation of literacy and Latin classics later provided a base for scholars like Alcuin (ca. 735–804) and John Scotus Erigena (ca. 810–ca. 877).[18] There was at least one systematic attempt to interpret all miracles naturally, to "demythologize" Scripture, as we might say today.[19]

Certain classical ideas carried into the early Middle Ages a sense of systematic coherence to the universe that the theoretical minds of the philosophers had produced. The Neoplatonic interpretation remained popular, guided by what Arthur Lovejoy has called the "Principle of Plenitude" and reflected in the writings of Pseudo-Dionysius.[20] This interpretation held that the universe was a "Great Chain of Being," hierarchically ordered from top to bottom. Each soul, as a microcosm, reflected that order and had the potential to make the "Soul Journey" from earthly interests toward mystical union with the One.[21] From the individual human life to the grand array of the cosmos there was one single schematic unity, with each possible niche filled to add up to a great Plentitude.

Attempts to understand other aspects of human life also had echoes of classical thinking. Medicine still used a theory of four humors that was based on the philosophical analysis of physical reality into four elements, which in turn was related to theories about four seasons, the four ages of a person's life, four eras of earthly history, and so on.[22]

The continuing apocalyptic thought had a classical element in its systematizing approach to history, even though it took an archaic story form like a myth rather than a classical analytical form. Julius Africanus (fl. ca. 221), building upon an idea in the early second-century Epistle of Barnabas,[23] had interpreted all of history as one single tale with six major chapters. Declaring the six days of creation in Genesis to be an allegory of creation as a whole, Julius divided all history into "dispensations" or major periods of time in which God dealt with people. One dispensation ran from Adam to Abraham, another from Abraham to Moses, and so forth. Julius concluded that his time was that of the sixth dispensation, the time of the Church. After an apocalyptic ending of this world order, the sixth period would be followed by a seventh period, the millennial reign of Christ, the Sabbath of creation. Eusebius, bishop of Caesarea (ca. 260–340 CE) and then Augustine accepted, modified, and handed this scheme down to the early Middle Ages (and also to modern dispensation-alists).[24]

In spite of the continued presence of some aspects of classical-style thought, from the sixth to the tenth century the archaic cognitive style reappeared more strongly than it had for centuries. This was mainly by default—that is, in the relative absence of theoretical rigor, the ordinary concrete operational style of thought used by most people most of the time in any culture dominated. Lower standards of rationality are visible in a variety of ways.[25]

The apocalyptic visions, for example, were not just systematic schemata of history; they were also larded with all sorts of specific mythical and legendary elements. The Sibylline prophecies, stories of the return of Alexander the Great as Last Emperor, and other fantastic tales filled people's imagination.[26] Much of biblical interpretation lacked any system. Individual stories were interpreted allegorically to find various messages to individuals on how to live and earn heaven.[27] The dominant mode of expression was no longer systematically organized argument and analysis.

Belief in miracles became so normal as to require no justification, and the notion of miracle tended to shift back toward the first of Augustine's four approaches, in which miracles are only specially significant events in a universe where everything might be due to the direct action of God rather than to any reliable and predictable laws of nature. Benedicta Ward confirms this: "Miracles were the rule rather than the exception, and the concept of the hand of God at work in the whole of life coloured the perception of miracles and their records." She cites some of the endless stories of miracles attributed to this or that set of relics.[28] To the early medieval mind the Eucharistic miracle was not something contrary to the laws of nature but a special marvel among many marvels in the events of history and nature.[29] The Germanic practice of trial by ordeal was commonplace. A person's innocence could be tested by calling upon God to miraculously produce proper healing of the hand of a person who had thrust it in boiling water or who had grasped a heated iron. Water in a pond was blessed so that a guilty person thrown into it would be rejected by the water and float to the top.[30]

Local loyalties once again became the dominant norm of behavior. After the sixth century "The bonds of society were personal and tribal and the idea of public authority progressively disappeared."[31] In Anglo-Saxon thought, crimes were not against the public order or against the rule of law or the laws as such, but against the person of the ruler.[32] Although there was a classical tradition in much of Europe that the king represented and administered a higher law, nonetheless there was no appeal beyond the king; in practice it was the person of the king that was law.[33]

There was no theory of individual rights. Kinship was more important than law, or was the major basis of law.[34] Friendship was defined as a matter of swearing allegiance, of contract or oath, rather than of inner affection.[35] Some justifications given were of a vaguely theoretical-systematic sort. Walter Ullmann cites the medieval idea of society as a large organism somehow manifesting a larger divine plan.[36] But the actual practice was a tribal conformity.

Although it was believed that each person had to work out his or her salvation individually, nonetheless the notion of the individual had grown weaker. Heresy was an intellectual arrogance that the person had no right to place superior to the needs of the society for peace and order.[37] Each person had to remain in the vocation or state to which the person was born.[38] There was an emphasis on external criteria rather than internal intentions or worth, much as had been the case in Homeric times. The externals of fame, honor, power were what counted.[39] The major importance of the saints was as powerful protectors of the territory in which their relics were located, rather than in their ability to inspire behavior worthy of a Christian.[40] As late as the eleventh century Anselm interpreted the heinousness of sin as an offense against God's honor. For the person "without name or honor"—the landless, the blind or deformed or crippled—there was no social standing at all.[41]

The veneration of saints and the use of their relics was a "growth industry" after the sixth century.[42] Patrick Geary, in analyzing the common practice of the theft of relics, highlights many aspects of the generally archaic cognitive style of the early Middle Ages.[43] "A world that looked to saints for identity, protection, and economic sustenance was far different from one that depended on national identity, central government, and fiscal planning."[44] Since it was family affiliation that provided a focal point for social organization, saints functioned as noble ancestors for monasteries, providing a familial character to the religious order. A monastery's pride and honor were at stake in disputes over the power of the relics it possessed of its "ancestral" saint. A means of persuading a saint to help was to humiliate the saint by taking the relic outdoors, perhaps covering it with thorns.[45] (Geary cites the case of a girl who *unknowingly* dishonored a saint by urinating near the saint's grave and was paralyzed until prayers released her.[46]) The relics of the saint were alive in a sense, part of the body to be resurrected at the Last Judgment, able to bleed under certain circumstances, possessed of legal rights.[47]

The long downhill slide from classical culture continued, with some ups and downs, through the tenth century. Five hundred years after Aristotle there was far less of the careful analysis and theoretical systematizing of ideas that had characterized his best work. Five hundred years more, and philosophy and science were represented in western Europe by the hand-me-down knowledge of Isidore of Seville and distorted through his imaginatively symbolic etymologies. It would take yet another five hundred years before western European thought had again clearly recaptured the kind of intellectual standards established one and a half millennia earlier.

This is evidence that systematic-theoretical thought is not easily sustained in a culture. Such thought may be part of the natural cognitive capacity of every human group, but it does not come "naturally," as we say. It requires cultural elements to sustain it. The European mind showed itself no more better endowed by nature than other minds in other cultures in other times. Primitiveness and archaic style in thought come quite naturally to us all, as the thought path of least resistance.

The Rebirth of Classical-Style Rationality in Western Europe

The resurgence of western Europe had begun with the creation of new wealth, perhaps as a result of many technological advances, such as the invention of the horse collar.[48] Marie-Dominique Chenu provides a list of technological developments in use by the end of the twelfth century, and suggests that these accomplishments encouraged people to trust that intelligence and ingenuity could give them understanding and control of nature.[49] Whatever the causes, within a couple of centuries there was a doubling of the land under cultivation and a tripling of population. Cities reappeared and expanded.[50] Not everyone was comfortable with the changes. Religious groups illustrate the tension: some, like Bernard of Clairvaux, fled the cities, those new worldly centers of pride and greed; others, like the followers of Dominic and Francis of Assisi, became mendicant friars, living in the towns on the surplus wealth donated to them, which enabled them to preach and to teach there.[51]

Learning also expanded greatly. When the scholarly Gerbert of Aurillac (946–1003) became Pope Sylvester II in 999, he had a few Arabic treatises translated and taught others the scientific ideas in them.[52] In 1085 Muslim Toledo fell to Christian armies, and Christian Europe soon had translations of Greek classics from its library. From various sources new parts of Aristotle's work, and eventually commentaries by Maimonides, Avicenna, Averroës, and others, provoked eager minds to take up old skills and analyze and dispute once again.[53] The classical cognitive style began to burn strongly in various centers of learning.

The individual reemerged into explicit awareness. A major sign of this new consciousness was the reappearance of a clear sense of interiority, of inner thoughts and feelings and choices and responsibility.[54] Where the early medieval Christ was a triumphant king in outward glory, the Christ of the twelfth century was also the suffering Lord on the cross, and the Christian was exhorted to feel the pain of Christ, to suffer inwardly with Christ.[55] The relation to God was to be one of each individual's interior love, affection, or friendship. Because every individual could establish a direct relationship with God, it now became more important that every person live out the fullest degree of perfection compatible with that person's station in life. The ideal of celibacy not just for monks but for all priests may be a sign of this.[56] Denis de Rougement even claims that "love" in the sense of an inner devotion to another was reinvented in the twelfth century after an absence from the literature of the previous eight centuries.[57] Peter Abelard stressed the renewed notion of the importance of intention in his moral theology.[58] At Cluny, Alger of Liège directed confessors to "investigate intentions scrupulously," and to "define carefully the role of the will in the offence."[59] Whereas the early medieval emphasis was on worship and penance done correctly, between 1050 and 1215 there was a shift toward the ideal of loving and serving one's neighbor.[60]

Inner, subjective faith could be efficacious even when using false relics for a cure. It was the inner devotedness rather than the miraculous power in the relic that made the difference. "This personal element in devotion marks a new religious sensibility."[61] Whereas the early Middle Ages had easily celebrated the external accomplishments of a powerful lord, great hero, or conquering king, the high Middle Ages perceived a conflict between the aspiration for outward glory and the inner demands of conscience. At the shrines of the saints it was no longer just the power of the saint to offer protection and miracles that was the center of attention. A high degree of inner virtue and holiness became the standard, so that miracles attributed to the saint were not sufficient for the new process of canonization if the person was not also one of great virtue.[62]

The renewed awareness of the individual was accompanied by a loosening of the tribal ties of loyalty and of conformity to the community as the basis both of a person's identity and of the norms of behavior (though clan identity remained strong, as evidenced by countless brutal interfamilial feuds[63]). Devotion to local saints was subordinated to the new European enthusiasm for the cult of the Blessed Virgin. The roles and rules for each person were no longer automatically established by birth. More choices of occupation had become possible, along with an increased need to reflect on what choice to make.[64] Social acceptance was contrasted with acceptance by God, marking an awareness that conformity to the standards of society stood under judgment of a higher standard.[65] By the thirteenth century, theorists were giving reasons why even the king was bound by a higher natural law, and speculating on when a king might be overthrown for failure to live by that law.[66]

The late medieval political order achieved new levels of complexity, requiring greater efficiency in the use of law and government policy. Church laws had accumulated somewhat randomly during the early Middle Ages. Some method was needed to bring order out of all the conflicting rules that had been established. In the twelfth century, following the rules provided by Abelard for dealing with conflicting testimonies from Scripture and other authorities, the great legal scholar Gratian brought rational coherence to canon law.[67]

In general there is a striking similarity between the shift in ancient Greece from archaic to classical cultural forms and the shift from early medieval to late medieval cultural forms.[68] The individual emerged out of traditional-tribal consciousness into explicit self-recognition. Conformity to external authority gave way partly to allegiance to inner principles. And, as in the case of individual development, it was a shift from the concrete operational style of thought typical of archaic cultures to the formal operational thought that attains public strength in a classical culture.

An Uneasy Mixture of Thought Styles

In the late Middle Ages archaic elements endured. Tradition and authority generally weighed as heavily as reason. Miracles were taken for granted, and belief in them even increased among the less educated. Scientific information was often an archaic-style collection of hand-me-downs from ancient times, in which the specific "correspondences" of one thing with another constituted significant knowledge.[69] Most important, there were numerous opponents to the renewed classical rational style. While the new mendicant orders, the Dominicans and Franciscans, supported "the flowering of questions" (the dialectical method of argumentation), the monastic mind still delighted in allegories.[70]

But classical-style consciousness grew rapidly. The intellectual renaissance of the twelfth and thirteenth centuries manifested a renewed confidence in the dialectical method of considering all the possible alternative ways of resolving the conflict, and then offering an argued case for picking one of these ways as the best. This often challenged the authority of tradition, even though the goal usually proclaimed was only to reconcile differences among the authorities and resolve problems raised. In fact, one of the great issues to be resolved in those and later centuries was precisely the relation between tradition, under the name of "faith," and the dialectical method and the evidence of the sense, under the name of "reason."[71]

In the eleventh century Otloh of St. Emmeram, in his *The Confession of My Deeds*, explained that he had once doubted God's existence and the validity of Scripture because of so much evil in the world and because of contradictions among the Old Testament, the New Testament, and the writings of the Fathers of the Church.[72] In response to Otloh, Anselm argued out the explanations for evil and the proof for God's existence, and Abelard constructed his *Sic et Non* to show how the various authorities could be reconciled by the application of a little reasoning.[73]

A renewed interest in physical and astronomical science appeared in the many cosmologies, though the twelfth century versions were often a mixture of archaic and classical styles. William of Auvergne's (ca. 1180– 1249) *De Universo* fit endless pieces of information about the world within the kind of universal cosmic structure that classical consciousness finds fascinating. Eduard R. Dijksterhuis, overlooking more advanced aspects of William's work, makes his cosmology sound clearly archaic, a catalog of traditional truths instead of knowledge gained by rational systematic standards:

> Here again we come across the vigorous medieval tendency to accumulate scientific facts, and the peculiar failure of the medieval scholar to make anything of them, largely because of his excessive credulity and his boundless confidence in the authority of ancient authors or in exotic reports.[74]

Dijksterhuis goes on to cite William's many examples of miraculous happenings and magical powers as a sign of his "archaic" style of thought. The mere attempt, however, to construct a whole cosmology represents the reemerging classical-style search for a universal order.

The renewed classical approach is clear in the earlier (ca. 1145) *Cosmographia* Bernard Silvester. His universe is similar to William's, but Bernard exhibits explicit awareness that many traditional images, stories, and symbols must be demythologized, as it were, to fit the rational universe.[75] The myths must be taken seriously but not literally. Bernard emphasizes the value of the old method of allegory for dealing with the limitations of a literal approach to traditional texts.[76] The cosmology of Thierry of Chartres also reflects classical concerns. Around 1140 he used the quadrivium, the "scientific" studies of arithmetic, geometry, music, and astronomy, to analyze Genesis "scientifically," in order "that the artifice of the Creator be made manifest in his works and, as I propose, that it be *rationally demonstrated*."[77] These cosmologies attempted rational interpretations of nature. They were doing to Scriptures what the Stoics had done to Homer.

Questions of cognitive method returned to center stage. John of Salisbury's *Metalogicon*, completed in 1159 (and sent to Thomas Becket, who was royal chancellor), analyzed verbal and logical skills. It is a learned, balanced, and realistic account of the processes of education. It is also a trenchant attack on those enemies of logic whose method is to cite authorities or toss around ideas without intellectual discipline or without attending carefully to evidence.[78]

The most massive and still best-known works bringing a fully rationalized order to human understanding were the theological summae of the thirteenth century, especially those of Thomas Aquinas. They were the high point, perhaps, of the school theology or "Scholasticism." These summae united theology and philosophy, including ethics and even much of what we would call science, in grand syntheses in which every individual belief or conclusion took on extra credibility because it was logically fitted into systematic relationship with all other beliefs or conclusions.

Scholasticism is a testimony to the ability of the mind to go beyond cataloging information in order to provide theoretical explanations for things and match up all the explanations in an ever-expanding web of coherence. The logical thoroughness is beautifully manifest in the diagrams provided by the English Dominicans in their translation of Aquinas's *Summa Theologiae*, diagrams like the team pairing charts for major sports tournaments, showing where each team stands in relation to every other in the overall structure of the tournament. Similarly, the structure of the *Summa Theologiae* can be charted to show how all the questions fit together in one logically comprehensive package.[79]

Like Aristotle, the Scholastics sought certitude by deducing truth from reliable premises with full logical rigor. In theology many of these premises came from Scripture and tradition with the certitude of God's authority behind them. Other premises came from argumentations of philosophers of the past or from what everyone could know from firsthand experience to be true. The intent was to show what logically *must* be the case, what *must* be true. The more extreme Aristotelians worked with as much respectful awe toward Aristotle's authority as toward their own rational analysis, but they often claimed for their conclusions a philosophical certitude that gave them grounds to challenge traditional religious beliefs.

Necessity in the Universe

Among the later medieval philosophers were many followers of the twelfth-century Muslim Aristotelian Ibn Rushd, known as Averroës by Christian Europeans. The rationalism of the Averroists directly challenged Christian tradition on several points. Averroists claimed that the intellectual powers of each person were not the powers of individual personal souls, but were participations in a single Intellect or Soul. This challenged traditional belief in the individual soul of the person and in the separate survival of each person's soul. More important, the Averroists accepted Aristotle's belief in the eternity of the universe, implying some degree of independence of the world in relation to God, and contrary to the traditional Christian belief that God had created the universe out of nothing a finite amount of time previous to any present moment. And the Averroists saw a high degree of necessity in the universe, a necessity that there be four basic elements (earth, water, air, and fire), that the heavens had to move in perfect circles, and so forth. This seemed to imply that God *had* to sustain the universe as it was and was not free to do otherwise. These latter two beliefs together seemed to give the universe some degree of autonomy from God's power and rule.[80]

These two claims struck the thirteenth and fourteenth centuries with the force that the fights over Copernican astronomy or Darwin's theory of evolution would have in later centuries. They sound quite abstractly theological to us now, as indeed they were. But they were also issues about the intelligibility of the universe and about the capacity of the human mind to grasp that intelligibility. They are issues of whether human inquirers can expect to find a world following its own reliable and necessary patterns, a world they can therefore understand and to some extent control through their own analysis and actions, or whether the active presence of an omnipotent and utterly free God places an effective and significant limit on the aspirations of humankind to understand things for themselves through the use of their own powers of reason.[81]

Miracles Again

These issues appear again in the case of belief in miracles. Belief in miracles was a practical necessity for the average twelfth- and thirteenth-century person. To question the reality of miracles would be to doubt the veracity of the Bible, which was the foundation of religious belief. It would challenge the ability of God to rule over the universe and do as God pleased, binding God instead to a Stoic necessity or calling into question God's omnipotence. It would pose a threat to popular beliefs in miracles produced by the intercession of saints, especially through their relics. The popular mental image of God's activity could suppose that God could simply do as God pleased, with no limit of any kind.

There were nonetheless signs of doubts among at least some of the cognitive elite about reliance on miracles or other supernatural powers.[82] Fewer miracles were recorded in the histories written at the end of the twelfth century, although the use of miracles in popular preaching and instruction increased.[83] Trial by ordeal, which relied on God's intervention to provide a sign of innocence or guilt, began to disappear.[84] By 1395 the Lollards argued against belief in any special power in holy water or consecrated bells or even the Eucharist.[85] In the case of the Eucharist, miracle stories had increased, says Gary Macy, though perhaps in reaction to Berengar of Tours, who in the eleventh century had cast doubt on the reality of Christ's literal—miraculous—presence under the appearance of bread and wine.[86]

Other philosophically trained theologians recognized problems with miracles. As had been agreed centuries earlier in disputes with Stoics, God could not do anything self-contradictory, such as making a rock so big that God could not move it. Anselm recognized another limit to God's power, saying that God was bound by the divine nature to be perfectly just.[87] This would be part of the controversy over whether God willed something because it was good, or whether something was "good" solely because God willed it. It was the intelligibility of the universe, however, that was also at stake, not just the image of God.

In the thirteenth century Thomas Aquinas provided an Augustinian-style account of how miracles could take place, an account that, like Augustine's, sacrificed some of the intelligibility of things. According to Aquinas, God as the primary cause of everything that exists is the absolute ruler of the universe. God made the universe to have its own "secondary" order of causality. But the natural order has a certain amount of slack in it. Nature is not rigidly ruled by necessity; what we call nature is in accord with what nature *usually* does. Thus, because most people are born with five fingers, we call that natural; but it is also within the limits of the natural for some people to be born with six fingers.[88] We give the name "miracle" to whatever is strikingly unusual. But that does not mean that such events are contrary to nature, since God made nature loose enough to allow for the unusual.[89]

In none of his miracles, Aquinas argues, does God act contrary to the nature that God created; instead, God is merely using opportunities to go beyond nature's *usual* activity in order to do something striking for the purpose of educating people, especially to give credibility to the words of prophets and apostles and evangelists.[90] Aquinas, like Augustine, thus provided a way of making rational sense of how God could be the Creator and Sustainer of an orderly nature but also could do what was miraculous. But Aquinas did this at the expense of putting nature itself somewhat beyond human intelligibility by keeping nature loose enough in its order that the unusual or unpredictable was intrinsic to it.

The Absolute and Ordained Powers of God

In late medieval times the main issue concerning God's power shifted from miracles alone to the larger question of whether God could do absolutely anything God chose. The problem was partly a logical-theoretical one. If God was perfect goodness and perfect power, then it would seem necessary for God to make as perfectly good a universe as could possibly be, so that given God's choice to make any universe at all (a puzzle in itself), this single universe which exists is the one that God had to make—"the best of all possible worlds," to use the phrase later inspired by Leibniz's thought.[91] Here the conclusion of theoretical thinking challenged traditional belief in divine omnipotence. Theorizing minds sought a full rationality to nature, while traditional believers did not want God's power subjected to the limits of rationality.

An odd comment from St. Jerome provided a focus for the dispute.[92] Jerome, speaking in praise of virginity rather than arguing over God's power, had declared that not even God can restore a virgin to her original virginity, once it has been lost. Peter Damian, in the late eleventh century, disagreed vehemently. He declared that God can do anything God chooses to do, without any limit or necessity of any kind. God can even change the past. No amount of arrogant theorizing by the dialecticians can ever determine how events must take place, or whether there has to be a reliable and therefore intelligible order to things. (The condemnation of Abelard in 1140 included the grounds that he agreed with Jerome rather than Peter Damian.)[93]

The answer that satisfied many theologians was used in the thirteenth century by Albertus Magnus as though it had already become commonplace, and was used also by Thomas Aquinas. It is the distinction between God's absolute power and God's ordained power.[94] The absolute power of God has no limit. The ordained power of God is the way in which God decided from all eternity to use the divine power—what God "ordained" to be so. What God has ordained is now necessarily the case, but only because God freely chose to act in that way, not because God had to act in that way. God chose to create a universe of usually reliable secondary causes, thereby freely choosing to limit the *application* of God's own absolute power.[95]

By this distinction Aquinas continued to walk the middle road, rejecting Peter Damian's flat denial of any limit at all to the application of God's absolute power, but also rejecting the insistence of several Aristotelian philosophers who argued that this world necessarily exists and is the sole way a universe could exist. After 1277, when 219 philosophical and largely Aristotelian propositions were condemned by the archbishop of Paris, among them even a few of Aquinas's, theologians took great care to preserve God's freedom and power from the constraints that some philosophers placed on them.[96]

Nominalism

Thirteenth-century nominalism focused on the dispute over God's power.[97] Nominalism insisted on the distinction between God's absolute power and God's ordained power in order to stress the freedom God had in making this world, to the point where the order of this world was portrayed as only one of a potentially infinite number of different worlds that God might have made out of God's infinite power. The regular patterns of this world were rather arbitrary, or at least certainly not necessary. The world was ruled not by "laws of nature but merely customs of God."[98]

William of Ockham (ca. 1285–1349) is the best-known nominalist. Some historians have emphasized the degree to which Ockham and other nominalists loosened the order of the universe, rendering it less intelligible by insisting on God's freedom and absolute power to do anything, and on the idea that this was only one of many possible universes.[99] Others historians argue that Ockham perceived a great amount of regularity in nature and wanted only to insist that this regularity could not be deduced theoretically, as though logic could show what kind of universe God would have to make. Instead, the order of this universe was so dependent on God's utter freedom that no amount of deduction could determine what it was like. Only by taking a careful look could one determine what in fact God had chosen to do.

Most philosophers and theologians of the time insisted that God had made a reliably regular universe.[100] They tried to preserve the intelligibility of reliable order in the universe; but they also insisted that it was not the intelligibility of necessity, of what had to happen. So the intelligibility in things can be discovered only empirically, rather than being deducible from first principles.[101] In principle God might even have made an infinity of universes, each with its own different order of secondary causes (natural causal patterns), if any. Duns Scotus, William of Ockham, Nicholas of Autrecourt, and others each found a different way to indicate that our knowledge of reality is conditional or approximate or contingent because of some lack of necessity or necessary intelligibility in things. Only empirical investigation could provide the answers about the world.

There is at least a small irony in the history of thought following upon this. Nominalism gave some reinforcement to Peter Damian's less philosophical view of God's total supremacy over all things. This meant that in principle Neoplatonic and Scholastic notions of a hierarchically ordered world system with its perfect chain of being and self-enclosed, goal-oriented harmony were challenged in order to provide more room for God's absolute power and freedom.[102] An earlier chapter described how in the early days of Christianity, many Christian thinkers defended belief in God's sovereign freedom over nature at least partly to defend belief in certain miraculous events, including the miracles in Scripture. Now the nominalists defended God's sovereign freedom to make any kind of universe with any kind of order or lack of order that God chose, thereby still providing a way to defend the notion of God intervening to work miracles. But in principle the nominalist position left open the possibility that God might have made this universe (or some universe) so tightly run by reliably regular secondary causes that there was no room for miracles. Nominalism argued for a need to investigate empirically to discover just what sort of order this universe does have. In the long run it has turned out that the degree of reliable orderliness in the universe is so great that miracles are no longer very plausible. The irony, therefore, is that the notion of God's sovereign freedom which first preserved space for God to work miracles, ended up making necessary the empirical method that has largely closed the universe to miracles.

In sum, the late Middle Ages recovered the classical style of formal operational thought and applied it widely. Concrete operational thought, including its openness to narratives full of wonders and marvels, remained in place as the normal mode of human thought. But formal standards of logic, of systematic coherence among ideas, an expectation of a rationally intelligible order to the universe, took their place as the standards of the cognitive elite, those educated in theology, philosophy (including science), and law. Much of what contemporary writers sometimes think of as "modern" scientific thought and its approach to reality began again in these times, not as something entirely new but as a renewal of the rationally systematic style of an earlier classical era. The words of Chenu, describing twelfth- and thirteenth-century thought show how much the later scientific approach we are familiar with was already present:

> In this mechanism-minded world [of the twelfth–thirteenth century] man moved away from a confused trial-and-error approach, became objective and impersonal in his efforts, and grew aware of the complex structures of realities governed by natural laws. Order was experimentally ascertained and systematically verified, for nature was seen as penetrable and predictable.[103]

Chenu's words suggest a stronger experimental practice than was actually the case. But the general idea is correct: The formal operational style of thought, trusting in logical and supposedly objective analysis, once strong among ancient philosophers of Greece as well as of China and India, guided the resurgent classical style in the late medieval period in Europe. At the same time the origins of a more modern empirical science are also visible.

Early Forms of an Empirical Approach

As was mentioned earlier, empirical observation had a place in the scientific method of Aristotle. In his *Posterior Analytics* he carefully analyzed ways in which observation was the starting point for formulating the general truths from which a person could logically deduce other knowledge. But Aristotle gave no explicit role to observation as an ongoing *testing* of truth-claims.[104] Others after Aristotle used some forms of experimentation. Hero of Alexandria, for example, borrowed from Strato, the intellectual grandchild of Aristotle at the Lyceum, specific directions on how to demonstrate experimentally the existence of a vacuum of sorts.[105] But theorizing by far outweighed experimentation or other forms of empirical investigation. In spite of advice such as Carneades', to inspect things carefully as a corrective to initial and possibly misleading impressions, the philosophers were mostly content to think things through without ongoing empirical inspection or testing.

The modern empirical approach has more recent roots in the thirteenth-century work of Robert Grosseteste (ca. 1175–1253) and his disciple Roger Bacon (ca. 1220–1292). Bacon had learned from Grosseteste to recommend in certain limited cases a practice that is now intrinsic to the scientific method: the idea of experimentation as the normal and necessary method for testing truth-claims.[106] Grosseteste had promoted the method of falsification: If a theory predicts certain consequences and those consequences do not occur, then something must be wrong with the theory.[107] Bacon added descriptions of ways in which careful observation and even experimentation could aid the philosopher.[108] (They had not arrived at the modern somewhat "skeptical" idea that such testing was in principle an open-ended matter with no absolute certitude at the end of it.)

The concern for empirical knowledge appears also in the thirteenth-century work of Albert the Great. Dijksterhuis has collated statements from the works of Albert that illustrate an empirical and experimental orientation:

> A conclusion that is inconsistent with the evidence of our sense cannot be believed; a principle that does not agree with experience gained by sense-perception is not a principle.

> The investigation of nature should be pursued even into individual things; knowledge of the natures of things in general is only rudimentary knowledge.

> Much time is required to conduct an experiment in such a way that it is not defective in any single respect; in fact, experimentation should not be effected in one way only, but under all possible circumstances, in order that a secure basis for the work may be found.

> Evidence based on sense-perception is the most secure of all in science, and is superior to reasoning without experimentation.[109]

Yet Scholasticism, the dominant approach through the thirteenth century, relied much more on achieving logical coherence among ideas—finding ways of explaining how to maintain Christian truth and philosophical truths—than on empirical tests of the ideas. The empirical was honored in theory but very little in practice.[110] (This is scarcely surprising. Philosophers and theologians still try to solve empirical issues by mental analysis alone.)

By the sixteenth century, interest in empirical study had increased greatly. Francis Bacon (1561–1626) manifests a strongly empirical spirit coupled with a detailed analysis of how to use evidence successfully.[111] He now has a reputation as an extreme inductivist, as though he claimed that good science would simply count individual instances until they added up to truth.[112] In fact he clearly recognized the need to form hypotheses and test them in a variety of ways. A famous metaphorical passage of his sums it up nicely: A mere empiricist is like an ant who only collects and uses things, while a rationalist is like a spider that spins its webs out of its own substance. The ideal method, however, is that of the bee, which both collects material from the flowers and also digests and transforms it (into honey).[113] Bacon's *Novum Organum* is a detailed and careful compendium of how induction may be used to generate hypotheses as the "first vintage" or preliminary interpretation, and how those hypotheses may be subjected to a wide variety of types of tests.[114]

An important implication of the empirical approach is that it provides no final proof of anything. There was long precedent for this. The astronomy of Ptolemy, even in his own time, was recognized as a model for dealing with how the heavens appeared but perhaps not a fully accurate picture.[115] There were a variety of models, each with problems. The model that placed the sun at the center would have made the stars so far from the Earth as to be an incredible distance away. More than one model placed the Earth at the center of the universe, and each caused some theoretical difficulties. A model that worked quite well was recognized as only one possible legitimate model, not the only workable one. (For example, there were at least two equally workable ways to account for the fact that from fall to spring in the northern hemisphere there are 179 days, and from spring to fall there are 186.)

A tactic for dealing with this plurality of models was to give up claiming that any one of them was the truth and to accept any such model as a good one only to the extent that it "saved the appearances"—it fit with how things appeared, and therefore at least did not go against the empirical evidence. The fifteenth-century translation of the skeptical writings of Sextus Empiricus cautioned against dogmatic truth-claims. In the sixteenth century Andreas Osiander, who published Copernicus's heliocentric theory, added a preface in which he claimed that the Copernican model was just another way of "saving the appearances" and not necessarily the truth, even though Copernicus apparently believed that it was. Nor was Francis Bacon seeking perfect truth through his method. His own metaphors again express it best: He wanted evidence as pledges of truth, as collateral or security, that limit risk of error but cannot banish it completely. Evidently, then, there is a long tradition behind some principles of modern science: testing theories by empirical evidence and treating scientific theories as workable models. We will see more about these two principles and about modern science in general in the next chapters. There we will also see more about the effect of modern science on different aspects of religious thought.

8

EARLY MODERN MODELS OF REALITY IN SCIENCE AND RELIGION

Modern science has slowly taken shape over the last four hundred or so years, although some of its characteristics already existed in classical philosophies of nature and of knowledge. Modern science has gradually produced a new model of the universe and how that universe operates, a model partly at odds with traditional Western religious belief, though it has contributed to some religious thought. This chapter will review major competing models of reality over the last few centuries, to see how the current scientific model emerged and whether either religious or antireligious motives helped determine which model would win out. Chapter 9 will look at scientific method. Chapter 10 will review the status of religious thought today, as a result of developments in science and its cognitive style.

The fourteenth century was the century of nominalism, as chapter 7 described. It was also a century important in literary history: Dante, Boccaccio, and Chaucer hold more than their own among the literary giants of the ages. It was also a century of disasters. Early droughts led to hunger, which in turn led to peasant rebellions. Bubonic plague touched Italian soil in 1347. Within a few decades almost half of Europe had died. By the fifteenth century, however, Europeans had entered into what they called a renaissance of ancient literature and arts. Scholars and aristocrats eagerly sought ancient texts, to translate the Greek into Latin, and even into vernacular languages. Hermetic literature, the skeptical writings of Sextus Empiricus, and newly found Epicurean texts all contributed to an intellectual ferment. Many of the texts had material relevant to the renewal of science in a Europe that had slowly become accustomed to using better mathematical notion and computational methods. The next centuries were rich ones for the mind.

For the last few centuries science has been sorting through various models of reality. The major contenders in the late sixteenth century and afterward were the long-standing Aristotelian model, a Neoplatonist model or two, and various forms of the Epicurean atomist model. The model that dominates science at the edge of the twenty-first century is none of these, though it is closest to Epicurean atomism. Some current writings speak of the relation between religious and scientific views of the universe as though there has been only a simple choice between two models, one a universe in which God acts, the other a naturalistic universe bereft of divine activity. But even a simplified review of scientific models of the universe over the last four hundred years shows that matters are far more complex than that. Out of multiple models of reality, one has emerged to dominate the sciences because it is the sole model that makes coherent sense out of the research and results in astronomy, physics, chemistry, biology, and geology all at once.

The dominant scientific model of the universe is indeed naturalistic. It is, for all that, not necessarily a Godless universe, as multiple twentieth-century theologies attest, some of them constructed to fit with the conclusions of science. But in those theologies the mode of divine presence and activity, as well as the basis for belief in God, appear in forms that earlier generations might well have considered inadequate, even as many of the current generation do, on the grounds that a naturalistic universe is not a religious one. (Chapters 9 and 10 will have more to say on all this.)

A Review of Models of the Universe

Suppose that classical thought is correct in its goal to discover a single, all-inclusive intelligibility that explains the events, structure, and stuff of the universe. Even on that assumption there are still many possible different models. Here is a list of some that have been proposed in Western thought during the last twenty-five hundred years, some of them overlapping quite a bit, some contradicting others:

1. A universe of basic inner essences (tree, star, dog, water), each of which is unchangingly true to its own nature as the source of nature's reliability, and each of which has its own inner goal-directedness to act in its own way.
2. A universe of geometric and essential (essences) harmonies that make up the macrocosmic order of the overall universe and that

exist all together in microcosmic complexity in each human person, thereby making the person the locus for natural magic.

3. A universe in which most events are due to "secondary" (i.e., natural) causes, but in which there are also divine interventions to produce effects that natural causes alone would not have produced.

4. A universe in which a divine Being (or beings) invisibly manipulate the patterns of things in the way any person can, by intimate knowledge of nature, thereby producing whatever this Being wants to happen but without suspending the laws of nature.

5. A universe in which permanent inner essences do not exist, so that one can only try to identify external reliable patterns, such as the pattern we call gravity, or characteristics, such as solidity, and then see how these basic externals in fact interact, perhaps describing these external patterns mathematically for maximum precision.

6. A universe of two major components: the first material, the dead and passive atoms physically kept in motion somehow, and collectively constituting all physical reality (including all animals and the human body); the second immaterial, the immortal and purely spiritual (fully nonmaterial) rational selves/souls of people, angels, and demons.

7. A universe in which inert physical matter is organized into life patterns by the presence of various nonmaterial "subtle spirits," which are fully natural rather than supernatural and which make inert matter operate in a certain way.

8. A fully material and evolving universe, which has within itself sufficient energy to account for all activities in the universe, including life and human conscious rationality as part of the material process.

9. A universe in which only mind is really real, with all seeming materiality only a way of perceiving things or a temporary process that mind itself is undergoing.

10. A self-contained, evolving universe in which the development of sequential levels of responsiveness and consciousness is due to a divine element that is part of the matrix of the universe and is nurturing this development.

Each of these models has been proposed and supported in the last four hundred years. It is not an exhaustive list. In physics today, for example, the notion of matter as a form that energy takes has shifted the description given in 8 above to an "energist" model rather than a materialist one. This idea was prefigured in the eighteenth century by the Jesuit Ruggiero Boscovich, who gave it a religious interpretation; on the other hand, the theory was taken quite seriously by Joseph Priestley who found that he could fit it with his unreligious views.[1] In either case it is energy, not matter, that is the basic "stuff" of things. And, of course, the list omits some models from other cultures, many of them religious. Hindu thought might add the model of an ephemeral universe of change that is not the really real but is a shadow alternative to the unchanging realm of true Being and Truth. Some other Hindus or some Buddhists will offer variations on this; Taoists will draw another picture. Evidently, the theorizing human mind is endlessly inventive. Formal operational thought can construct a variety of mental schemata to make sense of things.

In all this there has been no simple conflict between religious and nonreligious viewpoints. Contrary to some current arguments, we have more choices than between a cold, mechanistic, religionless view of the universe and a warm, organismic, religious view. We will see cases where one or more of these ten models was given both a religious and a nonreligious interpretation.

To get a sense of the competition among models of the universe, we can begin with the formative period for much of modern science, the seventeenth century, and some of the models in use then. By the seventeenth century Scholasticism still preserved much of Aristotle's science. But the excitement focused on two conflicting models, each of them also somewhat ancient, Neoplatonic hermeticism and mechanistic neo-atomism.

The Hermetic Philosophy

We have seen a little of Neoplatonic hermeticism in preceding chapters. Its resurgence was due to the recovery of the *Corpus Hermeticum* in the fifteenth century. For a century and a half these writings had a powerful influence on the new humanism of Heinrich Agrippa, Marsilio Ficino, Giovanni Pico della Mirandola, Giordano Bruno, Paracelsus, John Dee, and others. Their influence continues today, in fact, not only in Rosicrucian ideas developed by Johan Valentin Andreä (ca. 1614), and promoted by Robert Fludd in England, but in the many forms of New Age belief in crystal power, ESP, and so forth.[2]

The first book of the *Corpus Hermeticum*, the "Poimandres," promised godlike powers. Each person, as the juncture of material and spiritual forces, had the power of a gateway to let pass or inhibit or divert cosmic forces.[3] Those who were trained in the relevant skills of mind and soul, and had the innate spiritual instincts for taking advantage of this, would be able to manipulate these forces. Such a person was a "magus," a magician.[4]

Evidence today says the mind or feelings can indeed have a direct effect on physical reality. Psychosomatic influences exist in states of stress or in the placebo effect. Continued anxiety can produce high blood pressure. A person's belief that a sugar pill may actually be an effective medicine (or where the attention that comes from those providing the pills has an influence on the person's attitudes) can have an effect on the person's health. Neoplatonism had a somewhat different notion of mind-body interaction, but not one that was irrational in its own time, even though it expected a less rationally reliable universe than other philosophies. Neoplatonism was a model of how the universe works, a model that could function as a good hypothesis worth testing out. It also had the authority of antiquity on its side, a weighty consideration in the sixteenth century. Its apparent source, the divine being Hermes Trismegistus, had supposedly given information to both Moses and Plato. Had the many enthusiastic hermeticists managed to find reliable evidence for their general beliefs, their model of the universe would have had a better chance to survive and flourish as the leading science.[5]

Hermeticism obscured or eliminated the difference between the natural and the supernatural. Powers that most Christians then would have thought of as preternatural or supernatural powers—the ability to influence demons or angels, to send thoughts through the air at a distance, to cure people of disease through magical influence—were, according to the magi, all just part of the order of nature, able to be controlled by a magus precisely because it was the nature of the human person to be the microcosmic point of intersection of these natural forces. This blurring of the line between the natural and the supernatural often led traditionally religious people to oppose hermeticism.[6]

Another implication of hermetic thought, however, was that this universe is not as reliably intelligible as a classical mind might wish. It is a universe in which forces like those of gravity, electricity, magnetism, light could be increased or diminished, created or eliminated in certain places at certain times, by the variable mind influences of magi, by the unpredictable choices of humans, demons, and angels. Soul power could divert or suspend the laws of nature, thereby making them not strictly lawful at all. The problem that this created was similar to that created by belief in supernatural intervention. The only "science" that this would allow, as the magi proclaimed, was actually an artistry of the adept, the skilled manipulation of natural magic. Science would consist of some insights into the general essences of things, and the rest would be a craft, a practical application of soul power. "Science" would be a juggler's art.

A sixteenth-century magus could nonetheless claim that this model of the universe was quite plausible. The universe does seem to be full of variable forces. For though the seasons go round with regularity and acorns continue to produce oaks and not lilies, nonetheless some summers are too cool and some oaks outgrow all others. Evidently invisible forces can somehow vary the processes of nature. In a world of variable influences, no a priori rules could describe what would happen of necessity. A person could only experiment with various metals and crystals and harmonies, in conjunction with various moods and states of mind and decisions, at different times in the astronomical calendar, to see which combinations in fact have desired effects.[7] The fans of hermeticism could say that the search of the strictly formal operational thinkers for a more reliably intelligible order of events would have to give way to the fact of soul power as a large-scale unpredictable force.

Hermeticism lost ground in 1614 when Isaac Causabon showed by philological evidence that the hermetic writings had originated in a second-century CE Hellenic context, not in ancient Egyptian times.[8] But it also lost ground because natural philosophers like Galileo were beginning to provide the evidence that beneath the variabilities of nature were highly reliable physical regularities. The period of the pendulum's swing varies in direct proportion to the length of the rod from which it is suspended. The rate of acceleration of a ball rolling down an inclined plane is proportional to the angle of incline. The force of a cannonball can be divided into mathematically measurable components. Observations like these encouraged the search for other lawful patterns. William Gilbert, William Harvey, Rene Descartes, Blaise Pascal, Robert Boyle, and many hundreds of other "virtuosi" piled up observations, challenged each others' conclusions, established new tools and techniques for experiment or testing, and took measurement upon measurement. Hermeticism remained in the competition as a potentially valid model of the universe. But as more and more lawful patterns were found, soul power was not in evidence as an influence on any of them.[9] Perhaps the virtuosi were not looking hard enough for soul power, but the hermeticists were. They still are today—so far without reliable evidence in support of their model of reality.[10]

The Mechanical Philosophy

In the seventeenth century the new major contender for status as the true model of reality was what was sometimes called the mechanical philosophy. It was also known as the corpuscularist philosophy, a revival of aspects of the ancient Epicurean worldview (with Empedocles' idea of a *plenum* sometimes replacing the atomists' void). For anyone disdainful of Neoplatonic hermeticism and its magic, this corpuscular theory was an excellent antidote. A universe in which all events are part of the ongoing movements of atoms is one in which there is no need to postulate demons or angels or souls, or hidden magical forces ("occult powers"), as the hermetic magi did. Instead, every event could be interpreted as the result of plain physical contact among atoms.

The preeminent mechanist, Descartes, claimed that there were extremely fine particles (corpuscles, atoms) of different types and sizes that filled all of space and that flowed in currents in a way similar to the droplets of water which make up an ocean. This interplanetary ocean flowed in circular currents, carrying the planets along with it.[11] The effect of the moon on Earth's tides was due to the physical contact of the moon with the currents of particles surrounding it, which flowed against the currents of particles surrounding the Earth, and thence to the surface of the oceans.[12]

Descartes reaffirmed Aristotle's claim that there is no action at a distance, that is, no influences on physical bodies except through physical contact. This deliberately excluded belief in invisible and nonphysical "occult" forces such as soul power. Instead, every physical motion was due to other physical motions of atoms bumping and spinning and hooking up in relatively complex configurations such as trees and human bodies. Thus all physical events were mechanical in a strict sense. There was no void between particles; there were particles at every point in space. Even gravity and magnetism, invisible forces that seemed to work at a distance without physical contact, were in fact the result of physical contact among invisibly small particles rubbing against the Earth or against a magnet.[13]

There are four or more major forms of mechanistic philosophy, with four distinct models of the universe. Some mechanistic models were dualistic, dividing the universe into physical matter and nonphysical (nonmaterial or spiritual) souls; others were completely materialistic, claiming that even human thought is a product of matter rather than of a nonmaterial soul. Descartes was a leading dualist in the seventeenth century, sharply distinguishing matter from soul. To him, all animals as well as the human body were material machines, nothing more.[14] The human soul, by contrast, was a fully nonmaterial reality. Though animals had no souls (Latin: *anima*; French: *ame*), they nonetheless had various spirits, in the language of the day (Latin: *spiritus*; French: *esprit*). The animal spirits were refined matter like fire or air, which conveyed pressure and heat, and therefore caused activity within the animal. The active power of fire or air, however, was not an innate power or activity in matter, according to Descartes. All activity was derived from the initial impulse given by God to everything at the moment of creation. Matter itself was inert.

Thomas Hobbes, on the other hand, was a fully materialist mechanist, who argued against Descartes that even the inner thoughts of a human person were a product of matter.[15] Hobbes was in fuller conformity with the ancient Greek atomists, who said that events in the history of the universe come from chance and necessity, not from any divine plan or guidance. The Catholic priest Pierre Gassendi agreed with much of Hobbes's thorough materialism, even about the human soul, but he also insisted that the order and energy of the universe made it plain that there had to be a God who planned it all and put it in motion. It was evidently possible to be a religious person and hold a rather thoroughly materialistic model of the universe at the same time. Gassendi, in fact, supported a mechanistic philosophy precisely as a way of defending Catholic belief in dependence on God's activity against the Neoplatonists and their universe of natural magic.[16]

A second set of mechanistic models described matter as either totally inert, without any power or force or source of activity in it, or as intrinsically active, possessed of its own inner energy.[17] The notion that matter was lifeless and inert was quite traditional. Aristotle's notion of primary materiality as a principle that limited a being to a specific time and space had a long standing in the consciousness of Europe. In the thirteenth century Aquinas could sum it up: "Matter is not a principle of action, but is the subject that receives the effect of action."[18] Matter is lacking in any active power whatsoever. "Form," the essence force, acts upon matter to make it take particular characteristics. Furthermore, because atoms have no intrinsic principle of order (no forms or essences of particular kinds), God must have imposed upon them the lawful behavior that they exhibit. Otherwise, even a universe in motion would be one of only random atoms.[19]

But there were further aspects of material activity to consider that challenged the inert version. Some material things seemed to manifest quite active powers. Attraction, as in gravity and magnetism, was still difficult to account for, in spite of Descartes's claims about particles rubbing against each other. So was repulsion, as when two magnets pushed one another away. So also was cohesion; a theory was needed to explain why some things stuck together strongly and other things did not. The inert mechanists made various proposals to account for such things. But there was room for a more active view of matter.

In England, for example, William Harvey (1578–1657) had employed a philosophy that was also called "mechanical" even though it appealed to natural "spirits."[20] Harvey had to account for the fact that the process of the heart pumping and blood circulating continued. What was the source of the energy to keep this activity going? The language that Harvey used to explain this was fairly traditional. He said that blood is filled with spirits. The spirits in question are the principle of vitality and hence are vital spirits. But the word "spirit" can still be misleading. Harvey described this spirit as a kind of energy-laden fluid, something different from what we would mean by spirit, and employing a different analogy from Descartes's comparison of the spirits to fire or air. A belief in "subtle fluids," in fact, remained important for a while in biology. Harvey thought of this "spirit" energy as part of material reality itself. He was a "dynamic materialist."

These spirits are fully natural spirits, according to Harvey, not the sort of spiritual "soul" that his compatriot William Gilbert, influenced a little by hermetic philosophy, had earlier proposed as the cause of magnetic influence. With Gilbert in mind, Harvey wrote:

> There is no occasion for searching after spirits foreign to or distinct from the blood, to evoke heat from some other source, to bring gods upon the scene, and to encumber philosophy with any fanciful con-

ceits. We physicians at this time designate that as spirit which Hippocrates called *impetum faciens* or moving power. . . . In this sense we are accustomed to speak of spirit of wine, spirit of vitriol, etc. And therefore it is that physicians admit as many spirits as there are principal parts or operations in the body, viz. animal, vital, natural, visual, auditory, concoctive, generative, implanted, influent, etc., etc.[21]

Harvey insisted that the spirits in the blood are simply whatever is in blood that makes it alive, and denied that they are like the celestial forces Gilbert or the hermetic philosophy proposed.[22]

For Descartes, however, Harvey had not departed far enough from Gilbert's hint of hermeticism. This use of the idea of a spirit force was too close to Aristotelian belief in "forms," natural but immaterial inner principles of activity, life, and sensation. So Descartes proposed his theory of firelike spirit as an alternative to Harvey's spirits. Descartes said that it was the heat of the heart which provided the power to the blood. Just as heat provided power to make water boil, expand, and turn to steam, so the heat of the heart was part of a process whereby the heart expanded and contracted mechanically to pump the blood.[23] This heat was fiery "spirit," perhaps, but a very mechanical sort of "spirit." These distinctions seem a bit too fine to us, perhaps; but they show us the difficulty that early science had in arriving at ways to conceive accurately and adequately how nature operates. That is why so many different models could be proposed and defended.

Newton's philosophy of nature was also a form of mechanical atomism. He nonetheless gave his own version of it, one that the followers of Descartes would oppose. Newton thought of the physical universe as made up of inert particles or atoms, all of it created, organized, and set in motion by God.[24] But where Descartes sought to discover rationally the inner essence of matter and how it must operate, Newton declared that he would devise no such explanatory ideas and would settle instead for simply describing the patterns of behavior of material things. Hence, because his law of gravity merely described how physical objects behaved in relation to each other, he could say that he did not have to argue about what spirits might account for the activity. This allowed him to sidestep the challenge from Cartesians that his gravity was an *occult* power which created "action at a distance."

Newton was being at least mildly disingenuous. In his theological writings, the vast bulk of them not public at this time, Newton was proposing that the forces which held the universe together and made it operate—gravity, magnetism, life—were actually God's activity.[25] God kept the universe supplied with ongoing motive power and exerted the influence to make physical bodies attract one another in accord with the law of gravity. Newton lays out the basis for this in the General Scholion appended to the *Principia* even while he insists that he will "frame no hypothesis" about this spirit.[26]

In the seventeenth century, then, there were several currents of thought. The various mechanistic models shared in a search for a fully intelligible physical world. The Neoplatonists focused on the ability of soul power to influence the physical world. Aristotelians still found the idea of goal-directed forms or essences necessary to explain biological activities of various kinds. Traditional religion continued to uphold forms of supernaturalism in which God intervened miraculously, albeit perhaps in an otherwise natural universe that was generally mechanistic.

Miracles Once Again: Deism

The seventeenth and eighteenth centuries saw many specific arguments against belief in any miracles at all. Descartes responded to those who saw God's hand moving the clouds by saying that he would explain the nature of clouds through natural causes and remove any reason to marvel at them.[27] He offered the double support of experience and reason, arguing that even if our sense experience did not confirm that God has made the world to operate with complete regularity, we would still know from reason that because God is immutable, God would not act differently at some times and places, but rather would continue to sustain the same laws of nature always and everywhere.[28]

Descartes gave scant place to God as the originator of the universe and its motion. His contemporary, Robert Boyle, showed a more emphatic religiousness without recourse to belief in miracles. Boyle positioned himself over against the pernicious Aristotle, whose belief in the eternity of the world denied God's creation of it. In addition to creation, said Boyle, God continuously preserves and sustains the universe in its activity. God is also the providential Orderer of the universe, though not through any interventions in the natural order of things:

> I ascribe to the wisdom of God in the first fabric of the universe, which he so admirably contrived, that, if he but continue his ordinary and general concourse, there will be no necessity of extraordinary interpositions, which may reduce him to seem, as it were, to play after-games.

Boyle goes on to complain of those philosophers and physicists who nonetheless try to include divine interventions:

> Methinks the difference betwixt their opinion of God's agency in the world, and that, which I would propose, may be somewhat adumbrated by saying, that they seem to imagine the world to be after the nature of a puppet, whose contrivance indeed may be very artificial, but yet is such, that in almost every particular motion the artificer is fain (by drawing sometimes one wire or string, sometimes another) to guide and oftentimes over-rule the actions of the engine; whereas,

according to us, it is like a rare clock, such as may be that at Strasbourg, where all things are so skillfully contrived, that the engine being once set a moving, all things proceed, according to the artificer's first design.[29]

Those philosophers who came to be called deists had a mixture of ideas about divine interventions. Some allowed for a few miracles, in particular the miracles of the Bible, especially those of Jesus, as well as the miracle of God's inspiration of the Bible. Most, however, rejected miracles altogether, on the grounds that it was not reasonable to believe in them. The deists of the Enlightenment are marvelous examples of formal operational thought seeking universal and objective truth on the basis of highly rational systematic analysis.

John Toland, in his *Christianity Not Mysterious* (1696), allowed a few miracles. The work was banned by the Irish Parliament, in spite of its intended support of Christianity, because it revised Christian beliefs to fit the test of reasonableness. Toland allowed that God did miraculously reveal some things, that in fact it was reasonable to suppose that God would do this; but all of the revealed truths were also knowable by reason. Toland rejected what he called absurdities such as "transubstantiation and other ridiculous fables."[30] In his Boyle lectures published in 1742, a half-century later, Samuel Clarke still reserved room for the revelatory activity of God, who selected some people as his teaching instruments, as well as for miracles in biblical times done by God or Jesus to confirm the validity of revelation.[31] Clarke argued it was reasonable for God to do this.

Other deists, in keeping with their rationalist approach, sought a way around miracle stories. Thomas Woolston, in his *Discourse on Our Saviour's Miraculous Power of Healing* (1730), addressed the controversy over Jesus' miracles and proclaimed the miracle stories to be allegories. To accept them as literally true, Woolston argued, would be to accept absurdities, improbabilities, and incredibilities.[32] Matthew Tindal, in his *Christianity as Old as the Creation* (1730), challenged earlier works of Clarke in support of revelation, arguing that no external revelation could really be needed, because only reason could select which of the many purported revelations of the world's religions were true, and reason could do this only by first knowing through rational inquiry which beliefs are true.[33]

David Hume spoke for many later in the century when he declared that belief in miracles is not reasonable.[34] He argued that the most highly probable knowledge we have is of the consistent reliability of the basic patterns of nature, the "laws" of nature. A miracle, by definition a suspension or evasion of those laws, is therefore by its nature a highly improbable event; and we would need unusually powerful evidence to believe that something so improbable has occurred. Given the unreliability of secondhand testimony, given the fact that religions which we consider to be false also make claims of miracles, and given the need to balance even our own firsthand experience of what may be a miracle against the possibility of trickery, mistake, or illusion, there is altogether no good reason to believe in any miracle.[35]

The twentieth century has inherited a great deal of this skepticism about miracles. This is partly just a tendency of formal operational thought. The late medieval thinkers who distanced themselves from trial by ordeal or who argued that God was bound to create a maximally rational and good universe might have been comfortable with some of the deists (though most medieval thinkers would have refrained from doubting the miracles attested in Scripture).

Modern skepticism about miracles stems also partly from the success of the formal operational search for overall intelligibility in the form of the new and still developing science. In the late eighteenth century, Pierre-Simon Laplace showed mathematically that the wobbling in the orbits of Jupiter and Saturn did not require that God step in to keep the solar system steady. The orbit variations were regular and self-correcting, as it were. In chemistry, as we call it, Antoine Lavoisier and Priestley battled over phlogiston. With the contributions of dozens of experimenters the existence of a gas later called oxygen was established, along with "fixed air" (carbon dioxide) and nitrogen. When deism was fading and evolutionary ideas expanded, exploration into the elements continued. John Dalton and Joseph Gay-Lussac worked out most of what would go into Amedeo Avogadro's periodic table.[36] By 1838 Friedrich Wilhelm Bessel (as well as Friedrich Wilhelm Struve) had finally constructed the equipment to identify the stellar parallax that had to exist if Copernicus's theory was true. It did.[37] By the late eighteenth and early nineteenth centuries, physics and chemistry had achieved a great deal that was compatible with a mechanistic philosophy, and could do quite well without miracles or supernatural forces. Biology was perhaps another matter.

Biology and Vital Forces

Mechanistic philosophy was the main alternative to Aristotelianism, hermeticism, and traditional supernaturalism.[38] Yet the mechanistic philosophy could not explain certain biological realities very well. Bernard de Fontenelle expressed it vividly. If a male dog-machine and a female dog-machine were placed side by side, they could produce little dog-machines. But if two watches were placed side by side for however long, no little timepieces would result.[39] In addition to the bump and flow and cohesion of particles, there seemed to be a need for some additional force or guiding element to make the particles assemble and operate in the extraordinarily complex forms that constitute life. Of the various models of reality available, it looked as though Aristotle's goal-seeking forms were needed as guiding souls.

The inert materialists, like all the mechanists or corpuscularists, rejected Aristotle. In Italy, Giovanni Borelli (1608–1679) tried to show that physiology (biology) was a fully mechanical science. He worked out the mechanics of muscle movement and showed how the muscles moved the bones by their contractions, like mechanical levers. Borelli likewise explained digestion as a mechanical grinding and crushing process carried out by the intestines.[40] No spirits were needed to explain this activity (except perhaps the fiery or airy "spirits" of Descartes).

The active materialists had what seemed to be a better case. Atheists like Paul d'Holbach favored active materialism, perhaps for less-than-scientific reasons. They could eliminate the divine or supernatural elements by supposing that matter itself somehow had its own active powers, so that all the many activities of things—gravitational, magnetic, electrical, vegetative, animate, sensate, and even human thinking—were things that matter could do by its own powers.[41] On the other hand, it was with a deistic sort of religiousness that Leibniz proposed that the universe is made up of active little atom substances he called monads, each of which is alive in a sense. Their nature is that of force/activity, so their nature is to have something analogous to sense and to appetite.[42] John Locke disturbed people by claiming that had God wanted to, God could have made matter capable of thinking.[43] So a religious person might be on either side of this argument about active matter.

As the natural philosophers continued to investigate the properties of matter in general, including living things, some sort of active materialism became more and more plausible. We have seen that in the seventeenth century, materialists described both magnetism and gravity as intrinsic and active properties of the material universe. Harvey declared that the heat energy in blood, its vital spirit, was a quality inherent in blood of its own nature, not a nonmaterial principle. As experimentation and knowledge of electricity grew, Ben Franklin proposed to think of it as a subtle, fiery fluid, more etherial than solid matter, yet nonetheless a material stuff in its own way.[44] Electricity was obviously dynamic. It could account for biological activity, too, it seemed, as Luigi Galvani's experiments with twitching frog legs later showed. By the end of the eighteenth century the "inert" materialism of the early mechanists had been left behind. The accumulating evidence eventually made the mechanistic philosophy a "dynamic" materialism, contrary to what some early mechanists had first proposed.

It was one thing to show that the dynamic powers of matter could account for general activities of living creatures. But it was something else to show that matter, regardless of how dynamic, could account for the formation of *new* life. In the generation of offspring, the regeneration of wounded or severed parts, and in the spontaneous generation of life from non-life, as eighteenth-century physiologists believed (maggots from manure, for example), the dynamic forces of matter not only were active but also were being guided in certain extremely precise and complex ways, so that an acorn became an oak and a frog's eggs became tadpoles. What cause or principle or element could be at work, taking hold of the dynamic properties of matter and channeling its development along such very specific paths to make the nut or egg develop as it did—as it was *supposed* to, it seemed (i.e., as though each nut or egg fulfilled an inner goal orientation)? Perhaps some "final cause" (a goal-oriented principle) must be at work.

There were two general positions on this, the mechanistic (now a "dynamic" one) and the vitalist. Those who called themselves mechanists looked for some property of material processes that could account for the formation of new life. They expected that if we could learn enough about the physical and chemical processes of dynamic matter, we would discover an intelligible and natural set of events taking place that would explain the formation of new life. Those who were vitalists insisted that something besides matter, regardless of how dynamic that matter might be, was required to guide the active matter in the formation of new life. So they invoked the idea of some "vital principle" that was different from matter. This was not the dualism of Descartes, who distinguished between a purely spiritual human soul and materiality. It was an Aristotelian sort of dualism, which depicted non-material but natural animating principles, operating in now-dynamic matter.

There were, inevitably, various forms of vitalism. In the early twentieth century Hans Driesch offered a distinction between old and new vitalism.[45] The old vitalism, as he defined it, included the viewpoint shared by Aristotle and Harvey: that there was some proper informing, active power in each kind of thing, making it perform according to its nature. Driesch, on the other hand, promoted a new vitalism (he called it "neovitalism"), which supposes only a very general vital evolutionary force at work in the whole universe at once, manifesting itself in various "entelechies" or goal-directed tendencies on the part of life-forms.

It is difficult to identify clearly the various forms of vitalism, precisely because the vital principle sought tended to be thought of as the kind of reality that cannot be easily understood. Like Aristotle's essences, it was the whatever-it-is that produces certain characteristic forms or behaviors. For some the vital principle was best known through philosophical speculation such as that of Schelling and Hegel about the "Spirit" in the world, a kind of cosmic divinity (reminiscent of the World Soul of Neoplatonism and some Hermetic thought).[46] For others the notion of a vital principle kept open a realm for God, as the Creator of a principle that could not arise from matter itself. For others it was simply a label for some natural force that was rather mysterious. (Thus Driesch's search for some "law" of the phenomena of life was perhaps not really a search for a "law," for a fully reliable pattern that could become part of a reliably effective understanding of life.)[47]

An issue that illustrates the arguments well is the generation of offspring. By the early eighteenth century there were two major schools of thought: preformationism and epigenesis. The word "epigenesis" stands for a belief that life can come from nonliving material, though opinions differed on what this implied. Descartes favored epigenesis, because physical life for him was the mechanistic operation of subtle elements. Harvey favored a different notion of epigenesis, following Aristotle and Galen. For Harvey a seed that generates a new generation has within it, as blood does, its own active element or aspect to cause the production of a new complex offspring, such as a chick or a stalk of wheat, out of the material at hand.[48] By the middle of the eighteenth century a form of epigenesis was championed by Caspar F. Wolff (1733–1794), a thoroughgoing rationalist who sought a fully deductive explanation of life, between "the reductionism of mechanism and the inexplicability of vitalism."[49]

Preformationism offered an alternative to epigenesis. It was first articulated by Nicolas de Malebranche in 1674, says Shirley Roe. (We can recognize in it a rough similarity to the *rationes seminales* of Stoic and Augustinian thought.) Malebranche stretched the work of a biologist, Marcello Malphighi, to argue that every egg contained a preformed copy of the parent, so that each act of generation was simply a process whereby the seed or germ found a nourishing context (womb, warm earth) in which to develop what it already was in miniature. The biggest objection to this notion was the implication that at the creation of the universe, God would have had to create a nesting of egg within egg within egg within egg, and so on. Eve would have been created (or Adam, depending on the theory of reproduction involved) with a set of preformed humans, one nested within another. The egg of a child would have within it the eggs of the grandchildren, each containing the eggs of the great-grandchildren.

Albrecht von Haller (1708–1777) supported preformationism, partly in defense of God's role in creating life.[50] He was more willing than Wolff, says Roe, to accept limits to rational understanding. He acknowledged God's mysterious work as a mystery, not as a mechanical process to be rendered fully intelligible by human investigation. But new information about the age of the Earth made preformationism less plausible. By the mid-eighteenth century geological studies were extending the age of the Earth and its inhabitants to perhaps many tens of thousands of years. The number of nestings of eggs within eggs required for preformationism was being stretched beyond plausibility.

Of more immediate impact were the many and varied empirical studies of aspects of generation—of supposedly spontaneous generation, of parthenogenesis of aphids, of the regeneration of polyps, of the development of deer embryos, of the insemination and development and dissection of fish and frog eggs, of the effect of putting taffeta pants on male frogs during mating, of the sperm in mammals including humans, of careful embryological studies of chicks and other organisms, of monstrous births (e.g., two-headed calves), of the crossbreeding of tobacco plants, of the nature of living tissue, and of attributes of sensitivity and irritability. A great deal of evidence was being created or identified, collected, and compared.[51] As work continued, the theory of preformationism shifted toward a more general notion of a prior "mold" or format contained in an organism as the principle that formed new life in womb or egg. Perhaps careful investigation of such formats would yield precise intelligibility of the processes of generation.[52]

The Aristotelian account still remained, however, as an alternative nonmechanistic theory of life and generation. In this account the forms/ essences were technically nonmaterial but were nonetheless part of the natural world. Like Haller's mode of preformationism, this theory halted explanation. It just asserted that the form of dogginess caused dogs to be dogs, that chicken eggs developed into chickens because they had chicken nature. The Aristotelian theory, it should be noted, could also fit easily with a religious understanding of life. Aquinas had no trouble in supposing that the way God had set things up was to implant in nature the order of secondary causes whereby each kind of living being begat according to its kind, and that perhaps Aristotle had the right answer in describing how God had done this.[53]

Biological inquiry continued.[54] In 1824 Jean-Louis Prevost and Jean-Baptiste Dumas provided evidence that showed sperm were somehow necessary for fertilization, though why this was so was still not known.[55] Karl von Baer published his discovery of the mammalian ovum in 1827. Darwin's theory of how all present life forms could have evolved through natural processes appeared in print in 1859, about the same time Gregor Mendel was doing his work on inheritance. Study of the cell had revealed that it could live on after the death of a larger body of which it had been a part. If there were a need for some vital principle in addition to chemical activity to account for life processes, then each cell might need its own vital principle, in addition to whatever vital principles guided the cells to coordinate with each other when part of a living body. There were getting to be a lot of these vital principles. And unfortunately none of them really contributed to an understanding of life processes. These vital principles were still unknown forces, like Aristotle's forms.

Other discoveries made the notion of vital principles even less necessary. Lavoisier established a connection between respiration and fire. Both were a form of oxidation. Careful measurement of animal and human metabolism seemed to verify that the amount of energy going into a living being was balanced by the amount of energy expended. Later physiologists noted that injury to the medulla oblongata produced trouble with breathing. Apparently it was this physical organ, not a vital breathing principle, that regulated breathing. There was no need to postulate some extra vital force as an energy source.

In these cases, as with so many others in science, there were a great number of different lines of exploration of alternative hypotheses, different models, various kinds of evidence, to determine when some particular hypothesis might or might not be worth pursuing further.[56] Neovitalism continued into the middle of the twentieth century. Joseph Needham cites a meeting of neovitalists in 1924 at Oxford.[57] They could still argue that nothing so simple as a solitary fertilized cell could possibly guide the complexity of life development from single cell to a newborn organism such as a human being. As long as evidence was lacking that a cell could do this, their position had some plausibility. The identification of chromosomes as building blocks of biological inheritance, however, carried things further. In 1953 James Watson and Francis Crick, building on the work of Rosalind Franklin in X-ray crystallography, finally developed the evidence concerning the double helix pattern of DNA.

Because of molecular biology it is now possible to give a fairly good account of just how the information encoded in DNA may be quite sufficient to guide the development of the embryo and subsequent life activities, all in what contemporary biologist Ernst Mayr still calls a mechanistic account, one not requiring any hypothetical life force or soul in addition to the physicochemical activities.[58] But now this "mechanistic" account is not one that reduces life processes to physics and chemistry alone; it is one that must emphasize another layer of causality, that of the life-code information that evolved over billions of years through a process of variation and natural selection.

The Darwinian Revolution

As biology (still often called "physiology") continued to develop in the nineteenth century, it continued to impinge upon religious belief. Religion had adapted to new theories about the heavens. It was struggling with new information about the age of the Earth. It was entangled to some extent in arguments about vital forces. Charles Darwin's particular theory of how the evolution of life might have taken place had a strong impact on religious beliefs about the order of the world and about the nature of the human person.

When Darwin proposed his theory, the idea of evolution was not new. A hundred years earlier Pierre-Louis Maupertuis had speculated on whether the species on the Earth now could have descended from earlier species, through a process something like natural selection.[59] Darwin's grandfather, Erasmus Darwin, had written a lengthy poetic defense of a theory of evolution. And the French biologist Jean-Baptiste Lamarck was well known in Charles Darwin's youth as a promoter of a particular theory of how evolution had occurred as individual organisms changed in their own characteristics through adaptation to local conditions.[60]

Darwin's *On the Origin of Species* is a compendium of natural history ranging across a wide spectrum of information, some gathered by him directly in the field and some from a vast array of reports by others.[61] Darwin agreed with the idea that had been building up for some time, that current species on the Earth had descended from earlier and different ones. The sequence of fossils in the strata of the Earth implied an evolutionary process. Many species that had existed in the past were no longer found on the Earth. The fossils that were most like contemporary dry-land species were ones generally found in the upper geological strata. Lower strata had fewer or even none of the land-based organisms that exist today. The lowest strata of all had no discernible life-form fossils. Information had also accumulated about the distribution of various plants and animals on the surface of the planet. Alfred Russel Wallace arrived at his own notion of the mechanics of evolution partly through his very detailed knowledge of the distribution of species of beetles in a tropical forest. The information available could be made sense of if it were supposed that some populations descended from neighboring ones, which in turn had descended from yet others farther away. Darwin was not saying anything very startling by arguing for "descent," the notion that current species had descended from earlier ones.

One early nineteenth-century theory about the sequence of fossils was based on a striking oddity of the geological record. It looked as though there had been mass extinctions of species every so often. At certain points in the geological strata, entire groups of fossils of species that had been abundant up to this layer suddenly disappeared. A very few layers would then show relatively few fossils of any kind. Then there would be a great increase in the diversity and number of fossils, many of them from significantly new species. An opinion favored by many was that God, for God's own inscrutable purposes, had wiped out most life at various times, in fact up to eighty or more times, by one estimate, and then created new life-forms. The evidence of mass extinctions and then the appearance of multiple new species served as extra reason to see God's hand in nature.[62] Belief in a sequence of life-forms over millions of years was here used to *support* religious belief.[63]

A belief in God's active participation in, or at least planning of, evolutionary nature's course was common.When Robert Chambers argued in 1844 that the process of biological evolution was divinely guided, he was able to rely on similar ideas of others before him. Those who were religious in a less traditional way could accept the Romantic belief in a cosmic Force, Nature as a divinity. (Spinoza's *Deus sive Natura* was one version; Hegel's evolving *Geist* was another.) Even those somewhat skeptical about religion had some belief in a patterned purposefulness to nature. Thus, in England, Herbert Spencer's popular evolutionism was quasi-religious. He claimed that the process of evolution was a directional one toward higher moral sentiment. Spencer also argued that religious beliefs are products of "the religious sentiment," a feeling which arose as part of the process of evolution and should therefore be respected as part of evolution's purpose.[64]

The aspect of Darwin's theory most disturbing to religious thought was not that evolution had taken place. It was that the mechanism of evolution proposed by Darwin was a blind mechanism. The first part of Darwin's theory was to note the natural variation among the offspring in any species, especially through sexual reproduction. This seemed somewhat random. The second part was that there was a selection process which went on in a decidedly unplanned way, as far as Darwin could tell. It occurred most frequently through the struggle for survival. Most offspring die before they can reproduce. Their particular variant characteristics are not passed on by them. The selection process included sexual selection, wherein some males would fail to mate, often because they were rejected by a female or outcompeted by another male. In either case there was a "natural selection" that determined what the next generation would be like.

This was a "mechanism" of evolution in that it required no miracles, no vital force, no guiding telos, no world soul, to make it happen a certain way. It was also rather unmechanical, however, in that life-forms seem to be the products of an unplanned and undirected process. The process was "lawful" in the limited sense that the variations in the offspring at each stage were variations on a current species, not a wildly creative process producing utterly new forms of life in a single step. The process was also "lawful" in that there was a severe weeding out of possible life-forms by the environment and the competition for survival and reproduction. As a result of natural selection, surviving species would be fairly well adapted to their environmental situation—adapted in thousands, even millions, of very specific ways through a process of what seemed to Darwin to be a process covering well over half a billion years. (We now say over three and a half billion.)[65]

There were various major disagreements with Darwin's theory. Traditional religious people opposed its treatment of Genesis. Some argued about the validity of Darwin's inductive approach, which merely assembled instances to make a plausible case rather than to prove anything. Progressivists like Spencer thought Darwin not quite bold enough. German Romantics sought a more sweeping philosophy of nature.[66]

The other major disagreement with Darwin's theory was from biology. It was the conviction that there were still aspects of life which Darwin's mechanistic theory could not explain, in particular the regeneration of wounds or even missing parts in organisms. Driesch could still argue in 1914 that "The regeneration of the salamander confutes, as is well known, the orthodox Darwinism of Darwin's followers." "The whole life-process is in no way the result of physico-chemical events, but rather controls them."[67] It was one thing to show how an existing animal could give birth to a near copy of itself, as in Darwin's theory. It was something else to show how this little copy had within it the power to guide wounded tissue to heal itself or, in the case of the salamander, to produce an entire new tail. Not just "descent" but an additional guiding force still seemed to be needed to explain the whole range of life activities.

These objections to Darwinism make it clear that there were still various models of reality being proposed. In Germany, for example, "idealistic morphology" was popular in the early twentieth century.[68] According to idealistic morphologists, each species represents a morphological type. These types were similar to the natures or essences of Platonic thought, and the fundamental way of grasping these natures was through insight or intuition, rather than through a slow, empirical accumulation of phenomenal descriptions of their external characteristics and behavior. Insight provided knowledge of the inner essence. The position was a kind of vitalism in the minds of its adherents, who sought to grasp the basic types of life in order to know and influence the basic life forces that dwelt in living beings and gave them their type-form of life.

Nineteenth-century spiritualism also fit with the Neoplatonist model. Wallace ended up attending séances and became convinced of the validity of spiritualism. He was joined in this by other scientists, such as Francis Galton. Wallace used the séances as empirical evidence of the reality of the spirit domain.[69] The Society for Psychical Research was founded in 1882 by a group of people, who included bishops, astronomers, and chemists,[70] whose intent was to provide evidence for the reality of spirits. (The evidence has continued to elude them.)

Other hypotheses about life, spirit, and matter were proposed in the nineteenth century. For a while physiognomy (faces reveal character and abilities) was popular, followed by phrenology (which absorbed physiognomy). There was a materialist assumption here: that the physical brain and its shape provided sufficient indication of the state of mind, thereby implying that mind might be nothing more than brain.[71] But no amount of materialist bias was enough to provide the evidence to support either of these theories.

A major addition to arguments for a materialist and naturalistic model of the universe was Darwin's *The Descent of Man*, which presented careful and cumulative evidence about the similarity of the human to the ape.[72] This book compares homologous traits in apes and humans: some common mental abilities, language, emotions, facial expressions, moral sense (e.g., sympathy as an instinct), even behaviors that suggest similar religious sentiments.[73] Darwin noted degrees of intelligence among various animals. Monkey intelligence emerged out of lesser forms of materially based minds, such as snails. Yet a monkey's intelligence seems much closer to that of a human person than of a snail. So it is reasonable to suppose that human intelligence was produced by further processes of evolution. If even the human person is a product of material evolution, then energetic matter may indeed be adequate to account for all events in the universe.

Darwin's theories have had obvious effects on a number of religious beliefs. The working out of a theory of evolution has provided reasons to suppose that we humans are products of natural processes, with no evidence to support traditional belief in a special creative act by God to produce each person's soul. The element of randomness in this theory is easily at odds with belief in a divine Providence that guides the processes of the universe or a divine Plan that established an order to those processes. The amount of randomness, of what seems like "waste," and of what is even a kind of cruelty, perhaps, in the process of evolution has been used against belief in a divine Plan or Providence.[74]

Darwin's theories, and the modern neo-Darwinian synthesis, have had their effect on religious beliefs not by direct attack but mainly by making highly plausible an alternative model of the story of life, one that is consistent with an inclusive naturalistic model of the story of the universe and that provides no evidence to make a supernaturalistic model plausible. Moreover, Darwin's theory of evolution fits within a large general theory of cosmic evolution today. As Richard Dawkins has expressed it, the basic law of the universe is "survival of the stable." From the time of the Big Bang some fifteen billion years ago (or something like a Big Bang, depending on what Stephen Hawking and others do with the theories[75]), the basic energy of the universe exploded into a variety of forms, some extremely short-lived (not stable), some longer-lived (more stable). The more stable forms lasted, by definition.

As the Big Bang scattered outward, its energy dissolved partly into the four basic forces and then into subsubatomic particles, most of which then united into simple atoms, especially of hydrogen but also of helium. These stable atoms make up most of the universe. As clouds of hydrogen and helium flow and fall together under gravity's influence, some clouds are large enough to form stars. In the stars the thermonuclear reactions tear apart hydrogen, and out of its particles make even more helium and other light elements. In large stars the sequence of events produces stages in which even helium is torn apart and its particles are fused into large atoms like carbon and oxygen. In the largest stars this fusion can progress to a stage where even iron and nickel and similarly heavy elements are formed. Whatever is formed, the unstable falls apart; the stable remains.

The evolution of the physical universe thereby produces the stuff out of which planets can be formed, such as iron and nickel, silicon, carbon, oxygen, and nitrogen. In many places in the universe these elements form compounds, like water and methane and carbon dioxide, that will be important for life as eventually happened on Earth. On our planet, perhaps on millions of others in the universe, more complex compounds have formed, including chains of amino acids. At least one of these amino acid chains may have turned out to be self-replicating through a physicochemical process.

Because self-replicating amino acid chains are not perfectly stable, some variants can appear. The original self-replicating amino acid chains thus produced replicas of themselves with slight differences, some more stable and some less, some able to hang together longer or replicate more quickly or reliably. Even at this prelife point in the Earth's history, a process of random variation and natural selection was at work. Eventually some sequence of this prelife process could have produced a chain of amino acids that was the information code which was the relatively simple and prelife ancestor to the DNA information code present in all living cells on this planet. The early simple form would have needed only some millions of years to produce the variants that would make protective coatings around themselves, which in turn would need only some millions of years more before some of their offspring's offspring would be doing this so complexly and on such a large scale that they would be living cells.

There are conditional words in this account: "would" and "could have." The evidence is often either too indirect or too limited for us to know what actually took place at the main points of origin—of the universe as a whole or life as we know it. Yet the large-scale story of the evolution of the whole universe and of life here on Earth is a story that has coalesced out of the last four hundred years of argument about matter and spirits, about life and generation of life, about thousands of pieces of information and another thousand kinds of experiments in physics, chemistry, biology, geology, and astronomy. The careful work of people like Galileo, Gilbert, Harvey, Newton, Lavoisier, Priestley, Haller, Darwin, and Watson and Crick are but a few crests in a vast ocean of exploration.

The story fits together in such a way as to negate many models of the universe, not by disproving them directly but by rendering them unnecessary and unsupported. Vitalistic theories, which sought some principle or power at work that guided the material and "mechanistic" processes of life, have turned out to be unnecessary and unsupported. This is not proof that there are no "souls" to guide the processes of biology. But it makes the idea of soul unnecessary. "Soul" is a hypothesis without any evidence requiring a hypothesis to explain it. Similarly, the theories of cosmic evolution and the evolution of life may have rendered unnecessary belief that the processes of the universe must somehow have been guided by God or at least planned by God. Perhaps God did nonetheless plan and guide it all. But the evidence does not seem to require an explanation beyond a full naturalism. (Chapter 10, however, will note the Anthropic Principle as a theistic hypothesis.)

The scientific model of the universe is not as rationally complete as the classical mind-set might wish. Contrary to the hopes of the seventeenth-century mechanistic philosophers, reality has turned out to have indeterminacy built into it, as far as we can tell. The evidence has indicated that energy acts in quanta—minimum doses of energy, as it were. At the level of reality that lies behind these discrete doses of energy there is uncertainty, perhaps because when we try to look at this deeper level, we always add outside disturbance to it, perhaps because reality itself at this deeper level is indeterminate in some way. Physicists are blocked by this indeterminacy from getting at what earlier generations would have called the true essences of matter-energy states, and are compelled instead to deal with models of probability. Similarly, astrophysics seems unable to get behind the Big Bang to determine what could account for it, how probable it is, whether there can be endless numbers of such Bangs, and so on.

Yet within these limits to our knowledge, within these extreme edges of our universe and of our current understanding, the ordinary laws of physics and astronomy and chemistry and geology and biology still stand, reliable and effective. These laws together and the general theories by which science understands the connections among them form a coherent and workable model of a naturalistic universe. This model fits extremely well with the evidence, as no other model does. It is not just the result of the formal operational mind's simple preference for intelligibility. It is also the result of centuries of competition among various theories, competition that slowly produced modern science's general model of the universe. The same centuries also produced a new method for science. Chapter 9 will explore that method. That in turn will establish the context for a final chapter on the status of religious thought today, in response to the scientific revolution, as part of a larger evolution of cognitive methods.

9

THE METHOD OF
MODERN EMPIRICAL SCIENCE

The goal of this chapter is to describe and defend the method of modern science, in preparation for chapter 10, on religious responses to science. This chapter will begin with a general description of late formal operational thought, and with the claim that modern science is a major locale for such thought. A quick look at some critics of science will sharpen the issue of the method of science. A following section will describe that method in seven steps, which will lead to the last section, a defense of the validity of the method of science, especially in the face of postmodern interpretations.

Late Formal Operational Thought
in Science

Modern science has its roots in the classical search for reliable universal truths that constitute true knowledge of reality, as opposed to mere opinion. From early classical times, however, skeptics in different cultures gave reasons to doubt that there were universal truths which could be held with certainty. Skeptics showed that all human judgments of truth were subject to various limiting conditions. At the most, the skeptic Carneades declared, we can obtain only well-tested probable conclusions, not "truth" itself. In recent centuries science has adopted a Carneadean probabilism. This means it has a style of thought quite like late formal operational thought.

Recall that every culture lives by concrete operational thought to a large degree (with some people apparently more susceptible than others to a preoperational fuzziness about the difference between reliable truth-claims and vivid but fictional images). Concrete operational thought is the practical daily type of thought by which we manage this problem and that, without worrying about how it all fits into some large, logically coherent scheme. Wherever there is language, there is concrete operational thought. Where there is also literacy, longer and more complex narratives provide people with a sense of their identity, history, and place in a larger order of powers or beings. The axial age added formalized logic to literacy and language. A cognitive elite in more than one culture began to raise ultimate and universal questions, about the most basic stuff and context and forces that make reality be as it is. This same cognitive elite asked basic questions about language and thought, about clarity of concepts, about the origin and validity of one's knowledge, about logic and methods of systematic analysis. The sequential accretion of language, literacy, and logic flows from the less difficult to the more difficult, roughly from preoperational and concrete operational to formal operational modes of thought, in Piaget's categories.

Recall also that the developmental history of cognitive styles includes developments in religious thought. When literacy arrived, longer mythic visions of the world overshadowed many earlier and simpler folktales, and the arena of the activities of the gods enlarged a great deal. When the axial age arrived, the gods and the myths were in turn overshadowed by thoughts about a single Ultimate One; the mythic narratives were challenged by rational analyses. At both these points of change in cultural development, religious thought adapted to the new cognitive style. Many people today still live by a rather literal concrete operational style of religious thought, by a set of beliefs about invisible beings and sacred powers and places, beliefs accepted without large-scale rational analysis and defense. Others live by a much more formally systematized theological perspective, guided by rationally organized and criticized beliefs, by a formal operational style of thought. In the last four centuries a late formal operational style has been emerging. It is most visible in the growth of modern science. A great deal of religious thought has adapted to it also, as chapter 10 will indicate.

Late formal operational thought is first of all formal operational thought, skill at systematic or logical analysis.[1] Late formal operational thought includes the added awareness that however valuable and valid systematic analysis may be, it cannot guarantee that its results are correct. Late formal operational thought is conscious of the conditional nature of all human truth-claims.[2] In individual cognitive development this may be not so much a clear stage as simply a sophistication in the use of formal operational thought. Likewise in the case of cultural development. If it is true that modern scientific method is best understood as a late formal operational style of thought, it is also true that the basic elements of this method were expressed by Carneades and perhaps skeptics in other cultures long ago. It just took a long time for one particular culture to stumble into an awareness that this is a much more powerful method for figuring out what is probably true than it might at first seem.

An awareness of the conditionedness of all knowledge is not necessarily a sign of late formal operational thought. It can be just an everyday conclusion based on experience and common sense. A person need only live long enough to notice how often we make mistakes about things. We discover error in what was once thought to be truth, mistakes in what was once taken for granted, ordinary human fallibility where its presence had been overlooked. Thus even concrete operational thought can arrive at some sort of sense that knowledge is conditional, without having first to develop competence at formal operational thought. Late formal operational thought, however, is the work of a mind that has first learned to reason systematically and then to use that reasoning ability to recognize the *intrinsically* conditional nature of systematic reason.[3]

Reasoned reflection can show that it is impossible in principle to determine whether all the conditions have been met that would allow a person to say unqualifiedly that "x" is true. How does one know there is not some as yet unseen "anomaly" (as Thomas Kuhn has taught us to say, following Ptolemy) that would require an adjustment in our theories, a major change in our beliefs? How does one know there is not some basic distortion that our mode of perception always brings to our experiences (as ancient skeptics and Kant have taught us)? How does one know that the model of reality we have created is the only one which could fit with all the relevant available data (as Aristotle and Popper have taught us to worry about)?

The history of modern science has nonetheless made it clear that well-tested probable conclusions can become so well-tested as to achieve the functional equivalence of those reliable universal truths which the classical mind sought. Modern science achieves only probable truth. But within the limits described at the end of chapter 8—the "edges" of reality, the ultimate conditions of the cosmos—modern science has constructed an extremely reliable and logically consistent network of descriptions of reality that function time after time, in application after application, in locale upon locale, for endless numbers of persons, as though they were the simple truth. Modern science has attained at least the functional equivalent of truth, sets of explanatory descriptions about reality that function in practice as though they were true.[4]

Critics of Science

Many critics of modern science argue that it does not function very well at all. They point to ways in which the projects of science are guided by the interests of those who have money and power, even when this ignores the legitimate needs of the poor and powerless. The critics point to the disastrous application of science to produce tools for killing and coercion, to pollute the planet, to indoctrinate people into harmful desires.

These complaints, however, are so broad as to be pointed not at the method of science but at the funding and application of scientific efforts. When opponents of science argue against trusting science, they often blur the difference between the method of science for learning what is probably true and the *use* of science by people. Barry Barnes, for example is a proponent of a fairly "hard" sociology of knowledge which claims that all knowledge, including science's, is so conditioned by social factors that it is not reliable. But his arguments about the reliability of science's truth-claims are off the point:

> When esoteric, technical knowledge is encountered, like that of the physical sciences, then its *use and development* is intelligible in relation to specific, context-dependent technical predictive goals and interests rather than to abstract criterion or "correspondence rules" or any other verbal formulations.[5]

This reference to abstract criterion and correspondence rules would make sense only if the reliability of the truth-claims that were at issue here, not their use and development.

Complaints of misuse of science are certainly valid (though whether the good produced by science is outweighed by the evil is the larger question). But when I speak of science achieving the functional equivalent of truth, I am speaking of the sole thing that is precisely within the competence of the method of science. Science is a method for adjudicating truth-claims. As the introduction noted, science cannot determine values. The scientific method cannot determine whose interests should be served first by science. Ethics, morality, religion, or philosophy must make such determinations. It is important that moral reflection take command of decisions about the development and application of science precisely because the scientific method is so powerful. This is also why modern science has proven to be so challenging to religious thought, so hard to ignore, even when its conclusions do not fit well with aspects of religious tradition.

New Age forms of Neoplatonism are another source of objections to scientific standards. New Age writers say that science has a falsely limiting objective approach, which overlooks the spiritual dimension. Science rejects mystical or spiritual knowledge because scientists wrongly assume reality is totally material.[6] "An assumption of the importance of spirituality may impose restrictions on human curiosity that the scientist as such is unwilling to abide by," says Jean Hardy.[7] This correctly acknowledges a goal of science: to know whatever is knowable and not to allow prior limits to be set to what may be knowable. If "spirituality" here means an order of causality that is opaque to human inquiry, then science indeed will ignore it in favor of inquiry that may produce knowledge.

But the New Age person apparently does not think of spiritual causality as opaque. Consider a recommendation by Hardy. She claims that there is a nonscientific but valid mode of thought. This is "imaginal thought," which ranges from low-level primary process thought in infants, to "choosing states," to active imagination and creativity. Hardy implies that those who fail to appreciate imaginal thought may be threatened by it. In indirect language, however, she acknowledges the importance of the standards used by science to distinguish between fantasy and fact, to use logic and evidence. In her cautious wording, people who use this imaginal method of thought:

> can threaten the authority of dogma, the supremacy of rational thought, and an empiricism that relies heavily on sense data as a direct source of information about concrete reality. When imaginal thinking is developed to its highest level, however, the individual should have a well developed capacity for distinguishing between the imaginal reality and the ordinary consensual reality and should be able to combine imaginal thought effectively with rational thought and analytical observation.[8]

Like attacks on the method of science that are really attacks on the application of science, this is diversionary language with little substance. There is no question that scientists need imagination and that they may draw upon their own imaginings and those of nonscientists as sources of hypotheses. The goal of science is then to discriminate among imaginings in order to discover which of them will operate successfully in reality as valid truth-claims. This, in fact, is a valid goal for anyone, scientist or not. Science does this by combining "imaginal thought effectively with rational thought and analytical observation." The particular power of science's method is precisely to "distinguish between the imaginal reality and the ordinary consensual reality," depending on what is meant by "ordinary consensual reality." In science the consensus sought is agreement on what the evidence indicates. Hardy writes as though she could make valid truth-claims about spiritual realities that escaped the limits of the scientific method. But in fact she describes a good imagination that must then rely on criteria of rationality and observations to distinguish which imaginings are pleasant (or unpleasant) fantasies, and which might work successfully as hypotheses about how the world really is.

Other critics of science speak against the dangers of scientific dogmatism. Morse Peckham complains: "How often a European claim to have arrived at a 'truth,' that is, a linguistic construction deserving of 'belief,' has brought about the most hideous and destructive consequences so dreadful that there is some justice in calling, as has happened, the white race of Europe the cancer of mankind."[9] Ruben A. Alves puts it as harshly as Peckham: "The ideal of truth has been part of a totalitarian thera-peutic and political program for all discourse."[10] Like Hardy, Alves wants people to recognize that science is just one game among others for com-ing to terms with reality. This attacks not just the use or misuse of sci-ence, but also the claim that science can arrive at valid truth-claims.

A somewhat more balanced analysis is provided by Richard Schlegel.[11] He rejects the attitude that says the path of science "will one day bring us to the fullness of understanding that we seek in religion."[12] Schlegel recommends recognizing that science is quite limited, and cannot give a complete account of human life and the universe. He goes on to argue that religion is more adequate to deal with feeling and intuition, with values, and with the recognition of mystery. It is easy to agree with him on all of these points. But Schlegel leaves vague the question of whether science, limited as it is, is nonetheless a legitimate method for determin-ing the probable truth of specific truth-claims about the world, including those which religion makes. It is one thing to acknowledge—correctly, I believe—that science is limited and that religion is about more than truth-claims. It is something else to imply that there are truth-claims which can correctly be affirmed to be valid without submitting those truth-claims to the general test of the scientific method: overall fit with the relevant evidence, directly and indirectly. We are a bit ahead of our-selves, however, to sum up the scientific method that simply. A more thorough analysis of the method of science is needed first.

Major Elements of the Modern Scientific Method

We can distinguish seven major elements in the methods of science over the centuries, each of which has significant implications for religious thought, as evidenced by actual responses by religious thinkers. I will assign names to three different notions of science associated with differ-ent groups of these elements, so that it will be possible to refer briefly to them in later discussion.

The first two elements of modern science are also elements of classical science:

1. Unitary naturalism
2. Universalism

Unitary naturalism is the assumption that all events in the universe can be accounted for by aspects of the natural space-time, matter-energy world and its evolutionary history. As we have seen, naturalism could take a "binary" form. It could include a universe with many "natural" but nonmaterial (spiritual) invisible beings, as in the Neoplatonist universe with its demons and angels and gods and souls at work through soul power. Or a binary naturalism could portray a world with somewhat mysterious life essences, like Aristotle's animating forms operating on inert matter, to account for spontaneous generation and other life activities. As the result of the last four hundred years of scientific development, however, when modern science now calls itself naturalistic, it usually assumes that nature consists of matter-energy forming a space-time matrix of basic forces and particles that over billions of years have interacted and evolved into all that currently exists, including us human beings and our minds and mental processes. When current philosophers and scientists speak of naturalism, they usually mean this unitary form.[13] I will follow that usage.[14] (Note that naturalism does not of itself exclude a theism that postulates God as ultimate Cause.)

Naturalism could function quite well as merely a practical strategy for modern science. If a person supposes that all events can be explained as part of the regular and reliable natural process of the universe, then, to be tautological in a useful way, that person is supposing that the events of the universe can be explained. Whoever supposes this can feel justified in seeking the knowledge that will explain things. Whoever seeks this knowledge will be much more likely to discover it, if it is available to the human mind. So naturalism is a worthwhile strategy.[15] In practice it has proved to be an exceedingly fruitful strategy.

If science's unitary naturalism is only a strategy, then science does not truly know that all events are in fact due to the regular and reliable workings of the space-time matter-energy process. There could yet be some supernatural or preternatural events which science can never identify because its strategy excludes the hypothesis that some events are due to causes beyond nature. Science deliberately blinds itself, as it were, to what might be nonnatural. Sir Arthur Eddington's famous metaphor of the fishing net with four-inch gaps could apply here. It catches no fish small than four inches in diameter. But it would be false to infer from this that smaller fish do not exist.

The second element of modern science, however, extends the reach of science to all events that occur in the universe. The second element is implied in unitary naturalism. This second element is universalism, which says that there is some ultimate unity to all things. Universalism has been part of classical science from the beginning.[16] It is one of the fundamental hypotheses of the axial-age or classical consciousness. Universalism is also part of any ideal of intelligibility. As long as things or ideas fit together logically, then it all makes sense, at least so far. In practice, on any given topic, it is local fit that is the immediate concern of the scientist. The truth-claim being tested must fit with the available evidence most directly relevant to the claim being tested. But in principle, and ultimately also in practice, the criterion of fit is universal. Anytime and anywhere there is a lack of fit among any truth-claims, whether about fact or law or theory or results, something is wrong. In the long run all ideas about all thing must fit together logically; otherwise there is a lack of coherence, which is also a lack of intelligibility.[17]

The method of comparing ideas with each other and with the apparent evidence is not restricted to science. This is the everyday method used by any person attempting to figure out anything. Everyday language makes this clear. We all try to figure out whether ideas fit with each other and whether our ideas fit the evidence, whether we are thinking coherently (coherence among ideas is a logical fit among them) or whether our ideas correspond (fit) with how things are. To fail to make sense is to say things do not fit together logically or with the evidence (with rational thought and with analytical observations, as Hardy expressed it).[18] Modern science is a set of practices and rules that guide people in applying the general rule of "fit" very carefully and precisely.

Like naturalism, universalism might also be used as only a practical hypothesis. Whoever expects that ultimately all things will fit together into one grand systematic understanding is someone who will go on trying to discover the rational coherence of things. Whoever thus keeps on trying will be more likely to discover whatever intelligibility exists. Like naturalism this has proved to be at least an exceedingly fruitful hypothesis to work with.

Classical forms of universalistic naturalism included a search for certitude. As current philosophers of science have pointed out, this normally requires some undoubtable foundation on which to build the universalist scheme of the world. Ancient Greek philosophers trusted that clear vision or insight into the natures of things provided utterly reliable premises for further logical reflection. Descartes sought a similar foundation in clear and distinct ideas, along with a trust in an undeceiving God, for his intellectual enterprise. We can sum up the classical use of the naturalist and universalist assumptions as "certitudinism" (also usually a "foundationalism"). In modern science, unitary naturalism and the universalism it implies have a somewhat less absolute status; they are practical and effective hypotheses. The next four elements of contemporary science make this clear.

The next four related elements in modern science are much more clearly modern, in the sense of being postclassical. (The word "modern" has various meanings.) These elements are

3. That all hypotheses, theories, or truth-claims must be tested empirically,
4. That the testing must be public, open to criticism by opponents,
5. That there is no point at which the testing has been completed once and for all, and
6. That all scientific truth-claims are therefore tentative, at least in principle.

If classical science is "certitudinist," these four elements make modern science "probabilist." These four distinctly modern aspects of science can be stated more briefly: "Modern science operates by subjecting all ideas to public and open-ended empirical testing."[19]

The word "empiricism," as in element 3, has had different meanings. It has been used to refer to a strict inductivism seeking knowledge as the sum of empirical instances, with a minimum of rational deduction, if any.[20] Historically, however, the most important aspect of an empirical approach has been to grant a privileged place to empirical evidence as a *test* of any truth-claims. Science in any form has always been an interplay between empirical evidence and ideas (laws, theories, hypotheses, models, paradigms) used to make sense of that evidence. In the ancient Western world philosophy functioned as the basis of much of science. As we have seen, this philosophy tended to construct very large theories on the basis of inadequate empirical experience. Any person may be tempted to support a broad theory that makes wonderful mental sense, even when the evidence for it is scant. The formal operational mind can get carried away with the intellectual beauty of some systematic analysis. Modern science, by contrast, is highly aware that empirical testing of ideas is extremely important. It shares with late operational thought in general an awareness that intellectual beauty is not enough.

Francis Bacon's descriptions of types of empirical testing illustrate the open-ended character of such testing. He lists and describes at least twenty-seven different types of evidence. There is mathematically variable evidence, blatant evidence, hidden evidence, cumulative evidence, fingerpost evidence, manipulated evidence, singular instances, instances of limit, instances of opposition, and so on. The list is long enough to begin to make it clear that there could be endless variations in the ways any idea (fact, law, hypothesis, theory, paradigm) can be tested by reference to empirical evidence. Bacon calls these forms of evidence aspects of "induction," but his description of each shows that he is not just adding up instances until general truths appear. He uses the word "induction" as a name for whatever is not simply deductive science; he uses it as a synonym for a broadly empirical approach.[21]

There are different ways of identifying this style of science. Karl Popper sums it up in two words, "conjecture and refutation."[22] According to this, science has the double task of first devising ideas about the universe, about its composition, its processes, and its history; and then testing those ideas extensively, in formally planned tests or in ongoing application of the ideas to practical tasks. The goal is to put ideas to any and all tests that might show them to be mistaken. When the testing has been carried out at length, and when no alternative idea seems to make any good sense of the relevant evidence, then the scientists may arrive at the point where there is no practical reason to doubt that the descriptions will work quite reliably and precisely as the functional equivalent of truth.

David Oldroyd's metaphor of the method of science as "the arch of knowledge" provides a slightly more complete picture.[23] The arch begins with experiences of the world, the initial evidence to be explained. The arch rises to general theoretical statements that make sense of the evidence. The arch then returns to experience, as it looks for confirmation or negation in further evidence. Along the arch the scientist applies the single basic standard of "fit." The explanatory theory must fit with all relevant evidence so far. Further confirming evidence fits with the theory and with the original evidence; any other evidence negates the theory by failing to fit with the theory.

This metaphor of the arch is too limiting at the point where the criterion of "fit" becomes universal. Empirical science shares with certitudinism the criteria of unitary naturalism and universalism. The metaphor of the network must be added, implying that every instance of an "arch of knowledge" must be integrated with every other instance in a branching lacework.[24] Every piece of information, evidence, experience, theory, law, or hypothesis about reality must fit with every other. To whatever extent there is a failure of "fit," to that extent there is something wrong that must someday, somehow be resolved if the project of science to understand the natural world is to be carried forward successfully.

The next two elements of modern science (4 and 5) are the rules that the testing must be both public and open-ended. The public-testing rule evolved from various seventeenth-century practices: public meetings of the Royal Society, extensive letter-writing, literary symposia, and so on. Ironically, the rule of public testing may have evolved partly from the spread of "books of secrets," as they were known. The alchemy, astrology, and medicine of the Renaissance were often handed on as secrets of nature, as were the truths of hermetic revelation. These secrets were originally for the elite or the adept or the initiate. As printing presses made such books of secrets widely available, the information was widely tested in countless attempts to apply it. Out in the open, where thousands of people could test it, this once secret and awesome material turned out to be largely useless. The new scientists of the seventeenth century had thereby learned the value of public sharing and testing of ideas.[25]

It was not easy to learn to share ideas publicly because there were too few precedents. Rational analysis by the learned and intelligent individual, from Aristotle to Descartes, had been more usual. The early Royal Society of London therefore had to try out various procedures for public exhibition and testing of information.[26] These demonstrations appealed to sense evidence as much as to reasoning processes. Critics compared this to carnival shows, to spectacles of interesting phenomena. This was not rational science, said the critics. Replication of experimental evidence was also difficult. There were few standard procedures and tests, limited equipment, and poor measuring devices. It took centuries of invention, of both social procedures and mechanical devices, to make public sharing of ideas and tests highly effective. Each new segment of physics, astronomy, meteorology, geology, chemistry, and biology emerged out of such social and material inventions, which were then subjected to a public and open-ended series of challenges and changes. This is evidently a messy history, full of social influence and confusions. Yet science continued to discover ways to test ideas about reality so well that college-level introductory science textbooks today contain thousands of interlocking ideas, almost all of which work with a reliability and precision one could hope for from the truth itself.

The rule of modern science (5) that testing is open-ended, is partly the result of practical experience. Most achievements in science have come from a prolonged exchange of ideas, methods, and challenges among individuals and groups. There is no scientific canon that includes a statement to the effect: "Thou shalt keep up the testing of an idea forever." But neither is there a statute of limitations on testing. Anyone who finds reason to subject an old and well-approved idea to a new test or to test it in a new way is free to do so. If the old idea fails to pass the new test, there is a problem that has to be addressed. Newton's old idea of absolute space began to fail some tests. It took some decades, but finally Einstein's description of relativity fit both with the empirical data that Newton had to work with and with newer relevant data. In light of past successes of an idea, it may be reasonable to hold to it for a time, even in the face of anomalies (i.e., some lack of fit with new evidence). But the lack of fit remains as a warning that something is wrong somewhere. For well over a thousand years, for example, the anomalies in the geocentric model of the universe proposed by Heraclitus and refined by Ptolemy made it clear that there was something wrong somewhere in their portrayal of the universe.

The rule of open-ended testing is not just a result of historical experience. It is also logically implicit in the use of empirical tests. Aristotle pointed this out long ago. The logical form of an empirical test is the following: If the idea is correct, then the empirical results will be consistent (fit) with the idea. The bare form of this argument: If A, then B. Unfortunately, if B does occur, that does not logically prove that only A could have caused it. If an elephant walks on the bridge, it will collapse. Look, the bridge has collapsed. What can we conclude? Nothing certain. The bridge might have collapsed for any number of reasons. That is why Popper calls for attempts at refutation, rather than proof, of conjectures. If B does not occur, then at least we know that A is not the case. If the bridge is still standing, then no elephant walked on it.

The practice of empirical testing could work best if it were possible to limit the number of explanations of events and to rule out all of those possibilities except one. The goal is to be able to say: "*Only* if A occurs, will B occur." Nothing but an elephant can make that bridge collapse. But as Popper has also pointed out, there is no way of knowing that there really is only one possible explanation of a collapsed bridge or anything else. Termites, a local tornado, a nearby crane with a wrecking ball, UFOs, a divine miracle—the hypotheses can be multiplied endlessly.[27]

Actual empirical testing, however, is not artificially restricted to single instances. It is open-ended in more ways than one. The rule of "fit" applies to a test of fit between every idea and the available evidence relevant to it, between every idea and every other idea related to it in any way, and therefore indirectly to the evidence related to every other idea. The test of "fit," as was said, is a universal test. The search for relevant evidence can go forth in ever-widening circles. In the case of the bridge it is possible to look for evidence of termites, to consult the weather records about tornadoes, to question local construction companies about their equipment, to ask the sheriff about UFO sightings. Only the hypothesis of a divine miracle is probably beyond any further checking of evidence (an instance again of how belief in divine interventions can bring an end to inquiry).

An ever-expanding circle of evidence and ideas provides the network against which any idea or piece of evidence must be checked. Galileo's terrestrial mechanics turned out to be good for celestial mechanics also. Spectroscopy for earth elements turned out to tell us much about the sun. (These theories exhibit the "fruitfulness" that will be mentioned later as part of Kuhn's list of "values" in science.) Atomic theory eventually made sense of chemical bonding. Ideas that turn out to fit quite well with an extensive range of both evidence and other ideas, each of which in their turn fit with other evidence and ideas, are ideas that become highly probable. Not all truth-claims can be settled one way or another. The cause of a bridge's collapse may never be able to be resolved. But some ideas in science, like mitochondria, molecular bonding, and metamorphic rock, have fit so long with so much else in so many applications, that to question their effectiveness as truth-functioning ideas is now unreasonable, unless one has new relevant evidence that does not fit with some aspect of these concepts.

Public and open-ended empirical testing undermines certitudinist foundationalism, and replaces it with a "probabilist" style of science. Results of empirical testing that continue to fit well with the idea being tested do not give strict confirmation of the idea. These positive results only indicate that *so far* there is no conflict of the idea with other ideas or evidence. Scientific conclusions must therefore be held tentatively, in principle subject to revision (although in practice that rarely happens to publicly long-tested truth-claims), open to be tested further by their fit with any other truth-claim in the ideally universal network of ideas.[28]

On the other hand, the probabilists of the modern scientific enterprise have reason to be much more impressed than Carneades with the high degree of probability that can be achieved. That is not because current philosophy of science has established theoretically what the valid method of science must be. Probabilist science is impressive because of its immense practical success at its limited task. Probabilists today possess scientific descriptions of reality that in fact work in practice exceedingly more consistently and precisely than almost any of the claims of the sciences (the natural philosophy) of Carneades' ancient Athens. That which in theory is clearly tentative, in practice has become nonetheless amazingly reliable (save again at those "edges" of cosmic reality). Moreover, these descriptions function universally. When long-tested conclusions of science are applied in various places in the world by diverse people for different purposes, those conclusions continue to function as well as the simple truth might be expected to function.

The principle of open-endedness and the tentativeness it entails provides more leeway for various religious interpretations. This is especially so where relevant evidence is ambiguous, as on an issue such as the origin and purpose of the universe, as chapter 10 will discuss. But the universalist intent of the probabilist approach is an intention to find the single coherent model of the entire universe, into which religious truth-claims must fit as well as scientific ones, as though into the single truth of things. We will see more about this topic as we proceed.

A seventh major element is not so much part of modern science as an implication of philosophical reflection on science. This element is captured by the phrase "the turn to the subject."

7. All of science, process and conclusions alike, is a human construction.

The long history of philosophical attempts to figure out what good science should be, turned out to be a history of increasing awareness of the subjective element in science. Where science long has tried to pin down reality as the objective "known," the philosophy of science has shown the presence of the subjective "knower" more and more clearly in all supposedly objective knowledge. Historians of science have joined in this exposé. So have those doing sociology of knowledge. Unfortunately, philosophers, historians, and sociologists have sometimes concluded that because science is a human construction, it cannot also have universal validity and reliability.

Constructivist Theories of Science

This seventh element of modern science has been recruited in support of theories of "social constructivism." Countless social-historical-personal factors go into the construction and retention of all human ideas, including scientific conclusions. Social constructivism interprets science as a product of some particular, and therefore "local," social interaction or discourse. Science is located in time, space, and societies. It is conditioned by cultural interests, biases, vocabulary, beliefs, and values. It is located spatially, as in European culture rather than Chinese. It is located in the lives of a particular group of people who constitute, for example, the astronomers of sixteenth-century Catholic Italy or the chemists of Protestant areas in late eighteenth-century Europe and America.

The conclusion drawn by social constructivists from this is that science does not have any universal validity; nor is any validity it achieves at a certain time guaranteed to last. The science of today may not be valid tomorrow. Science is a particular language game among other and quite different types of language games.[29] Social constructivism is therefore at odds with classical universalism. It tends to reject even the criterion of "universal fit" as used by probabilist science.[30]

Constructivism has been supported by some historians of science, following Thomas Kuhn.[31] It has been promoted by philosophers, such as Richard Rorty.[32] It has quasi-philosophical status in the form of "the sociology of knowledge," in the early form given by Peter Berger and Thomas Luckman[33] (and Europeans of the Frankfurt school) or the later form, as given by Barry Barnes.[34] Some of those favoring a "local" view of science might not accept being swept into this single category, but discussions on the nature of science have become too varied and complex to treat each of them adequately here. The justification for lumping together a variety of localists is that reasons for treating science as "local" are often all cited together by the critics of science, regardless of whether those reasons are mainly historical, philosophical, or sociological, regardless of whether the critic identifies herself or himself as a historian, philosopher, or sociologist (or theologian or historian of religion, for that matter).

Religious thought challenged by science can find a source of relief in the social constructivist approach to science. If science is local rather than universal, then let it keep to its own place; let it leave room in other social spaces for various kinds of religious thought and practices. As we will see, this argument is a significant part of "postliberal" theology. It matters to religious thought, then, whether the probabilist or the constructivist account turns out to be more plausible in the longer run.

A priori it would seem difficult to begin to figure out whether a constructivist or probabilist account is more plausible without being utterly circular. On the constructivist assumptions, the plausibility of either of the accounts is a matter of social place. If the probabilist account wins an intellectual vote, for example, the constructivist will say that this victory is simply a matter of the social conventions of a certain group at a certain time and place. At a later time, a different account may become socially accepted. On the probabilist account, the one with the best evidence will win out. But the constructivists claim to have historical and social evidence on their side (even though it is not clear why they should appeal to evidence, as though empirical evidence were the determining factor, as the probabilists say it is). In spite of all the potential for confusion here, I will review some of the evidence used by the constructivists, to see how well it may support the constructivist case.[35]

There are five major points in the constructivist case. The first is the interdependent or "network" character of all knowledge. A foundationalist in science would need some initial knowledge that is not dependent on other knowledge. The constructivists follow W. V. Quine in arguing that there is no such independent knowledge.[36] Quine's famous illustration is the sentence "All bachelors are unmarried men." That sounds like a self-evident proposition because of the tautology it contains. Perhaps, then, it is an instance of foundational knowledge that is true of itself and not because it depends on other knowledge. Yet Quine points out that it is not true that all bachelors of arts nor all bachelor buttons are unmarried men. The first sentence seems self-evident, provided a person first knows what the word "bachelor" means in this particular context. This knowledge is dependent upon learning language use from the culture.[37] Quine goes on to show how all statements, whether analytic or synthetic (logical or empirical), are intelligible and/or valid only as part of a larger network of meanings. There is no knowledge not conditioned by other knowledge.[38] Quine's argument is more complete than this brief illustration might suggest. But we can grant his basic point: There is no set of foundational truths independent of other truth-claims.

Quine's idea of networks can be used to support a local-construction-of-knowledge theory. If there are many local and quite different networks of ideas, then each network appears more arbitrary. If science is itself a network, it must compete with other networks, including those from nonscientific cultures. But science is more ambitious than this. As a universalist approach to knowledge, it strives to construct a universal network of ideas (fact-claims, theories, laws, paradigms). Every event in the universe has the potential to put some scientific idea to the test of whether that idea fits with the evidence. Similarly, the network of scientific theories that fit well with a great deal of evidence and with other well-evidenced theories casts doubt on any truth-claims that do not fit with that network of ideas.

The universalist intent of science evokes the kind of charge leveled by Ruben Alves earlier in this chapter: "totalitarian." Here is science laying claim to be able to pass judgment on the probable validity of all truth-claims made anywhere in the world. Surely this is blind arrogance, the critics say.

We can acknowledge that the method of science is too limited for metaphysical truth-claims about the ultimate nature and source and destiny of everything. A later section in this chapter will elaborate on this.

What science tells us about the whole universe may incline us to speculate and even to feel some confidence about our speculations. But what the philosophers and theologians call the utterly transcendent or the truly ultimate context of all else escapes the grasp of the method of science.[39] Yet within that limit, within the realm of the universe as we have it, science indeed aspires to put every truth-claim in its single network.

Science will also fall short in another very important area, the area traditionally known as the humanities. Very much can be known scientifically about art, music, and literature. But the level of complexity of human experiences, feelings, and thoughts expressed in art, music, and literature is very high indeed. The inner and personal experiences of even one person can only be approached by the arts; the varieties of experiences and values among many people are more difficult yet to grasp. Science will contribute a great deal of background knowledge to enrich the humanities, but that will make human experiences of all of these even more complex and more difficult to capture. At the same time, the network of truth-claims that science constructs can be relevant to the art, music, literature, and experiences of people of all cultures.

When science challenges the traditional beliefs of a culture by its universalist claims, this is an old story, as old as the demythologization wrought by axial-age formal operational thought upon the myths of the gods. Anthropologists are correct in their value judgment, I believe, that scientific cultures have no right to insult or coerce peoples of other cultures. But the scientific method will still be quite effective in judging the probable accuracy of truth-claims made by those cultures—about the relative efficacy of medicinal plants, for example, or the power of sorcerers beyond their psychological impact. Likewise, it has been effective in judging whether some truth-claims in Western history were valid, from belief in various types of miracles, to the movement of the Earth around the sun, to belief in witches' demonic powers. The scientific method broke into the network of traditional Western ideas and proved effective in changing that network toward greater accuracy of truth-claims.

When deciding whether there can be a universalist network of scientific ideas, it is appropriate to remind ourselves of our common humanness. Cultural relativism claims that different cultures have radically different networks of ideas. But recall the claim in the introduction that in spite of manifold and deep differences among cultures, they are still all human cultures. A brief note in the introduction referred to Donald Brown's *Human Universals*. From his annotated bibliography at the end, here is an abbreviated list of things that humans in general share:

> bipedal walking, need for food, digestion, elimination, need for water, susceptibility to weather extremes, opposable thumbs, sleep and dreams, tiredness, vision, sense of smell, hearing, taste, fondness for sweets and fats, tactile information and pleasure, pleasure and pain,

comfort and discomfort, sexual interest and arousal, fear, anger, calmness, facial expressions correlated with emotions, normal range of personality, language use, innate tendency to practice sounds, universal grammatical forms, storytelling/narrative to interpret reality, kin favoritism, anthropomorphizing of natural forces and things, belief in entities not directly observed, a distinction between self and others, status and roles, division of labor by age and/or sex, group regulation of sex, marriage, and other behaviors, rules and leadership for allocation of resources, leadership practices, early socialization by parents and kin, interaction with children, caregiving, affection, distinction between public and private, etiquette, using facial and bodily expression to communicate, using hands interpersonally to fight, stroke, and groom, games, ritual, artistic expression, joking, procuring and processing raw materials, tool use, use of fire, body decoration, metaphor, daily routines, need for novelty, conscious awareness of memory, making of decisions, self-responsibility, psychological language, classification of things, consciousness of birth and death, care of ill or injured, knowledge of relationship between sickness and death, positive death customs.

Such human commonalities make it possible for people everywhere to learn each other's languages, to recognize common interests, needs, fears, and hopes. Our networks of ideas include these common elements in some form or another. Humans everywhere also share in modes of thought, in preoperational imagination, in concrete operational common sense, in the everyday "science" of formulating ideas and testing them by trial and error. We can presume that people in all cultures have the capacity for formal operational thought, including the later form of such thought that constitutes modern empirical science.

All in all, the network nature of our knowledge is indeed a legitimate basis for rejecting a certitudinists or foundationalist understanding of science. But it is indirectly a support for a science whose basic test of any truth-claim is "universal fit"—the ever-increasing network of coherence among the truth-claims in all the realms of science. It is in fact the method that has become foundational here, the method of devising ideas about reality and then testing them all by the criterion of fit, both locally and (in principle) universally. (We will talk more about this in relation to the fifth major point of constructivism.)

A second major point in the constructivist case is based on historical evidence of social determination of knowledge. Thomas Kuhn in particular, but also Paul Feyerabend and, more recently, Steven Shapin and Simon Schaffer, have appealed to this historical evidence.[40] Kuhn began with a book on the Copernican revolution.[41] He noted what he called various "biases" in the work of Copernicus and those who entered into the arguments after him. A Neoplatonist love of harmonies, a Hermetic glorification of the sun, an aesthetic appreciation of the heliocentric order, all contributed to the Copernican position.[42] Kuhn also suggests that the eventual victory of Copernicanism was due to social agreement. After a century of Copernicanism, says Kuhn, heliocentrism became accepted because even the strangest idea finally becomes plausible once people get used to it.[43]

This set the stage for Kuhn's full theory of the social dimension of science. In his *The Structure of Scientific Revolutions*, with its well-known use of the notion of "paradigms," Kuhn highlights instances of what he sees as changes in scientific knowledge that were produced not by an objective and consciously rational process which followed the evidence, but by the flow of social convention. He analyzes instances from the history of science, especially the Copernican revolution, the discovery of oxygen, and the shift from Newtonian space to Einsteinian space-time, and includes comments on the discovery of Uranus and X-rays, and the development of the periodic table. In his description of the histories, social approval overrides other criteria in determining which theories gain acceptance. Scientists ignore evidence contrary to a paradigm that is well-established in the scientific community, using "secondary elaborations" to protect theories against such anomalies. Social acceptance of the paradigm blocks new tests of its validity because scientists will ignore or explain away any anomalies.

But, ironically, as Kuhn reviews the historical evidence, he tends to overlook his own evidence that it was evidence, not social approval, which sifted through the various truth-claims and determined the winner. Kuhn's treatment of evidence stumbles partly because he says little about the long-term process of scientific disputes. Kuhn notes various short-term errors, concluding that because Galileo, for example, was wrong about the tides and the circular orbits of the planets, his Copernicanism must have won out because of rhetorical success or social pressures. In retrospect it is quite easy to see that the Copernican theory, adjusted by Kepler and others, "won" because long-term public testing and development and further testing of the ideas over a few centuries gradually produced a set of truth-claims about the structure of the solar system which fits the evidence quite precisely. The same is true of the decades of investigation leading to the discovery of oxygen, and the confirmation of this idea by its long and many successful applications, as well as by its good fit with the periodic table, with discoveries about the construction of the atom, and with the development of modern chemistry in general. Modern science is a long-term, open-ended process. All along the path, evidence counts.

Kuhn's case should not be that evidence counts for little in science. Kuhn spends a great deal of time citing specific evidence that made scientific inquirers change their minds, try new lines of thought, support certain conclusions. The strongest case he might make, given his own accounts of Copernicanism, the discovery of oxygen, and so forth, is that evidence was often ignored or badly interpreted out of conformity to social pressures, personal bias, or habitual acceptance of a reigning paradigm. Indeed, Kuhn cites various instances when awkward evidence was not allowed to serve as refutation of some hypothesis or theory.

The instances are illuminating. Kuhn praises Copernicus for "the painstaking detail" of his mathematical analyses of the skies, to show how his heliocentric theory fit quite precisely with the whole range of evidence. Kuhn explicitly attributes this, however, not to a concern for precise fit of theory with evidence, but to Copernicus's love of geometrical harmony. He treats Copernicus's concern for fit with the evidence as though it were just a matter of personal bias.[44] Kuhn lists other biases influencing Copernicus—Neoplatonist, Pythagorean, aesthetic.[45] But this list follows five pages describing ways in which Ptolemy's theory did not fit well with the evidence. As Kuhn notes, by the time of Copernicus, the small errors in Ptolemy's system had added up to many days of calendar error. Copernicus may well have had many biases, and in his writings made rhetorical appeal to the biases of readers. But by Kuhn's own account Copernicus appealed in detail to ways in which his version of a heliocentric system solved many of the problems by fitting better with the evidence.[46]

Kuhn also uses somewhat misleading language when he claims that it was aesthetic rather than "pragmatic" reasons which made Copernicus's theory attractive to others. The major aesthetic value Kuhn cites is the degree to which heliocentrism explained things more "neatly" than the geocentric theory.[47] But in Kuhn's own account this again means that Copernicus's theory fit well with various pieces of evidence. The apparently regular recurrence of retrograde motion of the planets, their variations in brightness, the duration and speed of planetary orbiting, the proximity of Venus and Mercury to the sun, the precession of the stellar order over centuries, were pieces of evidence that Copernicus could account for better than Ptolemy had. Later, Kuhn repeats his same theme: "Copernicus' arguments are not pragmatic. They appeal if at all, not to the utilitarian sense of the practicing astronomer, but to his aesthetic sense and to that alone."[48] Kuhn has a valid point, that even though Copernicus's system brought the calendar up to date, it was not going to be more exact and effective in astronomical calculations than Ptolemy's. Yet Kuhn's words are misleading. He has presented pages of Copernicus's careful appeal to specific evidence. Copernicus could say, as Kuhn himself tells us, that his system made sense of more pieces of evidence than Ptolemy's, even if it was not superior in practical application to navigation and timekeeping.

As Kuhn continues with a description of the reception of Copernicus's theory, the place of evidence in the subsequent arguments is front and center. Provide evidence, evidence, evidence was the call from Robert Bellarmine, Tycho Brahe, Johannes Kepler, Galileo, and others, even as

Kuhn tells the story. Make it all fit together coherently with the evidence. But Kuhn's interpretation of the result is again odd: "Somehow, in the century after Copernicus's death, all novelties of astronomical observation and theory, whether or not provided by Copernicans, turned themselves into evidence for the Copernican theory. That theory, we should say, was proving its fruitfulness."[49]

This statement is odd because of the "somehow" at the beginning and the expression "turned themselves into" toward the end of the sentence. Kuhn has himself piled up the evidence that Copernicans looked at. Some of it was old evidence seen in a new light. Some of it was new evidence: from Galileo's telescope, from Brahe's precise observations, from Kepler's discovery of elliptical orbits and his laws of the motions of the planets, from observation of the orbit of a comet, from the startling supernova of 1572. Though Kuhn himself cites the evidence, he then sums things up in such a way to obscure the role it plays, and appeals instead to bias and aesthetic values.

The tendency to obscure the role of evidence increases in Kuhn's later work, *The Structure of Scientific Revolutions*. Here he repeats the frequent theme in the earlier book, the role of bias and values. But now he emphasizes much more the factors that sustain "normal science" (i.e., a well-accepted paradigm) in the face of anomalies (evidence contrary to the paradigm). Kuhn's account of the response to such "crises" minimizes the impact of evidence. Normal science gets its criteria of success, he says, from the science itself. Results that confirm the normal science are good results; those which do not, must somehow be wrong. Students of science, Kuhn argues, learn by authority that the normal account must be the true one. They apply it; *it works*; they do not doubt it.[50] (Kuhn does not seem to notice that he has included continuing effectiveness of a theory as evidence in its favor.)

Kuhn's point is partly valid. When anomalies appear in applying a theory that has long functioned well, there are various good reasons why the anomalies should not be taken too seriously. Laboratory work, from high school chemistry onward, is subject to problems of measurement, instruments, temperature or other atmospheric conditions, and so on. Furthermore, it often happens that a theory needs adjustment or expansion in order to continue to work well. The discovery of different isotopes of basic elements, for example, started with some anomalies and ended up leading to a more precise and accurate knowledge of atomic weight and structure. Yet Kuhn also notes that when anomalies continue and accrue, scientists do take this evidence quite seriously. That is why there are "crises" in science, as Kuhn calls them.[51] There are no crises when a theory or paradigm is working well, which means it fits with expectations. This is confirming evidence. Kuhn's own description of the process of science acknowledges the controlling role of evidence in the work of science, even though his commentary on those descriptions points much more strongly to bias and interests and habit than to the role of evidence.

This is not the place to attempt a full analysis of Kuhn's theory of scientific developments.[52] It is important only to say enough to argue that any claim that science is merely a "local" enterprise, guided by subjective or social values of a given place and time, does not hold up. Current religious thinkers who dismiss challenges from science as from only another and different local community may have more work ahead of them. The universal validity of modern science for its limited task is difficult to deny.

A third major claim by constructivists is that science is guided by values rather than by objective criteria or evidence. We have seen Kuhn making this claim. He has provided a list of values used by scientists. Rorty cites this list as evidence that values, not evidence, guide science.[53] The list nonetheless shows a variety of ways in which any theory or concept might be checked to see how well it fits within the network of meanings of a culture. Here is the list, with bracketed comments added by me, to show how it is a list of checking for "fit" with the overall network.

> First, a theory should be accurate: within its domain, that is, consequences deducible from a theory should be in demonstrated agreement with the results of existing experiments and observations. [The theory should fit with observations.] Second, a theory should be consistent, not only internally or with itself, but also with other currently accepted theories applicable to related aspects of nature. [It should fit with other theories.] Third, it should have broad scope: in particular, a theory's consequences should extend far beyond the particular observations, laws, or subtheories it was initially designed to explain. [Its consequences should fit with other fact-claims and theories.] Fourth, and closely related, it should be simple, bringing order to phenomena that in its absence would be individually isolated and, as a set, confused. [It should show how many phenomena fit together.] Fifth . . . a theory should be fruitful of new research findings: it should, that is, disclose new phenomena or previously unnoted relationships among those already known. [It should fit increasingly with many other phenomena, theories, and fact-claims.][54]

Kuhn claims he is listing certain "values" that guide science. But the values turn out to be five different ways of speaking about how theories and observations can be checked for "fit." Someone else might find four or seven or twenty-nine ways, just as Bacon identified twenty-seven ways in which ideas can be checked against evidence. There is no single list of criteria concerning how science works because there are potentially endless ways of checking for "fit." This method of "fit" seems to be the sole effective means we have for checking on the reliability of any of our ideas, whether in science, philosophy, religion, or commonsense matters. Our truth-claims are sustained by the network of ideas according to how well they fit with each other. We all make exceptions to this. We all hold to beliefs that would not fit very well if we checked carefully. But we also end up having to admit that there is something wrong on those occasions when we do have to check carefully and discover that there is a lack of fit.

A fourth major point in the constructionist case is the claim that the idea of "fit" is hopelessly vague. If science, that enterprise which requires great precision, is to use "fit" as its criterion, then the word must be defined quite precisely and clearly, it would seem. Yet if there are indeed more than twenty-seven kinds of evidence, as Bacon argues—perhaps endlessly more kinds—then there are endless possible ways in which some evidence could "fit" with an idea. Precision appears impossible.

We cannot define with any precision what we mean by "fit" because this word stands for the most basic function of our minds. We put things into categories without knowing how we know that one thing fits there and another does not. We have learned the categories from our culture and have learned what fits into those categories by a continuing learning process. But we cannot say much about how our brains are able to do this. We likewise recognize logical fit or lack of logical fit, but we cannot say how our brains do this. We recognize when what we mean by a fact-claim does not fit with other fact-claims or other ideas (laws, theories, etc.) We can look at $2 + 2 = 4$ and say that is correct. We do not know what our mind has done except to "see" there is a logical fit between $2 + 2$ and 4. We do it instantly and with ease. We do not know how our brains do this, any more than we know how they make our feet move when we decide to walk. Yet we do walk; and in practice we do fairly well in judging for fit.

Thus science is a set of practices that aid people in applying the everyday mental ability of judging how well things fit or do not fit. The practices of science aid people in doing this with precision and exactness, with full reflective awareness of possible sources of error, and with long-term public criticism. The methods of science are techniques to aid us in that practice, so that our judgments are increasingly exact and reliable. Judging from the results, they are very productive practices.[55]

The fifth major point in the constructivist case hovers in the background, not often explicitly noted. It is the Kantian point: that all our ideas about reality, even if they were not socially conditioned and were not biased by values, are nonetheless constructions of the human mind and senses. Our cognitive abilities are not pure openness to truth; they are programmed, as we might say today, to reflect reality in certain unavoidable ways. Our sensations and ideas are forced into certain interpretive forms. Even more than Kant knew, we are products of an evolutionary history that has formed our neural system to perceive the world in certain ways. We never know the world directly as it is; we know only our own knowledge of the world—how it seems to us. This is the phenomenal world, the world as it appears, which is not necessarily the world as it is. Because the world as it appears to us is partly a product of human senses and image-making, it is to some indeterminate degree a "fictive" world.[56]

As Kant also said, however, this phenomenal world is our *entire* world. Whether there is some different noumenal world behind it is an interesting philosophical question, perhaps. If a person were seeking to establish a philosophical justification of science, a justification that achieved the kind of certitude that Descartes sought, then the possibility that there is a "real" world behind the world as it appears to us, a world significantly different from the world as it appears, would make such justification unachievable. But modern science is much more pragmatic in its approach to the world.

Modern science has accepted the world of appearances and has laid upon it the expectation that it will be an intelligible world, where the events are all part of a natural and "mechanical" (or energist) whole, where the validity of truth-claims can be tested by their fit with all other truth-claims. This expectation might not have worked. The world as it appears to us might have turned out to be chaotic and largely unintelligible. As we have seen, it might have turned out that a careful attentiveness to the world of appearances would yield a polytheistic, concrete operational result: a world of events that do not cohere in any overall way. Or it might have turned out to be a monotheistic world in which a high degree of "slack" and a lot of divine interventions obviated the effective use of the criterion of universal fit. Or it might have been a world of Neoplatonic forces subject to magical control, or a world of Aristotelian essences opaque to further inquiry. But after more than twenty-five hundred years of attempts at understanding the world (perhaps minus the half-millennium of the early Middle Ages), of speculation and trial and error, a scientific model of reality has emerged that works so well that philosophical uncertainties do not stand in the way of its effectiveness at its limited task. It may be only the world of appearances with which science deals. But that is the entire and single human world of appearances. It is the whole unitary and universal nature that we encounter and interpret in an increasingly complex and wide-reaching, coherent network of ideas. The only other universes are indeed "imaginal."

An important final aspect of modern science is the degree to which certain values are unavoidably connected with it. Scientists uphold an ideal of objectivity. In spite of the various inescapable subjective factors in every human endeavor, including science, the method of public and open-ended testing means that a variety of people, with different subjective interests, biases, and habits, place demands on each other to take perspectives other than the individual person's original views. By seeking a universally workable set of ideas, science is seeking that which can function as objective truth, truth-claims not dependent on subjective factors except those shared by intelligent human beings anywhere. This value guides people to stretch beyond individual and local perspectives to find what might work as valid truth regardless of local perspective. As Ian Barbour puts it, science seeks "intersubjective testability" and "commitment to universality" as its equivalent of "objectivity."[57]

Bernard Lonergan speaks of "intellectual conversion," using the religious metaphor deliberately. The conversion to the general empirical method of science is an opening of oneself to the possibility of evaluating truth-claims not on the basis of what one would like to be the truth, not because a certain belief is imaginative and fun, or traditional and cherished, or socially approved or emotionally comforting, but on the basis of adequate evidence and reasoning. (In Lonergan's scheme this parallels a moral conversion in which a person learns to seek broadly valid values instead of just personal satisfaction.) Another way of saying this is that modern science places a demand of intellectual honesty on the person. Scientists are perhaps no more honest as persons than are people in general. But the rule that every truth-claim must be submitted to the court of public long-term testing is a rule that enforces a kind of honesty in the end.

Science is thus also antiauthoritarian. It is legitimate for any person to doubt any conclusion of science, to dissent from whatever scientific tradition has thus far held strong. This implies a certain degree of individualism as well. Each person has the right to challenge the conclusions of others. Science is egalitarian in that any person may make these challenges. There is a significant practical limit to egalitarian individualism. Scientific practices include the expectation that a person raising a doubt has evidence which justifies the doubt. Any person can proclaim a state of doubt on the general basis that some alternative account is always in theory possible, that science does not know everything, that the conclusions of science must in principle be open to revision. Who knows, after all, that there really exist such things as bridges and elephants, or that UFOs are not visiting nightly? General doubts of this sort are useless. They are the intellectual equivalent of saying that the history of Earth, after all, just *might* be guided by the Buddha and Jesus working in tandem from Venus and Mars, where they now dwell. Indeed, anything is possible; on the basis of consistent experience as evidence, however, we know that some truth-claims are not to be taken very seriously as truth-claims.

Others have argued that there is a basic faith operating in science, a faith in the validity of the scientific method as well as a faith that reality is intelligible. Perhaps we can legitimately call it a faith, or at least a hope or expectation, that reality is intelligible. But it is by no means a blind faith or an unjustified faith. This faith was once just a hopeful hypothesis. It has been confirmed by the ongoing success of science in living by it. This success confirms the practical efficacy of the scientific method. Science contains a further faith in the human capacity to discover more and more of the intelligibility of reality through the exercise of reason and empirical investigation, following the basic rules about public and long-term testing. This faith also is confirmed by science's success, in the limited but important realm of determining which truth-claims about reality will work so reliably and accurately that they function as though they were the simple truth. Continued success makes all these kinds of faith well justified.

A more difficult faith may lie in the trust that is it truly worthwhile to discover more and more of the truth (or its functional equivalent). This is faith in the ultimate worthwhileness of being a knower in this universe.[58] The ongoing enterprise of science is perhaps an implicit act of trust that human achievements in science have fundamental meaning or value. There are obvious pragmatic values: We can prevent polio and feed more millions than we once could. But implicit in every human activity is the existential and religious question of whether any activity finally has value. Time comes and time goes, and everything might grow cold in the end. Like every human activity except suicide, perhaps, the enterprise of science may have an implicit religious affirmation hidden within it. This religious question, however, is a topic for chapter 10.

10

RELIGIOUS RESPONSES
TO MODERN SCIENCE

Previous chapters recounted the stages of cognitive styles through millennia of cultural development, the effect of those cognitive styles on religious thought, and their part in the development of scientific thought. A purpose of tracking both religious and scientific thought through so many centuries is to be able to make sense of aspects of the current cultural cognitive context—where we are today. Interactions between religious thought and science illustrate major alternative options available to us on how to think about whatever it is we consider worth thinking about. The various forms that religious thought takes today illustrate basic human alternatives about how to be rational, or whether to try to be rational at all.

We have seen that throughout history, religious thought has had multiple kinds of relations with science. In both primitive and archaic cultures, religion was not really distinguishable from what might be called the science of those cultures. Primitive religion explained many events in the universe as the effect of invisible beings and forces, of spirits and magic, that were thought of as part of the natural order. The same is true of the great cosmogonic myths of archaic literate cultures. These explained the natural universe as the outcome of the activities of gods. The relation between science and religion became more ambivalent with the appearance of the great classical philosophies in major cultural centers. The new philosophies opposed or transformed the old polytheistic religion. Yet many of these philosophies were still religious, giving a new universalizing form to religion rather than abolishing it. At the same time these classic philosophies were a kind of science. They did not have a careful method of public and long-term "conjecture and refutation," but they did attempt to explain the basic forces and processes and stuff of the universe.

The troubled interaction among natural philosophies and the older religious views in classical times was a foretaste of later problems and possibilities, from the tensions in late medieval theology and natural philosophy, through the centuries of early modern science. In each of these periods the formal operational thought style in theology and philosophy was somewhat at odds with religious thought, which kept the universe open to unpredictable and irregular miraculous interventions or to ongoing supernatural activities. Most recently, both the conclusions and the methods of modern science are putting new pressures on traditional religious beliefs. Religious thinkers vary in their responses.

Modes of Religious Thought Today

The Method of "Personal Appeal": Imagination and Credulity in Religion Today

In both individual and cultural development, there are signs of an inventive imagination as soon as there is language. The ability to develop new ideas or new combinations of old ideas is the core of creativity. This is a valuable talent. It remains valuable through the whole history of life, individually or culturally. It works best, though, if it is taken up and transformed by more complex overall thought patterns and experience.

The products of imagination may remain relatively simple for people growing up in a society with relatively limited experiences and with relatively limited vocabulary. Cultural development aids creativity and inventiveness by providing more mental and experiential material for each person to work with. Thus people in primitive cultures, as intelligent as people everywhere, do not produce such an extensive range of art, music, architecture, and science as do people of other cultures. Equally important are means of distinguishing between imagination and sound factual judgment. To imagine that there are berries in the field will not feed one's family; the berries must actually be there, or at least there must be a reasonable basis for assuming the berries might be there, for one to use time and energy to go out looking for them.

In individual development, imagination is at first poorly constrained by reality. Preoperational thought in children lacks the ability to distinguish very well between ideas that are vivid and appealing and ideas that are also probably true. There are a variety of popular beliefs today among adults that seem to represent a similar lack of skill, or perhaps a lack of interest, in making such distinctions. New Age beliefs in general suffer from this. The New Age repertoire of beliefs constitutes a contemporary animism, with spirits and magic abounding. Crystals alter a person's mood. Adept individuals channel the spirits of ancient beings. Strange new stories, with no community tradition to support them, attract believers. UFO abductions have multiplied in recent years, for example.[1]

Belief in strange beings or powers does not arise from preoperational credulity alone. Primitive people make an intelligent inference when they conclude that events with no visible causes must have invisible causes. These people then rely on community tradition as a depository of explanations. Similarly, an adult in the era of modern science may be persuaded by what looks like good evidence for an otherwise improbable power or event. But crystal power and channeling seem remarkably short on evidence or on a community tradition to vouch for them. Simple credulity must receive much of the credit for the popularity of such beliefs.

Credulity is often harmless. It is a benign credulity to believe that the image of the Blessed Virgin in a tortilla, or the face of Jesus on an oil tank, is a supernatural miracle. But there are dangerous forms of credulity. Innocent people have been sent to jail because "therapists" managed to get little children to testify that their teachers sexually molested them over long periods in classrooms, killed animals as sacrifices to Satan, and engaged in other behaviors that collectively are so incredible that one wonders at the credulity of the therapists (as well as of the prosecutors). Parents have been accused of extraordinary kinds of sexual molestation by their adult children, who had no memory of this until some therapist helped the person "recover" these memories.[2] The evidence in many of these cases is about as good as the evidence of witchcraft in the seventeenth and eighteenth centuries.

Whether credulity is a sign of genuinely preoperational thought is difficult to say. We can suppose that credulity in adults is not identical with a child's inability to understand the difference between a vivid and appealing idea and actual reality. The point here is only to indicate that there is a kind of credulity, one associated at times with religious beliefs, which is highly similar to the uncritically imaginative thought style that appears in early childhood and in cultures where further means of evaluating truth-claims are not well developed.

If one had to assign a name to the *method* used here, it would be "personal appeal." It is enough that an idea appeal strongly to a person for the idea to be accepted as true. Every person undoubtedly has this inclination. There are many ideas we would like to be true. It would be fascinating if UFOs were spaceships piloted by alien beings, and comforting if those beings were also benevolent. It would be handy to have crystal power at one's fingertips, ready to alter one's mood or character as needed. Fortunately, however, "personal appeal" is not the sole method most of us rely on when making judgments of truth or falsity, fact or fiction.

The Method of Relying on the Authority of Community Tradition in Religion Today

In later childhood, from around the age of seven or so, distinguishing between fact and fiction gains importance. Imagination is trimmed to fit both daily evidence and the authority of older people, who, it is assumed, know the truth of things. In everyday life the package of truths possessed by the community stands as a corrective to wild imagining. So community tradition provides significant control over the output of imagination. This is true for the individual person in childhood; it is true also for cultures that have not yet developed skills at formal operational analysis and therefore must rely more on a concrete operational trust in authority.

Concrete operational thought does not look for an overall logical unity to the universe. It does not try to construct a coherent analysis that makes all aspects of reality fit into one logical system. Instead, it collects facts and tells stories. When literacy is added to this normal human means of understanding reality, the stories may become long and complex, with a degree of internal coherence to the sequence of events. But these stories, like life itself, contain surprises, historical contingencies, and, in most cultures, unpredictable interventions by invisible beings.

As earlier chapters have said, this is the normal thought style of most of us most of the time. Religious thought also is mostly of this normal human type. The great mythologies of preclassical literate cultures are outstanding examples. So are the classic epics of India, and stories in the Hebrew Bible and the Christian New Testament. These stories gain most of their authority from their status as revered tradition. Even the formal doctrines of classical religions are usually accepted by most religious people as authoritative and true because those doctrines are tradition, not because they live up to some systematically rational criteria.

Like other modes of thought, the concrete operational style has both good and bad aspects. Stories have power to guide and inspire, much more than bald fact-claims or abstract analyses. The testing of stories by their application in the life of a community probably molds the stories into forms that often benefit those who tell them. Nevertheless, stories can also promote rules that hurt. When community tradition and its stories are unbounded by any higher criteria of truth and value, they can be rather destructive. Some mythic tales have justified human sacrifice; others have promoted the destruction of outsiders. Archaic societies dominated by concrete operational thought are quite normal in their tendency to disparage those in their group who are different from societal norms. They are normal in their tendency to defend their traditional ways by attacking foreigners. Today Christians find texts in their tradition that justify anti-Semitism or hatred of homosexuals. Muslims in some countries have pushed women back behind layers of veils and repression. Not all the many antagonisms in the world between different religious groups can be attributed to a concrete operational style of thought, but allegiance to the identity-giving stories of the community and its tradition is often precisely what drives some of the destruction done in the name of religion.

Unfortunately, traditionalism is not very reliable for judging the validity of *truth-claims*.[3] It may be that most religious traditions function quite well in providing moral guidance, inspiration in crises, a sense of identity and belonging. These are valuable functions. A tradition that does all these things well is perhaps worth cherishing. But it is nonetheless possible that the same tradition may have errors in its truth-claims. In religion in particular it is quite easy to see that different communities, each with different traditions, make different truth-claims, some of which conflict directly with one another. Some additional basis is needed for determining which, if any, are more probably true or at least more probably closer to the truth. Furthermore, historical research sometimes shows that over the history of a single religious community the tradition has changed. People follow their community's truth-claims as though they constituted the single unchanging truth, even when the community has modified or rejected aspects of the tradition over the centuries. The question then is how the community knows that it is correct to change tradition in a certain way. It would need some other standard besides loyalty to tradition in order to evaluate the truth or falsity of tradition.

There is more than one kind of traditionalism. A first obvious kind is Fundamentalism. This was first the name for the early twentieth-century Protestant movement that reaffirmed traditional belief in the literal inerrancy of the Scriptures and in the many miracles attested to in the Scriptures. The name has often been extended to any religious movement that seeks to reestablish older tradition in a fairly literalist way. Thus Islamic movements in Egypt and Iran, or Hindu movements in India, have been called Fundamentalist. Other forms of traditionalism have shown more openness to negotiate, as it were, with the conclusions and methods of formal operational philosophical theologies. This was a major project of the late Middle Ages for Christianity. It was received less well among earlier Islamic leaders. There are traditionalists today who will at least enter into constructive dialogue with the late formal operational approach of science. The last few sections in this chapter will look at some instances.

The Method of Coherence:
Formal Operational Theologies in
Religion Today

I will use the word "theology" to stand for that part of a religious community's thought which is formal operational thought, even though a given religious group may use the word more broadly than that. Theology defined in this way is usually a systematic analysis of the tradition of a religious community. This can include not only beliefs about what is true, but also doctrines about moral rules and ritual practices and forms of authority. It is a universalist style of thought, expecting that all things cohere rationally, that the test of "fit" can apply across the board among all the truth-claims. From within a religious perspective, this coherence flows from the single common divine or sacred reality that lies behind the multiplicity of things. If a single God has created the universe, then all things and events must somehow fit within the purpose and plan of that God, it seems.

The importance of formal theology varies with the tradition. In the Muslim seminaries in Qom in Iran and in the Catholic seminaries in Rome, formal theology has great authority. Its analyses of the sacred sources, Qur'an or Bible and councils, built upon earlier centuries of reflection and conclusions, are highly authoritative. Ironically, formal operational modes of theological analyses may receive some of their legitimacy from the concrete operational criterion of community tradition. The formal analyses provided by Shankara or Al-Ghazali or Aquinas might be received with respect by later generations because tradition has certified these analyses, rather than because they are appreciated for their rationality.

A systematically logical approach to religious beliefs has both good and bad aspects. It produces coherence among beliefs, making them less vulnerable to charges of irrationality. It seeks out doctrines and values that are of universal validity, in the expectation that there are basic truths and values in life that all people can use as a basis for harmony. Classical theologies have traditionally supposed that human beings everywhere share in some universal basic worth. The systematically logical approach thus has a principle whereby it can overlook differences in favor of what is common to us all as human. In principle, classical theology ought to be opposed to slavery, gender discrimination, racism, and other antiuniversalist interpretations of human worth.

History makes evident a dark side to this universalist expectation, however. Formal operational thought may trust dogmatically in rational analyses without the late formal operational reflexive awareness of the conditional nature of all doctrinal formulations. To the eye of a dogmatist, the rich diversity of human life appears as a threatening problem rather than a wonderful resource. A rigid, dogmatic theology may join forces with the clannish tendencies of concrete operational thought to condemn the outsiders who fail to conform to the single universal truths and moral norms. Outsiders are then branded as weak or ignorant or malicious.

Systematic thought also has to face the awkward fact that there are many large-scale coherent worldviews, ones that apparently integrate life experiences and beliefs for those who accept these worldviews. Aquinas and Shankara provide two quite distinct metaphysical ones; Empedocles, philosophical Taoism, and Madame Blavatsky offer different cosmological ones. Each has a great deal of internal coherence, yet some conflict with others; they cannot all be true. Formal operational theology has some advantages over the methods of personal appeal and relying on the authority of tradition, but is still not quite enough. Large-scale internal coherence (logical fit) is necessary but not sufficient in determining what is probably true.

The Critical-Empirical Method: Reflexive Thought in Religion Today

Late formal operational thought has been described in chapters 1 and 9. It is formal operational rationality qualified by the reflexive awareness that all human thought processes and truth-claims are the work of finite and imperfect humans, whose categories and conclusions are conditioned by personal and social elements, in ways often difficult to detect. Out of this reflexive awareness two distinct kinds of theologies have emerged, the deconstructive and the reconstructive. We will turn to these shortly. First, we need to consider other possible methods. The method of modern science is to accept as probably true those fact-claims, laws, and theories which are shown to fit well with the available relevant evidence through ongoing and extensive public testing. Those defending religious beliefs against challenges from science sometime assert that there are other methods for determining what is true.

There may well be other methods; but the question is whether any of those methods is reliably effective. A person can toss bones in the dirt and have them interpreted by a mystic. That is a method. But does it work effectively and reliably to determine what is probably true? (It may, of course, "work" in other ways, psychological and social and moral.) We have already described four methods of determining what is true, methods that closely imitate four Piagetian stages of cognitive development: the "personal appeal" method, the "community tradition" method, the "coherence" method, and the empirical-critical method of modern science (postmodern variations on it in religious thought are yet to be discussed). There are two more potential candidates for the status of alternative method to that of science for determining what is probably true.

In addition to the four just named, a fifth alternative for determining what is true is to trust our deepest and most intense inward experiences as a kind of evidence. Call it the "depth-experience" method. In religion in particular, it has often been claimed that individual religious experience is sufficient evidence for the existence of a divine or sacred reality. Christian theologians such as Friedrich Schleiermacher and Rudolph Otto have appealed to religious experience in a way that is supposed to make such experience an undoubtable foundation for all else they say. Thus Otto argues that to those who have had the experience it is self-evidently true, and those who have not had it will not understand.[4]

One obvious problem with the depth-experience method is precisely one that those skeptical about science cite, though in this case it applies to religious belief: that of possible distortion through bias and interest or through cultural indoctrination. Whatever seems most intensely and deeply true in our inner experience may appear that way not because of the truth of it, but because of factors cited in the prior methods for determining what is true. We are all somewhat susceptible to personal appeal. Furthermore, whatever our community and tradition have accustomed us to believe will seem most intensely and deeply true. To take a stand contrary to community tradition may even evoke in us a deep uneasiness, a fear of anomy.[5] Our individual inclinations will follow that enculturation. Whatever we have been raised to believe will easily feel to us to be the most well integrated with our life experiences. Its inner coherence will appear to be strong, regardless of any actual logical flaws.[6]

Modern science has discovered the effectiveness of public and long-term testing of its experiences to compensate for community bias and individual enthusiasm. Through such public testing it uncovers many errors. Those who employ religious experience as evidence of the reality of the supernatural or of a divine plan within the natural or of a divine (metaphysical) reality behind the natural do not seem to have any method of compensating for bias and emotional investment. (Religious believers sometimes say that the object of religion lies beyond the realm of public testing against evidence. The next section, "Three Types of Religious Truth-Claims,"[7] will address this.)

An analysis of religious experience by Wayne Proudfoot illustrates the problem with trusting inner experience very far.[8] He points out that people can be convinced they have a culture- and bias-free experience of the sacred even while they are in fact experiencing things precisely as their religion has taught them. Proudfoot appeals to experiments by two psychologists, Schacter and Singer, to illustrate his point. They administered adrenaline to various subjects, sometimes forewarning them of the specific results to expect, other times only giving vague indications. Those not told precisely what to expect experienced deep anger that they were sure was caused by the disrespectful behavior of other people toward them. Other subjects, who were forewarned, recognized similar inner experiences as a product of the adrenaline, and did not impute to others any bad behavior toward them. Proudfoot's point is to show how expectations can influence interpretation. It may be that religious experiences are "religious" if people have been taught to experience them as religious. To know whether such experiences are anything more than interesting but fully natural psychological states, would require some evidence that is not preinterpreted as religious.

Another evident difficulty with the depth-experience method is, once again, that different traditions make different truth-claims, even while many of these traditions also say that they have intense inner experiences of the divine that are the source of certainty about their beliefs. The Hindu guru experiences the inner spark of divinity that all people possess in their innermost nature; the Buddhist mystic has experienced a small moment of what nirvana or Buddha nature is like; the Jewish cabalist has discovered the inner power with which God has endowed us; and so forth.

The appeal to inner religious experience would carry more weight, perhaps, if there were some clearly similar depth experience within all religions, or within all intense and deep religious experiences. Schleiermacher, Otto, W. C. Smith, Mircea Eliade, and others have proposed this.[9] Unfortunately, they do not all agree on the nature of this experience. Otto said Schleiermacher was not quite correct in his understanding of the primordial religious experience. Moreover, Schleiermacher told his readers that true religion did not hope for individual spiritual existence after death. Eliade seems to want to retain room for belief in spirit beings as a form of the sacred.[10] The Taoist speaks of oneness with the order of nature; the Hindu rejects nature to experience Atman, and so on.[11] When it becomes clearer what this religious experience is—whether it is metaphysical in nature, or whether it is experience of spirits—it will be easier to judge the validity of truth-claims based on it.[12]

A sixth and final alternative method for evaluating religious truth-claims might be to accept a set of truth-claims as probably true if the witnesses to these truths are exemplars of special moral qualities or if the religion provides a believer with life-enhancing values.[13] Call it the "moral witness" method. There are at least four different reasons why it is not workable to try to validate truth-claims on the basis of the moral quality of the persons witnessing to these truth-claims or on the moral effect in people's lives.

A first reason why moral witness cannot establish true belief, at least within many religious traditions, is the ambiguous record of actions by religious people acting in the name of God. A Jew who lived in Europe anytime from the twelfth to the twentieth century would frequently have had a good experiential basis for judging Christian morals rather harshly.

So would certain Christians, from persecuted Donatists in northern Africa in Augustine's times, to Eastern Christians attacked in Constantinople during the Fourth Crusade, to the families of those burned as heretics or witches in later centuries. Here the moral witness is a negative one, acknowledged as negative even by later believers.

A second reason why moral witness does not establish what is true, is that even if it were easy to agree on what is moral, it seems clear that many people who adhere firmly to high values nonetheless make factual mistakes. Love of one's neighbor is a moral value almost everyone would agree on. Yet it is possible to love one's neighbor and make quite serious mistakes about how to prevent the neighbor from getting sick. We no longer think that warding off demons or asking God to prevent demons from doing harm is the way to prevent disease. A person of otherwise high moral standards may mistakenly think that the Bible is correct in saying that children not hit with the rod now and then will grow up spoiled. A person of great virtue may oppose a sound scientific idea for no better reason than that it seems to conflict with a religious belief. So moral rectitude does not assure the validity of truth-claims.

A third reason why moral witness is not sufficient as a trustworthy criterion for what is true is that people who have fairly impressive moralities support different religious traditions. Christian Scientists and Mormons profess high standards of morality; in his own mind and that of his followers, so did the Ayatollah Khomeini. Yet each of these religious movements judges at least some of the beliefs of the others to be false. If a group of Buddhists is highly compassionate, and Jews very humane, and Jains respectful of all life, how should we judge which of these different religious traditions, if any, has truth-claims that are more probably true? Similarly, many find the atheistic vision of secular humanism to be morally inspiring. Does the high moral witness of this movement indicate that atheism is more probably correct in making its truth-claims about the nonexistence of God or spirits?

The search for alternative methods of determining what is true might still be a path worth exploring. People have defended many or all of the five alternatives to the critical-empirical method used by science in order to support religious truth-claims. Any one of them might lead to truth-claims that *happen* to be correct. But so far in history only the kind of careful empirical testing used by science has been *shown* to be a reliably effective method for determining which truth-claims are actually most probably correct and which are not, and in precisely which aspects. It has taken thousands of years of cultural development to arrive at a good grasp and appreciation of this method. It takes years of individual cognitive development to learn to understand and use this method. But it has turned out to be highly effective, and is the only one shown to be effective. It is not surprising, then, that most religious thinkers have found it necessary to take science very seriously, in one way or another, in interpreting their beliefs and reformulating their methods. Before reviewing these religious responses, however, we should first distinguish among three different types of religious truth-claims, to see whether the empirical-critical method of science can really apply in any way to truth-claims made by religions.

Three Types of Religious Truth-Claims

The conclusions of science have sometimes been at odds with specific traditional religious beliefs. The specific theory of Copernicus challenged the specific belief that God had placed the Earth motionless in the center of the universe; Darwin's specific theory that humans had descended from primates challenged the specific belief that humankind is a special creation of God. Many such specific theories in science, however, have also been added up to create a more general overview that challenges the entire worldview of most religious traditions. Thus Stephen Jay Gould and Richard Dawkins situate human life in the midst of cosmic aimlessness.[14] Relations among scientific conclusions and religious beliefs can be discussed more clearly if we first sort out some of the different general types of beliefs involved. One convenient division identifies three major types of religious truth-claims: the miraculous, the cosmological, and the metaphysical.

The Miraculous

The category of the miraculous includes all beliefs about interventions into the natural order by a supernatural (or preternatural) Being or beings. Such interventions accomplish what reliable patterns of nature would not or even could not have produced on their own. This is the category of ancestral spirits who bring sickness to a village, of a demon who dwells inside an insane person, of miraculous intervention by a saint to send plague upon the enemy, of house-haunting poltergeists. It may well be the category of Pentecostal healings, or of special revelation by God to the chief elder of the Mormon Church, or of the transformation of bread and wine into the body and blood of Christ, depending on how these beliefs are interpreted.

Such truth-claims are about events that take place in this empirical world of time and space. They are about sickness and cures, about ideas received by people, about changes in physical objects. It seems legitimate to inquire whether there is reason to be confident that (1) these events do in fact take place as described, and (2) their causes are not natural causes. A scientific approach is thus appropriate for investigating specific claims of supernatural interventions.[15] As Hume pointed out long ago, events are deemed miracles precisely if they look as though they could not be due to natural causes. The only way to justify a claim that a certain event is not due to natural causes is to know enough about it to judge that it is beyond the powers of nature to accomplish. That requires a careful investigation into exactly what has taken place, considering all the relevant evidence. It requires a comparison of the event with what nature is already known to be able to accomplish in the way this event took place. Clearly this is all a matter of empirical investigation.

There is no way to disprove all miracles.[16] A supernatural intervention could be too subtle to be detected; or it could be disguised to look natural. Even demons are tricky enough for this, on some traditional accounts; surely God could do even better at evading empirical detection. But to say God evades all empirical detection is the same as saying that there is no evidence at all of any supernatural cause at work.

Neither is it possible to prove that no natural cause could account for a given event. Every claim that a miracle has taken place is a form of an argument from ignorance. "We do not see how natural causes could account for this" is the plainest form of an argument from ignorance. The stronger form is a flat claim: "We know that natural causes could not account for this." This sounds like an argument from knowledge, from what "we know" rather than from ignorance. But the next question to ask is how "we know" natural causes could not account for it. One can hope to slowly eliminate possibilities until one is left with no alternative except miraculous intervention. But it is true, as critics of science sometimes say, that science does not know everything. It is always possible that an event not due to a known process of natural causality might be due to a natural causality of which we know too little. Continual empirical investigation is relevant here. The record so far shows extensive success in finding natural causes for what were once taken to be unnatural events. This success seems to justify science's unitary naturalism, an approach that challenges belief in miraculous interruptions of the natural order.

Cosmological Beliefs

The second type of religious belief potentially related to standards of scientific method is the cosmological. This is belief that the overall *natural* order of reality is indicative in some way of a divine reality or presence. Interpreting the order of nature in such a way as to be able to perceive the Intelligence of God at work, and thereby support belief in God, has been part of natural theology for centuries. Minucius Felix used Stoic arguments to do it in the second century; Anselm and Aquinas made their contributions; natural theology writers like William Paley excelled in it; Catholic neo-Thomists practiced it extensively in the twentieth century. Langdon Gilkey, an American Protestant expert on belief in God, found the "Anthropic Principle" plausible for supporting belief in an Intelligent Designer.[17] So have other theologians and scientists. Numerous Christian and Jewish theologians have developed interpretations of their traditions to make them fit well with the general evolutionary cosmology of modern science.[18] When it has seemed as though the arguments of natural theology could indeed prove God's existence, Christian theologians have been happy to rely on these arguments. In all such arguments there is a clear appeal to empirical evidence. The evidence indicates that there has been a multibillion-year process, beginning with an explosive moment (the "Big Bang"), which has produced ever-greater levels of complexity and, eventually, life and consciousness, at least on this planet. This is consistent with a theistic claim that the process of the universe has a purposeful direction and thus suggests intelligent design. At a minimum, religion seems at least compatible with the evidence.

A cosmological religious view of the universe is also compatible with the methodological naturalism of science. Science operates by supposing that every event can be explained as part of a reliable natural order. A deistic cosmology can agree with this by assuming that God is Creator and Planner, that God is the sustaining power in all that happens, even that the eventual outcome of the natural processes will achieve some sort of divinely intended fulfillment. This is compatible with a belief that God leaves all specific events in the universe to the working of what medieval theology called secondary causality, the created causal order intrinsic to the universe. There are sharply diverse opinions today on whether the process of the universe is clear and sufficient evidence for God the Intelligent Designer.[19] But many theologians are happy to discover what they see as a complementarity between religious and scientific views of the cosmos. We will see more of this when we look at a few correlational theologies later.

Metaphysical Religious Beliefs

There is a third type of religious truth-claim, which I will call the metaphysical. That word is used in many senses, unfortunately, including as a label for belief in spirit realms and visits to the astral plane. By "metaphysical" I mean the level of thought the human mind reaches when it asks questions about the ultimate ground or source of everything. The metaphysical questions concern that which is more fundamental than or prior to anything else. There are few such questions. One is whether the time of the universe extends endlessly backward, whether the universe has always existed, or whether it required some sort of beginning. There seems to be no rational way of discovering the correct answer to this question, as Aquinas and Kant both insisted. The theory that the current universe originated in a Big Bang does not quite answer the question, for one may ask where the Big Bang came from. The law of the conservation of matter-energy seems to imply that the energy-stuff of which everything is composed, is everlastingly the same in quantity (whatever that might mean). But if this is so, that raises a further question: Why is matter-energy such that it never diminishes but only changes in distribution and form? The deepest form of this metaphysical question is why there is something at all rather than nothing. Regardless of whether the Big Bang started it all, or whether there have been endless Bangs, why is there "stuff" or energy to go bang at all?

A second metaphysical question is whether there is a basic plan or purpose to the whole of what exists. Perhaps, as the atheistic existentialist and many evolutionists and cosmologists assure us, things just are, and whatever happens is not the result of any deeper value or goal. It is in fact difficult to imagine what such a cosmic meaning or goal might be, though theologians and religious philosophers have offered answers. Perhaps the goal of all things is to return to some sort of fulfilling relation with the Origin. Or perhaps, as the Whiteheadians have it, the goal of cosmic processes is to enrich ever more the inner life of God. Or perhaps there is no ultimate purpose at all.

It is difficult to make reliable judgments about the truth or falsity of metaphysical theories. It is first of all difficult to know what evidence could count for or against any truth-claims about the ultimate source or goal of all things, especially if we include among "all things" the hypothetical universes, of which there may be an infinite number. No matter how things may look in the universe we know, if it is one of an endless set of universes, this tiny single universe would not be an adequate clue to any larger patterns or purposes. Our minds can allow us great liberties on the metaphysical level. A metaphysics that even goes contrary to constant experience can nonetheless find support. A Hindu who follows Shankara's interpretation will claim that the universe of events and people is not really real, is only a shadow world; that the infinite and incomprehensible Brahman alone has true existence. A Christian who believes that there is an all-powerful, all-knowing, and perfectly loving God, affirms this belief in the face of suffering on the part of billions of people over the last ten thousand years. God's ways are beyond human comprehension, say Jews, Christians, and Muslims; we cannot use historical evidence of suffering as evidence that God does not exist or that God is not good, because God transcends all that we can really understand.[20]

Theologians on Miracles, Cosmic Order, and the Ultimate

The three types of truth-claims have suffered different fates in the course of modern scientific rationality. Miracles have fared least well. The overall patterns of the cosmos no longer are clear evidence of intelligent design, though there is room for various interpretations here. The metaphysical claim that behind all specific events, as well as behind the general course of nature, there is some Ultimate in which humans may place some sort of religious hope or trust is the claim perhaps least able to be adjudicated by appeals to empirical evidence.

It is worth repeating once more that religions are complex realities in which truth-claims are only one element intermeshed with others.[21] Judgments of value, moral exhortations, rituals and symbols whose function it is to reinforce a sense of community or to express inner feelings, are all part of religion. But religions also make truth-claims. Because conclusions of science have challenged some of those truth-claims, and because science has so effective a method for judging the probable validity of truth-claims, religious thinkers have found it necessary to formulate their own conclusions and methods at least partly in response to science.

Miracles

The history of modern science presents an obvious challenge to the plausibility of belief in miracles. The range of knowledge of natural causality has expanded until supernatural interventions have been squeezed into a few remaining gaps. As belief in ordeals and succubi and demonic possession has decreased, the gaps have gotten smaller. The regularity of nature, its intelligibility, its mathematical reliability, have become increasingly well attested by the practical success of science. The strike of a lightning bolt was to Benjamin Franklin a manifestation of a natural fluid (later called electricity), not a warning from God. The appearance of a comet to Halley was not a special sign sent by God but rather part of an orbit that could be explained by natural causes. The irregularities in the orbiting speeds of Saturn and Jupiter were to Pierre-Simon Laplace part of a natural oscillation rather than a sign that the universe needed divine tending to keep it running smoothly, as Newton had briefly supposed. As we have seen, such scientific advances made deism more plausible.

Perhaps it was in reaction to this that on a popular level there was a resurgence of belief in the miraculous. Keith Thomas claims that belief in healings and prophecies increased enormously, in particular among the sectarians.[22] In the sixteenth and seventeenth centuries the terrible witch-hunts with their burnings and hangings represented a widespread belief in the presence of supernatural beings and powers. Traditional religious believers accepted the reality of pacts with real demons.[23] The beliefs typical of primitive or archaic culture remained as part of the culture. The new natural philosophy, however, gave reasons to disbelieve such things. The supernatural was being squeezed out.[24]

By the end of the eighteenth century in Europe, many of the well educated no longer believed either in miracles or in deistic proofs for God. They were also disdainful of the emotional excitement of various religious enthusiasts. So Schleiermacher proposed as a solution his idea of a kind of God-consciousness, which did not depend at all on miracles or on rational proof.[25] A consciousness of the Whole, said Schleiermacher, is an inner experience (an intuition or *gefühl*) of a divine reality. This experience is sui generis, as historians of religion express it. It justifies itself by the inwardly perceived evidence of its truth. It is an experience of absolute dependence on the ultimate Whole.[26] It is "God-consciousness."

Schleiermacher followed where science had been leading, and gave up belief in supernatural interventions. He proclaimed that belief in miracles was contrary to true religion. Genuine religious sentiment was a perception of the wholeness of the universe. Belief in miracles was belief that the unity of all things could be broken up by interventions from a supernatural world.

> Where . . . a conception of miracles is commonly found, namely, in conditions where there is least knowledge of nature, there, too, the fundamental feeling [of God-consciousness] appears to be weakest and most ineffectual. . . . It follows from this that the most perfect representation of omnipotence would be a view of the world which made no use of such an idea.[27]

Schleiermacher also claimed that the search of science for coherent understanding of the universe was actually dependent upon a prior religious intuition into the unity of all things. His disbelief in miracles was therefore declared by him not to be a result of scientific skepticism. But in fact this rejection of miracle appears only after more than a century years of scientific rationalism that cast doubt on miracles.

The resulting theology is famous as "liberal theology." Each of the beliefs of Christianity that had traditionally been supernaturalist, presupposing a miraculous intervention by God into nature's order, was reinterpreted by Schleiermacher. The incarnation of God in Jesus, for example, was not the descent of a supernatural being into human history. It should instead be understood as a way of expressing recognition that of all the people of history, Jesus had the greatest God-consciousness, and was therefore the one in whom the creation of the human reached maximum perfection.[28] Because of this, Jesus is the one who should be accepted as the truest guide to full and genuine religiousness. Similarly, belief in a life after death should be thought of as a symbol of human confidence that the meaning of our lives is somehow ultimately vindicated.[29]

Early in the twentieth century Karl Barth promoted the odd theological combination that came to be known as neoorthodoxy. Barth's ideas often seemed to be traditionally supernaturalistic, in that he asserted the centuries-old doctrine that true faith was the product of God's grace, that God gave this grace to those whom God chose. He declared that God acts to reveal truth, guide history, and judge human behavior. Schleiermacher's liberal theology, however, continued on in Barth's approach. God does all these things, Barth says, yet not through any sort of supernatural intervention. Barth tried to combine the affirmation of traditional doctrines with a liberal interpretation of those doctrines. His way of expressing belief in eternal life, for example, does not quite affirm traditional belief in an individual life beyond this natural order:

> What is the meaning of the Christian hope . . . ? A life after death? An event apart from death? A tiny soul which, like a butterfly, flutters away above the grave and is still preserved somewhere, in order to live on immortally? That was how the heathen looked on the life after death. But that is not the Christian hope. . . . Resurrection means not the continuation of this life, but life's completion.[30]

Langdon Gilkey none too gently summarized the overall result of Barth's ideas as an affirmation that God acts in history, but with words that say God does not really act in history.

> The God of neo-orthodoxy "spoke," but no concrete divine words resulted; he "acted," but not in miraculous or otherwise identifiable or even specific ways; he "ruled," but not by omnipotently willing any particular and certainly no evil events; and he "judged," but not in terms of divine punishment either presently evident or even to be expected eternally.[31]

The influential Scripture scholar Rudolph Bultmann went further. His accomplishment was to give wide currency to the expression "demythologize," something that he thought Christians needed to do.[32] If there is a story in the Bible that tells of a miraculous act in which the laws of nature are suspended or exceeded by some divine activity, the contemporary Christian is to understand that this is only a mythological way of speaking appropriate for people of long ago. Contemporary people are supposed to know better. They should seek to find in such stories not literal historical truth but rather existential symbols. Thus the stories of Jesus' miracles in the New Testament are to be interpreted as an expression of faith that God is at work in the world, in a way, however, that is not an interruption of the natural order of causality.[33]

Religious believers have usually resisted the demythologization of their beliefs. The Second Great Awakening in the United States in the early nineteenth century led people to experience the miraculous powers of the Holy Spirit in their own lives, in conversion and healing and signs. Their descendants are today's Pentecostals and other Fundamentalists,

Christians who unabashedly reject the stratagems of liberal theology in order to reaffirm the reality of miracles, especially those of the Bible and concerning Jesus, but also contemporary interventions by God in history and in the lives of individuals.[34] The Fundamentalist method is to rely on a sacred text, attested to by their community and tradition, as a miraculously revealed source of truth.[35]

Fundamentalists nonetheless sometimes grant legitimacy to a quasi-scientific style of analysis. "Scientific creationism" tests the ideas of evolutionists for logical inconsistencies and even look for evidence that would falsify the theory of how evolution took place. But they do not do a very good job.[36] Fundamentalists also argue rationally in defense of miracles. Norman Geisler, the less fundamentalist Douglas Geivett and Gary Habermas, and T. C. Williams, all use the rational criteria of logical coherence and fit with the evidence. In fact, they often then use miracles as empirical evidence for the validity of the Bible as a whole.[37] Fundamentalists, then, may argue rationally yet reject science's conclusions where these conflict with seemingly clear biblical assertions. In the end they trust the sacred text of their tradition, and the interpretations held by their community and leaders, more than they trust the rational methods of science. Like Clement of Alexandria and Augustine, they first believe and then seek an understanding within the framework of that belief.

There have been various other suggestions on how to affirm that God intervenes in history without interfering with the laws of nature. John Polkinghorne has recommended more than once that we think of divine agency as intervention done without energy. Quantum theory says that there is an indeterminacy on the subatomic level so equally balanced between two outcomes that no energy would be required to select one rather than the other.[38] Perhaps so; it would be difficult to prove or disprove that God is at work in this way.[39] Because all the things in the entire universe are made of atoms, God could certainly be exceedingly influential by nudging every subatomic possibility in one direction or another. Yet as far as the evidence goes, the indeterminacy on the quantum level nonetheless eventuates in the enormously reliable laws of nature that operate at the atomic level and above. The result of any ongoing divine activity on the quantum level turns out to *look* just like what naturalism expects: The events of the universe can be successfully treated as due to built-in, reliably regular, natural causes.[40] This theology is carefully formulated not to be in conflict with science. The divine activity it proposes is so thoroughly disguised that the universe gives no evidence of anything except natural causes at work.

A blunter approach to miracles is represented by the firm way in which an Anglican chaplain tries to promote religion without miracles: "An outmoded theology which smuggles God into the system to interfere with the laws of nature is much less sophisticated than a scientific account which sees all the emergent richness of life as the true glory of chemistry. The scientific account has the touch of *true* mystery."[41] The presence of God is found implicit within the bounds of nature, here in its chemistry, not in any miraculous exceptions to the natural order.[42] Science here has defined the boundaries of plausibility for religious beliefs. Many theologians have in fact accepted those boundaries, even though they sometimes seem to say otherwise.

Theologies in Response to Modern Cosmology and Evolution

The second large category of religious beliefs is composed of beliefs about the general order of nature (rather than about supernatural powers and acts). The large-scale theories about the evolution of the universe and the evolution of life on Earth have been the focal point of disputes here. To construct a religious hypothesis adequate to the whole of the universe and all of its history as portrayed by modern science is an adventure of imagination. Many have tried, and the results are interesting. It is apparently difficult to prove or disprove any of these hypotheses, though the evidence from science does impose some limits. It is no longer possible, for example, to sustain a hypothesis that says the universe was made six thousand years ago and has remained unchanged in its essential form. It is contrary to the evidence to claim that every niche in the universe has its ideal form or thing or living being to fill it up, all in a neatly ordered hierarchy of value. Where the scientific conclusions seem clear and firm, religious thinkers have reinterpreted traditional beliefs to fit the scientific conclusions.

By the late 1920s the universe had continued to grow in size, so to speak. Edwin Hubble used the 100-inch mirror of the Mount Wilson telescope to provide evidence that there were multitudes of galaxies of stars, not just our own Milky Way, and that each of the galaxies seemed to be rushing away from our own, as though the entire universe were expanding. Theories about the eventual extinction of our own sun had bothered some people in the nineteenth century; the new picture of the enormous and expanding universe made it even more difficult to find a meaningful location and purpose for humankind. Cosmological questions were pressing in upon the consciousness of the educated.

One response to this sort of information is Bultmann's: to stand up to science and proclaim that he would believe nevertheless, by making an existential choice to affirm life's ultimate meaningfulness even in the face of science's disturbing conclusions. He asserts his right to interpret life's events as signs of loving concern for him by a personal God, in spite of the apparent impersonalness of the order of the cosmos. Like Schleiermacher, Bultmann finds his answer to science in subjectivity, this time in the courageous inner choice to assert ultimate personal meaningfulness in spite of science. Yet this is the same Bultmann who had abandoned traditional Christian belief in the literal truth of miracles and had demythologized such stories. He has clearly taken modern science quite seriously, simultaneously accepting its skepticism about miracles and its portrait of the universe as apparently aimless. This is the context that provokes his existential decision to have faith.

Other theologians have found it possible and even necessary to integrate the scientific portrait of the universe with their religious beliefs in God's creativity and purposes. Pierre Teilhard de Chardin composed hymns to the evolving universe as the manifestation of the workings of God. Numerous theologians and religiously minded scientists have supported some version of the Anthropic Principle, a claim that the conditions of the universe from the beginning are fine-tuned so precisely to make the evolution of human life possible, that it is reasonable to conclude that the order of the universe had to have been planned for this purpose.

Alfred North Whitehead went further than most theologians in finding a religious interpretation of the process of the universe.[43] Whitehead constructed a new model of the universe, using a peculiar language of his own to make the shift in models more noticeable. Reality is a process, a flow of event-moments rather than a universe of stable or permanent things, each with its proper essence. The universe is made up basically of happenings, not things, because all things are collections of happenings (atomic "particles" and energy waves, etc.) in a process. The fact that the universe has actively produced more complex forms all the way up to human consciousness is startling and requires special explanation. Evidently there is something about the universe, some characteristic of it or some "principle" within it, that has produced the eons-long history of creative development of ever more complex interconnected interconnections. To Gould or Dawkins the answer is that it is all part of a cosmic lottery based on a few basic rules of the game of variation and selective survival. For Whitehead the process of reality must be influenced by a principle that somehow draws forth from event-moments, as they happen, at least some small tendency to develop in the direction of more complex interconnectedness and the fuller levels of consciousness which that includes. On this basis Whitehead proposed a notion of God as a divine principle of directional creativity, as an intrinsic part of the natural universe, rather than the totally transcendent creator of more traditional Western theologies.

Not all theologians change traditional beliefs as much as Whitehead in order to create a theology compatible with the conclusions of modern science about the overall order and history of nature. But most non-Fundamentalist theologians who are also knowledgeable about science consider the scientific story of cosmic history to be so well established as to require that traditional relevant religious doctrines be reinterpreted to fit with that story. The twelve billion-year-old evolving cosmos is the way God has exercised the divine creative and providential power.

God's activity, many of them say, is best understood as sustaining and empowering the cosmic process rather than as intervening in it in irregular ways. The appearance of humankind on this planet is part of an overall biological process of evolution. Perhaps even the old doctrine of the creation of souls by God must be understood as brought about through the process of evolution, not by any later special divine acts of creation.[44]

Rarely, one finds a theologian who not merely accepts the conclusions of science but also recommends its *method* for theology. Wolfhart Pannenberg argues that there must be some rational way of determining what general worldview is more probably true, and that "It cannot be a mere existential certainty which is incapable of adducing any premises or arguments in its support." Pannenberg says that religious truth-claims must also fit with the best evidence available, even though the most basic claim of all, about the existence of the Ultimate which is God, cannot be checked up on in the way finite realities can be.[45]

The adaptation of religious belief to the conclusions of science can be dangerous for religion. The conclusions of science can change. Religion traps itself into opposition to a culture's advances in knowledge when religion clings to old science.[46] For a time, many Christians remained tied to Ptolemy's old science of the heavens and could not adapt to Copernicus and Kepler's new science. Some Christians are still bound to an archaic science reflected in the first book of Genesis about the construction of the Earth and cannot accept Darwinian science. Many now cling to a Platonic or Cartesian matter-spirit dualism that once represented the best natural philosophy (science) of its time, and cannot find a way to accept the more unitary naturalism of contemporary science.[47]

Metaphysical Truth-Claims in Current Religious Thought

The third kind of religious belief is the metaphysical, about the nature or character of whatever is truly ultimate. Theistic theologians perceive this as the question of God—whether the ultimate is a "Personal" Reality, Creator, Sustainer, Empowering Presence, and/or Purpose of all things. Many Buddhists would understand the topic differently. So also might Vedantic philosophers. Atheists, ancient and modern, differ from all of these, though they might agree partly with some Buddhists. As the brief earlier section on metaphysical ideas indicated, this whole question is the least amenable to any sort of empirical or even logical test, at least if the question is taken to be one about the factual status of the ultimate (how one may psychologically or existentially choose to deal with ultimacy may be another matter).

The question of the metaphysical ultimate carries us closer to the topic of how the scientific *method* (as opposed to science's conclusions) has affected religious thought. So it will be best to allow metaphysical questions to arise as we look more directly at how the method of science has had an impact on methods in religious thought. The method of science is an empirical-critical one. It trusts theories or truth-claims only to the extent that they can be tested empirically. If they cannot be tested, then one cannot know whether they are true or not (or are the functional equivalent of truth). It maintains a "critical" awareness of the conditional nature of even well-tested truth-claims, as the product of a human process of investigation, theorizing, and testing in a public and open-ended way.

Religion resolves threatening mysteries of life for people, by providing reassuring answers as well as rules for life, forms of community, inspiring symbols and rituals, and so on. These answers and patterns provide a sense of secure boundaries and well-defined paths. A critical style in theology, however, turns the boundaries into open horizons and the paths into multiple options. Neither the archaic nor the historic style of religious thought expects its beliefs to be changeable, so these two styles of thought provide more security than a critical mode of thought. Some theologians, however, have found opportunity instead of threat in a critical approach to religious beliefs. They have adapted their mode of theologizing to include a critical element.

There are two general methods of theology that are self-consciously critical. One of them is the general method of correlation, a method both empirical and critical, which seeks to discover compatibility, even integration, between science and religious thought. The other is the general postmodern approach, a method that is hypercritical, which seeks to exempt religious belief from the criteria of scientific or perhaps any other rationality. The language use gets a bit out of hand here; many things have been called "postmodern."[48] The correlational approaches might also be called constructive, or even reconstructive, postmodernist; and the second type of approach often labeled "post" something might be called deconstructive postmodernist. They are "deconstructive" inasmuch as they participate in the relativizing and localizing effect of deconstruction in literature and history. They take their cues from the relativizing and localizing postmodern sociology, history, and philosophy of science described in chapter 9. The two approaches might also be labeled the "integrative" and the "exemptive." The correlational seeks to make religion and science compatible or even integrated into a single worldview. The deconstructive postmodern exempts religion from any criteria except its own internal ones. Both of these approaches are identifiable by their methods of thought more than by the collection of beliefs they represent. Correlational theologies have been overshadowed to some degree by deconstructive postmodern theologies.

Deconstruction and Other Ways to
Exempt Religious Belief from
Scientific Standards

There are at least four ways in which religious people have tried to exempt religious beliefs from being judged by the methods of science. The
first is well known. It is the fundamentalist conviction that the revelation
of God is always superior to the products of the weak and sinful human
mind. Where science and the Bible are truly in conflict, science must be
wrong.

The other ways are less well known, except to theologians and philosophers. The second strategy to exempt religious beliefs from the criteria
of science arises from Schleiermacher's and then Otto's grounding of true
religion in a special experience. This strategy argues that religious beliefs
are about the "sacred," a dimension quite distinct from empirical reality,
which is therefore exempt from scientific investigation. The sacred is sui
generis, and so are religious claims about it.[49] Mircea Eliade says that the
sacred shows itself as "a wholly different order, a reality that does not
belong to our world." He concludes that the test of empirical evidence
used by science does not apply to religious beliefs.

But whatever there is about religion that is unique to it, making
truth-claims is not on the face of it a uniquely religious act.[50] Once again,
as in the general use of religious experience as a method of discerning
truth, the advocates of the sui generis nature of religious experience are
not very clear. If the only reality that is called the Sacred is the metaphysical Ultimate, then indeed we are getting to a sui generis reality. If,
however, it includes spirits or magic or gods or some general numinous
power in nature or miraculous interventions, then we are talking about
specific finite things or aspects of the world. Such religious truth-claims
are empirical, about specific factual (or nonfactual) events. The two basic
questions can still be asked: Is there something really "there"? And is
that something truly "nonnatural"?

The third strategy for exempting religion from science's standards was
mentioned in the introduction. This has been to deny that religions make
truth-claims. D. Z. Phillips,[51] for example, seems to say that his own religiousness is not about truth-claims, and goes on to say that this is the
truth about all religion.[52] Nonetheless, most religious people are quite
sure that their religious tradition makes a number of very important
truth-claims. The history of disputes over heresies in Christianity or in
Buddhism illustrates this. Regardless of what Phillips says, it would seem
that such believers must be allowed to define their own beliefs as truth-
claims if they so choose.[53] On the other hand, if Phillips wishes to promote a religion that makes no truth-claims at all, then indeed he will
have a religion exempt from scientific criteria for judging truth-claims.

The fourth strategy has been to say that science, religion, and other aspects of life are each part of a different language game and are therefore incommensurable. If religion wishes to give up making all truth-claims, as Phillips seems to recommend, then it is certainly a different kind of "game" than science. But as long as it does make truth-claims, it must show that its truth-claims are so different from those of science that the method of science does not apply. Of the three kinds of truth-claims—miraculous, cosmological, and metaphysical—at least the first two are within the realms of what can be investigated empirically. Moreover, Phillips's strategy is challenged by the history of changes made in religious beliefs to conform to science. We have seen in these pages that there is a long history of religious beliefs that have changed to fit what seemed to be good science. If religion does make truth-claims of a kind that even its adherents and defenders change or reinterpret in order to conform to the conclusions of science, it no longer looks very much like a different language game.

The introduction also briefly mentioned George Lindbeck's influential postmodern religious view (that depends at least partly on a Wittgensteinian model). He calls his approach "postliberal." He offers three major ways to interpret religion. One is cognitive or propositionalist. This interpretation of religion emphasizes its function as a depository of doctrinal truths. Religion in this guise is analogous to philosophy or science as a source of knowledge. The second way is the experiential-expressive. This supposes that there is some basic form of religious experience which major religions of the world share, an experience of the "sacred." Each religion expresses a different response to this basic experience. The expressions constitute different religious traditions. Lindbeck's postliberal position is a third way. He calls it the "cultural-linguistic" interpretation. Religions, in this reading, are each a "comprehensive interpretive scheme." The doctrines and stories and ethical standards are intimately tied to rituals and sentiments and institutional forms. Lindbeck insists that though a religion's truth-claims, such as those of Christianity, may have great importance, they are subordinate to the larger pattern of the overall interpretative scheme. "The cognitive aspect, while often important, is not primary."[54]

Doctrinal statements must meet an "intrasystematic" criterion of truth; they must be coherent with the overall scheme of the religious tradition, with its stories and values and practices and symbols. Lindbeck struggles, however, with the question of whether religious doctrines are also "ontologically" true, as he calls it; that is, whether they are valid truth-claims about how the world really is, "objectively," as we might say. Certain doctrinal statements, such as "God is love" or "The soul is immortal," sound like ordinary truth-claims.[55] From within a tradition, Christianity in this case, these doctrines may be intended as universal truths about how reality really, objectively, is. But from the reflexively critical perspective of Lindbeck, different religions may each legitimately make different and conflicting universalist-style truth-claims.

Lindbeck stands outside religions in order to interpret them in this reflexive way, seeing them each as a human language game or a form of life. But most religious believers, living within their religious community as their own form of life, assert their doctrines as genuinely valid and reliable truth-claims, as ontologically true, perhaps on the grounds that community tradition supports them, perhaps on the grounds that good theological analysis confirms them. It is not quite clear what a whole community of believers would have in mind if they shared Lindbeck's reflexive critical distance from their own set of beliefs. On the one hand, they might share in a liberal notion that serious truth-claims made by their tradition are not meant as literal truth-claims about how things really are, but instead are symbolic expressions of a deeper, ultimate truth. In the liberal framework also, these symbols are recognized as having an "intrasystematic" function of providing a guiding set of images for the life of the community. But in his choice of the label *post*liberal, Lindbeck seems to reject the liberal approach. Lindbeck wants postliberal believers to have the right to insist on the genuine (literal?) truth of their intrasystematic beliefs, even while acknowledging that these beliefs may not be true by "extrasystematic" criteria.[56]

This is a rather sophisticated philosophical position, from which one analyzes all other systems. It is a position of "epistemic cognition," as Karen Kitchener labeled it, acknowledging the existence of various intrasystematic positions (the various religions of the world), some of which see themselves as the universally valid truth for humankind. Lindbeck recommends choosing this postliberal extrasystematic position as a way to justify restricting oneself to one intrasystematic viewpoint, that of a given religious community of believers.

Religions themselves have traditionally used other extrasystematic criteria. They have challenged other religious traditions by appeals to what might even be called suprasystematic criteria, if I may add one more awkward word here. They have appealed to evidence and logic. Jew and Christian and Muslim, Buddhist and Taoist, Hindu and Sikh, have acted as though evidence and logic could count as valid criteria for everyone. They have pointed to their own history of fulfilled prophecies and of miracles. They have argued that other prophecies have not been fulfilled, or that miracles in other religions were done by demons, and so on.

But the major challenge to traditional religious belief in recent centuries has come precisely from the sciences, using evidence and logic as though they were "suprasystematic," universally valid criteria. Lindbeck adopts a postmodern position precisely because it denies that there are any suprasystematically valid criteria for evaluating and judging truth-claims. To sustain this, he must join with the Wittgensteinians (whether or not Wittgenstein took this position himself) and insist that there are no such suprasystematically valid criteria. He seems to think he must deny that modern science has a universally effective method for evaluating and judging truth-claims about events which are part of the universe of time and space—all truth-claims except the metaphysical, perhaps. Chapter 9 makes it clear that there is very good reason to say that modern science is in fact a highly effective method for judging the validity of truth-claims. Earlier segments of this chapter make it clear that there are good reasons to mistrust alternative methods. There remains also the history of changes in religious doctrine to fit with science, changes that in retrospect look well justified.

Finally, Lindbeck appears to be using logic and evidence in defense of his own conclusions. Perhaps he thinks that logic and evidence are valid criteria only within his own particular tradition. But we might then ask which tradition this is—whether it is the religious tradition he wants to defend that has evidence and logic as criteria for its truth-claims, or whether he belongs to two (or more) traditions, one of which relies on evidence and logic, the other of which says it is only necessary to be faithful to the life-form of one's (religious) community. In the latter case it would be interesting to find out what rules Lindbeck follows in applying the standards of one tradition to an analysis of another. A major point of the history of thought in religion and science provided in this book is to argue that evidence and logic are universally valid as criteria for determining which truth-claims are reliable. I suspect Lindbeck implicitly accepts the universal validity of evidence and logic, though his postliberal stance obscures this.

A further problem with the postliberal approach is that it seems suited for the extreme few, though this is a problem that all highly reflexively critical approaches share, whether religious or not. Lindbeck is inviting people to join him in a perspective on their own traditional religious beliefs that asks them to stand simultaneously inside and outside of their own tradition. From within the tradition many an ordinary believer will follow tradition in a fairly concrete operational way, trusting religious leaders to pass on correctly the doctrines that they may accept as true. From within the tradition many another ordinary believer will be convinced that a set of rational arguments, with evidence and logic, has established the reasonableness of the tradition. But the postliberal stands inside and outside the tradition at the same time. The postliberal person shares with fellow believers the affirmation of traditional truths. This person also has a reflexively critical position which acknowledges that this particular tradition is one among others, and that there are nowhere any valid suprasystematic criteria for determining which tradition, if any, is likely to be true or not. By denying the validity of the scientific method, the postmodern person can tell other, less reflexively critical, believers to go on believing, free from worry that there is any way to cast legitimate doubt on their beliefs. But the postmodern person, if this person really believes in the postmodern position, has taken up residence halfway outside of the tradition, in the strange land of postmodernity.

The land is strange because it is one in which the inhabitants declare that there is no universally valid perspective for judging various language games or forms of life, and take this declaration to be a universal truth.[57] If postmodernism is itself only a local system of thought, relative to a certain point of North Atlantic culture in the late twentieth century, then an alternative view on criteria for truth-claims, such as that of modern science can propose itself as superior to the local prejudice of postmodernism. Only if postmodernism can somehow establish that it is itself the suprasystematic, universally valid position, can it place limits on other perspectives. In any case, it is at least implicitly a universalist position, claiming to have the truth about the nature of all other positions.

Those who dwell in postmodern thought in religion have another problem to consider. The position they take puts them at ease with their own religious community, even while they continue to live in the larger world to which they are accustomed. But in principle they are cutting that community loose from the patterns of the larger world. They are adopting a position analogous to that taken by the Amish long ago, when their way of life was not all that different from life in general, except for some specifically religious elements. Now, to preserve that way of life, they use horse-pulled carriages and end the schooling of their children at the eighth grade. We may suspect that postliberals do not intend to segregate their "form of life" from the larger cultural life in so many respects as the Amish. Postliberals may simply wish to preserve certain religious beliefs and practices and moral norms, while at the same time being able to communicate with the larger world and even share in much of its life. Even to use postmodern philosophy is to borrow from the larger world in which the religious community finds itself. Postliberals may also want to maintain the moral witness that most religious traditions believe they have to offer to the larger world. With these and other forms of communication with the larger world in place, it seems artificial to cut the lines between religious thought and science. It seems more to be a ploy, a special pleading, than a general position on how a religious community relates to other forms of life or other language games.

Learned journals contain endless theoretical arguments on all this. The arguments are sometimes illuminating because they differentiate among different aspects of religion and among different types of ordinary and/or scientific knowledge. But skill in theoretical argumentation will probably not get us much further by itself than it did when the major ancient schools of Greek philosophy battled each other to an impasse. The practices of modern science have shown us that balancing theoretical reflections with careful and controlled attention to evidence is much more effective. Like postmodernism, science is also universalist, though more coherently so. Science does not have to deny the universal validity of standards of truth, even as it speaks of itself as universally valid (for the limited goal of determining which truth-claims about reality will function as though they are simply true). Science is also highly successful in practice, again for its limited goal. We have already seen briefly that as a result of the success of science, there are many theologians who, like Teilhard de Chardin, Pannenberg, and the philosopher Whitehead, have found ways to integrate their scientific worldview with their overall religious tradition. There is another twentieth-century theological approach that accepts the validity of science for judging truth-claims, at least truth-claims that are short of the metaphysical. It provides a model of how religious thought and scientific method and conclusions can find at least a high degree of compatibility.

Correlational Theologies

By the early twentieth century, as we have seen, liberal and existential theologies had dealt with the challenge of scientific rationality and conclusions by extracting religion from the realm of science. In the middle of the twentieth century, the development of a correlational approach opened a door toward greater cooperation between religion and science. The first well-known correlational theology was Paul Tillich's attempt to relate the basic human experience of existential dismay to a rather liberalized Christianity as a relation of question to answer.[58] His starting point was the existential-metaphysical. Borrowing images from German philosophers of his time, he addressed the fundamental human question of being and non-being, of ultimate meaning or ultimate meaninglessness. The human person, he said, can perceive an ultimate threat in the possibility of endless meaninglessness. Looking around for evidence that there is ultimate meaning, like others of our times Tillich did not find it possible to believe in miracles as a means to attest to the reality of an Ultimate called God; nor could he perceive in the order of the universe a basis for an argument from design for the existence of God. Where evidence failed, he found he could still turn, in a manner similar to Bultmann's, to the inner possibility of courage in face of the threat of meaninglessness. He could find in himself the power to affirm being over non-being. Like Bultmann also, he derived his courage partly from the inspiration of traditional Christian images. He "correlated" his existential and metaphysical needs with the possibility of faith and courage he found in religious symbols. Tillich was critically aware that the images and doctrines of his Christian heritage are symbols that must not be taken as simple literal truth. They are "broken myths," in his terminology. They are broken because we recognize that they are symbols and not literal truth.[59] On this point, Tillich was doing little more than repeating the liberal position on the symbolic nature of traditional doctrines.

Later in the century, a critical yet more traditional theology appeared in the work of the Roman Catholic theologian Karl Rahner. Like Tillich, he emphasized the issue of ultimacy. We are indeed the being with the capacity for the infinite, as Ludwig Feuerbach said. Our core humanness is our capacity for a the critically reflective openness to the infinite. This capacity for the infinite presents us with the problem that Feuerbach, as well as Tillich and Rahner, saw in their different ways: The infinite threatens the meaning of our lives by presenting the possibility of endless aimlessness. All that we do and value and devote ourselves to, may in the end be swallowed up in the utterly mindless processes of an awesomely immense universe. The experience of infinite mystery, as Rahner puts it, is an intrinsic capacity of the human person. But Rahner notes another special aspect of most human experience: that we find ourselves able to act and choose and make lasting commitments, sometimes for the sake of others even at great personal sacrifice. All this is a stance toward life that treats life as though it were ultimately worthwhile. Even many an atheist, proclaiming that the final truth about reality is that there is no ultimate value or meaning to anything, still finds the faith or hope or courage to live for certain values.

To make sense of this human condition, Rahner turns to his own Christian tradition, just as Tillich does. He finds in the traditional doctrine of grace a way to interpret human faith and courage in the face of infinite mystery. This doctrine proclaims that it is by the power of God within a person that the person is able to have such faith and courage. The fact of human courageous faith correlates here with the Christian understanding. But Rahner goes much further than Tillich in seeking an overall correlation among various aspects of life, including a correlation between the empirical contents of science and the doctrines of his religious tradition. Rahner accepts the scientific picture of the universe as an immense evolutionary process. Like Teilhard de Chardin, he correlates this scientific understanding with his traditional belief that the mystery is actually the Creative Mystery called God, which accounts for the reality of the universe and its basic processes. The "grace" that empowers people to hope and have trust in life's meaning is, traditionally, a name for the empowering presence of God. This is a single sustaining presence for the universe as a whole. Rahner reinterprets a number of major traditional doctrines, but not as symbols standing in for a more literal truth. He affirms the literal truth of doctrines such as the incarnation of God in Jesus, or the resurrection of Jesus from the dead. He reinterprets them, however, as *instances* of the more general truth that God's sustaining presence is "incarnate" in everyone, that at death everyone enters into their final relationship with the Eternal Mystery, and so on. Rahner elim inates individual miraculous interventions and translates such beliefs into instances of the single "miracle" of divine creation and sustenance of the universe.[60] The metaphysical perspective of Rahner thereby provides him a way to affirm the literal truth of traditional doctrines even while understanding that literal truth in a way which is compatible with the method and conclusions of modern science.

Rahner integrates a number of elements. He first points to the normally vague human experience of mystery, as well as to the basic trust or hope in the face of mystery. Second, he applies philosophical reflection to bring the experience of mystery and of hope or trust to explicit consciousness. Third, he correlates this with his Christian tradition, which describes a God who is Absolute Mystery, who creates, sustains, and in the end redeems all, by bringing it to an ultimate fulfillment (one beyond human imagination). To all this Rahner adds science, as the method that establishes what should be accepted as true about anything in the created and therefore finite order—whatever is not Ultimate Mystery. Rahner thereby tries to integrate basic aspects of experience, philosophical reflection, his Christian tradition, and science.

Rahner and Tillich both demythologize claims of miraculous interventions in history. Both claim that this demythologizing is not something forced upon religion by the external requirements of scientific rationality. They both insist that the absolute infiniteness of the divine mystery places God beyond activity more appropriate for a limited god. Precisely because God is the ultimate, says Tillich, all human formulations about God are necessarily limited and tentative, symbolic expressions rather than immutable and univocally accurate truths. Because God is infinite Mystery, says Rahner, all doctrinal formulations belong in a hierarchy of truth wherein lesser doctrines must always be understood as humanly intelligible ways of categorizing what is beyond all categories. So religion of its own nature, not because of a science external to it, must always demythologize itself in relation to the Ultimate or Mystery. They thereby make it possible for a person to integrate science and religious thought.

Tillich and Rahner thus found a *theological* reason to affirm a reflexively critical approach to the religious truth-claims of their Christian tradition. The method of these theologies is in harmony with the modern empirical-critical method in science. If the practices of modern science have made contemporary people more aware of themselves as limited knowers, at work in an evolving universe, then science may be directing people's awareness to what Tillich and Rahner see as the real issue of God: Ultimacy or Infinite Mystery. The focus on Ultimacy or the Infinite allows these correlational theologies to leave it to science to determine the probable validity of all truth-claims about the finite processes and events of the universe, including those which have in the past been interpreted as miraculous interventions.[61]

Conclusion

The evolution of thought styles in human history has swept along the whole range of human thought—philosophical, scientific, and religious. At each major point of cultural cognitive development, at least some traditional religious beliefs were undercut by the new thought style. The village shaman faced city priests who claimed priority for the gods over local spirits. In the axial age the gods were demoted or shunted aside to make room for an Ultimate Power or Reality. At each of these points religious traditionalists could well feel they were losing something they cherished. In the last two or more centuries, traditional religious believers have met similar threats to what they cherish. Belief in miracles, already long challenged by the search for intelligibility, became doubly doubtful as the new science found natural explanations for what once seemed miraculous. Scientific understanding of the processes of nature makes nature no longer seem clearly planned and purposeful. Finally, the reflexively critical awareness of current philosophy and science challenges traditional religious certitude. A person at home with a late formal operational style of thought may find it comfortable to interpret religious belief in the style of postliberalism or correlational theology. But to translate traditional religious doctrines into anything but the simple truth will feel like a loss to many religious people.

If the analysis of cognitive styles in these pages is correct, it suggests that most of the people in any large population will live their lives mainly by concrete operational thought with perhaps some extra guidance from formal operational thought. They will not maintain a steadily reflexive awareness of the limitations of language and thought, in such a way as to hold the truth-claims of their religious tradition as historically conditioned and symbolic expressions of a fundamental trust in the ultimate worthwhileness of life because of some not-quite-clear presence and power of a divine reality. They will not find sentences like the previous one to be of much use in either religion or life in general.

At this point the science-minded skeptic may recommend abandoning religion for a more "scientifically" rational stance. But life confronts us all with experiences that make life deeply difficult. Pain, sickness, handicaps, loss, loneliness, and death may require something more than rational skepticism. Certainly people today who have lost traditional beliefs often seem to turn to New Age or other beliefs that offer them a basis to hope or trust that life can be made whole or at least meaningful in the face of these threats. Most people seem also to need something more definite than just trust; more, even, than trust and hope and courage together. Nor is a general metaphysical affirmation of life's meaning enough. Specific beliefs in resurrection or rebirth, heaven or nirvana, Jesus or Amida Buddha convey a much more reassuring message.

Let me speak, then, of how religious philosophers and theologians might respond to this. These religious thinkers often have special training not only in the content of their religious tradition but also in cognitive methods as sophisticated as the late formal operational style of science, postmodernism, and correlational theologies. From this suprasystematic position, they have many options about both beliefs and methods. They have a very large, and therefore very difficult, task of dealing not only with the truth-claims of their traditions but also with many other aspects and functions, individual and communal, moral and emotional and symbolic. I do not want to underplay the difficulty of this project, nor do I want to dismiss any of the many forms of religious thought as useless or unimportant.

I can speak only to one point: a concern for standards of truthfulness. I believe contemporary religious thinkers, the philosophers and theologians, recently have been far too eager to release their religious communities and traditions from the standards of modern science for evaluating truth-claims. Let me repeat: These standards are not restricted to science. Science has merely brought intensity and exactitude to what we all must do daily to make our beliefs more reliably accurate. To judge whether the newly installed front porch is firmly footed and nailed, we need to examine it closely. Careful measurements tell us how level it is; jumping on it determines how steady it is; finding the nails in the studdings tells us how well it has been hammered together. It will help to get a neighbor or two over to find things we have overlooked, to put our evaluation to a further test. Science is just a highly refined version of these methods. Let me also repeat: Science is the only method that has shown itself to be effective at all, and it has shown itself to be highly effective for the limited task of determining which truth-claims will function reliably as the equivalent of truth.

Religion ought to promote standards of truthfulness. Religious thinkers do not serve humankind well by undercutting the method of science; they do not serve religion well in the long run by evading the method and conclusions of science. Concern by theologians and philosophers for the community of religious believers is commendable. But undercutting the best means available for judging the validity and reliability of truth-claims will hurt people in general, including those in communities of religious believers.

Chapter 9 ended with a brief mention of a basic faith implicit in science. This is faith that being a human person, exercising curiosity and intelligence, seeking to know more about reality, is worthwhile. If the scientist will go so far as to claim it is ultimately worthwhile, this is an act of at least implicit religious faith. Religious believers have a fairly simple choice. One option is to evade, attack, reject, or vilify the method of science in order to safeguard traditional religious belief. The other option is to acknowledge the power of that method to discriminate well between truth-claims that work reliably and universally and those that do not. Only the second option is consistent with the actual history and success of science. Science has discovered an enormous amount of fundamental intelligibility to the universe, and has thereby also vindicated the hopes of generations that such intelligibility does exist and that our minds can come to grasp it. Religious thought which does not take this quite seriously as one of its starting points will serve neither itself nor humankind well. Religious thought which does accept this may also find in it a fundamental reason to affirm the ultimate, and therefore religious, validity of being a knower in the world.[62]

NOTES

Introduction

1. Talcott Parsons, *The Evolution of Societies* (Englewood Cliffs, NJ: Prentice-Hall, 1977). Niklas Luhmann, *Religious Dogmatics and the Evolution of Societies*, trans. Peter Beyer (New York: E. Mellen Press, 1984), is an excellent set of reflections on the place of religious thought in Parsons's theory of cultural evolution.

2. James Peacock and A. Thomas Kirsch, *The Human Direction: An Evolutionary Approach to Social and Cultural Anthropology* (New York: Appleton-Century-Crofts, 1970; 3rd ed., Englewood Cliffs, NJ: Prentice-Hall, 1980). At the time the first edition (1970) was available to me.

3. See Alexander R. Luria, *Cognitive Development: Its Cultural and Social Foundations*, trans. Martin Lopez-Morillas and Lynn Solotaroff (Cambridge, MA: Harvard University Press, 1976). Michael Cole's introduction provides background on Luria's speculation.

4. See Alexander R. Luria, *Cognitive Development*, 8–12.

5. Haydn White, *Tropics of Discourse: Essays in Cultural Criticism* (Baltimore: Johns Hopkins University Press, 1978). I agree with the sequence of development in White's comparison of literary tropes, cultural stages, and Piagetian categories, though not with his precise parallels.

6. Bernard Lonergan compares his "four realms of meaning" to stages of cultural development, in *Method in Theology* (New York: Herder and Herder, 1972), 257–265. He makes comparisons between the cognitive development of the individual and shifts in cultural thought styles in his *Philosophy of God and Theology* (Philadelphia: Westminster, 1973), 1–8. For a profound expansion of Lonergan's theory, see Robert M. Doran, *Theology and the Dialectics of History* (Toronto: University of Toronto Press, 1990).

7. James W. Fowler, *Stages of Faith: The Psychology of Human Development and the Quest for Meaning* (San Francisco: Harper & Row, 1981).

8. James W. Fowler, *Faithful Change: The Personal and Public Challenges of Postmodern Life* (Nashville, TN: Abingdon Press, 1996).

9. Richard H. Schlagel, *From Myth to Modern Mind: A Study of the Origins and Growth of Scientific Thought*, vol. 1, *Theogony Through Ptolemy* (New York: Peter Lang, 1995), 46.

10. I must credit Kieran Egan for the contrast between Vygotsky and Piaget, in his *The Educated Mind: How Cognitive Tools Shape Our Understanding* (Chicago: University of Chicago Press, 1997), 29. Piaget treats all the stages as part of a natural development, whereas Egan thinks that only the first stages, up through concrete operational, are natural, and that formal operational kinds of thought are products of culture that must be learned. I think Egan is correct.

11. Donald E. Brown, *Human Universals* (Philadelphia: Temple University Press, 1991), lists numerous such universals in a long argument against the almost pure social determinism that has reigned in much of anthropology. Bradd Shore, in *Culture in Mind: Cognition, Culture, and the Problem of Meaning* (New York: Oxford University Press, 1996), recounts that he experienced great psychic difference between himself and Samoans, but went on to discover how much they shared cognitively. What we humans share allows anthropologists to understand other cultures. See Merlin Donald, *The Origins of the Modern Mind: Three Stages in the Evolution of Culture and Cognition* (Cambridge, MA: Harvard University Press, 1991), for an excellent review of our common genetic and linguistic heritage.

12. Mark Turner, *The Literary Mind* (New York: Oxford University Press, 1996), argues that even our basic declarative sentences are small stories. James B. Wertsch, *Voices of the Mind: A Sociocultural Approach to Mediated Action* (Cambridge, MA: Harvard University Press, 1991), emphasizes cultural diversities but nonetheless describes shared basic human traits of learning and thinking.

13. Donald Brown, *Human Universals*, 3, makes this point by reference to Lyle B. Steadman, "Neighbours and Killers: Residence and Dominance Among the Hewa of New Guinea" (Ph.D. diss., Australian National University). Steadman lived and worked among the Hewa of New Guinea, a people who were in an "uncontrolled" area (one off-limits to Europeans, including missionaries [but not, apparently, to anthropologists]). Steadman learned the Hewa language eventually, and in spite of having been taught the lack of universals in humankind, he found that the Hewa and he understood each other quite well. Brown quotes Steadman: "Living, traveling, working and hunting with the Hewa, made it clear to me that their basic concerns, the concerns motivating their behaviour, were similar to my own" (26).

14. Jared Diamond, *The Third Chimpanzee: The Evolution and Future of the Human Animal* (New York: HarperPerennial, 1993), 51.

15. Charles M. Radding provides an outstanding review of the medieval decline and rebirth of cognitive styles, using Piaget's categories to interpret them, in *A World Made by Men: Cognition and Society, 400–1200* (Chapel Hill: University of North Carolina Press, 1985). I have somewhat different examples and have taken a different approach by stressing the religious aspect, particularly in relation to miracles, and by providing some background for the rise of empiricism. Nonetheless, Redding and I agree substantially. See also Don LePan, *The Cognitive Revolution in Western Culture*, vol. 1, *The Birth*

of Expectation (London: Macmillan, 1989); LePan agrees with Redding and offers further support for the Piagetian interpretation of this era.

16. *The Positive Philosophy of Auguste Comte*, trans. Harriet Martinau, 2 vols. (London: John Chapman, 1853), 2–3. Comte presents an early instance of the notion that cultural development is like individual development: "the phases of a mind of a man correspond to the epochs of the mind of the race" (3). Or see *Auguste Comte and Positivism: The Essential Writings*, ed. Gertrude Lenzer (Chicago: University of Chicago Press, 1975), 71–72.

17. Donald Wiebe, *The Irony of Theology and the Nature of Religion* (Montreal: McGill-Queens University Press, 1991), 33.

18. Stewart Elliott Guthrie, *Faces in the Clouds* (New York: Oxford University Press, 1993), 32–36.

19. One account is Bruce D. Lawrence, *Defenders of God: The Fundamentalist Revolt Against the Modern Age* (San Francisco: Harper & Row, 1989). He recommends extending the label "Fundamentalist" to literalists in Islam and Judaism.

20. Friedrich Schleiermacher, *The Christian Faith* (Edinburgh: T. & T. Clark, 1928; 1968), 156–160, 161–170, 178–184. He did link morality and science to religious feeling by his claim that awareness of the Whole is in fact what leads to morality's search for positive unity among people and science's search for a unified understanding of the universe.

21. Mircea Eliade, *The Sacred and the Profane* (New York: Harper Torchbook, 1961), 10. Eliade says he is concerned with "the sacred in its entirety," not just with nonrational forms. See also Rudolph Otto, *The Idea of the Holy* (New York: Oxford University Press, 1958), e.g., 117–129. Otto thinks that religious feeling may exist within cognitive beliefs, but that there needs to be a further evolution of feeling to achieve true religiousness.

22. Michael J. Buckley, S. J., *At the Origins of Modern Atheism* (New Haven, CT: Yale University Press, 1987), 358–361.

23. George Lindbeck, *The Nature of Doctrine: Religion and Theology in a Postliberal Age* (Philadelphia: Westminster, 1984).

24. Norman Malcolm, "The Groundlessness of Belief," in *Reason and Religion*, ed. Stuart C. Brown (Ithaca, NY: Cornell University Press, 1977), 143–157.

Chapter 1

1. It may help from the first to distinguish the general notion of cultural evolution from Herbert Spencer's "recapitulation" theory. Spencer proposed a fairly rigid and inexorable law of human progress, and then proposed that each human child would ideally recapitulate the cognitive development of the human race. Unlike Spencer, I do not see any iron law of progress at work, no inevitable upward trend. Nor is there a law of nature or history creating the parallel between culture and individual.

2. This is a point made in Joseph Lopreato, "From Sociological Evolutionism to Biocultural Evolutionism," *Sociological Forum* 5:2 (June 1990): 187–212.

3. David Levinson and Martin J. Malone, *Toward Exploring Human Culture* (New Haven, CT: HRAF Press, 1980). This is a highly empirical review of various studies. Robert Boyd and Peter J. Richardson, *Culture and the Evolutionary Process* (Chicago: University of Chicago Press, 1985), constructs a de-

tailed model of major aspects of cultural evolution. This ambitious attempt to correlate many aspects of culture reaches a bit beyond even the extensive evidence they cite.

4. Merlin Donald, *The Origins of the Modern Mind: Three Stages in the Evolution of Culture and Cognition* (Cambridge, MA: Harvard University Press, 1991). A wonderfully detailed and argued book, it has been criticized only on the grounds that it could have benefited from even more archaeological information. See also Kieran Egan, *The Educated Mind*.

5. Ernest Gellner, *Plough, Sword, and Book: The Structure of Human History* (London: Collins Harvill, 1988).

6. Robert Bellah, "Religious Evolution," in his *Beyond Belief* (San Francisco: Harper & Row, 1970), reprinted from *American Sociological Review* 29 (1964): 358–374. Bellah's thesis is like that in Auguste Sabatier, *Outlines of a Philosophy of Religion Based on Psychology and History* (New York: George H. Doran, 1902; repr. New York: Harper Torchbook, 1957), esp. 96–104. Sabatier proposed that a basic common religiousness, both mystical and practical, evolved from a primitive stage of family/clan animism, to "national" forms of polytheism, to universalist moral monotheism.

7. See Christopher Hallpike, *The Principles of Social Evolution* (Oxford: Clarendon Press, 1986), 372, for comments to this effect. Hallpike should also be credited with the observation that social conversations tend to a lower common denominator; see his *The Foundations of Primitive Thought* (New York: Oxford University Press, 1979), 60.

8. For his views on how his theory is a form of a structuralism, see Jean Piaget, *Structuralism*, trans. Chaninah Maschler (New York: Basic Books, 1970).

9. For brief summaries by Piaget, see his *The Child and Reality: Problems of Genetic Psychology*, trans. Arnold Rosin (New York: Grossman, 1973), 57–61; or Barbel Inhelder and Jean Piaget, *The Growth of Logical Thinking: From Childhood to Adolescence* (New York: Basic Books, 1958), 245–257.

10. Piaget thought he could apply his theory to historical developments. In a book written with Rolando Garcia, for example, he made an attempt to apply his theory to the development of aspects of scientific thought in Western culture. Rolando Garcia and Jean Piaget, *Psychogenesis and the History of Science* (New York: Columbia University Press, 1989). This was based on the 1983 French edition, yet in Jean-Claude Bringuier, *Conversations with Jean Piaget* (Chicago: University of Chicago Press, 1980), "Ninth Conversation," 91–109, Piaget comments on *Psychogenesis* as though it were already written. Piaget begins with Aristotle, and except for a side comment here and there does not try to analyze the history of any but Western culture and science. In *Conversations*, 100, he indicates that the development of thought in China might be much different from that in the West, but does not say further what he means.

11. James Fowler, *Stages of Faith* (San Francisco: Harper & Row, 1981), esp. 149–150, 172–173, 182–183, 197–198. See also Fritz K. Oser and Paul Gmunder, *Religious Judgment: A Developmental Perspective* (Birmingham: Religious Education Press, 1991), for a report on a major research project using Fowler's categories and finding them valid. Their one major criticism of Fowler's work is that his definition of "faith" is broader than religion (44), an aspect that turns out to be rather advantageous, I believe. His general descriptions of the various stages eventually came to provide me with heuristic

guides even better than Piaget's formulations. It is only very recently that he has applied his descriptions—accurately, I think—to the evolution of thought styles in North Atlantic culture over the last few hundred years. See Fowler's *Faithful Change: The Personal and Public Challenges of Postmodern Life* (Nashville, TN: Abingdon Press, 1996), 145–147.

12. Egan, *The Educated Mind.*

13. See Lawrence Kohlberg, *The Philosophy of Moral Development* (San Francisco: Harper & Row, 1981) and *The Psychology of Moral Development* (New York: Harper & Row, 1983), for collected articles. See also Leonard T. Hobhouse, *Morals in Evolution: A Study in Comparative Ethics* (London: Chapman and Hall, 1951 [repr. of 1906 original]). This careful and insightful comparison of widespread empirical data apparently faded from view because of strong antievolutionary thought at the beginning of the twentieth century. Hobhouse's work deserves attention.

14. Robert Kegan, *In over Our Heads: The Mental Demands of Modern Life* (Cambridge, MA: Harvard University Press, 1994).

15. Haydn White, *Tropics of Discourse: Essays in Cultural Criticism* (Baltimore: Johns Hopkins University Press, 1978). The sequence of development in White's comparison of literary tropes, cultural stages, and Piagetian categories is relevant.

16. Karen Strohn Kitchener, "Cognition, Metacognition, and Epistemic Cognition," *Human Development* 26:4 (July–August 1983), 222–232.

17. Bernard Lonergan, *Method in Theology* (New York: Herder and Herder, 1972), 257–265. He compares the cognitive development of the individual and shifts in cultural thought styles in *Philosophy of God and Theology* (Philadelphia: Westminster, 1973), 1–8.

18. William Perry, *The Forms of Intellectual and Ethical Development in College Years* (New York: Holt, Rinehart, and Winston, 1970). The comparison is made in Carol Gilligan and John Michael Murphy, "Development from Adolescence to Adulthood," in *Intellectual Development Beyond Childhood*, ed. Deanna Kuhn (San Francisco: Jossey-Bass, 1979), 85–99.

19. C. Daniel Batson and W. Larry Ventis, *Religious Experience: A Social-Psychological Perspective* (New York: Oxford University Press, 1982).

20. See Ronnie Lesser and Marilyn Paisner, "Magical Thinking in Formal Operational Adults," *Human Development* 28:2 (March–April 1985): 57–70. See also Richard Shweder, "Likeness and Likelihood in Everyday Thought: Magical Thinking in Judgements About Personality," *Current Anthropology* 18:4 (1977): 637–658.

21. Alex Shoumatoff, *The Rivers Amazon* (San Francisco: Sierra Club, 1986), 66.

22. Marjorie Rutter and Michael Rutter, *Developing Minds: Challenges and Continuity Across the Life Span* (New York: Basic Books, 1993), 195. The Rutters offer criticism of Piaget that the next chapter will discuss.

23. See Dorothy G. Singer and Jerome L. Singer, *The House of Make-Believe: Children's Play and the Developing Imagination* (Cambridge, MA: Harvard University Press, 1990), esp. ch. 5. The authors suspect similarities between childhood imaginings and adult beliefs (89–91).

24. Margaret Mary Wilcox, *A Developmental Journey* (Nashville, TN: Abingdon Press, 1979), 63, 67, uses this expression.

25. Ernest Gellner, *Reason and Culture: The Historic Role of Rationality and Rationalism* (Oxford: Blackwell, 1992), 31–32, notes that the sympathetic and

homeopathic forms of magic identified by Frazer are merely expressions of the mind's natural tendencies in all of its thinking.

26. D. Kuhn, J. Langer, L. Kohlberg, and N. S. Haan, "The Development of Formal Operations in Logical and Moral Judgments," *Genetic Psychology Monographs* 95 (1977): 97–188, discusses types of reasoning adults can ordinarily use.

27. Kitchener does not use it in quite the same way, however. In her usage "metacognition" seems to apply even to ways in which concrete operational thinkers learn to organize their thoughts, as in arithmetic classes.

28. See Fowler, *Stages*, 183–184.

29. Piaget and Inhelder, *The Growth of Logical Thinking*, 345.

30. There is less careful research on patterns of cognitive development past late adolescence. Fischer and Silvern note that while there is clearly continuing development, it is not certain that these changes should be labeled technically as new developmental stages or levels. See Kurt W. Fischer and Louise Silvern, "Stages and Individual Differences in Cognitive Development," *Annual Review of Psychology* 36 (1985): 613–648. Also see Michael L. Commons, Jan D. Sinnott, Francis A. Richards, and Cheryl Armon, eds., *Adult Development*, vol. 1, *Comparisons and Applications of Developmental Models* (New York: Praeger, 1989).

31. Piaget's description of the awareness of the limits of knowledge leads Walter E. Conn to call Piaget a "critical realist." See his "Piaget as a Critical Realist," *Angelicum* 54:1 (1977): 67–88.

32. Lucretius, *De Rerum Natura*, trans. W. H. D. Rouse (Cambridge, MA: Harvard University Press, 1975), 451–491. In the last third of book 5, lines 915–1457, Lucretius gives a sweeping story of the evolution of culture from before language and fire up to city life and the arts. He explains the origin and nature of worship of the gods in lines 1161–1236, pp. 469–475, citing dreams and visions, and the order and power of nature, as the basis of belief. His explanation is "intellectualist," saying belief in the gods answers questions the mind raises when confronting nature and the human condition.

33. *Turgot on Progress, Sociology, and Economics*, ed. and trans. Ronald L. Meek (Cambridge: Cambridge University Press, 1973), 9.

34. *Turgot on Progress*: "The original aptitudes are distributed equally among barbarous peoples and among civilized peoples; they are probably the same in all places and at all times. Genius is spread throughout the human race very much as gold is in a mine" (88). It is education that makes the difference in the *use* of the mind. A notable aspect of his thought: "Inequality between the sexes, like slavery, is a product of barbarism" (81).

35. Ronald L. Meek, *Social Science and the Ignoble Savage* (New York: Cambridge University Press, 1976), 177–219. Meek (5–36) traces the theory back to Lucretius, and then to Jean Bodin (d. 1596) and to Hugo Grotius in his *The Laws of War and Peace* (1625).

36. Donald's *The Origins of the Modern Mind* analyzes the results of psychoneurology, compares them against what is known about early hominids from paleontology, adds studies from current primatology, and offers detailed hypotheses about how the transition to speech took place.

37. Genuinely human language with many specific sounds of high information content existed by late paleolithic times (ca. forty thousand to ten thousand years ago). Philip Lieberman, "The Origins of Some Aspects of Human Language and Cognition," *The Human Revolution: Behavioral and Biologi-*

cal Perspectives on the Origin of Modern Humans, ed. Paul Mellar and Chris Stringer (Princeton: Princeton University Press, 1989), 391–414, reviews fossils and comparative studies of primate vocalization ability. Recent paleontology suggests that Neanderthals had much greater speech abilities than we have suspected.

38. Steven Mithen, *The Prehistory of the Mind: The Cognitive Origin of Art, Religion, and Science* (London: Thames and Hudson, 1996), provides an impressive estimate of the thinking processes of hominids up through Cro-Magnon, based on archaeological evidence.

39. Chapter 3 will provide sources and further analysis on this primitive thought.

40. Contrary to the claims by Lévi-Strauss. See Thomas Gregor, *Mehinaku* (Chicago: University of Chicago Press, 1977), 56, on how these people, whom Lévi-Strauss claimed to have studied, classify and organize. Or see Jaan Puhvel, *Comparative Mythology* (Baltimore: Johns Hopkins University Press, 1987), 18, on Lévi-Strauss's categories as gimmickry.

41. There are disputes about whether this should be called religion. Segal suggests Lévy-Bruhl was correct to interpret the most primitive ideas and activities as "prereligious" on the grounds that the rituals and accompanying stories did not include worship. See Robert Segal, "Mythopoeic Versus Religious Thought: A Reply to Michael Barnes," *Religion* 24:1 (January 1994): 77–80.

42. Bronislaw Malinowski, *Magic, Science, and Religion* (New York: Doubleday Anchor, 1954), 87–90, argues that the two are quite distinct. There have been a variety of positions on this since then.

43. Ibid., 25–36, reviews ideas in Malinowski's time. More recent discussions of this have focused on articles by Robin Horton, e.g., his "African Traditional Thought and Western Science," *Africa* 37:1 (January 1967): 50–71, and 37:2 (April 1967): 155–187. He responds to his critics is in "Tradition and Modernity Revisited," in *Rationality and Relativism*, ed. Martin Hollis and Steven Lukes (Cambridge, MA: MIT Press, 1982), 201–260. Robin Dunbar, *The Trouble with Science* (Cambridge, MA: Harvard University Press, 1995), argues that a kind of science—hypothesis and testing—is done even by pigeons and rats, that science is a name for what all higher organisms must be able to do to survive. It is not surprising that he supports Horton's claim that primitive religion and mythical thinking are a kind of primitive science (56).

44. Karl A. Wittfogel, *Oriental Despotism; a Comparative Study of Total Power* (New Haven, CT: Yale University Press, 1957), 3.

45. As in ancient Sumer or China. See the discussion of this in chapter 3.

46. Karl Jaspers, *The Origin and Goal of History* (New Haven, CT: Yale University Press, 1953), esp. 1–27.

47. A useful work on this topic is Shmuel Noah Eisenstadt, ed., *The Origins and Diversity of Axial Age Civilizations* (Albany: SUNY Press, 1986). See chapter 5 of this volume for more on this.

48. See Joseph Needham, *Science and Civilization in China* (New York: Cambridge University Press, 1956), 165–188, on this period in China as its axial or classical age. John B. Henderson, *The Development and Decline of Chinese Cosmology* (New York: Columbia University Press, 1984), portrays classical Chinese thought as somewhat more archaic in some aspects than the

classical eras of Greece and India. Chapter 5 of this volume will discuss this further.

49. Robert D. Baird and Alfred Bloom, *Indian and Far Eastern Religious Traditions* (New York: Harper & Row, 1972), 19–21, 42–43.

50. The often quoted locus is book X of the Rig Veda, ch. 129, verses 1–7, beginning: "Non-being then existed not, nor being. . . . " See Sarvepalli Radhakrishnan, Charles Moore, eds., *A Sourcebook in Indian Philosophy* (Princeton, NJ: Princeton University Press, 1957), 23–24. A. L. Herman suggests that earlier ideas, such as those about Varuna in book VIII, already ascribed a greatness to the Divinity that approximates a belief in omnipotence and omniscience, but he is clearly arguing as to what he thinks the text only *implies*. See his *An Introduction to Indian Thought* (Englewood Cliffs, NJ: Prentice-Hall, 1976), 82. Radhakrishnan lists many passages from earlier Vedas under the heading "monotheistic and monist *tendencies*." *Sourcebook*, 16–25. Again, see chapter 5 of this volume for more on the topic.

51. Edward E. Evans-Pritchard, *Theories of Primitive Religion* (New York: Oxford University Press, 1965), 121, says those who believe in souls, spirits, and gods grasp the inner life of religion better than nonbelievers. He seems to want to defend such beliefs.

52. Richard A. Shweder, *Thinking Through Cultures: Expeditions in Cultural Psychology* (Cambridge, MA: Harvard University Press, 1991), 52–55. Shweder does not say whether he finds such beliefs rationally legitimate within his own culture.

53. Mircea Eliade, *The Sacred and the Profane* (New York: Harper Torchbook, 1961), 2. Eliade says something similar in his *Patterns in Comparative Religion* (New York: World Publishing, 1967), 462–465.

54. Jacques Kamstra, "Changes in the Idea of God in Non-Western Religions and Culture," in *New Questions on God*, ed. Johannes B. Metz (New York: Herder and Herder, 1972), 123–133. Kamstra borrows categories from David Smith (128). Richard W. Comstock, *The Study of Religion and Primitive Religion* (New York: Harper & Row, 1972), uses similar language even while he denies that there is an evolution of religion!

55. See Lesser and Paisner, "Magical Thinking in Formal Operational Adults," and Shweder, "Likeness and Likelihood in Everyday Thought."

56. Robert Wuthnow, *Meaning and Moral Order: Explorations in Cultural Analysis* (Berkeley: University of California Press, 1987), 187–190.

57. Fowler also claims many adults operate with what he calls a stage three style of life. His description of this style fits with concrete operational thought. *Stages of Faith*, 172–173.

58. John McLeish, *Number: The History of Numbers and How They Shape Our Lives* (New York: Fawcett Columbine, 1992), 8, agrees. Montessori, Piaget, and Vygotsky remind us, he says, that learning to think abstractly is a long, hard process.

59. See Dunbar, *The Trouble with Science*, 44–55.

Chapter 2

1. Franz Boas, *The Mind of Primitive Man* (New York: Macmillan, 1991 [a revision of Boas's 1938 revision of the 1911 original]). Chapters 1 and 2 summarize his antiracist arguments.

2. Ibid., p. 12.

3. Ibid., p. 173. Boas argues against various highly specific theories (e.g., economic theories that are so detailed as to portray the gradual steps by which agriculture appeared). He offers specific counterinstances in which the theoretical sequence did not occur, probably because of local conditions, and goes on to argue that local conditions in general are probably stronger determinants of development than any logical sequencing could predict. See ibid., pp. 175–193.

4. Ibid. See ch. 11, "The Mind of Primitive Man and The Progress of Culture," 197–225.

5. Ibid., 224–225.

6. Ibid., p. 223.

7. Consider also Paul Diener's claim that the biological model of "punctuated equilibrium" helps interpret "civilizational history." See his "Quantum Adjustment, Macroevolution, and the Social Field: Some Comments on Evolution and Culture," *Current Anthropology* 21:4 (August 1980): 423–431. See also the articles in *Sociological Forum* 5:2 (June 1990) on current thinking about social evolution. T. R. Burns, and F. H. Buttel, and T. Dietz, "Evolutionary Theory in Sociology: An Examination of Current Thinking," 155–171, are excited about work that compares cultural evolution with biology or that links it to sociobiology. They make no mention of Piagetian schemes and give no attention to specifically cognitive dimensions. P. L. van den Berghe, "Why Most Sociologists Don't (and Won't) Think Evolutionarily," 173–185, makes this a question of why sociologists will not incorporate concepts from biological evolution into sociological theories. They give five major reasons, none of them having much to do with arguments about evolution of cognitive methods or styles. Joseph Lopreato, "From Social Evolutionism to Biocultural Evolutionism," 187–212, contrasts the new social evolutionism with the old. The new is closer to biological evolution as understood since the neo-Darwinian synthesis (i.e., not as a simple progressivist ladder but as a multiply branching tree, in which many aspects of societies—war, production, incest avoidance, sex-ratio control, gender preferences, etc.—may vary in many ways). The "coevolutionary model" of Charles J. Lumsden and Edward O. Wilson, *Genes, Mind, and Culture* (Cambridge, MA: Harvard University Press, 1981) and *Promethean Fires: Reflections on the Origin of Mind* (Cambridge, MA: Harvard University Press, 1983), focuses on the origin of mind from brain, not on the evolution of mental techniques. Lumsden and Wilson raise the issue of "enthnocentrism," of why we tend to divide everyone into us and them and hate them, and attend (rightly) to the sociobiological basis of this. This list could be extended; the purpose is to suggest the great support that exists for theories of cultural evolution.

8. John D. Y. Peel, "History, Culture, and the Comparative Method: An African Puzzle," in *Comparative Anthropology*, ed. Ladislav Holy (Oxford: Basil Blackwell, 1987), 88–118. Peel's fivefold set of options is not the end of complexities. Anthropologists who suppose it is worth seeking out large-scale patterns in the development of cultures may add their own specific theories.

9. Steven Pinker, *The Language Instinct: How the Mind Creates Language* (New York: Harper Perennial, 1994), breaks language use into several major aspects, each with a distinct effect common to humans in general.

10. See Donald E. Brown, *Human Universals* (Philadelphia: Temple University Press, 1991), for a thorough discussion of human universals. He provides extensive lists, though he does not claim that any one universals is

"necessary." The bibliography is especially useful for identifying sources and possible universals.

11. An excellent example of (4) is Nicholas Thomas, *Out of Time: History and Evolution in Anthropological Discourse* (New York: Cambridge University Press, 1989). This includes careful critiques of the limits of evolutionary theories, but also shows the necessity of tracking the history of changes in a cultural development, particularly in a single region. Thomas rejects progressivism, on the grounds that he can show instances of "devolution" (65–66). He is also is skeptical of the value of cognitive interpretations of cultural development. The specifics of the thesis of this book, however, are not in direct conflict with his analysis.

12. In an earlier article Durham rejects stage like sequences, linking them to what he calls the "archaic and prejudiced" concepts of Spencer. William H. Durham, "Advances in Evolutionary Culture Theory," *Annual Review of Anthropology* 19 (1990): 187–210. His own theory of "ramification," however, does not by itself account for any patterns in the evolution of culture. Durham has been at work for some years on "Evolutionary Culture Theory," which he labels ECT. He also follows Peel's method (2) but adds a specific Darwinian note, interpreting the process of cultural change as "descent with modification," in Darwin's famous phrase. Durham's goal is to treat the history of cultures as family trees, with various aspects of the culture drifting and diversifying much as language has over the last twenty thousand years.

13. Ernest Gellner, *Plough, Sword, and Book* (London: Collins Harvill, 1988), 15.

14. Ibid., 20.

15. Leslie White proposed a similar model in *The Evolution of Culture* (New York: McGraw-Hill, 1959). He divided societies into three strata, the technological-material at the bottom, the philosophical-cognitive at the top, and the "social" in between. These three aspects develop together.

16. Gellner, *Plough, Sword, and Book*, 71.

17. Ibid., 79.

18. Ibid., 122, 202–204.

19. Tim Ingold, *Evolution and Social Life* (New York: Cambridge University Press, 1986).

20. Stephen K. Sanderson, *Social Evolutionism: A Critical History* (New York: Cambridge University Press, 1990).

21. Ibid., 224–226.

22. Ruth Finnegan, *Oral Literature in Africa* (Oxford: Oxford University Press, 1970), 34–36, 319–320.

23. Ronald M. Berndt and Catherine H. Berndt, *The World of the First Australians* (Chicago: University of Chicago Press, 1964 [repr. of 1954]), 326–347. Their account of the tales about the two sisters from whom the human race descended, for example, does not really have a plot; it is a collection of brief descriptions of a variety of rather disconnected activities by the sisters.

24. Bruce Chatwin, *The Songlines* (New York: Viking Penguin, 1987). Chatwin adds extra weight to the stories by capitalizing many words. In his text it is "the story of the Lizard who ate some Dingo pups at the Middle Bore Hill."

25. Ibid., 106–107.

26. Edwin Hutchins, *Culture and Inference* (Cambridge, MA: Harvard University Press, 1980), 11. Hutchins notes also that before him Malinowski had

also discovered some doctrines of law, but ones that "are not, of course, codified in any explicit native tradition" (18). Hutchins describes islanders as making disjunctions between factual and hypothetical claims, but the instances given are all very concrete, lacking any of what later chapters of this volume will describe as analytically systematic thought.

27. Ibid., 11, 117.

28. Christopher Vecsey, "The Story and Structure of the Iroquois Confederacy," *Journal of the American Academy of Religion* 54:1 (Spring 1986): 93.

29. Aletta Biersack, "The Logic of Misplaced Concreteness: Paiela Body Counting and the Nature of the Primitive Mind," *American Anthropologist* 84: 4 (December 1982): 811–829.

30. Claude Lévi-Strauss, *The Savage Mind* (Chicago: University of Chicago Press, 1966), 127–128, 250–262.

31. Edward E. Evans-Pritchard, *Witchcraft, Oracles, and Magic Among the Azande* (Oxford: Clarendon Press, 1937), 70; see 314–322 for other instances of similar lack of analysis by the Azande.

32. Horton calls them "theories," but as always it is necessary to be cautious in the use of such labels. Robin Horton, "African Traditional Thought and Western Science," in *Rationality*, ed. Bryan R. Wilson (Evanston, IL: Harper & Row, 1970), 145.

33. Ibid.

34. See also Robert A. LeVine, "Properties of Culture," in *Culture Theory*, ed. Richard A. Shweder and Robert A. LeVine (New York: Cambridge University Press, 1984), 67–85, for similar comments about and analysis of the beliefs of the Gusii of Kenya in a number of inner spirits, beliefs that function as a substitute for an awareness of the inner complexity of the individual person's thoughts and feelings. See especially 82–85.

35. Mircea Eliade, *Patterns in Comparative Religion*, trans. Rosemary Eliade (New York: Sheed and Ward, 1958; New American Library, 1963), 33.

36. In Mircea Eliade, *Myths, Dreams, and Mysteries: The Encounter Between Contemporary Faiths and Archaic Realities*, trans. Philip Mairet (New York: Harper Torchbooks, 1967), 191–192.

37. Marjorie Rutter and Michael Rutter, *Developing Minds: Challenge and Continuity Across the Life Span* (New York: Basic Books, 1993), 195. See ch. 6, "The Growth of Intelligence and Language."

38. Alison Gopnik and Andrew N. Meltzoff, *Words, Thoughts, and Theories* (Cambridge, MA: MIT Press, 1997), 51.

39. Ibid., 83.

40. In addition to other sources cited in this section, see Kurt W. Fischer and Louise Silvern, "Stages and Individual Differences in Cognitive Development," *Annual Review of Psychology* 36 (1985): 613–648, an inclusive summary of significant studies and the state of the question at the time.

41. Rutter and Rutter, *Developing Minds*, 193–194.

42. Robbie Case, *Intellectual Development: Birth to Adulthood* (New York: Academic Press, 1985), 50. Other important sources include Sara Meadows, "Piaget's Contribution to Understanding Cognitive Development: An Assessment for the Late 1980's," in *Cognitive Development to Adolescence*, eds. Ken Richardson and Sue Sheldon (Hove, East Sussex: Lawrence Erlbaum Associates, 1988), 19–31; and Robbie Case and Wolfgang Edelstein, ed., *The New Structuralism in Cognitive Development: Theory and Research on Individual Pathways* (New York: Karger, 1993).

43. See Susan Carey, "Are Children Fundamentally Different Kinds of Thinkers and Learners Than Adults?" in *Cognitive Development to Adolescence*, ed. Ken Richardson and Sue Sheldon (Hove, East Sussex: Lawrence Erlbaum Associates, 1988), 105–138, for a summary of many relevant studies.

44. See Thomas R. Bidell and Kurt W. Fischer, "Cognitive Development in Educational Contexts: Implications of Skill Theory," in *Neo-Piagetian Theories of Cognitive Development*, ed. Andreas Demetriou, and Anastasia Efklides, Michael Shayer, (New York: Routledge, 1992), 11.

45. An analysis parallel to Carey's appears in work by John E. Biggs, a longtime leading scholar and sometime critic of Piagetian theory. He subdivides forms of knowing into more categories than Piaget and gives a long list of neo-Piagetian issues that are as yet unresolved. Biggs remains a neo-Piagetian, however, one who recognizes a general validity of Piaget's descriptions of cognitive stages and skills. See Andreas Demetriou, Anastasia Efklides, and Michael Shayer, eds, *Neo-Piagetian Theories of Cognitive Development* (New York: Routledge, 1992), 31–43, 277–294.

46. Howard Gardner, *Frames of Mind: The Theory of Multiple Intelligences* (New York: Basic Books, 1983), 281–282. Gardner agrees with the cognitive psychologist D. Alan Allport that the various modules simply interact, like a group of experts in different fields whose opinions carry varying weight in different contexts. See Jerry Fodor, *The Modularity of Mind: An Essay on Faculty Psychology* (Cambridge, MA: MIT Press, 1983).

47. Steven Mithen, *The Prehistory of the Mind: The Cognitive Origins of Art, Religion, and Science* (London: Thames and Hudson, 1996).

48. Dan Sperber, *Explaining Culture: A Naturalistic Approach* (New York: Blackwell, 1996), 146.

49. This is perhaps less true for the seven intelligences that Gardner identifies: linguistic, musical, logico-mathematical, spatial, bodily kinesthetic, self-awareness, and sociality. But this list also takes us beyond the scope of what Piaget studied and what we will examine here. The cognitive styles at issue here are those related mainly to linguistic and logical modes of thought.

50. Case and Edelstein, *The New Structuralism in Cognitive Development*.

51. Fischer and Silvern, "Stages and Individual Differences in Cognitive Development." This is a long review of many studies over the previous decade. The conclusions are fairly clear and consistent: in spite of great variations that exist among children, whether because of individual differences or particular environment, the child's stage of general cross-skill ability is a good predictor of how easily the child can learn any single skill. In other words, there is evidence for something like an underlying structure of thought at each stage of development. See other articles in this volume for more evidence along the same lines.

52. Case, *Intellectual Development*, 50.

53. For example, Jean Piaget, *The Child and Reality: Problems in Genetic Epistemology*, trans. Arnold Rosin (New York: Grossman, 1973), 26–28.

54. Annette Karmiloff-Smith, *Beyond Modularity: A Developmental Perspective on Cognitive Science* (Cambridge, MA: MIT Press, 1992). As she puts it, she wants to get beyond "a cute empirical database about *when* external behavior can be observed" to "a discussion on *how* the human mind is organized internally" (xiii).

55. Case, *Intellectual Development*, 377–380.

56. R. W. Thatcher, R. A. Walker, and S. Guidice, "Human Cerebral Hemispheres Develop at Different Rates and Ages," *Science* 236 (May 29, 1986): 1110–1113.

57. Richard A. Shweder, *Thinking through Cultures: Expeditions in Cultural Psychology* (Cambridge, MA: Harvard University Press, 1991), 2. Shweder declares that the work of both Piaget and Gellner is based on a devotion to the idea of the modern autonomous individual ego and a rejection of the claims of tradition. He attributes this rejection of tradition to a universalism like that of Plato and Descartes and the modern structuralists, who are looking for some abstract universals or "pure being" rather than the particulars of real human history.

58. Ibid.

59. Ibid., 31–32. See also Richard Shweder and Edmund J. Bourne, "Does the Concept of the Person Vary Cross-Culturally?" in *Culture Theory: Essays on Mind, Self, and Emotion*, eds. Richard A. Shweder and Robert A. LeVine (New York: Cambridge University Press, 1984), 158–199. Here he asserts relativism about the concept of the person. As part of his exchange with Hallpike in the *American Anthropologist*, however (87 [1985]: 138–144), Shweder cites a study by Thomas Schultz on causal thinking in children. The study compares the thinking of illiterate children in Mali with that of Western children. Shweder approvingly quotes Schultz that "the essential similarities between the results for Malian children and those obtained for Western children are many and striking" (141). This implies a cross-cultural similarity that would fit well with either a universalism or with some developmentalisms.

60. Shweder, *Thinking Through Cultures*, 33–39.

61. On Neitzschean thought, see ibid., 39–40; on belief in witches, jinns, gods, etc., ibid., 43–46.

62. Ibid., 50.

63. Ibid.

64. Ibid., 43–44.

65. Richard A. Shweder, "Rationality 'Goes Without Saying,'" *Culture, Medicine, and Psychiatry* 5:4 (1981): 348–358.

66. See his attack on Christopher Hallpike's ideas: Richard A. Shweder, "On Savages and Other Children," *American Anthropologist* 80:1 (1982): 354–366. In subsequent issues of the *American Anthropologist* Shweder and Hallpike continued to argue. See Hallpike's response in 85 (1983): 656–660; and the final sorties by each of them in 87 (1985): 138–144 and 144–146. There will be more on Hallpike in chapter 3. See his summary criticism of Piaget in his "Anthropology's Romantic Rebellion against the Enlightenment," in *Culture Theory*, eds. Richard A. Shweder and Robert A. LeVine (New York: Cambridge University Press, 1984), 49–51.

67. Shweder, "On Savages and Other Children," 356.

68. Shweder, *Thinking Through Cultures*, 129–136.

69. Shweder complicates the issue by using instances concerning value judgments, aesthetics, feelings, and thought all together. This is more than Piaget tried to cover. To introduce these related issues may be important in the long run, but the effect at this point is just to muddy the waters.

70. See Levine and Shweder, *Culture Theory*, 51. Shweder cites nine studies of "magical" thinking among American adults, 36–37.

71. A point also made by Biggs, in Demetriou et al., *Neo-Piagetian Theories*, 43.

72. Shweder, *Culture Theory*, 54.

73. Richard A. Shweder, "Has Piaget Been Upstaged? A Reply to Hallpike," *American Anthropologist* (1985): 87 138–144.

74. Karen Strohm Kitchener, "Cognition, Metacognition, and Epistemic Cognition: A Three-Level Model of Cognitive Processing," *Human Development* 26:4 (July–August 1983): 222–232.

75. Shweder, "Has Piaget Been Upstaged?" 51, 54.

76. Ibid., 36–37, 51–57.

77. Shweder, "On Savages and Other Children," 359.

78. Shweder refers to W. C. Ward and H. M. Jenkins, "The Display of Information and the Judgment of Contingency," *Canadian Journal of Psychology* (1965): 19:231–241.

79. Pierre R. Dasen and Alastair Heron, "Cross-Cultural Tests of Piaget's Theory, in *The Handbook of Cross-Cultural Psychology*, vol. 4, *Developmental Psychology*, ed. Alastair Heron and Harry C. Triandis (Boston: Allyn and Bacon, 1981), 295–341.

80. E.g., Irven DeVore and Richard B. Lee, eds., *Man the Hunter* (Chicago: Aldine, 1968), likewise surveys many studies. Or see Thomas Gladwin, "Culture and Logical Process," in *Explorations in Cultural Anthropology*, ed. Ward H. Goodenough (New York: McGraw-Hill, 1964), 167–177. There are studies of many individual tribal groups, such as Gavin Seagrim and Robin Lendon, *Furnishing the Mind: A Comparative Study of Cognitive Development in Central Australian Aborigines* (Sydney and New York: Academic Press, 1980); or Seagrim's article on Piagetian categories applied to the Aborigines, "Caveat Interventor," in *Piagetian Psychology: Cross-Cultural Contributions*, ed. Pierre Dasen (New York: Gardner Press, 1977). John W. Berry, *Human Ecology and Cognitive Style* (New York: John Wiley and Sons, 1976).

81. There are also intriguing parallel studies on aspects of life that indirectly reveal something of the cognitive styles. Brian Sutton-Smith and John M. Roberts, for example, report that the simplest cultures play no games or just games of physical skill. Only more complex cultures add games of chance or games of strategy. See their "Play, Games, and Sports," in Triandis and Heron, *Handbook of Cross-Cultural Psychology*, vol. 4, 425–471. Raoul Naroll, "Holocultural Theory Tests," in *Main Currents in Cultural Anthropology*, eds. Frada Naroll and Raoul Naroll (New York: Appleton-Century-Crofts, 1973), 309–384, surveys other common patterns among primitive peoples. More on this in the next chapter.

82. LeVine, "Properties of Culture," 82–83.

Chapter 3

1. Much of this chapter appeared as part of Michael Barnes, "Primitive Religious Thought and the Evolution of Religion," *Religion* 22 (1993): 21–46.

2. Richard B. Lee, "Art, Science, or Politics? The Crisis in Hunter-Gatherer Studies," *American Anthropologist* 94 (1992): 31–54, summarizes this point along with others. Also see Barbara Bender and Brian Morris, "Twenty Years of History, Evolution, and Social Change in Gatherer-Hunter Studies," in *Hunters and Gatherers*, vol. 1, *History, Evolution, and Social Change*, eds. Tim

Ingold, David Riches, and James Woodburn (New York: St. Martin's Press, 1988), 4–14.

3. Anna C. Roosevelt, "Secrets of the Forest," *The Sciences* (November/December 1992): 22–28.

4. Barbara Rogoff, "Schooling and the Development of Cognitive Skills," in *Handbook of Cross-Cultural Psychology*, vol. 4, *Developmental Psychology*, eds. Harry C. Triandis and Alastair Heron (Boston: Allyn and Bacon, 1981), esp. 258–265.

5. Daniel A. Wagner and Harold W. Stevenson, eds., *Cultural Perspectives on Child Development* (San Francisco: W. H. Freeman, 1982), 161.

6. Michael Cole, John Gay, Joseph A. Glide, and Donald A. Sharp, *The Cultural Context of Learning and Thinking* (New York: Basic Books, 1971), 213–216, takes note of this problem in the summary conclusions of many years of investigating and comparing modes of thought in some West African societies.

7. John F. Peters makes this point about the "egalitarian" social structure in his *Life Among the Yanomami: The Story of Change Among the Xilixanna on the Mucajai River in Brazil* (Orchard Park, New York: Broadview Press, 1998), 61.

8. Dean Sheils, "An Evolutionary Theory of Supportive Monotheism: A Comparative Study," *International Journal of Comparative Sociology* 15:1–2 (1974): 47–56, surveys a wide variety of studies to arrive at this conclusion.

9. Pascal Boyer, *The Naturalness of Religious Ideas: A Cognitive Theory of Religion* (Berkeley: University of California Press, 1994), 93.

10. Ruth Finnegan, *Oral Literature in Africa* (Oxford: Oxford University Press, 1970), 361–367, a defender of the beauty and power of oral literature as well as an opponent of evolutionary theories of culture, nonetheless says that the preliterate cultures of Africa have no clearly religious "myths" but only many stories about origins of things, about various spirit beings.

11. Radin chose the word "folktale" for his collection of "myths" from Africa. Paul Radin, ed., *African Folktales* (New York: Schocken Books, 1983), extracted from his *African Folktales and Sculpture* (New York: Pantheon, 1952). On the other hand John Bierhorst, whose selection of Native American folktales has stories of the same general brevity and simplicity, titles his book *The Mythology of North America* (New York: William Morrow, 1985).

12. Timothy K. Earle, "Chiefdoms in Archeological and Ethnological Perspective," in *Annual Review of Anthropology* 16 (1987): 279–308, says chiefdoms are important intermediate-level societies, an evolutionary bridge between acephalous primitive cultures and bureaucratic states. He notes that even while evolutionary theories are unpopular, ethnological studies do in fact use this threefold division (280).

13. Some of this material on "high gods" has appeared in Barnes, "Primitive Religious Thought and the Evolution of Religion."

14. The idea was not new. Fr. Joseph François Lafitau, S.J., lived in North America as a missionary, and wrote *Manners of the American Natives Compared with the Manners of Earliest Times* (1724), to argue that all barbarians had the concept of God, and God therefore must have engraved the idea in our hearts. So says A. Owen Aldridge in "Primitivism in the Eighteenth Century" in *Dictionary of the History of Ideas*, ed. Philip Warner, vol. 3 (New York: Scribner's, 1973), 599. (Calvin had proposed this too, and so, perhaps, did Augustine.)

15. Fr. Schmidt provides his own summary of all his work in *The Origin and Growth of Religion* (New York: Cooper Square, 1972 [repr. of the 1931 original]). See also Paul Radin's early and good criticism of Schmidt's approach in his *Primitive Religion: Its Nature and Origin* (New York: Dover, 1937), 255–262. For a current Catholic semicritic, see Jacques Kamstra, "Changes in the Idea of God in Non-Western Religion and Culture," in *New Questions on God*, ed. Johannes B. Metz (New York: Herder and Herder, 1972), 123–133. Kamstra notes that when the idea of a universal God is imported into a primitive culture, the God tends to become shrunken down to a local god. Kamstra uses this and other ideas to distinguish between tribal, national, and universal religions, nicely paralleling the division of primitive, archaic, and classical or axial.

16. Robert K. Dentan, *The Semai* (New York: Holt, Rinehart, and Winston, 1968), 23–24.

17. As reported in Carleton S. Coon, *The Hunting Peoples* (Boston: Little, Brown, 1971), 298–299, with other examples of exaggerated claims for the existence of a high god at, 299–301.

18. Also see John Middleton, *Lugbara Religion* (London: Oxford University Press, 1960), for a summary of one of the sources of Horton's information about high gods among African tribespeople. The word "God" is used by Middleton to translate *Adro*, but this is a slippery word. Middleton's own descriptions of it make it sound as though it actually names the supernatural (to use our categories) *in general*, as it exists in magic and in spirits, rather than a specific high god, much less a supreme God. Horton, however, speaks of cannibalistic *Adro* spirits. "African Traditional Thought and Western Science," in Bryan R. Wilson, ed., *Rationality* (Evanston, IL: Harper & Row, 1970), 151. See note 69 in this chapter.

19. See Jonathan Z. Smith, *Imagining Religion: From Babylon to Jonestown* (Chicago: University of Chicago Press, 1982), ch. 5, pp. 66–89.

20. According to Robin Horton, many tribespeople balance a local polytheism, which satisfies their usual interests, with access to the idea of a God, which is relevant to the occasional large questions about life. Horton acknowledges, however, that ideas about God are rather undeveloped and not of much interest, and concludes therefore, that "The idea of God seems more the pointer to a potential theory than the core of a seriously operative one." "African Traditional Thought and Western Science," 144.

21. Michael Gelfand, *An African's Religion* (Cape Town: Juta and Co., 1966), 111, 118–129. See also Alice B. Child and Irvin L. Child, *Religion and Magic in the Life of Traditional Peoples* (Englewood Cliffs, NJ: Prentice-Hall, 1993), 50, 59, 124–127. As a final note on the issue of high gods, at least one person casts doubt on a seemingly obvious instance of belief in a high god: the ancient Chinese belief in the will of Heaven. Jordon Paper provides numerous instances of errors that Westerners have made about Chinese thought. One of these, he claims, was made by the sixteenth-century Jesuits when they identified Heaven as a personal being, and therefore at least a high god (and perhaps close to belief in God). See his *The Spirits Are Drunk: Comparative Approaches to Chinese Religion* (Albany: SUNY Press, 1995).

22. Percy Amaury Talbot, *Tribes of the Niger Delta* (New York: Barnes and Noble, 1967), esp. 253.

23. Middleton, *Lugbara Religion*, esp. 250–258.

24. Guy E. Swanson, *The Birth of the Gods: The Origins of Primitive Beliefs* (Ann Arbor: University of Michigan Press, 1964). See 65 for a summary chart of the relation of social organization to beliefs in a high god. Swanson discusses exceptions and problems in the subsequent pages.

25. Phillip Guddemi, "When Horticulturalists Are like Hunter-Gatherers: The Sawiyano of Papua New Guinea," *Ethnology* 31:4 (October 1992): 303–314.

26. Bruce Lincoln, *Priests, Warriors, and Cattle: A Study in the Ecology of Religions* (Berkeley: University of California Press, 1981), 14–23.

27. Talcott Parsons, *The Evolution of Societies* (Englewood Cliffs, NJ: Prentice-Hall, 1977), 45.

28. Emile Durkheim, *The Elementary Forms of the Religious Life* (New York: Free Press, 1965 [repr. of 1915 ed.]), 54.

29. Mircea Eliade, *The Sacred and the Profane* (New York: Harper Torchbook, 1961), 11.

30. Ibid., 8–10.

31. Steven Lukes summarizes the results of ongoing anthropological research on this point in his *Emile Durkheim: His Life and Work* (New York: Harper & Row, 1972), 24–28.

32. Joachim Wach, *Types of Religious Experience* (Chicago: University of Chicago Press, 1951), 32–37.

33. Äka Hultkrantz, "The Concept of the Supernatural in Primal Religion," *History of Religions* 22:3 (February 1983): 231–251.

34. Peter Worsley, *The Trumpet Shall Sound* (New York: Schocken Books, 1968), xxvii–xxviii, xxxii–xxxiii, 240.

35. Douglas Lienhardt, *Divinity and Experience: The Religion of the Dinka* (Oxford: Clarendon Press, 1961), 29–31.

36. Robert Baird and Alfred Bloom, *Indian and Far Eastern Religious Traditions* (New York: Harper & Row, 1972), 316.

37. Ronald M. Berndt and Catherine M. Berndt, *The World of the First Australians* (Chicago: University of Chicago Press, 1964 [repr. of 1954]), 137, 149 describes the bull-roarer and its use.

38. Napoleon Chagnon, *Yanomamö: The Fierce People*, 3rd ed. (New York: Harcourt Brace Jovanovich, 1992), 140–141.

39. Colin M. Turnbull, *The Forest People: A Study of the Pygmies of the Congo* (New York: Simon and Schuster, 1962), 75–76.

40. Edward B. Tylor, *Religion in Primitive Culture* (New York: Harper & Row, 1958; [reprint of 1873 2nd ed.]), vol. 2, 2. Tylor gives only this reference: J. D. Lang, "Queensland."

41. Ibid., vol. 2, 2–3, with reference to Lang's "Queensland," 340, 374, 380, 388, 444, as evidence of special dealings with spirit beings.

42. Child and Child, *Religion and Magic*, 79.

43. Tylor, *Religion in Primitive Culture*, vol. 2, 8.

44. Some of this material is taken from Michael H. Barnes, "Rationality in Religion," *Religion* 27 (1997): 375–390.

45. Robert Segal has called attention to this in his, "Mythopoeic Versus Religious Thought: A Reply to Michael Barnes," *Religion* 24:1 (January 1994): 77–80.

46. Lucien Lévy-Bruhl, *Primitive Mythology: The Mythic World of Australian and Papuan Natives*, trans. Brian Elliott (New York: University of Queensland Press, 1983), 37–39. First published as *La mythologie primitive*. 1935.

47. Ibid., 37–38.

48. Ibid., 39.

49. Edward Burnett Tylor, *Anthropology: An Introduction to the Study of Man and Civilization* (New York: D. Appleton and Co., 1898), 336–337.

50. Ibid., 338–341.

51. Lucien Lévy-Bruhl, *How Natives Think*, trans. Lilian Clare (New York: Allen and Unwin, 1985), 24–27.

52. Ibid., 25.

53. Ibid.

54. Steven Lukes, argues that religions make cognitive claims and that there are valid standards of rationality by which to judge such claims. "Some problems about Rationality," in Bryan Wilson, ed., *Rationality* (New York: Harper & Row, 1970), 194–213. Augustine Shutte, "A Theory of Religion," *International Philosophical Quarterly* 16:3 (September 1976): 289–300, agrees. Humans desire to know and need completeness; we find it through the concepts and practices given us by a social tradition including religious beliefs. Terry Godlove, "In What Sense Are Religions Conceptual Frameworks?" *Journal of the American Academy of Religion*, 52:2 (June 1984), 289–305, argues each religion is a conceptual framework and can be judged by conceptual truth standards to that extent. William Bainbridge, *The Future of Religion* and Rodney Stark, also interpret religion as a search for rational understanding, substantive empirical data and analysis in support of their theories in their books *The Future of Religion* (Berkeley: University of California, 1985) (New York: Peter Lang, 1987). See Bainbridge's summary in "Is Belief in the Supernatural Inevitable?" *Free Inquiry* 8:2 (Spring 1988): 21–26.

55. As a side point, we might note that Tylor did not restrict his analysis of primitive religion to beliefs alone. But even in his description, say, of rituals or the use of drugs in religion, he elaborated on the beliefs associated with them. *Religion in Primitive Culture*, vol. 2, 448–496, 502–507.

56. See Dewi Z. Phillips, "The Devil's Disguises: Philosophy of Religion, 'Objectivity,' and 'Cultural Divergence,'" in *Objectivity and Cultural Divergence*, ed. S. C. Brown (New York: Cambridge University Press, 1984), 61–77.

57. Perhaps a reference to Tylor, *Religion in Primitive Culture*, vol. 2, 17. Tylor here is speaking of the Seminole practice of holding a child over the face of a dying mother. Tylor does not explicitly say it is a false belief, though Phillips is undoubtedly correct in assuming that is Tylor's position.

58. Dewi Z. Phillips, *Faith and Philosophical Enquiry* (New York: Schocken Books, 1971), 9. Phillips and other "Wittgensteinian Fideists" like Peter Winch and Norman Malcolm support a noncognitive notion of religion. See the list and criticisms of Wittgensteinians like Winch and Phillips in Edward L. Schoen, *Religious Explanations* (Durham, NC: Duke University Press, 1985), 188–200. Schoen describes those who use a "noncognitive Christianity" model as a refuge to make religion safe from all rational questioning because it is not rational at all, because all of its apparent fact-claims about supernatural realities are really just expressions of deeply felt emotions and commitments. He argues that some religious beliefs are truth-claims and must be subject to rational-scientific tests (15–18). On "Wittgensteinian Fideism," see Kai Nielsen's article by that title in *Philosophy* 42 (1967): 191–199; and Thomas Ommen, "Wittgensteinian Fideism and Theology," *Horizons* 7:2 (Fall 1980): 183–204. An extreme instance is that of Norman Malcolm, who calls the demand for justifying evidence "the pathology of philosophy." See his

"The Groundlessness of Belief," in *Reason and Religion*, ed. Stuart C. Brown (Ithaca, NY: Cornell University Press, 1977), 150. For Winch's position see Peter Winch, "Understanding Primitive Society," in *Understanding and Social Inquiry*, eds. Fred Dallmayr and Thomas McCarthy (Notre Dame, IN: University of Notre Dame Press, 1977), 159–188. Winch allows some fact-claim functions to mingle with emotional ones. Reasonably enough, he thinks the Azande use magic both as a technology to make crops grow and to express their feelings of concern (180–181). See also I. C. Jarvie's reply to Winch, in Dallmayr and McCarthy, 189–206.

59. David Hoy makes a similar charge against the general Eliadean claim that there is but one underlying experience of the sacred in all religions. It is quite ethnocentric, says Hoy, to thus suppose that all religious experience must be like one's own. David Hoy, "Is Hermeneutics Ethnocentric?" in *The Interpretive Turn: Philosophy, Science, Culture*, eds. David Hiley et al. (Ithaca, NY: Cornell University Press, 1991), 155–175.

60. Peter Winch made a similar claim for primitive thought in general in his "Understanding a Primitive Society," first printed in *American Philosophical Quarterly* (1964), to which Horton responded in his "Professor Winch on Safari," repr. in his *Patterns of Thought in Africa and the West* (New York: Cambridge University Press, 1993), 138–160. Winch argued that the Azande were not concerned with "explanation, prediction, and control," says Horton (150), who then shows at length that Winch is wrong in this.

61. Lucien Lévy-Bruhl, *The Notebooks on Primitive Mentality*, trans. Peter Riviere (New York: Harper & Row, 1975), 37–39. In passages dated 1938 he is still struggling for clarity. See esp. 37–43, 56–57.

62. E.g., ibid., 36–38.

63. E.g., ibid., 38.

64. E.g., ibid., 44–45, or all of ch. 2.

65. Much the same set of ideas appears in Lucien Lévy-Bruhl, *Primitive Mentality* (New York: Macmillan, 1923), trans. by Lilian A. Clare of *La Mentalité Primitive*, based on 1919 Lowell lectures in Boston, which he called "volume 2" of *How Natives Think* (p. 5). Still later his *Primitive Mythology* was meant to add further support. In all of these works there is the same attempt to delineate a mode of consciousness that he calls "mystical participation."

66. Horton's original presentation of his ideas was in "African Traditional Thought and Western Science," *Africa* 37:1 (January 1967): 50–71 and 37:2 (April 1967): 155–187. Horton abbreviated his ideas for publication in *Rationality*, ed. Bryan R. Wilson (Evanston, IL: Harper & Row, 1970), 131–171.

67. Horton has his own further theory about why modern industrial people use nonpersonal theories—gravity, force, mass—rather than personalist ones such as spirits or gods. Wilson, *Rationality*, 147. Later we will look at a historical account of the shift, and at a different theory to account for the shift.

68. Ibid., 147–148.

69. Horton provides instances that are rather speculative. He suggests, for example, that the Lugbara *Adro* spirits are incestuous cannibals, contrary to what humans are allowed to be, because the Lugbara need to have some spirits that represent the contrast between the settled and orderly life of the village and the wilder life of the bush, where the *Adro* live. This is another example to Horton of a "theoretical" scheme used to make sense of the world

through the extension of an analogy about how people might behave were they wild like the *Adro*. Ibid., 151.

70. Ibid., 162–164.

71. Christopher Hallpike, *The Foundations of Primitive Thought* (New York: Oxford University Press, 1979), 58. My apologies for the many footnotes here, but Hallpike's critics attribute to him many statements he does not make. The many references can guide the reader to see for herself or himself.

72. Ibid., 59.

73. Perhaps because of the anticolonialism of recent postmodern thought, cross-cultural studies of cognition seem to have decreased. Michael Cole, *Cultural Psychology: A Once and Future Discipline* (Cambridge, MA: The Belknap Press of Harvard University Press, 1996), a work by one of the great experts in the field, lists Hallpike's study in the bibliography, but not in the text, even though cognitive development is one of the topics. David Matsumoto, *People: Psychology from a Cultural Perspective* (Pacific Grove, CA: Brooks/Cole, 1994), a useful textbook, ignores Hallpike's work entirely, including in chapter 7 on cognitive development.

74. Hallpike, *Foundations of Primitive Thought*, 51.

75. Ibid., 64.

76. Ibid., 64, 485–486.

77. Ibid., 65.

78. Michael Cole et al., *The Cultural Context of Learning and Thinking* (New York: Basic Books, 1971).

79. See Ibid., 213–235, for conclusions and qualifications.

80. Hallpike, *Foundations of Primitive Thought*, 114. Ch. 5 "Classification," 169–236, recounts a number of studies on this aspect of thought.

81. Ibid., 110–114.

82. Bernard Lonergan, "Philosophy and the Religious Phenomenon," *Method: Journal of Lonergan Studies* 12:2 (Fall 1994): 142.

83. Hallpike, *Foundations of Primitive Thought*, 114.

84. Alexander Luria briefly summarizes and illustrates the use of the problem of the white bears in his *Cognitive Development* (Cambridge, MA: Harvard University Press, 1976), 110–112. He notes that one person who had received formal schooling did conclude that the bear was white. School culture can teach formal operational cognitive skills.

85. See Christopher R. Hallpike, *Bloodshed and Vengeance in the Papuan Mountains: The Generation of Conflict in Tauade Society* (Oxford: Clarendon Press, 1977). See also his *The Konso of Ethiopia: A Study of the Values of a Cushitic People* (Oxford: Clarendon Press, 1972).

86. Hallpike, *Foundations of Primitive Thought*, 234. Hallpike here credits Jack Goody with this comparison.

87. Ibid., 236.

88. Ibid., 296–313.

89. Ibid., 340–383.

90. Ibid., 415–420.

91. Ibid., 409–413.

92. Ibid., 388–401.

93. Ibid., ch. 10. This is the point of the whole chapter, but see esp. 466–470. As an aside, I might note that the tendency of the human mind to postulate a specific cause for each event may be hardwired into us. Infants

appear disconcerted when psychologists test them by creating an event where the normal cause is missing.

94. Foundations, 409–413, provides references to Hallpike's other studies.

95. Richard A. Shweder, "On Savages and Other Children," *American Anthropologist* 84 (1982): 354–366; T. O. Beidelman, "Review of Hallpike's *The Foundations of Primitive Thought*," *American Ethnologist* 8 (1981): 812–813.

96. Gustav Jahoda, *Psychology and Anthropology: A Psychological Perspective* (New York: Academic Press, 1982), 224–235. Brian Morris, *Anthropological Studies of Religion: An Introductory Text* (New York: Cambridge University Press, 1987). Ch. 6, "Religious Thought: Structure and Hermeneutics," 264–328, contains a great deal on Hallpike, though the relevant parts end at 312.

97. Marshall H. Segall, Pierre R. Dasen, John W. Berry, and Ype H. Poortinga, *Human Behavior in Global Perspective: An Introduction to Cross-Cultural Psychology* (Oxford: Pergamon Press, 1990).

98. Shweder's attack is the most thorough. In spite of his qualified acceptance of Piaget in some of his other writings, in his review of Hallpike's book, Shweder tries to show that Piaget's theory has fallen flat and cannot be used successfully for measuring any culture's modes of thought. (Ch. 2 of this volume has already responded to this.) Both Morris and Jahoda use Shweder's writings to criticize Hallpike; Beidelman wrote independently but has a few of the same concerns as Shweder.

99. Jahoda, *Psychology and Anthropology*, 224–228; Morris, *Anthropological Studies*, 311.

100. Hallpike, *Foundations of Primitive Thought*, 24.

101. Jahoda, *Psychology and Anthropology*, 229; Beidelman, "Review," 812.

102. See Hallpike, *Foundations of Primitive Thought*, 24–39, for many observations about similarities and continuities between primitive and modern people in their thought styles.

103. Morris, *Anthropological Studies*, 311, with a reference to Hallpike, *Foundations of Primitive Thought*, 33.

104. Hallpike, *Foundations of Primitive Thought*, 142.

105. Ibid., 58–62.

106. Shweder, "On Savages," 358. See also 355, 358–359, 361 for Shweder's fuller case.

107. Segall et al., *Human Behavior*, 152.

108. Beidelman, "Review," 812.

109. See John R. Snarey, "Cross-Cultural Universality of Social-Moral Development: A Critical Review of Kohlbergian Research," *Psychological Bulletin* 97:2 (1985): 202–232, for a review of over thirty studies.

110. Morris, *Anthropological Studies*, 311.

111. I suspect that Morris is alluding to the claims of Lévi-Strauss about the marvelous categorizing done by primitive people. A critique of the claims of Lévi-Strauss, however, would require many more pages here. Hallpike addresses those claims quite well, I believe.

112. Jahoda, *Psychology and Anthropology*, 221–222.

113. Ibid., 229. Jahoda takes the word of Gluckman on the Lozi of Barotseland and their legal logic, and that of Hutchins on the legal thought of the Trobrianders, that there is sophisticated thought here beyond what Hallpike's analysis seems to allow. Having read both of these works, as well as other

writings by Hutchins on the navigators of the Caroline Islands, I disagree. All of the skills as described in these various works strike me as lacking in any "metacognition," to return to that word. The categorization of ownership, land, lines of travel on the ocean, and so on, used in the various cases is held in memory and repeatedly appealed to as established fact. The law arguments mainly pit one set of ideas or memories against another, with some condensation of information. Rather than argue this at length in the text, this footnote will have to stand as unsupported claim, open to further argument in other circumstances.

Chapter 4

1. Samuel Noah Kramer proposes that the ancient Sumerians first governed their cities through a council of free citizens rather than by royal power. Samuel Noah Kramer and Diane Wolkstein, *Inanna, Queen of Heaven and Earth* (New York: Harper & Row, 1983), 116.

2. The development of ancient Greek society has been extensively analyzed. But Henri Frankfort's older studies of Egyptian and Mesopotamian modes of thought needs to be carried forward. Henri Frankfort et al., *Before Philosophy* (New York: Penguin, 1949).

3. David W. Anthony, "Shards of Speech," *The Sciences* 36:1 (January–February 1996): 34–39.

4. See, for example, Miranda Green, *The God of the Celts* (Totowa, NJ: Barnes and Noble, 1986), 7–17, on the sources of knowledge of the non-literate centuries of this people's religion.

5. Jaan Puhvel, *Comparative Mythology* (Baltimore: Johns Hopkins University Press, 1987), describes the means used to get behind the texts. The task is companion to philology, following words and phrases backward, discovering certain quite similar written stories from widely different locales but with common linguistic roots. Judgments of when the languages began to diverge provide a basis of how far back the common story may go. See ch. 1, 7–20.

6. "Particular word clusters . . . reveal rituals and beliefs beyond the reach of archaeological evidence alone. They show that the speakers of PIE [proto-Indo-European] probably practiced patrilineal descent and patrilocal . . . residence, recognized the authority of chiefs who were associated with a residential-kin group, had formally instituted warrior bands, practiced ritual sacrifices of cattle and horses, drove wagons, recognized a male or father sky deity, and avoided speaking the name of the bear for ritualistic reasons. They even demonstrated two senses of the sacred: 'that which is imbued with holiness' and 'that which is forbidden.'" Anthony, "Shards of Speech," 36.

7. Green, *God of the Celts*, 32. The presence of many animal carvings in contexts suggestive of ritual prompts Green to spend some time discussing the "animism" of the Celts. Ibid., 167–189.

8. Norman J. Girandot, "Behaving Cosmogonically in Early Taoism," in *Cosmogony and Ethical Order*, eds. Robin Lovin and Frank Reynolds (Chicago: University of Chicago Press, 1985), 70, makes a special point of this: "The common conception of 'primitive' cultures constantly and necessarily ordering their existence through the actual telling of coherent mythical narratives is in many ways nothing more than another mesmerizing scholarly myth about myths."

9. Denise Schmandt-Besserat, "From Accounting to Written Language: The Role of Abstract Counting in the Invention of Writing," in *The Social Construction of Written Communication*, eds. Bennet A. Raforth and Donald L. Rubin (Norwood, NJ: Ablex, 1988), 119–130. Roy Harris, *The Origins of Writing* (LaSalle, IL: Open Court, 1986), 71–73, disputes some aspects of Schmandt-Besserat's case but not the general outline of development.

10. At the least Samuel Noah Kramer's title, *History Begins at Sumer* (Philadelphia: University of Pennsylvania Press, 1981 [3rd rev. ed. of 1959 original]), is peculiarly correct: History, defined as the writing of events, began with writing, at Sumer. Nicholas D. Kristof reports in the *New York Times Magazine* on the Internet (June 13, 1999), with no source given, that Chinese explorers may have made contact with the Mayans in the fifth century CE].

11. Colin McEvedy, *The Penguin Atlas of Ancient History* (New York: Penguin, 1967), 26.

12. Flourian Coulmas, *The Writing Systems of the World* (Oxford: Basil Blackwell, 1989), 180–183.

13. McEvedy, *Penguin Atlas*, 32–34, claimed a Mesopotamian influence was discernible in the form of the inscriptions. He connects this with the technological leap in China from Paleolithic directly to Bronze Age tools. If China managed to shift this suddenly without going through the long copper–stone (chalcolithic) intermediate stage, it may well be that China learned bronze-producing techniques along with the *idea* of literacy from Mesopotamian influence. Coulmas, *Writing Systems*, 93–94, notes that the Mesopotamian connection is not established and prefers to see writing in China as an independent development. The use of bronze may have come from Southeast Asia, where bronze had been in use since at least 2000 BCE. Time-Life Editors, *The Age of God-Kings* (Alexandria, VA: Time-Life Books, 1987), 144–145. On the other hand, David N. Keightley, "The Origins of Writing in China: Scripts and Cultural Contexts," in *The Origins of Writing*, ed. Wayne M. Senner (Lincoln: University of Nebraska Press, 1989), 171–202, flatly claims that "Chinese writing was entirely indigenous" (187) and provides a summary of archaeological evidence. This includes the use of carved symbols for an eye and for the sun found on a turtle-shell box that apparently dates to about 6000 BCE. To my amateur's eye, Senner's side-by-side comparison of Sumerian, Egyptian, Hittite, and Chinese signs gives no reason at all to suspect any connection between Chinese writing and that of the other cultures. *The Origins of Writing*, 6.

J. T. Hooker argues that Egypt and China must be credited with inventing writing on their own. To say they borrowed the idea from Mesopotamia "would imply that the Egyptian and Chinese, with their aptitude for the higher arts of civilization, were incapable of devising a simple series of signs in which a round disk stood for 'sun.'" And so on. Historical questions are not safely solved by invoking implications of this sort. Evidence must establish the probabilities here. Moreover, if it took Sumer as much as eight hundred years to move from tokens to marked envelopes to early writing, it would not be surprising if Egyptians and Chinese were smart enough to grab a good idea when they saw it rather than wait a few centuries for their own process of development to produce writing. J. T. Hooker et al., *Reading the Past: Ancient Writing from Cuneiform to the Alphabet* (Berkeley: University of California Press, 1990), 7.

14. Walter Ong, *Orality and Literacy: The Technologizing of the Word* (New York: Methuen, 1982); *Interfaces of the Word: Studies in the Evolution of Consciousness and Culture* (Ithaca, NY: Cornell University Press, 1977); *The Presence of the Word* (New Haven, CT: Yale University Press, 1967); and *The Interface Between the Written and the Oral* (New York: Cambridge University Press, 1987).

15. Jack Goody and Ian Watt, "The Consequences of Literacy," *Comparative Studies in Society and History* 5 (1962–1963): 304–345. Also see Jack Goody, *The Domestication of the Savage Mind* (New York: Cambridge University Press, 1977) and *The Interface Between the Written and the Oral* (New York: Cambridge University Press, 1987).

16. Ong, *Presence of the Word*, 28–31.

17. Ong, *Orality and Literacy*, 31–32.

18. Ibid., 151.

19. Ong, *Presence of the Word*, 31. Ong says this of the medieval mind, meaning early medieval. A later chapter will take this up.

20. Goody and Watt, "Consequences of Literacy," 310.

21. Morris Edward Opler, *Myths and Tales of the Jicarilla Apache Indians* (New York: Dover, 1994 [repr. of 1938 ed.]), records what four Jicarilla informants told him. Each version is somewhat different from the others, and the stories of primal times have anachronistic additions. The spirit beings, for example, show the original people how to roll cigarettes and use the "thunder-stick" (rifle) to make noise (151, 157). One informant even discredits a competitor's version by calling it "shaman" knowledge, as though there were something inferior about traditional shamanism (162).

22. Goody and Watt, "Consequences of Literacy," 341–342.

23. Goody, *Domestication of the Savage Mind*, 43–47.

24. Ibid., 15.

25. Ong, *Orality and Literacy*, 133.

26. Goody and Watt, "Consequences of Literacy," 334.

27. Merlin Donald, *The Origins of the Modern Mind* (Cambridge, MA: Harvard University Press, 1991), 314–332, gives an excellent description of these external storage systems, their function, and their impact.

28. Ibid., 320. Donald notes here that 15 percent of the more than 100,000 cuneiform texts available are lists of words and numbers used for training scribes.

29. Brian V. Street, *Literacy in Theory and Practice* (New York: Cambridge University Press, 1984), 31, notes this basic form of abstraction in defense of primitive peoples' ability to do abstract thinking. The real issue is the levels of abstraction that are employed and the explicitness of the logic in using them. See below for more on Street's ideas.

30. Goody, *Domestication of the Savage Mind*, 71. Goody reminds us again that the various primitive "classificatory" schemes anthropologists have described are more in the minds of anthropologists than of primitives (52–53). The highly important kin relationships, for example, of which anthropologists draw complex diagrams, cannot be articulated by primitives. The branching genealogy, which traces not merely a maternal or paternal line but the geometrically expanding number of progenitors back numerous generations, is a topic of interest in oral cultures because of the importance of kinship ties and rules. But without literacy, branching genealogies cannot be created and remembered.

31. Ong, *Orality and Literacy*, 51–52. Here Ong uses Alexander Luria's work as major evidence. See ch. 3 of this volume.

32. Goody and Watt, "Consequences of Literacy," 339.

33. Ibid., 337.

34. Donald M. Topping, "Literacy in the Pacific Islands," *Interchange* 18: 1/2 (Spring/Summer 1987): 48–59.

35. Ibid., 56.

36. Ibid. Topping cites Ong, Lev Vygotsky, and Christopher Hallpike, among others. His own description of the Pacific Islanders fits well with Hallpike's description of nonliterate culture, though Topping might be unhappy to know this.

37. Stephen F. Mason, *A History of the Sciences* (New York: Macmillan, 1962), 17.

38. Ibid., 19.

39. George Sarton, *A History of Science: Ancient Science Through the Golden Age of Greece* (New York: W. W. Norton, 1952), has a wonderfully complete description of ancient Egyptian and Babylonian science. Henry W. F. Saggs, *The Greatness That Was Babylon* (New York: New American Library, 1962), 420–453, describes Babylonian sciences, including mathematics, astronomy, medicine, and chemical technology, in the larger context of Babylonian culture. Also see Mason, *History of the Sciences*, ch. 2.

40. Street, *Literacy in Theory and Practice*. Though he often mentions Ong and Goody, his actual targets are mainly the work of Angela Hildyard and David Olson in an unpublished manuscript at the Ontario Institute for Studies in Education (19) and the 1977 writings of Patricia Greenfield on the Wolof of Senegal (20–23).

41. The list and the conclusion are based on ibid., 3–4, 8–9.

42. Steven Shapin and Simon Schaffer, *Leviathan and the Air-Pump: Hobbes, Boyle, and the Experimental Life* (Princeton, NJ: Princeton University Press, 1985).

43. See, for example, the comment of Kwasi Wiredu, a member of the Akans tribal group of Ghana educated in British schools: "The principle that one is not entitled to accept a proposition as true in the absence of any evidential support is not Western in any but an episodic sense." Like any people anywhere, Africans use evidence as a means of assessing claims and as part of a "method of objective investigation." Kwasi J. E. Wiredu, "How Not to Compare African Thought with Western Thought," in *African Philosophy: An Introduction*, ed. Richard A. Wright, 3rd ed. (Lanham, MD: University Press of American, 1984), 152–153.

44. Street, *Literacy in Theory and Practice*, 26.

45. Ibid., 35.

46. Street cites Shirley Brice Heath, *Way with Words* (New York: Cambridge University Press, 1983), which compares ways of talking among people of three subcommunities to which Heath gives fictional names: "Mainstream," white and middle-class; "Roadville," populated by poor Christian whites of less education, and "Trackton," a black area of town. The contrasts she draws between Roadville and Mainstream kids are strikingly close to contrasts between concrete operational and formal operational thought. Street, *Literacy in Theory and Practice*, 121–123.

47. Street, *Literacy in Theory and Practice*, 26. The summary of Labov and the two quotations that follow in the text are all from 26.

48. Similarly, David Keightley explains the continuous development of writing in China as a result of a need to keep track of complex undertakings, whether the building of the great earthen wall around the Shang capital about 1500 BCE, the assembly-line procedures for the commercial production of bronze castings, or the construction of huge underground royal tombs. "Origins of Writing in China," 194–195.

49. Street, *Literacy in Theory and Practice*, 44–45.

50. Ong, *Orality and Literacy*, 140–143. See below for more on this.

51. Ibid., 104.

52. Walter Ong, "Technology Outside Us and Inside Us," *Communio* 2 (Summer 1978): 17.

53. Jeffrey H. Tigay, *The Evolution of the Gilgamesh Epic* (Philadelphia: University of Pennsylvania Press, 1982), 19–20, attributes to S. N. Kramer's 1944 study a claim that the epic was based on originally disconnected earlier tales. According to Tigay (43–46), there probably was an integrated text (i.e., one in which many tales had been revised and new material added to create a complexly plotted story), in the Old Babylonian period, about 2000–1600 BCE, and certainly by the Middle Babylonian period, about 1600–1000 BCE.

54. Liu Wu-Chi, *An Introduction to Chinese Literature* (Bloomington: Indiana University Press, 1966), 35, for example, cites the classic *Commentary of Tso* (fifth/third century BCE) as a revision, expansion, and compilation of briefer narratives. China may nonetheless be a partial exception here because it did not always integrate old stories into longer ones. Anne Birrell, *Chinese Mythology: An Introduction* (Baltimore: Johns Hopkins University Press, 1993), 17–18, says that the old myths often were not integrated into large epics but were preserved piecemeal in classic texts from the fourth century BCE to the third century CE.

55. Albert B. Lord, *The Singer of Tales* (Cambridge, MA: Harvard University Press, 1964), 129, argues that Homer's poems were products of orality and that the singer of oral poems cannot simultaneously be a writer of texts. He notes, however (8), that literacy was part of Homer's time and culture.

56. See Albert Lord's response to Ruth Finnegan in Richard S. Shannon III and Benjamin A. Stoltz, eds., *Oral Literature and the Formula* (Ann Arbor: Center for the Coordination of Ancient and Modern Studies, University of Michigan, 1976), 175. He says that the only distinction he wants to maintain is between the "oral mentality," which allows itself flexibility in the composition of the song as it is sung, and the textual approach, which seeks to memorize a single version. Hugh Lloyd-Jones provides a nice history of arguments about Milman Perry's work in "Becoming Homer," a review of three books, by Lord, Barry Powell, and Martin Bernal, *New York Review of Books* (March 5, 1992): 52–57.

57. Theodore M. Andersson, *The Problem of Icelandic Saga Origins* (New Haven, CT: Yale University Press, 1964), 75–83, says that the earlier theory that the sagas were oral was based on speculation about what went on during long winter nights in a small community. Though they draw some material from earlier oral tradition, says Andersson, the sagas as we have them are clearly literary, part of a Scandinavian literary tradition of the times.

58. Puhvel, *Comparative Mythology*, 69–71, discusses the general structure.

59. Both the *Mahabharata* and the *Ramayana* were composed in something like their current form after axial-age thought appeared in India. Post-

axial thought does not eliminate late archaic-style mythic narratives. As Shweder, Street, and I agree, more than one style of thought may mingle in a given culture.

60. Joseph A. Russo, "Oral Theory: Its Development in Homeric Studies and Applicability to Other Literature," in Herman L. Vanstiphout and Marianna E. Vogelganz, eds., *Mesopotamian Epic Literature: Oral or Aural?* (Lewiston, New York: Edwin Mellen, 1992), 16.

61. James B. Pritchard, *Ancient Near Eastern Texts Relating to the Old Testament* (Princeton, NJ: Princeton University Press, 1955), 405–407.

62. Julian Jaynes notes that this attribution of inner thoughts or feelings to a god or spirit being is a characteristic of preaxial Greek thought. *The Origin of Consciousness in the Breakdown of the Bicameral Mind* (Boston: Houghton Mifflin, 1976).

63. These unusual cases raise again the possibility that individuals even in foraging societies engage in such inner dialogues. On the one hand we can guess that some do, at least a genius or two. On the other hand even anthropologists trying to affirm the cognitive abilities of primitive people indicate otherwise. We have more to learn about the effect of more complex religio-socioeconomic life, and especially of literacy, on what a person is able to think and how a person is able to think it.

Chapter 5

1. Geoffrey Lloyd makes this point in his comparative analysis of ancient Greek and Chinese thought, *Demystifying Mentalities* (New York: Cambridge University Press, 1990). He shows that in axial times both of these cultures were arenas where different modes of thought mingled and competed. He delineates differences between Greek and Chinese thought, providing evidence that there is no single way in which formal operational thought (a terminology he does not use) may manifest itself. Because his emphasis is on the differences between China and Greece, he concludes that axial-age China and Greece did not share the same "mentality." He nonetheless provides the kinds of specific evidence that fit well with the thesis that axial thought is a shift from concrete mythical to formal operational systematic thought.

2. Jerome Bruner comes close to doing this with contemporary thought in *Actual Minds, Possible Worlds* (Cambridge, MA: Harvard University Press, 1986). Echoing C. P. Snow, perhaps, he argues that today there are "Two Modes of Thought" (ch. 2, 11–43) that are irreducibly different. Narrative thought creates scenes of action and feeling. Logical systematic thinking, on the other hand, seeks the regular and reliable causal patterns of things. Narrative is concerned with particulars; logical systematic thought says truth resides in the universals. Logic heartlessly goes wherever logic leads it; narrative goes where feeling and values lead it (12–13).

3. We can speculate that formal operational thought will be easier for those adults whose whole developmental history has included exposure to such thought. Just as learning a second language or becoming adept at music is easier for the person who has engaged in these activities from childhood, so perhaps before or during adolescence the brain slowly develops neural pathways to facilitate for formal operational thought if the person receives training in such thought during these years. Even if this is so, while this affects brain development, it does not affect the person's genes. Any innate

basis of intelligence would be passed on intact (as much as intelligence is indeed passed on). To repeat: this is speculation.

4. It is often difficult to determine where to draw lines between archaic and classic thought. Joseph Needham, *Science and Civilization in China*, vol. 2 of *History of Scientific Thought* (New York: Cambridge University Press, 1956), reports this ancient Taoist technique to create ideal health: Hold the breath; it expands. When it expands, it goes down. When it goes down, it becomes quiet. When it has become quiet, it will solidify. . . . There are more steps in this process. The description is a very orderly one, explicit in its sequencing, logical in its progression (143–144). In comparison with primitive people's difficulty in articulating their own procedures, as Hallpike noted, this represents a more consciously rational level of thinking, yet it is also quite concrete. Whether this Taoist teaching implies a formal operational style of thought is difficult to determine. It was written to educate, not to satisfy Piagetian scholars.

5. In addition to the logic of the *Samkhya* school discussed briefly below, see Robert D. Evans and Bimal Krishna Matilal, eds., *Buddhist Logic and Epistemology: Studies in the Buddhist Analysis of Inference and Language* (Boston: D. Reidel, 1982). These proceedings of a conference at Oxford on the *pramana* school of Buddhist philosophy, based on the writings of Dinnaga (ca. 480–540 CE), analyze word meanings and references, sentence meanings, and methods of valid inference.

6. Percival Spear, *India: A Modern History* (Ann Arbor: University of Michigan Press, 1961), 59.

7. Ibid.

8. "Literature" is a partial misnomer. The Vedic traditions were preserved orally, until apparently about the sixth century BCE, when writing appeared again in India. If it is true that after its early use in Harappan culture, writing disappeared from India, as scholarly opinion now seems to have it, then the development of the Vedas stands as evidence that Walter Ong and Jack Goody may overestimate the importance of writing for the development of complex thought. But the dates both of writing in India and of various Vedic texts are highly uncertain.

9. Dating ancient texts of India is difficult. Jeanine Miller, *The Vision of Cosmic Order in the Vedas* (Boston: Routledge and Kegan Paul, 1985), 3, says "Western scholarship" dates the *Rig Veda* about 1500–1200 BCE. Not all of the *Rig Veda* is this old. Wendy Doniger O'Flaherty, *Textual Sources for the Study of Hinduism* (Totowa, NJ: Barnes and Noble, 1988), gives a general date of 1000 BCE for the *Rig Veda*, but says the first and tenth books "are thought to be somewhat later" (1). She dates the Upanishads about 700 BCE. Louis Renou, *Hinduism* (New York: George Braziller, 1962), 24, dates the Upanishads to the fifth or fourth century BCE. Hajime Nakamura, *A History of Early Vedanta Philosophy* (Delhi: Motilal Banarsidass, 1983), 10, claims that "All Indian scholars have a tendency to think that the dates of the Upanishads are ancient." He notes that Radhakrishnan puts the dates at 1000 to 300 BCE, and that Paul Deussen sorted the fourteen principal Upanishads into early, middle, and late periods, from the eighth to fourth century BCE.

10. See Sarvepalli Radhakrishnan and Charles Moore, eds., *A Sourcebook in Indian Philosophy* (Princeton, NJ: Princeton University Press, 1957), 5, 16–17. They list many passages from earlier Vedas under the heading of "monotheistic and monist *tendencies*," 16–25.

11. Barbara Stoler Miller, *The Bhagavad Gita: Krishna's Counsel in Time of War* (New York: Bantam, 1986), 168.

12. Jaan Puhvel, *Comparative Mythology* (Baltimore: Johns Hopkins University Press, 1987), 46.

13. O'Flaherty, *Textual Sources*, 1, gives the number as 1,028. Radhakrishnan and Moore, *A Sourcebook*, 4, says there are 1,017.

14. Radhakrishnan and Moore, *A Sourcebook*, 5–8.

15. O'Flaherty, *Textual Sources*, 2.

16. A. L. Herman, *An Introduction to Indian Thought* (Englewood Cliffs, NJ: Prentice-Hall, 1976), 137–141.

17. Puhvel, *Comparative Mythology*. For instance, Indra breaks contracts and even the bonds of kinship, says Puhvel (54). The evolution of morality deserves its own book. For an analysis of forty-five anthropological studies on comparative moral development, see John R. Snarey, "Cross-Cultural University of Social-Moral Development: A Critical Review of Kohlbergian Research," *Pyschological Bulletin* 97:2 (1985): 202–232.

18. Others perceive greater sophistication in the Vedas. Radhakrishnan and Moore, *Sourcebook*, 5, note claims that the Vedas are "allegorical representation of the attributes of the supreme Being." The Stoics and Philo likewise tried to rescue Homer and the early Hebrew Scriptures, respectively, by an allegorical approach.

19. Renou, *Hinduism*, 67.

20. See Herman's *An Introduction to Indian Thought*, 82. Moore and Radhakrishnan classify this hymn as having "monotheistic tendencies." *Sourcebook*, 16–18.

21. The principal Upanishads may be as many as fourteen, depending on who is doing the counting. See Herman, *An Introduction*, 110–124, on the teaching of the Upanishads.

22. Moore and Radhakrishnan, *Sourcebook*, 42.

23. Ibid., 46–47.

24. Ram Shankar Bhattacharya and Gerald J. Larson, eds., *Samkhya: A Dualist Tradition in Indian Philosophy*, vol. 4 of *Encyclopedia of Indian Philosophies* (Princeton, NJ: Princeton University Press, 1987), provides a current summary and commentary. Richard Gorbe calls *samkhya* "one of the oldest philosophies in the Indian tradition" because reference to it appears in the *Arthasastra* of Kautilya, which he dates to about 300 BCE. "Critical Review of Interpretations of Samkhya," in Bhattacharya and Larson, *Samkhya*, 15. Gorbe says there is evidence that *samkhya* rose in Kshatriya circles (18).

25. The original text is not known. We have a Chinese copy translated about 560 CE. And Shankara's much later rejection of *samkhya* contains many lines from the missing text (just as we have Celsius's attack on Christianity from Origin's rejoinder to it).

26. Bhattacharya and Larsen, *Samkhya*, 9–10.

27. S. Radhakrishnan and C. Moore, *Sourcebook*, 227, 228–235 has texts from this school.

28. Robert D. Baird and Alfred Bloom, *Indian and Far Eastern Religious Traditions* (New York: Harper & Row, 1972), 86–88.

29. Moore and Radhakrishnan, *Sourcebook*, 237.

30. Ibid., 227.

31. I. M. Bochenski, *A History of Formal Logic*, trans. Ivo Thomas (New York: Chelsea, 1970 [repr. of 1961 "rev." trans.]), part VI, "The Indian Vari-

ety of Logic," 416–447. He cites numerous particular arguments from different sources, and sums up his conclusion thus: "That it really was a formal logic is shown by the fact that the formulae constructed by the Indian thinkers concern the fundamental question of logic, the questions of 'what follows from what.' These formulae, moreover, were thought of as universally valid" (446).

32. See Baird and Bloom, *Indian and Far Eastern Religious Tradition,* 76–80.

33. Herman, *An Introduction,* 162–165.

34. Jonah Blank, *Arrow of the Blue-Skinned God: Retracing the Ramayana Through India* (New York: Doubleday Image, 1992), offers many stories of current-day India to give a sense of religion there.

35. Anne Birrell, *Chinese Mythology: An Introduction* (Baltimore: Johns Hopkins University Press, 1993), 26.

36. Ibid., 24. The other Semitic source with a similar cosmogony is, of course, the book of Genesis. As with the question of the origin of literacy, there does not seem to be enough evidence to determine to what extent the Chinese myths might have been influenced by the stories of other cultures.

37. Ibid., 17–20. Birrell notes, however, that the writers who preserved them may have altered them to fit their own viewpoints.

38. See Daniel L. Overmyer, *Religions of China* (San Francisco: Harper & Row, 1986), 24–27, for a very brief survey of preaxial beliefs in divination, gods, and so on. Or see Lawrence G. Thompson, *The Chinese Way in Religion* (Belmont, CA: Wadsworth, 1973), 1–45, for a collection of readings and commentaries on the archaic religious tradition of China.

39. See some of the stories in Robert Shannu Chen, *A Comparative Study of Chinese and Western Cyclic Myths* (New York: Peter Lang, 1992), 9–29.

40. Benjamin I. Schwartz, *The World of Thought in Ancient China* (Cambridge, MA: Harvard University Press, 1985), 23–24.

41. Ibid., 23.

42. See Wing-Tsit Chan, *A Source Book of Chinese Philosophy* (Princeton, NJ: Princeton University Press, 1963), 16, for the observation that Confucius never refers to *Ti* (Lord) but only to *T'ien* (Heaven).

43. A summary given by Schwartz, *World of Thought,* 62–68. The norms of behavior in Confucianism are part of *li*. But apparently that word does not appear in the *Analects*. Chan, *Sourcebook of Chinese Philosophy,* 14.

44. Schwartz, for example, argues against Fingarette's claim that *li* is about only external behavior. Schwartz believes that the *Analects* are concerned with the inner self and good intentions, which is part of postaxial thought, and not just with outward conformity, which counted most in archaic thought. The issue is whether the "Superior Man" of the *Analects* is an individual self or is a reflector of group standards. Schwartz, *World of Thought,* 72–75.

45. Liu Wu-chi claims that while the *Analects* of Confucius and the *Book of Tao* are conglomerates of ideas, "extensive, carefully organized, and well-developed discourses" based on them are extant from shortly thereafter. *An Introduction to Chinese Literature* (Bloomington: Indiana University Press, 1966), 38. Mencius (ca. 371–ca. 289 BCE) was perhaps a bit more philosophical in his doctrine of the goodness of human nature, but he seems to have remained more concerned with loyalty to the family than with universal love of others, as the Mohists preached. Neo-Confucian thought in later centuries

reflected further on such issues, but that takes us far beyond the original axial period. Cho-yun Hsü, "The Unfolding of Early Confucianism: The Evolution from Confucius to Hsün-Tzu," in *Confucianism: The Dynamics of Tradition*, ed. Irene Ebert (New York: Macmillan, 1986), 22–38, describes a development of Confucian thought up to the time of Hsün-Tzu that is increasingly philosophical in content, in form of expression, and in its criteria of what counts as valid thought.

46. Angus C. Graham, *Disputers of the Tao: Philosophical Argument in Ancient China* (LaSalle, IL: Open Court, 1989), 6–7, claims the rational element of the axial period was almost lost, with the Sophist and later Mohist texts in obscurity until the sixteenth century. (Europe also had its Dark Ages.)

47. Benjamin Schwartz, "Transcendence in Ancient China," *Daedalus* 104:2 (Spring 1975): 57–68.

48. Toshihiko Izutsu, *Sufism and Taoism: A Comparative Study of Key Philosophical Concepts* (Berkeley: University of California Press, 1983), esp. 300–333, provides a study of Chinese thought that describes a movement from mythic to metaphysical thought, with accompanying changes in concepts of morality and the self.

49. Or, in a different interpretation, the heaven above, the primordial waters below the earth, and the earth between.

50. See Schwartz, *World of Thought*, 391–392.

51. Needham, *Science and Civilization*, 50. James Thrower, *The Alternative Tradition: Religion and the Rejection of Religion in the Ancient World* (The Hague and New York: Mouton, 1980), 114.

52. Thrower, *Alternative Tradition*, 111–114.

53. Chan, *Source Book of Chinese Philosophy*, 211–212.

54. Graham, *Disputers*, 97.

55. Angus C. Graham, *Unreason Within Reason: Essays on the Outskirts of Rationality* (LaSalle, IL: Open Court, 1992), uses his expert knowledge of Chinese thought to explore the general issue of rationality in culture. He describes the original appeal by Confucius to tradition as irrational, in that it appeals to authority rather than thinks for itself. But after Confucius all other positions had to develop rational arguments to show they were better than Confucian thought. Thus Graham calls the Chinese Sophists and Mohists instances in China of the kind of rationalism we also find in ancient Greece (98–99). But he also says that Chuang-Tzu's antirationalism proved stronger.

56. Chan, *Source Book of Chinese Philosophy*, 220.

57. Ibid., 221–226.

58. Needham claims that arguments about the relative value of empirical investigation and theoretical deduction were plentiful. *Science and Civilization*, 72–73. Needham even says that the work of the Logicians in the third century BCE was superior to that of Plato and Aristotle on issues of scientific method (186–188). (In this context Needham tells the wonderful Taoist story on the danger of theoretical thinking. A man was told not to build his house of green wood. But he reasoned it out: green wood is hard and grows softer with age; plaster begins soft but grows harder with age. If he combined the two of them, they would make a perfect house. So he built his house of green wood and plastered it well inside and out. Before long it fell down.)

59. Chan, *Source Book of Chinese Philosophy*, 233.

60. Ibid., 235–237.

61. Paul Kjellberg and Philip J. Ivanhoe, eds., *Essays on Skepticism, Relativism, and Ethics in the Zhuangzi* (Albany: SUNY Press, 1996), 20. A later chapter by Mark Berkson, "Language: The Guest of Reality—Zhuangzi and Derrida on Language, Reality, and Skillfulness," 97–126, finds a similar apophatic element in Zhuangzi, Derrida, Plotinus, and Nagarjuna.

62. Edward Motley Pickman, *The Sequence of Belief: A Consideration of Religious Thought from Homer to Ockham* (New York: St. Martin's Press, 1962). See also Jane Harrison, *Prolegomena to the Study of Greek Religion*, 3rd ed. (New York: Meridian Books, 1955), viii–xii.

63. John H. Finley, Jr., *Four Stages of Greek Thought* (Stanford, CA: Stanford University Press, 1966), ch. 1.

64. Julian Jaynes, *The Origin of Consciousness in the Breakdown of the Bicameral Mind* (Boston: Houghton Mifflin, 1976). Eric R. Dodds, *The Greeks and the Irrational* (Berkeley: University of California, 1959), 3–17, explicitly compares the thought style of the Homeric Greeks and of current natives of Borneo and Central Africa in this regard (13), though it is unclear how well he knows the cultures of these places.

65. William Irwin Thompson, *The Time Falling Bodies Take to Light* (New York: St. Martin's Press, 1981), 181–208, argues against Jaynes that there was a fuller sense of self present in the Gilgamesh Epic and other ancient writings, prior to the time when Jaynes discovers the first integrated selfhood. Thompson also says, however, that it was only in the sixth century BCE that conscious selfhood intensified through the civilizational process to the point of finding a new kind of answer to the problems of selfhood in the ideas of the Buddha, Pythagoras, Second Isaiah, Lao Tzu, and others. Bruno Snell had proposed in *The Discovery of the Mind* (Cambridge, MA: Harvard University Press, 1953), that in Homeric times there was a lack of inner self-consciousness. What Snell actually describes is not a lack of inner reflection but a lack of a sense of objectively universal moral standards, such as honesty and justice, for people to use in their inner reflections concerning what action to take. Lionel Pearson disputes Snell's thesis in his *Popular Ethics in Ancient Greece* (Stanford, CA: Stanford University Press, 1962), 208–209.

66. Arthur W. H. Adkins, *Moral Values and Political Behaviour in Ancient Greece* (New York: W. W. Norton, 1972), 16.

67. Dodds, *Greeks and the Irrational*, 1–4. As always in making general statements about a culture, the emphasis has to be on publicly shared values and cognitive techniques. This or that individual may have had skills and values of greater sophistication, though this is less likely in a culture in which the only accepted models or techniques are those of a preliterate culture.

68. Dodds, *Greeks and the Irrational*, 17–18. Taken from Ruth Benedict, *The Chrysanthemum and the Sword* (Boston: Houghton Mifflin, 1946), 222–224. The notion of guilt, like that of individuality, is not always clear. Japan's public norms have emphasized group conformity over allegiance to universal objective principles. The major reinforcement of group conformity is shame. Conformity to principles taken to be objective and universal might on some occasion require accepting public shame for the sake of obeying such higher principles. The word "guilt" was used by Benedict to stand for the inner sanction that could lead a person to endure shame rather than violate the objective principle. But neither Benedict nor Dodds defines or describes the nature of this inner sanction called guilt.

69. John Passmore, *The Perfectibility of Man* (New York: Scribner's, 1970), in a work describing the history of Western culture's ideas about human perfection or lack of it, contrasts the Homeric sense that the gods were morally no better than humans with the later Hellenic sense that the divine was perfect and that humans have the divine spark within them. See esp. 28–31, 46–67.

70. Ibid., 28–31; Dodds, *Greeks and the Irrational*, 32.

71. Edward Hussey, "Matter Theory in Ancient Greece," in *The Physical Sciences Since Antiquity*, ed. Rom Harré (New York: St. Martin's Press, 1986), 10–28, points to the absence in Ionia of a traditional wealthy class with vested interests to get in the way of new ideas.

72. Needham, *Science and Civilization*, 130–132, argues that democracy, at least in the sense of an open society not controlled by the traditional norms of an established elite, seems to be a precondition for scientific development. He cites the instances of ancient Greece and China as well as recent Europe.

73. Giovanni Reale, *A History of Ancient Philosophy*, vol. 3, *The Systems of the Hellenistic Age* (Albany: SUNY Press, 1985), 5–15, summarizes the impact of the political changes brought about by Alexander and the demise of the independent city-state on Hellenic philosophy.

74. See Joseph Owens, "The Aristotelian Conception of the Sciences," in *The Collected Papers of Joseph Owens*, ed. John A. Catan (Albany: SUNY Press, 1981), 23–34.

75. Ibid., 61.

76. E. O. Wilson celebrates the search for unity of ideas as the guiding belief of modern science in his *Consilience: The Unity of Knowledge* (New York: Alfred Knopf, 1998).

77. James Peacock and A. Thomas Kirsch, *The Human Direction* (New York: Appleton-Century-Crofts, 1970), 63–64, use similar words to describe the nature of ethics in any historical society.

78. For the text see N. Fleming and Alexander Sesonske, eds., *Plato's Meno: Text and Criticism* (Belmont, CA: Wadsworth, 1956). For the interpretation used here, see Adkins, *Moral Values and Political Behaviour in Ancient Greece*, 131–133.

79. Reale, *History of Ancient Philosophy*, 71.

80. Ibid., 161–182, for a summary of Epicurean ethics.

81. Ibid., 261–288, for a summary of Stoic ethics.

82. Dodds, *Greeks and the Irrational*, 237.

83. S. A. Nigosian, *The Zoroastrian Faith: Tradition and Modern Research* (Montreal: McGill-Queen's University Press, 1993), reviews theories about dates. Zoroastrian tradition says Zoroaster lived in the seventh to sixth centuries BCE (11). Dates vary from 630 or 618 BCE to as late as 588 BCE (15–16). Some obviously unreliable Greek texts claim he was born before 6000 BCE (15). Evidence from the Gathas, in the form of "linguistic antiquity and the socio-cultural allusions," place him about 1400–1200 BCE (16). Nigosian has doubts about the linguistic evidence, and so accepts the Zoroastrian tradition for lack of a better option (16). Mary Boyce, ed. and trans., *Textual Sources for the Study of Zoroastrianism* (Totowa, NJ: Barnes and Noble, 1984), 11–12, favors 1400–1200 BCE for Zoroaster on the basis of linguistic clues, especially references to Bronze Age warfare. Whether Zoroaster was a monotheist is also in dispute, according to Boyce, who reviews various positions but notes

the "ancient Iranian myth of 'the two uncreated Mainyu' (Spirit/Being)" (22–23). William W. Malandra, ed. and trans., *An Introduction to Ancient Iranian Religion* (Minneapolis: University of Minnesota Press, 1983), 19–20, calls early Zoroastrianism an approximation of monotheism.

84. Robert Gnuse, *Heilsgeschichte as a Model for Biblical Theology* (Lanham, MD: University Press of America, 1989), points to numerous similarities between Mesopotamian and Hebrew developments. See 110–111 and 141–148 on possible origins of Hebrew monotheism. For a similar analysis of the development of concepts of God in Hebrew thought, see Mark S. Smith, *The Early History of God: Yahweh and the Other Deities in Ancient Israel* (San Francisco: Harper & Row, 1990).

Chapter 6

1. See Sarvepalli Rhadakrishnan and Charles Moore, eds., *A Sourcebook in Indian Philosophy* (Princeton, NJ: Princeton University Press, 1957), 230, for a relevant selection from the *Sarvadarsanasamgraha*, a fourteenth-century CE document, citing the four elements. See 227–249 for other extant passages of the *carvaka* system.

2. See Cyril Bailey's trans. and note in *Epicurus: The Extant Remains* (Hildesheim: Georg Olms, 1970 [repr. of 1926 ed.]).

3. Epicurus, "Letter to Menoeceus," in ibid., nos. 123–125, pp. 83–85.

4. See Marcia Colish, *The Stoic Tradition from Antiquity to the Early Middle Ages*, vol. 1, *Stoicism in Classical Latin Literature* (Leiden: E. J. Brill, 1985).

5. Marcus Tullius Cicero, *Brutus; On the Nature of the Gods; On Divination; On Duty*, trans. Hubert M. Poteat (Chicago: Unviersity of Chicago Press, 1950), "On Divination," I.55, p. 392. Cicero puts these words into the mouth of his brother Quintus in favor of belief in divination. Cicero was an official Roman augur, but his philosophical mind rejected belief in augury, prophecy, and divination except as public ritual for reinforcing civic virtues and confidence. See II.32–62, pp. 257–287, as a source on the Stoic argument for the existence of a Divine principle in nature.

6. Pierre Pellegrin, *Aristotle's Classification of Animals: Biology and the Conceptual Unity of the Aristotelian Corpus*, trans. Anthony Preus (Berkeley: University of California Press, 1986), at the end of his notes on the text, says classifying organisms was "non-scientific" by Aristotle's standards because the classifications were not rationally deducible. Yet Aristotle says in the text (141) that from the data, principles of interrelations among organisms can be known, and that the correlations among animal parts "conform to reason" (148). The search for ultimate causes is evident in the *Metaphysics*, where Aristotle seeks to get beyond the four elements and the four basic causes to discover the ultimate cause of generation and destruction. See Aristotle, *Metaphysics*, Hippocrates G. Apostle, trans. (Bloomington: Indiana University Press, 1966).

7. Jaakko Hintikka, "On the Development of Aristotle's Ideas of Scientific Method and the Structure of Science," notes that Aristotle first emphasized dialectic or argumentative discussion, later emphasized syllogistic reasoning as the key to science, and later yet reflected further on the source of the premises of syllogisms and other problems associated with achieving true knowledge and new knowledge. In *Aristotle's Philosophical Development: Problems and Prospects*, ed. William Wians (Lanham, MD: Rowman and Littlefield,

1996), 83–104. Articles in this volume address other ways in which Aristotle's thought was not a static system but a life of exploration.

8. Lawrence P. Schrenk, ed., *Aristotle in Late Antiquity* (Washington, DC: Catholic University of America Press, 1994), assesses Aristotle's longer-term impact in comparison with Stoic, Platonist, and Neoplatonist philosophy.

9. See Dominic O'Meara, "Plotinus on How Soul Acts on Body," in *Platonic Investigations*, ed. Dominic O'Meara (Washington, DC: Catholic University of America Press, 1985), esp. 254–260.

10. John Roche, "The Transition from the Ancient World Picture," in *The Physical Sciences Since Antiquity*, ed. Rom Harré (New York: St. Martin's Press, 1986), 29–40, for example, describes early alchemy in Alexandria as part of natural magic in an animistic universe.

11. See "Letter to Menoeceus," in Bailey, *Epicurus*, no. 123, p. 83, of Bailey on this as basis for knowing the existence of the gods. "Immediate mental perceptions," Bailey calls them in his commentary (329). According to George K. Strodach, *The Philosophy of Epicurus* (Chicago: Northwestern University Press, 1963), 43, Epicurus also relies on a logically invalid criterion, "non-impossibility." Strodach cites various places where Epicurus writes as though a conclusion has been established merely because there is no reason why it may not be so.

12. I do not know whether Descartes derived his "clear and distinct idea" criterion from this. John A. Schuster, "Descartes Agonistes: New Tales of a Cartesian Natural Philosophy," *Perspectives on Science* 3:1 (Spring 1995): 99–145, cites Gaukroger's 1995 claim that Descartes got the idea from the Stoics by way of Cicero and Quintilian, whom Descartes had read at La Flèche.

13. See Myles Burnyeat, ed., *The Skeptical Tradition* (Berkeley: University of California Press, 1983), 78–85, for background to skepticism. Burnyeat includes Protagoras the Sophist (ca. 490–420 BCE), who was active when Socrates was a child. Fragments from him and from Gorgias (ca. 485/ca. 410) reveal strong doubts both about the gods and about certainty of knowledge or morals. David Sedly, "The Motivation of Greek Skepticism," in ibid., 9–29, provides a history of skepticism, and what this or that ancient skeptic must have thought or should have thought.

14. Trans. Julia Annas and Jonathan Barnes, with the British spelling *Scepticism* (New York: Cambridge University Press, 1994). References to the text here are from this translation. Also see Julia Annas and Jonathan Barnes, *The Modes of Scepticism* (New York: Cambridge University Press, 1985), for informed analyses of the formal "modes" or arguments used by various skeptical groups.

15. See Giovanni Reale, *A History of Ancient Philosophy*, vol. 3, *The Systems of the Hellenistic Age* (Albany: SUNY Press, 1985), 309–323, for a review of what is known of Pyrrho.

16. See Sextus Empiricus, *Outlines*, I.230–232, as an example of historical information.

17. See ibid., Annas and Barnes trans., 12–46, for a presentation of these various modes in I.35–184.

18. Ibid., I.165–177, Annas and Barnes, trans., 41–43.

19. Ibid., I.181–184, Annas and Barnes, trans., 45.

20. II.18–20, Annas and Barnes, trans., 72.

21. I.227–229, Annas and Barnes, trans., 60. R. G. Bury translates the three criteria in simpler English in the Loeb ed. (Cambridge, MA: Harvard

University Press, 1939), vol. 1, 41: "probable, tested, and irreversible" ['*aperis-paston*]. Sextus then observes that while Carneades would give strong assent to ideas which passed this triple test, Arcesilaus and he are both closer to true Pyrrhonic skepticism, neither assenting nor not assenting.

22. Reale sums it up as a matter of first accepting evidence, then looking for other evidence to confirm or disconfirm, and, if time allows, then connecting the impression thus received with other relevant impressions. *Systems of the Hellenistic Age*, 337–338. The reference is to Sextus Empiricus, *Adversus Mathematicos*, 7.166–189 (Bury trans., vol. 2, 91–103). In the realm of values, Cicero proposes a similar goal: "The aim of a skeptic is not to destroy ethical hypotheses, but to undermine the certainty with which they are held, and substitute probability in its place." *De Officiis*, John Higgenbotham, trans. (Berkeley: University of Calfornia Press, 1967), 20.

23. It also appears to be the kind of cognitive style that James Fowler calls stage five and associates with a fully developed formal operational style of thought. See his *Stages of Faith* (San Francisco: Harper & Row, 1981), 184–188, 197–198. This includes a sense that though all truth is relative, there can be reasonable commitments to a worldview.

24. Reale, *The Systems of the Hellenistic Age*, 369–372.

25. Eric R. Dodds, *The Greeks and the Irrational* (Berkeley: University of California Press, 1959), 243.

26. Reale, *Systems of the Hellenistic Age*, 373–376.

27. Robert M. Grant, *Miracle and Natural Law: In Greco-Roman and Early Christian Thought* (Amsterdam: North-Holland, 1952), provides a thorough survey of the decline of scientific attitudes and the rise of a new credulity. Elizabeth Rawson, *Intellectual Life in the Late Roman Republic* (Baltimore: Johns Hopkins University Press, 1985), says that in general, Romans had little expectation of improving on the Greek achievement and thus did not try very hard. See 317–325 in particular for a summary.

28. Grant, *Miracle and Natural Law*, 86.

29. Edward Hussey, "Matter Theory in Ancient Greece," in *The Physical Sciences Since Antiquity*, ed. Rom Harré, (New York: St. Martin's Press, 1986), 10–28.

30. See Geoffrey E. R. Lloyd, *Magic, Reason, and Experience: Studies in the Origin and Development of Greek Science* (New York: Cambridge University Press, 1979), 10–51; Dodds, *Greeks and The Irrational*, 244; and Grant, *Miracle and Natural Law*, 58.

31. Luther Martin argues in his *Hellenistic Religions* (New York: Oxford University Press, 1987), that when the Stoics changed the gods into allegorical images of the single and universal divine Logos inherent in all nature, the new syncretist and mystery religions provided a less intellectual way to appropriate this new sense of the universe.

32. Grant calls the *Natural History* a scissors-and-paste set of borrowings, often inaccurate. *Miracle and Natural Law*, 64–65.

33. The same shift to concrete operational thought is evident in law. The Stoics had legal theory. By the early fifth century Emperor Theodosius II established the "law of citations." Not theory but the number of previous jurists favoring a position established the law. Alan Watson, *The Law of the Ancient Romans* (Dallas: Southern Methodist University Press, 1970), 91–97. (Watson does not note that U.S. law is similarly concrete, unlike the Napoleonic code.)

34. Dodds, *Greeks and the Irrational*, 189–193.

35. Ibid. See ch. 8, "The Fear of Freedom," for the overall argument. I. F. Stone, "Was There a Witch Hunt in Ancient Athens," *New York Review of Books* (January 21, 1988): 37–41, argues that Dodds exaggerates the reaction against the new thought among Athenians.

36. Lloyd, *Magic, Reason, and Experience*, 234–246, 264–267. In his *Demystifying Mentalities* (New York: Cambridge University Press, 1990), Lloyd also attributes to the public disputes of Athens a formative and supporting role in the development of a classical rationality.

37. See Hussey, "Matter Theory," 25–27; he believes that a lack of trust in the empirical was an important factor in the decline of ancient science.

38. Joseph Owens thinks Aristotle avoided the empirical whenever it would have required math to make sense of it and restricted himself to things like biological observation, where math was not necessary. A distaste for mathematics, Owens said, is not uncommon among philosophers, and might account for the lack of empirical work as much as any aristocratic prejudice against hands-on efforts. "The Aristotelian Conception of the Sciences," in *Aristotle: The Collected Papers of Joseph Owens*, ed. John A. Catan (Albany: SUNY Press, 1981), 33–34.

39. Reaffirmed in the twentieth century by, among others, Karl Popper, *Objective Knowledge: An Evolutionary Approach* (Oxford: Clarendon Press, 1972), 264–265.

40. Frances A. Yates, *Giordano Bruno and the Hermetic Tradition* (Chicago: University of Chicago, 1964), 4.

41. Plotinus argues from the *fact* of magic as though its efficacy were so real as not to be doubtable: "But magic spells, how can their efficacy be explained?" On this basis he offers the idea of spiritual sympathies as the answer. "The magician . . . draws on these patterns of powers and by ranging himself also into the patterns is able tranquilly to possess himself of these forces." See Plotinus, *The Six Enneads* (Chicago: Encyclopedia Britannica, 1952), 180; selections from Ennead IV, tractate 4, secs. 40, 41. *Enneads* is vol. 17 of the Great Books.

42. See ibid. on reading portents in the stars (Ennead II, tractate 3, pp. 42–50); in support of the efficacy of magical spells (Ennead IV, tractate 4, sec. 40, p. 180); on dissolving incantations by counterincantations (Ennead IV, tractate 4, sec. 43, pp. 181–183); and so on. In the Loeb Classical Library, see translation by A. H. Armstrong in 7 vols. For IV, 4, sec. 40, p. 261; for IV, 4, sec. 43, pp. 269–270.

43. Edward Grant, *Physical Sciences in the Middle Ages* (New York: John Wiley and Sons, 1971), 2.

44. See Christopher Stead, *Philosophy in Christian Antiquity* (New York: Cambridge University Press, 1994), part II, "The Use of Philosophy in Christian Antiquity," and part III, "Augustine." Also see Henry Chadwick, *Early Christian Thought and the Classical Tradition* (New York: Oxford University Press, 1966), for descriptions of ways in which early Christian writers reacted to ideas from Hellenic philosophy, in particular the Platonist and Stoic traditions. William H. McNeill, *Plagues and Peoples* (New York: Doubleday, 1976), 121–139, proposes to understand why Christianity or any movement would ingest ideas from competing systems. Ideas are like germs, McNeil argues. When taken into a system, they create an immune reaction. Thus Hindu thought became immunized against Buddhist ideas by incorporating part of

them into itself. So Christians became immunized to Platonist thought by accepting aspects of it into itself.

45. Samuel Sandmel, *Philo of Alexandria: An Introduction* (New York: Oxford University Press, 1979), 146, agrees with Goodenough's earlier judgment that Philo's Hellenized Judaism aided the process of the Hellenization of Christianity. Harry Austryn Wolfson, *Philo: Foundations of Religious Philosophy in Judaism, Christianity, and Islam* (Cambridge, MA: Harvard University Press, 1962 [rev. of 1926 ed.]), 439–460, delineates major ways in which Philo may have set all subsequent Western philosophy and theology on a new course. See also Andrew Louth, *The Origins of the Christian Mystical Tradition: From Plato to Denys* (Oxford: Clarendon Press, 1981), 18–34, for Philo's influence.

46. A. A. Barn, "The Survival of the Magical Arts," in Arnaldo *The Conflict Between Paganism and Christianity in the Fourth Century*, ed. Momigliano (Oxford: Clarendon Press, 1963), 115. Lactantius says Jesus did miracles "not through the treachery of magic, which shows nothing true and solid, but by the strength and power of heaven." *The Divine Institutes*, vol. 49 of The Fathers of the Church (Washington, DC: Catholic University of America Press, 1964), bk. IV, ch. 12, p. 280.

47. "The First Apology of Justin Martyr," in *The Early Christian Fathers*, vol. 1 (Philadelphia: Westminster Press, 1953), 242–276.

48. Avery Dulles says Aristides' *Apology* (ca. 125 CE) appeals more to the evidence of high Christian morality than to biblical miracles, and cites other apologists whose emphasis was similarly on virtues and faith rather than miracles. Avery Dulles, *A History of Apologetics* (Philadelphia: Westminster Press, 1971), 24–31. (Compare with Cicero's skepticism about prophecies in *De Divinatione*.)

49. Amos Funkenstein, *Theology and the Scientific Imagination from the Middle Ages to the Seventeenth Century* (Princeton, NJ: Princeton University Press, 1986), 125.

50. *The Octavius of Marcus Minucius Felix*, trans. G. W. Clarke (New York: Newman Press, 1974). Minucius may have been responding to Celsus (fl. ca. 150 CE). The philosopher Porphyry (fl. 270) similarly raised philosophical challenges to the notion of an ultimate being that changed his mind about salvation or who set up a natural order and then violated that order by miraculous interventions. See Funkenstein, *Theology and the Scientific Imagination*, 124–127.

51. See Minucius Felix, *Octavius*, 117–118, on sending unbelievers to hell.

52. See Robert Grant, *Miracle and Natural Law*, 131, 198–206. Grant refers also to Henri de Lubac, *Surnaturelle* (Paris: 1946), 355–373, for the claim that this is the origin in Christian writings of the precise idea of the supernatural, though not yet the word.

53. Funkenstein, *Theology and the Scientific Imagination*, 125. See his whole discussion on the point at issue in ch. 3, "Divine Omnipotence and Laws of Nature," 117–152.

54. See Robert L. Wilken, *The Christians as the Romans Saw Them* (New Haven, CT: Yale University Press, 1984), 78–79, for references to other sources at that time.

55. Irenaeus, *Against Heresies*, book II, ch. 28.2–3, in vol. 1 of *The Writing of Irenaeus*, which is vol. 5 of Ante-Nicene Christian Library (Edinburgh: T. & T. Clark, 1868), 220–221.

56. Dodds, *Greeks and the Irrational*, 249, says the first-century Stoic philosopher Seneca "quotes with approval the view that we should not trouble to investigate things that it is neither possible nor useful to know, such as the cause of the tides or the principle of perspective."

57. Irenaeus, *Against Heresies*, book III, ch. 21.2–3 (pp. 352–353).

58. Lactantius, *The Divine Institutes*, 269. Ch. 15 asserts the importance of belief in various miracles, especially those done by Jesus. (Augustine repeated the story of wind-fertilized horses.) The editor cites Virgil's *Georgics* 3.274 as the source of this idea.

59. Dodds, *Greeks and the Irrational*, 209–213.

60. Celsus criticized Christians precisely for following faith without reason. *On the True Doctrine*, R. Joseph Hoffman, trans. and reconstructor (New York: Oxford University Press, 1987), 54. (In his *Contra Celsum*, I.10, Origen takes a middle and more rationalist stand, saying that people who are too busy for philosophy can rely on faith.)

61. Clement of Alexandria, *Stromata*, book II, chs. 2–4, in, *The Ante-Nicene Fathers*, vol. 2 (New York: Scribner's, 1926), 350. (Echoes of this can be found in Alvin Plantinga's notion of properly basic beliefs.)

62. Ibid., book II, ch. 2, 349 (New York: Doubleday, 1966), 1153. For example, The Jerusalem Bible, has "If you do not stand by me, you shall not stand at all." Isaiah 7:9.

63. *Physiologus*, trans. Michael J. Curley (Austin: University of Texas Press, 1979), 1–2.

64. Edward Grant, *Physical Sciences*, 5–8, 118; see also Robert Grant, *Miracle and Natural Law*, 118.

65. "The intense and bitter polemic against pagan learning and religion which had marked the long struggle of Christianity, cast a pall of suspicion over Greek philosophy and science." And, similarly, "With the triumph of Christianity in the fourth century, that small but essential handful of men who in previous centuries had somehow managed to . . . perpetuate an inherited body of high-level theoretical science, was no longer produced." Edward Grant, *Physical Sciences*, 4.

66. William M. Thompson, *Christ and Consciousness* (New York: Paulist Press, 1977), 65–67, using Bellah's (and Kohlberg's) ideas, claims Jesus' resurrection represents a degree of individual self-realization beyond that of the Hellenic philosophers. Without presuming to know Jesus' own consciousness, I would guess that belief in resurrection for early Christians in general would have been the sort of belief that an archaic commonsense cognitive style would have, a style that readily believes in miracles of various sorts. Thompson reads into the early belief his own much later way of interpreting things.

67. McNeill speculates that the evidence may have favored Christian belief also. The great plague of the Roman world in roughly 165–180 CE, as well as the plague of 251–266, challenged philosophical theory. Stoics had no explanation for such a disorderly and irrational event; Christian belief in divine justice was at least an explanation of sorts. *Plagues and People*, 116–123.

68. As in Augustine, *The Literal Meaning of Genesis*, trans. John Hammond Taylor, vols. 41 and 42 in Ancient Christian Writers (New York: Newman Press, 1982).

69. See Peter Brown, *The Cult of the Saints* (Chicago: University of Chicago Press, 1981), esp. ch. 4, "The Very Special Dead," 69–84. Also see A. H. M. Jones, "The Social Background of the Struggle Between Paganism and Christianity in the Fourth Century," in *The Conflict Between Paganism and Christianity in the Fourth Century*, ed. Arnaldo Momigliano (Oxford: Clarendon Press, 1963), 17–32.

Chapter 7

1. Support for the Piagetian interpretation of this period appears in Charles M. Radding, *A World Made by Men: Cognition and Society, 400–1200* (Chapel Hill: University of North Carolina Press, 1985). See also Don LePan, *The Cognitive Revolution in Western Culture*, vol. 1, *The Birth of Expectation* (London: Macmillan, 1989), who reaffirms Radding's Piagetian interpretation.

2. Francis Oakley, *Omnipotence, Covenant, and Order* (Ithaca, NY: Cornell University Press, 1984), 78, describes a similar position in the work of Al Ash[c]ari, a tenth-century CE Muslim thinker, and of the Asharites, in which there is little room for "that instinctive confidence in the existence of a rational order without which the natural sciences . . . could scarcely be developed."

3. *On the Trinity*, III.5., trans. Stephen King, *Fathers of the Church*, vol. 45 (Washington, DC: Catholic University of America Press, 1963), 106. See similar comments by Augustine in *The City of God*, book XXII, chs. 8–9, *Fathers of the Church*, vol. 24, 431–450. Also see the *Retractions*, *Fathers of the Church*, vol. 60, 55 and 61–62, where Augustine denies that he ever meant that all miracles ended in Christ's time. This is not entirely original with Augustine. Epictetus says in his *Enchiridion* (second century CE) that perfect order on Earth is from God's bidding that the plants flower, ripen, bear fruit, drop their fruit, and then let their leaves fall. See *The Discourses of Epictetus*, P. E. Matheson, trans., in *The Stoic and Epicurean Philosophers*, ed. Whitney J. Oates (New York: Modern Library, 1940), 250. Nonetheless, Augustine's God is different from that of the Stoics.

4. In Oakley's words, referring to the similar Asharite position: "All 'natural' processes were at best sacramental rather than natural." *Omnipotence*, 78.

5. Jules M. Brady, S.J., has surveyed Augustine's use of "seminal reasons," an idea borrowed from the Stoics, and concludes that Augustine was sure God could intervene to change even this set of natural potentials. See his "St. Augustine's Theory of Seminal Reasons," *The New Scholasticism* 38 (1964): 141–158.

6. *The Literal Meaning of Genesis*, trans. John Hammond Taylor, S.J., vol. 41 in Ancient Christian Writers Series (New York: Newman Press, 1982), book V, chs. 20–23, pp. 162–175. See also book VI, ch. 13, pp. 194–195.

7. Composed 401–414, after an incomplete earlier start on the topic ca. 393. See the chronology in Peter Brown, *Augustine of Hippo* (New York: Dorset Press, 1967), 74–75, 184–187.

8. *Literal . . . Genesis*, book VI, ch. 18, p. 199.

9. *City of God*, book 21, ch. 8. This segment was written ca. 425–427, according to Brown, *Augustine of Hippo*, 376–377.

10. As late as the seventeenth century the distinction between preternatural and supernatural deeds was maintained. Stuart Clark, "The Scientific Status of Demonology," in Brian Vickers, ed., *Occult and Scientific Mentalities in the Renaissance* (New York: Cambridge University Press, 1984), 359–360, cites four categories of demonic activity, none of them strictly miraculous because all are done within the limits of nature, albeit by speedy, crafty, and well-experienced beings who can create the illusion of doing miracles.

11. In *The City of God*, book X, ch. 18. See "The Writings of St. Augustine," part 7, in *The Fathers of the Church*, vol. 14 (New York: Fathers of the Church, 1952), 150–151. Augustine notes that some say no miracles are done by the gods. While he agrees that "no written record can be relied on in such matters," he says nonetheless that only miracles done by the gods could make people worship them. Book X, ch. 18, p. 140.

12. *City of God*, book X, ch. 16; *Fathers of the Church*, vol. 14, 146.

13. Ibid., book XXI, sect. 5, pp. 770–771.

14. Augustine *Enchiridion*, ch. IX. See also ch. XVI, in which Augustine declares that there is no need to know the cause of earthquakes but only the causes of good and evil.

15. E.g., book I, chs. 1–17, or book III, chs. 1–22.

16. Henri Marrou's comment is that Augustine wrote *de deo* and *de anima* but not *de creatione*. In *Saint Augustine and His Influence Through the Ages* (New York: Harper and Bros., 1957), 72. This is only partially correct, in that Augustine did write about the first book of Genesis, but it approximates Augustine's attitude quite well. Not long after Augustine, we have Cosmas Indicopleustes, who wrote the *Topographic Christiana* ca. 535 CE. As a sailor he had visited India, Ceylon, and Ethiopia; later he moved to a monastery on Mount Sinai. He there condemned the heathen Hellenistic theory of the Earth as a globe and promoted belief in a rectangular earth under a barrel sky and surrounded by an ocean. Jon R. Stone, "The Medieval Mappaemundi: Toward an Archeology of Sacred Cartography," *Religion* 23:3 (July 1993): 203.

17. Colin Morris, *The Discovery of the Individual: 1050–1200* (New York: Harper & Row, 1972), 20, looks back into the early Middle Ages and indicates the mixture: "Some scholars have suggested that the Western kingdoms of the Dark Ages must be considered on the analogy of primitive societies in other continents" but "the barbarian nations of the Dark Ages were heirs to complicated and sophisticated cultural traditions." Henri-Jean Martin, *The History and Power of Writing*, trans. Lydia G. Cochrane (Chicago: University of Chicago, 1994), 120, comments on Gregory of Tours's sixth-century literary product, the *Historia Francorum*: It "shows little capacity for discerning cause and effect, and faith alone cannot explain the credulity and naiveté of his lives of the saints and his *Miracula*."

18. Note the *Libri Carolini* (790–793) of Theodulf of Orléans, aided by Alcuin and others, the official reply by Charlemagne's theologians to Nicaea II on iconoclasm. It dares to criticize the Byzantines for their poor writing. See Edward D. English, *Reading the Wisdom: The* De Doctrina Christiana *of Augustine in the Middle Ages* (Notre Dame, IN: University of Notre Dame Press, 1995), 3–9.

19. Amos Funkenstein, *Theology and the Scientific Imagination: From the Middle Ages to the Seventeenth Century* (Princeton, NJ: Princeton University Press, 1986), 126–127. He refers to *De Mirabilibus Sacrae Scripturae*, attributed

to a seventh-century "Augustinus." Carol Susan Anderson's 1982 Ph.D. dissertation (UCLA) on this topic says this work was quite popular in the twelfth century, according to her dissertation abstract. I have not read either *De Mirabilibus* or Anderson's work.

20. See Arthur O. Lovejoy, *The Great Chain of Being* (Cambridge, MA: Harvard University Press, 1936), 52–56, on the "the Principle of Plenitude," as he calls it, cherished by Augustine and Pseudo-Denis.

21. See Morton W. Bloomfield, *The Seven Deadly Sins* (East Lansing: Michigan State University Press, 1952), esp. 1–41, 43–66, on the early medieval notion, based on Neoplatonic thought, of the ascent of the soul through the spheres of the skies, past each of the heavenly powers there: the moon, Mercury, and so forth.

22. See Elizabeth Sears, *The Ages of Man: Medieval Interpretations* (Princeton, NJ: Princeton University Press, 1986). Sears describes the medieval attempts to divine human life into distinct periods and to assign to each certain characteristics in accord with various other theories. This is not modern science, but it may reflect some historic interest in coherent, unified explanations for things.

23. See *The Letter of Barnabas* (ca. 130 CE) in Edgar J. Goodspeed, trans. and ed., *The Apostolic Fathers* (London: Independent Press, 1955), 23–45. The letter (ch. 15.5) declares that since God created the world in six days and rested on the seventh, six thousand years from the beginning will be the time "when his Son comes and destroys the lawless one and judges the ungodly and changes the sun and the moon and the stars, then he will rest well on the seventh day."

24. Stephen Toulmin and June Goodfield, *The Discovery of Time* (Chicago: University of Chicago, 1965), 50–60, provides a description of early dispensationalism and its effects. William Cook and Ronald B. Hertzman, *The Medieval World View* (New York: Oxford University Press, 1983), 103–104, has brief references to Augustine's role in passing this on.

25. Timothy J. Reiss, *The Discourse of Modernism* (Ithaca, NY: Cornell University Press, 1982), 13, 55–90, compares the medieval way of patterning ideas with that described by Lévi-Strauss in his works on the structure of primitive thought. I think this judgment is close to correct, but Lévi-Strauss's theory is too vague to be of much help.

26. Bernard McGinn, *Visions of the End: Apocalyptic Traditions in the Middle Ages* (New York: Columbia University Press, 1979), part 1.

27. Robert E. McNally, *The Bible in the Early Middle Ages* (Atlanta: Scholars Press, 1986 [repr. of 1959 ed.]).

28. Benedicta Ward, *Miracles and the Medieval Mind* (Philadelphia: University of Pennsylvania Press, 1982), 33–66. Also see Christopher Brooke and Rosalind Brooke, *Popular Religion in the Middle Ages* (London: Thames and Hudson, 1984). Of William of Canterbury they say: "William and his like looked for a miraculous explanation in every strange event, where we would look for coincidence or a natural scientific cause (42–43). Both Ward and the Brookes cite materials mostly from 1000 or later, partly because of a relatively smaller number of sources from earlier.

29. Ward, *Miracles*, 13–16.

30. Peter Brown provides a description of the forms that predominated from about 800 to 1000 CE in "Society and the Supernatural: A Medieval Change," *Daedalus* 104:2 (Spring 1975), 131–151.

31. Morris, *Discovery of the Individual*, 20.

32. Crane Brinton, John B. Christopher, and Robert Lee Wolff, *A History of Civilization*, vol. 1 (Englewood Cliffs, NJ: Prentice-Hall, 1984), 6th ed. 132–135.

33. Walter Ullmann, *The Individual and Society in the Middle Ages* (Baltimore: Johns Hopkins University Press, 1966), 25–27, 30–31.

34. See Joseph H. Lynch, *Godparents and Kinship in Early Medieval Europe* (Princeton, NJ: Princeton University Press, 1986), for a very thorough survey of ideas of kinship and its importance.

35. Morris, *Discovery of the Individual*, 36. John Boswell, *Same-sex Unions in Premodern Europe* (New York: Villard Books, 1994), interprets formal vows of friendship as part of a much more personal relation than Morris.

36. Ullmann, *The Individual and Society*, 40–46.

37. Alexander Murray, *Reason and Society in the Middle Ages* (Oxford: Clarendon Press, 1978), 36–37.

38. Ibid., 42.

39. Morris, *Discovery of the Individual*, 34. It was important in the early Middle Ages, says Alexander Murray, that Jesus was a royal descendant of David and that his mother was also "of royal and free descent," as the synod of Frankfurt declared. *Reason and Society*, 328–329.

40. Ward, *Miracles*, 33–36.

41. Ullmann, *Individual and Society*, 36–37.

42. Eric Waldram Kemp, *Canonization and Authority in the Western Church* (London: Oxford University Press, 1948), 24–35.

43. Patrick J. Geary, *Furta Sacra: Thefts of Relics in the Central Middle Ages* (Princeton, NJ: Princeton University Press, 1978). This contains a good collection of specific references to medieval documents.

44. Ibid., 21.

45. Ibid., 23, 70.

46. Ibid., 129.

47. Ibid., 152.

48. See Lynn White, Jr., *Medieval Technology and Social Change* (London: Oxford University Press, 1962).

49. Marie-Dominique Chenu, *Nature, Man, and Society in the Twelfth Century* ([1957] Chicago: University of Chicago, 1969), 43–45.

50. Lester K. Little, *Religious Poverty and the Profit Economy in Medieval Europe* (Ithaca, NY: Cornell University Press, 1978), 3–26.

51. Ibid., 59–96, provides a summary of the variety of new religious movements in the eleventh and twelfth centuries.

52. Edward Grant, *Physical Sciences in the Middle Ages* (New York: John Wiley and Sons, 1971), 13–20. This was an age rich in changes. Alexander Murray, for example, in *Reason and Society*, 165–167, notes the reintroduction of the abacus. The ancient Romans had known of it, but in a clumsy form. Its use had died out. Between 1000 and 1300 it reappeared and spread. Murray calls this "a stimulus towards an accurate concept of numbers." Thanks to Arabic transmission of mathematical notation from India, an empty column on the abacus now had a notation for it, the zero.

53. William R. Cook and Ronald B. Hertzman, *The Medieval World View* (New York: Oxford University Press, 1983), 275–292, describes the return of rational order in the twelfth century and its influence on law, architecture, and interiority.

54. Ibid. describes the reappearance of interiority in literature (290–292), as part of a general cultural change (275–289). See also Radding, *A World Made by Men*, 105–108, on a lack of interiority in early medieval times and, 210–213, its rebirth.

55. Morris, *Discovery of the Individual*, 140–142.

56. Ann Llewellyn Barstow, *Married Priests and the Reforming Papacy* (New York: Mellen, 1982).

57. *Dictionary of the History of Ideas* (New York: Scribner's, 1973), vol. 3, 97.

58. Little, *Religious Poverty*, 173–175, 188.

59. Quoted in Jacques Le Goff, *The Birth of Purgatory* (Chicago: University of Chicago Press, 1981), 209.

60. Caroline W. Bynum, "The Spirituality of Regular Canons in the Twelfth Century: A New Approach," in *Medieval and Renaissance Spirituality*, ed. Paul Maurice Clogan (Denton: North Texas State University Press, 1973), 3–24.

61. Ward, *Miracles*, 104.

62. Ward, *Miracles*, 98–99.

63. John Bossey, "Blood and Baptism," in *Sanctity and Secularity: The Church and the World*, Derek Baker, ed. (New York: Barnes and Noble, 1973), 129–143.

64. Morris, *Discovery of the Individual*, 121–122. Morris claims that individualism lost ground in the twelfth and thirteenth centuries because of the development of systems in theology and in government (164–165). But he defines "individual" in a somewhat existential way.

65. Norman T. Burns and Christopher J. Reagan, *Concepts of the Hero in the Middle Ages and the Renaissance* (New York: SUNY Press, 1975), 42–44.

66. See Walter Ullmann, *Law and Politics in the Middle Ages* (Ithaca, NY: Cornell University Press, 1975), 77–84.

67. Ibid., 137–139, 165.

68. Francis E. Peters, *Aristotle and the Arabs: The Aristotelian Tradition in Islam* (New York: New York University Press, 1968), describes arguments among Muslims over the use of philosophy, arguments that follow the same pattern of conflict between a more literal, episodic, archaic, and concrete operational style of thought and the systematic, logical, formal operational style of thought of a classical culture. See especially 69–71, on Quranic Hadith as piecemeal use of authority and tradition, and 136–146, on the autonomy of reason.

69. It was the thought style characterized by Haydn White as understanding things through the concrete operational style of metonymy—that is, by placing elements in a series without the thoroughgoing integration of the formal operational style of synecdoche. See Haydn White, *Tropics of Discourse* (Baltimore: Johns Hopkins University Press, 1978), 6–12, for his interpretation of the relation of this to Piaget's theory. (I think he matches up Piaget's stages and language categories incorrectly.)

70. Brian Stock, *Myth and Science in the Twelfth Century: A Study of Bernard Silvester* (Princeton, NJ: Princeton University Press, 1972), 251–252.

71. Tiina Steifel, *The Intellectual Revolution in Twelfth Century Europe* (New York: St. Martin's Press, 1985), ch. 3, "The New Conception of Science," 50–77, reviews major arguments of the time. William of Conches said God used natural laws to make Eve; Thierry of Chartres referred to various empir-

ical experiences as evidence; John of Salisbury discussed degrees of probability of knowledge, from probable to necessary; and so on.

72. Morris, *Discovery of the Individual*, 80–81.

73. Ibid. See also Peter Abelard, *Sic et Non* (Chicago: University of Chicago Press, 1976–1977). In the prologue, 89–112, Abelard reviews the problems and offers methods for resolving them.

74. Edward R. Dijksterhuis, *The Mechanization of the World Picture* (Oxford: Clarendon Press, 1961), 158.

75. See Stock, *Myth and Science*, 31–61.

76. "Throughout the *Cosmographia*, allegory is not only a literary device through which diverse ideas may be synthesized; it is a serious philosophical tool for which Bernard sees no alternative. Stock, *Myth and Science*, 230.

77. Ibid., 241. Emphasis added.

78. John of Salisbury, *The Metalogicon*, trans. Daniel D. McGarry (Berkeley: University of California Press, 1955), 12. John agreed that nature did not follow strict necessity. Whereas normally sexual intercourse is needed for pregnancy, yet there was at least one virgin birth. John concluded with a comment the nominalists would like: "Is it not easier to recognize what exists than to decide what is possible?" (104). Check the facts instead of theorizing on what must be the case. (Here also is the famous passage that resurfaced in Newton's time: "Bernard of Chartres used to compare us to [puny] dwarfs perched on the shoulders of giants" [book III, ch. 4, 167).

79. *Summa Theologiae* (New York: Benziger Bros, 1947). The title page refers to these diagrams as "synoptical charts."

80. Gordon Leff, *The Dissolution of the Medieval Outlook* (San Francisco: Harper & Row, 1976), describes the issues and the tensions that arose from them.

81. Oakley, *Omnipotence*, describes this well.

82. Alexander Murray calls them the cognitive elite, and properly so. *Reason and Society*, 233.

83. Ward *Miracles*, 205–207.

84. Peter Brown, "Society and the Supernatural."

85. See Keith Thomas, *Religion and the Decline of Magic* (London: Weidenfeld and Nicolson, 1971), 51–52. See also 656–657, on belief in an orderly, rational world as a basis for diminishing belief in magic.

86. Gary Macy, *The Theologies of the Eucharist in the Early Scholastic Period* (Oxford: Clarendon Press, 1984). See also Radding, *A World Made by Men*, 166–172.

87. Anselm of Canterbury, *Basic Writings*, trans. S. N. Deane (LaSalle, IL: Open Court, 1962), "Cur Deus Homo," book I, ch. 13, pp. 206–207.

88. Thomas Aquinas, *Summa Contra Gentiles* (Notre Dame, IN: Notre Dame University Press, 1956), book III, part II, chs. 99–101, pp. 78–82. Also see Aquinas's *Summa Theologiae*, I, 105, 6 and 7, and I–II, q. 178, art. 1, *resp.*

89. Funkenstein cites an earlier idea from Maimonides on the slackness or "indeterminacy of nature" that God makes use of in doing miracles. Maimonides' example, though, is more precisely honed than Aquinas's, to suggest a fully reliable world order within which God does miracles without conflicting with nature. *Theology and the Scientific Imagination*, 227–231.

90. *Summa Contra Gentiles*, 79–80; and *Summa Theologiae*, I–II, q. 178, art. 1, *resp.*

91. Steven J. Dick, *Plurality of Worlds: The Origins of the Extraterrestrial Life Debate from Democritus to Kant* (New York: Cambridge University Press, 1982), 31–32, notes the early history of this question from its mention by Peter Lombard in his *Sentences*: "whether God is able to make the world better than he has made it." Commentary on the *Sentences* was a standard practice for theologians up to the seventeenth century. Aquinas approved: "Given the things which actually exist, the universe cannot be better"; *Summa Theologiae*, I, 25, 6, *ad.* 3.

92. Oakley, *Omnipotence*, 41–65.

93. Ibid., 43–45.

94. A review of this issue from patristic times to the fifteenth century is the main topic of Funkenstein's excellent book, *Theology and the Scientific Imagination*, 124–150.

95. Miracles can be thought of also as part of God's ordained power, inasmuch as they were choices God made from all eternity about what would actually take place, as opposed to all the countless things that might have taken place through God's absolute power. But eventually miracles were associated with God's absolute power alone by some. Others defined nature's order as God's general ordained power and miracles as God's special ordained power. Ibid., 58–59.

96. Pierre Duhem traces the origin of modern science to this, because it opened the way for empirical studies, an idea later supported by Stanley Jaki. Edward Grant agrees on the greater openness to experiment but notes that the condemnation also undercut science by reducing the expectation that nature had to be rational. Grant, "Science and Theology in the Middle Ages," in *God and Nature: Historical Essays in the Encounter Between Christianity and Science*, eds. David Lindberg and Ronald Numbers (Berkeley: University of California Press, 1986), 54–58.

97. The term "nominalism" covers a variety of similar positions. See, e.g., the list of meanings provided in Alister McGrath, *The Intellectual Origins of the European Reformation* (Oxford: Basil Blackwell, 1987), "Nominalism: The Problem of Definition," 70–75. It can be defined in such a way, McGrath notes, that Ockham would not be a nominalist.

98. The expression is from Colin A. Russell, *Cross Currents: Interactions Between Science and Faith* (Downers Grove, IL: InterVarsity Press, 1985), 95.

99. See Leff, *Dissolution of the Medieval Outlook*, 67–70, 78–81. Leff's judgment is that "The renunciation of previous attempts to unite all knowledge and belief within a single system . . . marks the beginning of the dissolution of the medieval world outlook" (145). Other historians, however, note that even during Scholasticism's high point there were countercurrents, some of them more pious than intellectual, others intellectual but humanistic or vitalist rather than logical-dialectic-scientific in approach. Hiram Hayden's work still provides an excellent survey of this: *The Counter-Renaissance* (New York: Harcourt, Brace and World, 1950).

100. See Oakley, *Omnipotence*, 77–84, for instances.

101. See Edward Grant, "Science and Theology in the Middle Ages," for a survey of twelfth- and thirteenth-century thought, including various early kinds of nominalism and their effects on theology.

102. Hiram Hayden summarizes the elements of this "classical Christian" hierarchical universe, in *The Counter-Renaissance*, 293–324.

103. Chenu, *Nature, Man, and Society*, 43.

104. See the summary in John Losee, *A Historical Introduction to the Philosophy of Science* (Oxford: Oxford University Press, 1972), 6–11.

105. As described in Marshall Clagett, *Greek Science in Antiquity* (Freeport, New York: Books for Libraries Press, 1971 [repr. of 1955 ed.]), 29.

106. See Peter Urbach, *Roger Bacon's Philosophy of Science: An Account and a Reappraisal* (LaSalle, IL: Open Court, 1987), ch. 6, "The Role of Experiment," 149–171. Also see A. C. Crombie, *Robert Grosseteste and the Origins of Experimental Science* (Oxford: Clarendon Press, 1953).

107. Losee, *Historical Introduction*, 36–37. See also Henry Guerlac, "Newton and the Method of Analysis," in *Dictionary of the History of Ideas* (New York: Scribner's, 1973), vol. 3, 378–391, for some ideas on the impact of Grosseteste and Bacon.

108. Losee, *Historical Introduction*, 31–36.

109. Edward R. Dijksterhuis, *The Mechanization of the World Picture* (Oxford: Clarendon Press, 1961), 133. (He lists the specific place of each idea in Albert's work on 508.)

110. "The strong interest in the theory and logic of experimental science and in related philosophical conceptions of nature, sustained from Grosseteste down to the threshold of Galileo's activities, stands in striking contrast with the comparative scarcity of actual experimental investigations." A. C. Crombie, *Medieval and Early Modern Science*, rev. ed., vol. 2 (Garden City, New York: Doubleday Anchor, 1959).

111. Though he himself condemned "the Empirical school of philosophy," which in his time was the school of the alchemists and of natural magic. These were empirical inasmuch as they experimented with various compounds and chemicals. See Francis Bacon, *Essays, Advancement of Learning, New Atlantis, and Other Pieces*, ed. Richard Foster Jones (New York: Odyssey Press, 1937), 293.

112. Urbach, *Francis Bacon's Philosophy of Science*, 17–24, describes the standard interpretation of Bacon as a pure inductivist. Bacon actually explicitly rejects this approach, says Urbach, 30–35.

113. *The Works of Francis Bacon*, ed. Robert L. Ellis, Douglas D. Heath, and James Spedding (London: Longman and Co., 1857), vol. 3, 583; my translation/paraphrase. Dijksterhuis, *Mechanization of the World Picture*, 139, claims that when Bacon recommended using experience in his *Scientia Experimentalis*, he meant not only that sense experience should be used to gather information and evidence, but also that a person should rely on inner experiences of illumination or intuition, which were so important in religious matters and also in Neoplatonic natural magic. I find this interpretation surprising in view of how strongly Bacon rejected the natural magic aspects of William Gilbert's work on magnetism (see ch. 8) and in general.

114. Francis Bacon, *The New Organon and Related Writings*, ed. Fulton H. Anderson (New York: Liberal Arts Press, 1960). On 151–164 he describes "aids to understanding" in interpreting evidence to generate hypotheses; on 164–265 he lists twenty-seven different *types* of evidence or tests for distinguishing trustworthy hypotheses from untrustworthy. See 156 for the vintage image.

115. William P. D. Wightman, *The Growth of Scientific Ideas* (New Haven, CT: Yale University Press, 1951), 29–40, notes that Hipparchus in the second century BCE acknowledged two major ways to "save the appearances" (i.e., to portray the heavens in a way consistent with the evidence or appear-

ances), in relation to the odd fact that there are 186 days from the spring equinox to the autumn equinox but only 179 from the autumn equinox to the spring equinox. See Clagett, *Greek Science in Antiquity*, ch. 7.

Chapter 8

1. See John W. Yolton, *Thinking Matter: Materialism in Eighteenth Century Britain* (Minneapolis: University of Minnesota Press, 1983), 107–114.

2. Brian Easlea names Andreä as the founder in his *Witch Hunting, Magic, and the New Philosophy* (Atlantic Highlands, NJ: Humanities Press, 1980), 106.

3. See Stephen A. McKnight, *Sacralizing the Secular: The Renaissance Origins of Modernity* (Baton Rouge: Louisiana State University Press, 1989), for a thorough description of hermeticism, its supporters, and its influences. The message of the Poimandres is summarized on 41–43.

4. The skills and opportunities of the magus were laid out in the second major book of the *Corpus*, the "Asclepius." See ibid., 43–45.

5. Researchers still search for such mental powers, but so far supporting evidence is lacking, and there are some good theoretical reasons to be skeptical. See Ray Hyman's lengthy and careful report, "A Critical Overview of Parapsychology," in *A Skeptic's Handbook of Parapsychology*, ed. Paul Kurz (Buffalo, New York: Prometheus, 1985), 3–96, on the lack of evidence.

6. In defense of hermetic magic, Pietro Pomponazzi (1462–1525) explained that speaking with tongues and other *mirabilia* in this lower world are due to natural causes. In response, a Jesuit complained that Pomponazzi thereby ascribed all miracles to the stars, natural forces, instead of to God. As reported in Easlea, *Witch Hunting*, 95–96.

7. The work of William Gilbert on magnetism is a mixed example. He did extensive empirical work with magnets, laying down rules of magnetism that now sound quite scientific. But he concluded from all this that magnetism was a manifestation of "souls," perhaps even the universal soul such as recognized by Hermes, Zoroaster, and Orpheus. See Gilbert's *On the Lodestone and Magnetic Bodies* (Chicago: William Benton, 1952), 104B.

8. McKnight, *Sacralization*, 41.

9. The competing philosophies were not always clearly in opposition to each other. Hermeticism and mathematical measurements and Aristotelianism could all be used by a single person. This was the case with John Dee, for example, as reported by Peter French in *John Dee: The World of an Elizabethan Magus* (New York: Dorset Press, 1972). In fact, Dee emphasized the value of experience as promoted by Bacon (163). He favored applying mathematics to areas not recommended by Aristotle (162), yet used much of Aristotle (171).

10. I have now twice in this chapter referred to "reliable evidence" as a criterion for the acceptance of a model of reality. Modern science relies precisely on this criterion as the single most necessary way to distinguish between a mere idea about reality and a probably true claim about reality. Whether science should trust this as a valid criterion or not will be part of the discussion in chapter 9.

11. See Descartes's "Principles of Philosophy," part 3, no. 29, in *The Philosophical Writings of Descartes*, vol. 1, trans. John Cottingham, Dugald Mur-

doch, and Robert Stoothoff (New York: Cambridge University Press, 1984), 253.

12. Descartes alludes to this by listing the tides as an item to be accounted for by the corpuscular hypothesis, in "Principles of Philosophy," part 4, nos. 49–56, *Philosophical Writings*, vol. 1, 271.

13. Not all mechanistic atomists were Cartesian. Boyle, later Newton, and many on the Continent gradually filled empty space with ether rather than particles, and acknowledged the possibility of at least an approximate vacuum.

14. *Discourse on Method*, part V, no. 54, in *Philosophical Writings*, vol. 1, 138. The significant aspect here is not the distinction between material body and immaterial soul. That was a very old and well accepted idea, especially among Christians. What was striking in Descartes's thought was his acceptance of the ancient atomists' belief that matter is fully inert, that every animal body is really just mechanical matter living off of the aboriginal energy imparted by God to the universe. Up to this point in European natural philosophy, Aristotle's animating essences had performed the function of accounting for growth and motion and sensation in living things.

15. Half of Hobbes's *Leviathan* (New York: Collier/Macmillan, 1962) is devoted to religion, primarily attacking superstitions and promoting a more rational, mechanistic viewpoint.

16. See Pierre Gassendi's defense of thought as corporeal activity against Descartes's dualism in the "Fifth Set of Objections," to which Descartes responded in *Philosophical Writings*, vol. 2, 182, 232–239.

17. Definitions vary with the context. With an eye to the arguments in biology that loomed large in the eighteenth and nineteenth centuries, Rainer Schubert-Soldern defines mechanistic philosophy as one that imputes to matter its own powers of activity or life. He thereby unwittingly excludes Descartes and Hobbes from the list of mechanistic philosophers. In *Mechanism and Vitalism: Philosophical Aspects of Biology* (Notre Dame, IN: Notre Dame University Press, 1962), 10–14.

18. Thomas Aquinas, *Summa Theologica* (New York: Benziger Brothers, 1947), I, 105, 5, resp.

19. See Gary B. Deason, "Reformation, Theology, and the Mechanistic Conception of Nature," in David Lindberg and Ronald Numbers, eds., *God and Nature* (Berkeley: University of California Press, 1986), 178–183. See also Ernan McMullin, *Newton on Matter and Activity* (Notre Dame, IN: University of Notre Dame Press, 1988).

20. Richard Westfall, *The Construction of Modern Science: Mechanisms and Mechanics* (New York: John Wiley and Sons, 1971), 86–92, describes the history of Harvey's thought. It began with Galen's physiology, which employed the idea of various kinds of "natural spirits," but also used the model of a mechanical pump as a way to describe the heart's action.

21. *On Animal Generation*, in *The Works of William Harvey*, trans. Robert Willis (New York: Johnson Reprint, 1965), 502.

22. Ibid., 503, 507.

23. See also Richard Westfall's description of differences Descartes himself saw between his position and the ideas of Harvey, in *The Construction of Modern Science*, 86–94.

24. Isaac Newton, *Optics* (New York: Dover, 1952 [copy of 4th ed., 1730]), book 3, part I, p. 402. Newton rejected Descartes's speculation that the world could arise out of chaos by mere laws of nature.

25. H. McLachlin, who edited Newton's religious writing, published some of them as Isaac Newton, *Theological Manuscripts* (Liverpool: Liverpool University Press, 1950). McLachlin calculated that there were 1.3 million words in Newton's manuscripts on religion and theology, including ideas on prophecy, apocalypticism, Romanism, Sibylline oracles, New Testament criticism, Arius, Athanasius and the Trinity, God's activity in nature, and so on.

26. Newton, *Principia*, ed. Florian Cajori (Berkeley: University of California Press, 1960), 544–547.

27. As noted by Richard Westfall, "The Rise of Science and the Decline of Orthodox Christianity," in *God and Nature*, ed. David Lindberg and Ronald Numbers (Berkeley: University of California Press, 1986), 227.

28. "The World or Treatise on Light," ch. 7, in *Descartes's Philosophical Writings*, vol. 1, 92–97.

29. "A Free Inquiry," sec. I, in *The Works of the Honourable Robert Boyle in Six Volumes* (Hildesheim: Georg Olms, 1966 [1772]), vol. 5, 163.

30. In E. Graham Waring, ed., *Deism and Natural Religion: A Source Book* (New York: Frederick Ungar, 1967), 11–12. The words quoted are on 8.

31. Ibid., 49–51. The many references to Waring's book are references to the writings of the deists that Waring reprints in this source book.

32. Ibid., 66–81.

33. Ibid., 145–152.

34. "Of Miracles," sec. 10 of *An Inquiry into Human Understanding*, in David Hume, *On Human Nature and the Understanding*, eds. Crane Brinton and Paul Edwards (New York: Collier, 1962), 115–136. Deistic thought appeared into the nineteenth century, as in the works of William Paley.

35. It sounds a naive approach now, but note Frances Galton, who in 1872 used statistics against the belief that prayers evoked miracles: clergy lived no longer than physicians or lawyers; ships with missionaries sank as often as others, religious lands had their full share of evil. Robert J. Richards, *Darwinism and the Emergence of Evolutionary Theories of Mind and Behavior* (Chicago: University of Chicago Press, 1987), 337.

36. Derek Gjersten, *The Classics of Science* (New York: Lilian Barber Press, 1984), ch. 11, on the development of modern chemistry, tells the general story. James Bryant Conan et al., eds., *Harvard Case Histories in Experimental Science*, vol. 1 (Cambridge, MA: Harvard University Press, 1964 [1948]), offers a fuller account: Leonard K. Nash, "The Atomic-Molecular Theory," 215–321.

37. J. Levy, "The Exploration of the Stellar Universe," in *History of Science*, vol. 3, *Science in the Nineteenth Century*, ed. René Taton, trans. A. J. Pomerans (New York: Basic Books, 1965), 124.

38. Some of the material here on vitalism and Darwin has appeared in slightly different form in Michael Barnes, "The Evolution of the Soul from Matter and the Role of Science in the Theology of Karl Rahner," *Horizons* 21: 1 (Spring 1994), 85–104.

39. Cited in Shirley A. Roe, *Matter, Life, and Generation: Eighteenth Century Embryology and the Haller-Wolff Debate* (New York: Cambridge University Press, 1981), 1.

40. As described by Thomas L. Hankins, *Science and the Enlightenment* (New York: Cambridge University Press, 1985), 115.

41. Hobbes's *Leviathan*, for example, half of which is on religion, is not only antimiracle (usually as part of the anti-Catholic position) but also anti-spirit and anti-God, and rather mechanistic.

42. As described by Stuart Brown, *Leibniz* (Minneapolis: University of Minnesota, 1984), 170, based on Leibniz's *New System of the Nature and Communication of Substances*, no. 3 (written in 1695).

43. Yolton, *Thinking Matter*, 14–29.

44. William P. D. Wightman provides a brief description of Franklin's ideas in *The Growth of Scientific Ideas* (New Haven, CT: Yale University Press, 1951), 215–222. Joseph Toaldo at the University of Padua in 1774 had described the effect of this electric fire and how it might excite bodily fluids. It was not long before Mary Wollstonecraft Shelley told a tale of Dr. Frankenstein's creature vivified by this electrical fire. See Richard Burkhardt, Jr., *The Spirit of System: Lamarck and Evolutionary Biology* (Cambridge, MA: Harvard University Press, 1977), 64–67.

45. See Hans Driesch, *History and Theory of Vitalism*, trans. C. K. Ogden (London: Macmillan, 1914).

46. See David Knight, *The Age of Science: The Scientific Worldview in the Nineteenth Century* (Oxford: Basil Blackwell, 1986), 56–57. Bernard M. G. Reardon classifies all this as part of the religious romanticism of the late eighteenth and early nineteenth centuries. *Religion in the Age of Romanticism* (New York: Cambridge University Press, 1985), esp. vii, 21–27. See also Isaiah Berlin, "The Counter-Enlightenment," in *The Dictionary of the History of Ideas*, vol. 2 (New York: Scribner's, 1973), 100–112, for a summary of antirationalist support for some forms of vitalism.

47. For Driesch the question to ask was a very general one: "Do the facts compel us to assume that the phenomena of life have a law of their own, or do they not?" He said yes. *History and Theory of Vitalism*, 144.

48. See *On Animal Generation*, 272–273, for brief use of Aristotle.

49. The words are Shirley Roe's, from her *Matter, Life, and Generation*, 103.

50. Ibid., 90–91.

51. See Hankins, *Science and the Enlightenment*, 130–144, for a review of these and other studies in the early nineteenth century.

52. This account is in ibid., 125–127, 141–145.

53. Roe, *Matter, Life, and Generation*, 3. Jacques Roger cites an earlier epigeneticist, a Catholic priest named John Turberville Needham (1713–1781). He admired God's skill in creating a nature that could produce life. Roger, "The Mechanistic Conception of Life," in *God and Nature*, eds. David Lindberg and Ronald Numbers (Berkeley: University of California Press, 1986), 289. Roger agrees, however, that by the mid-nineteenth century, mechanistic theories were often used as a weapon against religious belief (292). Note also Lamarck (1744–1829). In early writings he spoke of life as a manifestation of a vital principle. In 1794 he made the flat assertion that life was a mysterious principle not explained by matter, though always dependent on matter. Eventually he interpreted life in a less vitalistic way. Animal heat came from decomposition, he thought, specifically the loss of "fixed fire" from the blood. He began to think in terms of a variety of subtle fluids—heat, electricity, magnetism—that could explain irritability and sensitivity and growth. Later

in his life (1802, 1809), Lamarck argued that life is not some special principle but a natural physical phenomenon. Lamarck was decidedly materialist, yet he believed in an "economy of nature" organized by the Wisdom of the Creator. It was evidently possible to be a mechanist and still be religious. Burkhardt, *The Spirit of System*, esp. 59–72, 151–157.

54. See the summary by Joseph Needham in "Mechanistic Biology and Religious Consciousness," in *Science, Religion, and Reality*, ed. Joseph Needham (New York: George Braziller, 1955), esp. 237–238.

55. See Claire L. Parkinson, *Breakthroughs: a Chronology of Great Achievements in Science and Mathematics, 1200–1930* (Boston: G. K. Hall, 1985), 276, for dates on this and related matters.

56. It is ironic that biologists were at first leery of Mendelism because it seemed too similar to preformationism by supposing that some preformed structure or characteristics were passed on from parent to offspring. See Stephen G. Brush, *The History of Modern Science* (Ames: Iowa State University Press, 1988), 136.

57. Ibid., 239.

58. Ernst Mayr, *Toward a New Philosophy of Biology: Observations of an Evolutionist* (Cambridge, MA: Belknap Press, 1988), 245–249.

59. See Roger Hahn, "Laplace and the Mechanistic Universe," in *God and Nature* (Berkeley: University of California Press, 1986), 265–266.

60. See John Durant, "Darwinism and Divinity: A Century of Debate," in *Darwinism and Divinity: Essays on Evolution and Religious Belief*, ed. John Durant (New York: Basil Blackwell, 1985), 15–17.

61. He was compelled to publish his theory in 1859 because Wallace was about to publish his own version of natural selection. (Darwin had circulated a brief version of his theory for others to read in 1844.) Feeling rushed, he took pains to indicate that the single volume of 1859 was an abstract of the relevant information he had. He would have liked to produce the sort of many-volume work that other Victorians took pride in offering to the public.

62. Louis Agassiz, the famous antievolutionary naturalist, strongly supported Georges Cuvier's view that the sixty to one hundred mass destructions of old life-forms and the appearance of new ones had religious implications. "Here again, the intervention of the Creator is displayed in the most striking manner, in every stage of the history of the world." Agassiz, *Essay on Classification* (Cambridge, MA: Belknap Press, 1962 [1857/1859]), 103–104.

63. See John Hedley Brooke, *Science and Religion: Some Historical Perspectives* (New York: Cambridge University Press, 1991), 194, 253–254. Chs. 6–8 provide a good history of various and sometimes opposing ways in which religious thinkers opted for one model or another in response to new evidence concerning geology and fossils.

64. Herbert Spencer, *First Principles* 4th ed. (London: A. L. Burt Home Library, 1880), 11–13.

65. Georges Buffon's eighteenth-century estimate of the age of the Earth was about 130,000 years. Lord Kelvin estimated the Earth's age (based on the rate of cooling of the Earth) at about 500 million years, which Kelvin thought too short a time for the gradual process that Darwin portrayed. Darwin agreed that this was too short a time. See Stephen Toulmin and Jane Goodfield, *The Discovery of Time* (Chicago: University of Chicago Press, 1965), 141, 222.

66. See Robert J. Richards, *Darwinism and the Emergence of Evolutionary Theories of Mind and Behavior* (Chicago: University of Chicago Press, 1987), ch. 8. The Englishman George Romanes, won a prize in 1873 for arguing that God could have guided evolution in ways not detectable (though he eventually abandoned this position). Richards, *Op. cit.*, 337–342, 543–544.

67. Driesch, *The History and Theory of Vitalism*, 138.

68. Wolf-Ernst Reif, "Evolutionary Theory in German Paleontology," in Marjorie Grene, ed., *Dimensions of Darwinism* (New York: Cambridge University Press, 1983), 173–203.

69. See Richards, *Darwinism and the Emergence*, 178–183.

70. Knight, *The Age of Science*, 194–203.

71. Ibid., 71–77.

72. Richards, *Darwinism and the Emergence*, 190–192, 195–201.

73. See Philip Appleman, ed., *Darwin* (New York: W. W. Norton, 1979), 132–208.

74. For example, see Stephen Jay Gould, *Hen's Teeth and Horses' Toes* (New York: W. W. Norton, 1983), for a description of the process of evolution as a crude one, using not the best possibilities but whatever is available as the basis of the next change (ch. 12); on the "nonmoral" character of nature (ch. 2); on the mass destruction of species on occasions (chs. 26–27). Given the available evidence, Gould's interpretation is a plausible one.

75. Stephen Hawking offers a variant of the Big Bang theory in his quasi-popularized book, *A Brief History of Time: From the Big Bang to Black Holes* (New York: Bantam Books, 1988). I confess I do not understand this version.

Chapter 9

1. Some have used the word "postformal" to name a mode of thought that follows formal operational thought. I wish to avoid any implied association with "postmodern," however, a word with troublesome connotations. For a description of postformal thought, see Fredda Blanchard-Fields, "Postformal Reasoning in Socio-Emotional Context," in *Adult Development*, vol. 1, *Comparisons and Applications of Developmental Models*, eds. Michael L. Commons, Jan D. Sinnott, Francis A. Richards, and Cheryl Armon (New York: Praeger, 1989), 73–94. Suzanne Benack and Michael A. Basseches use the expression "dialectical" thought for this. See their "Dialectical Thinking and Relativist Epistemology: Their Relation in Adult Development," Ibid., 95–109. Other articles in this book are also on "postformal reasoning."

2. D. Kuhn, J. Langer, L. Kohlberg, and N. S. Haan, "The Development of Formal Operations in Logical and Moral Judgment," *Genetic Psychology Monographs* 95 (1977): 97–188, reviews a variety of investigations on adult reasoning processes. More up-to-date is B. Leadbeater, "The Resolution of Relativism in Adult Thinking: Subjective, Objective, or Conceptual?" *Human Development* 29:5 (September–October 1986): 291–300. He notes that there is no agreement among the experts on which type of formal operational thought is "more mature." Also see Deirdre A. Kramer and Diana S. Woodruff, "Relativistic and Dialectical Thought in Three Adult Age-Groups," *Human Development* 29:5 (September–October 1986): 280–290, comparing young, middle-aged, and older adults. Flexibility of thought increases with age, but sex and the nature of the problem influence the style of thought as well.

3. William Perry, *Forms of Intellectual and Ethical Development in College Years* (New York: Holt, Rinehart, and Winston, 1970), tells a poignant story of Harvard undergraduate males who gradually perceived the fallibility of professors, books, and tradition. Some accepted a life of commitment to reasonable and valuable probabilities; others returned to the more dogmatic and comfortable certitudes they had possessed as freshmen; still others just remained confused.

4. As Ernest Gellner says, "it is stunningly effective" at its limited task. *Plough, Sword, and Book* (London: Collins Harvill, 1988), 202. Also see Larry Laudan, "Explaining the Success of Science: Beyond Epistemic Realism and Relativism," in *Science and Reality: Recent Work in the Philosophy of Science*, eds. James T. Cushing, C. F. Delaney, and Gary M. Gutting (Notre Dame, IN: University of Notre Dame Press, 1984), 83–105. Or Rachel Laudan: "It is a truism, but one worth remembering, that what sets natural science off as a distinct field of human activity is the success with which scientists have investigated the natural world in the past three or four centuries. Some critics dismiss this success as merely apparent, as a giant confidence trick that should be unmasked. But for those historians of science who disagree—and they are the majority, I believe—the central problem is to trace the history of scientific ideas and, if possible, to shed some light on why they seem so accurately to describe the world." *From Mineralogy to Geology: The Foundations of a Science* (Chicago: University of Chicago Press, 1987), 17–18.

5. Barry Barnes, *T. S. Kuhn and Social Science* (New York: Columbia University Press, 1982), 103 (emphasis added). Note that Barnes appeals to empirical evidence to determine the many ways in which people are influenced by social bias and individual interest in the ways they use and develop science.

6. As someone sympathetic to this view, Helga Novotny cites three kinds of critics: the antiscience romantics, pseudoscientists, and self-critical scientists. See her "Science and Its Critics: Reflections on Anti-Science," in *Counter-Movements in the Sciences*, eds. Helga Novotny and Hilary Rose (Dordrecht: D. Reidel, 1979), 1–26.

7. Jean Hardy, *A Psychology with a Soul: Psychosynthesis in Evolutionary Context* (New York: Routledge and Kegan Paul, 1987), p. 99.

8. Ibid., 168.

9. Morse Peckham, *The Birth of Romanticism, 1790–1815* (Greenwood, FL: Penkevill Publishing, 1986), iv. Worth raising is the distorted understanding of history this sentence contains. The empires of the invading Aryans in India, some Chinese dynasties, Mongolian conquerors, Islamic imperialists, ancient Tanzanian rulers, and so forth have no better a record than those of Europeans.

10. Ruben A. Alves, "What Does It Mean to Say the Truth?" in *The Sciences and Theology in the Twentieth Century*, ed. Arthur R. Peacocke (Notre Dame, IN: Notre Dame University Press, 1981), 168.

11. Richard Schlegel, "Is Science the Only Way to Truth?" *Zygon* 17:4 (December 1982): 343–359.

12. Ibid., 350.

13. This is Carl Sagan's famous position, in his *Cosmos* (New York: Random House, 1980), 4, 21.

14. I avoid calling it a "materialist" naturalism, because that word carries too much baggage. The discussion of "matter" in chapter 8 shows mate-

rialism has taken many forms. I likewise avoid the word "dualism" because of similar weight and ambiguities. Bernard Lightman, *The Origins of Agnosticism* (Baltimore: Johns Hopkins University Press, 1987), 28, defines nineteenth-century English "scientific naturalism."

15. Eugenie C. Scott and Robert M. West, both of the National Center for Science Education, say that the method of science includes methodological naturalism, not philosophical naturalism. See their "Again, Johnson Gets It Wrong," *Creation/Evolution* 37 (Winter 1995): 26–27.

16. Lonergan, seemingly to the contrary, claims classic scholarship promotes the aims of a particular culture, whereas modern scholarship is universalist. But other comments make it clear that classic scholarship nonetheless assumed it had the universally valid truth. Bernard Lonergan, "Aquinas Today: Tradition and Innovation," in *Celebrating the Medieval Heritage (Journal of Religion* supp.) 58 (1978): S4.

17. David R. Oldroyd, *The Arch of Knowledge: An Introductory Study of the History of the Philosophy and Methodology of Science* (New York: Methuen, 1986), 159–160, notes an early use of the criterion of fit in William Whewell's "conciliance of inductions," wherein theories from diverse fields turn out to reinforce each other. Popper analyzes the theory of complementarity by showing how it is in tension with the mind's test of ideas, "by whether they fit with other ideas. Where there is a lack of fit we recognize inadequacy of understanding." See Karl Popper, *Conjectures and Refutations* (London: Routledge and Kegan Paul, 1963), 113–114. George Gale, *Theory of Science: An Introduction to the History, Logic, and Philosophy of Science* (New York: McGraw-Hill, 1979), 275–285, describes all science as varied applications of the criterion of good "fit."

18. This is not a new observation. Michael J. Buckley, S.J., for example, in his "Transcendence, Truth, and Faith: The Ascending Experience of God in All Human Inquiry," *Theological Studies* 39:4 (December 1978): 633–655, quotes Einstein approvingly, to the effect that science is just a form of the normal human way of knowing (638). "The scientific way of forming concepts differs from that which we use in our daily life, not basically, but merely in the more precise definitions of concepts and conclusions; more painstaking and systematic choice of experimental material; and a great logical economy" (Einstein, *Out of My Later Years* [New York: Philosophical Library, 1950], 95).

19. These elements changed science from the classical certitudinism sought in the Enlightenment to a modern (or postmodern, depending on one's definition) probabilist form slowly accepted over the next few centuries. Various antiscience and constructivist writers attack what they call Enlightenment standards of rationality, such as foundationalism. These charges do not fit contemporary probabilist science very well.

20. I have not found anyone who has actually recommended strict inductivism. Certainly, neither Francis Bacon nor Auguste Comte did, in spite of what others have sometimes said about their methods, and in spite of Bacon's use of the word.

21. Francis Bacon, *The New Organon and Related Writings*, ed. Fulton H. Anderson (New York: The Liberal Arts Press, 1960), *Aphorisms*, book II, secs. XXII–LII, pp. 162–266. Peter Urbach, *Francis Bacon's Philosophy of Science: An Account and a Reappraisal* (LaSalle, IL: Open Court, 1987), 39–41, agrees that Bacon sought only "pledges of truth" from this evidence, not certitude.

22. Popper highlights the limits of science as well as its power, but against the Wittgensteinians he declares that scientists are concerned with truth, not just the usefulness of their ideas. See Popper, *Conjectures and Refutations*, 113–117. In ch. 3, 97–119, Popper refers frequently to refutation as a process of checking for "fit." In his later *Objective Knowledge: An Evolutionary Approach* (Oxford: Clarendon Press, 1972), 264–269, Popper repeats his claim that science is "conjecture and refutation." He emphasizes the continuously conditional and tentative character of all scientific truth-claims, but still insists that science searches for truth.

23. Oldroyd, *The Arch of Knowledge*.

24. Larry Laudan, *Science and Values* (Berkeley: University of California Press, 1984), has proposed a "reticulated model of justification" of ideas in science. The actual process of science is not a neat progression from fact-claims to generalizations and theories, and then on to empirical tests. It is a messy process in which ideas and fact-claims of various sorts are bumping up against each other in ways both planned and unplanned. But all such ideas are then evaluated by how well they reticulate—network—with each other. I have not read this; I depend on John Losee's summary in his *Philosophy of Science and Historical Inquiry* (Oxford: Clarendon Press, 1987), 130–134. Though the actual process is messy, the standard and helpful way to grasp the scientific justification of any idea after the fact is to sort out the elements into the shape of Oldroyd's arch for publication in professional journals.

25. William Eamon, *Science and the Secrets of Nature: Books of Secrets in Medieval and Modern Culture* (Princeton, NJ: Princeton University Press, 1994). Ch. 1, 15–37 is on the origin of books of secrets in late antiquity (though the chapter is entitled "The Literature of Secrets in the Middle Ages"). Chs. 9 and 10 provide detailed historical information on the shift toward public sharing and testing of ideas, 301–318, 319–350.

26. Jan V. Golinski, "A Noble Spectacle: Phosphorus and the Public Cultures of Science in the Early Royal Society," *Isis* 80:301 (March 1989): 11–39, gives an informative illustration.

27. As noted earlier, this is in Sextus Empiricus's *Outlines of Scepticism*, book I, sec. xvii, no. 181, in trans. by Julia Annas and Jonathan Barnes (New York: Cambridge University Press, 1994), 45: "Some people often give an explanation in only one way, although there is a rich abundance enabling them to explain the object of investigation in a variety of ways."

28. Christiaan Huygens defined the price: sacrifice certitude but achieve reliable knowledge through the process of conjecture and testing. See Ernan McMullin, "The Shaping of Scientific Rationality: Construction and Constraint," in *Construction and Constraint: The Shaping of Scientific Rationality*, ed. Ernan McMullin (Notre Dame, IN: University of Notre Dame Press, 1988), 32. (Huygens's words are taken from his introduction to his 1690 *Treatise on Light*.)

29. An ironic aspect of constructivism is that it uses *classical* standards of truth. Constructivism implies that science would be universally valid if it had an undoubtable foundation and true objectivity. It is because science fails these two classical tests that constructivism says it has only local validity. Rorty seems to accept probabilist standards of science when he says he judges science pragmatically, on how well it works. But the pragmatic test he wants to apply to science is the degree to which it may help him achieve

various social values, not the degree to which it gives him something like objective and universal truth, which he holds no hope of achieving. He never indicates how he will determine when in fact his values are being achieved. (See note 32.)

30. One can divide interpretations of science into "realist" and "antirealist." Thus a number of philosophies of science or of knowledge are antirealist in the sense that they deny that science attains to a knowledge of reality. Realist schools say science does know reality, albeit "critically." To avoid the intricacies of these arguments, I am not asserting that probabilism is a successful critical realism. I say only that the truth-claims which probabilism produces are often indistinguishable in practice from what realism seeks. They can *function* as the truth.

31. Thomas Kuhn, *The Structure of Scientific Revolutions*, 2nd ed. (Chicago: University of Chicago Press, 1970 [1962]). He prefigures the ideas presented here in many side comments in his earlier *The Copernican Revolution* (Cambridge, MA: Harvard University Press, 1957).

32. Richard Rorty, *Philosophy and the Mirror of Nature* (Princeton, NJ: Princeton University Press, 1979). He acknowledges his debt to Sellars and Quine in ch. 4, and to Kuhn in the second section of Ch. 7 (to the collection of Kuhn's essays titled *The Essential Tension* as well as to *Structure*).

33. Peter L. Berger and Thomas Luckman, *The Social Construction of Reality* (New York: Doubleday, 1966). They begin with "Our undertaking has been theoretical. Yet theory, in any empirical discipline, must be relevant in a double fashion to the 'data' defined as pertinent to the discipline. It must be congruent with them, and it must be geared to further empirical inquiry" (7). They treat their own theory as not socially constructed, or not simply so, but based upon good empirical data.

34. E.g., in Barnes, *T. S. Kuhn and Social Science*. He promotes a strong program in the sociology of knowledge, providing social reasons why science has developed as it has. He appeals to many facts, seemingly as evidence, to conclude that evidence is not that important in determining scientific conclusions. He says we blame foreign ideologies on bias, but "Where goals or interests of which we do approve bear upon evaluation, we do not speak of bias" (107). I must say I know many people who are willing and able to acknowledge their own biases. They may do this imperfectly, but they strive for an honest objectivity.

35. For a much more thorough review of the issues here, see Noretta Koertge, ed., *A House Built on Sand: Exposing Postmodernist Myths About Science* (New York: Oxford University Press, 1998). Alan Sokal and Jean Bricmont, *Fashionable Nonsense: Postmodern Intellectuals' Abuse of Science* (New York: Picador USA, 1998), is excellent as a critique of some particularly bad uses of science by postmodern critics of the claims of objectivity in science.

36. Credit also goes to Wilfred Sellars. He set out to destroy "the myth of the given" in his article "Empiricism and the Philosophy of Mind," in Herbert Feigl and Michael Scriven, eds., *The Foundations of Science and the Concepts of Psychology and Psychoanalysis* (Minneapolis: University of Minnesota Press, 1956), 253–329. There is precedent for this in Comte's observation that our knowledge of the facts is colored by the theories we bring to them, an early instance of the notion of "theory-laden" facts.

37. Willard Van Orman Quine, *From a Logical Point of View* (New York: Harper Torchbook, 1963), 20–37, part of the well-known essay "Two Dog-

mas of Empiricism." This point apparently was made by William Whewell in the early nineteenth century. The "fact" of 365 days to a year, he said, presupposes notions of time, of recurrence, and so forth. So reports John Losee, *A Historical Introduction to the Philosophy of Science* (London: Oxford University Press, 1972), 119–121.

38. If this is an accurate description of science and a valid extension of Sellars and Quine, then it undercuts the position of Alvin Plantinga on "properly basic" ideas. No truths are properly basic. The only foundational aspect here is the method of open-ended empirical testing of all ideas for fit. The basis for using this method is that it seems to work exceedingly well. The remaining issue is a Kantian one: whether it is properly basic to trust this method, or whether trust in this method has a hidden faith in empirical evidence, etc. The Kantian issue will appear shortly.

39. See chapter 10's section on metaphysical beliefs for a more thorough definition and a discussion of the implications for religious belief.

40. Steven Shapin and Simon Schaffer, *Leviathan and the Air-Pump: Hobbes, Boyle, and the Experimental Life* (Princeton, NJ: Princeton University Press, 1985).

41. Thomas Kuhn, *The Copernican Revolution* (Cambridge, MA: Harvard University Press, 1957).

42. See, e.g., ibid., 139–140, 171, 180, 183 (and 214 on Kepler).

43. Ibid., 229–230.

44. Ibid., 183.

45. Ibid., 139–140.

46. Ibid., 135–139.

47. Ibid., 171.

48. Ibid., 180, emphasis added.

49. Ibid., 208.

50. All this is from one of the strongest passages in *Structure* (80–81) on the way scientists ignore anomalies. For a careful testing of Kuhn's claims against the evidence available, see Arthur Donovan, Larry Laudan, and Rachel Laudan, eds., *Scrutinizing Science: Empirical Studies of Scientific Change* (Boston: Kluwer Academic Publishers, 1988). In this work sixteen scholars empirically test the main claims of Kuhn, Feyerabend, Lakatos, and Laudan about how scientists actually operate, using examples given by those writers and looking further into the historical record. These scholars identify in detail ways in which that record does not support Kuhn et al.

51. Kuhn's examples of theories that seem immune to falsification because anomalies are ignored or covered over with secondary elaborations are necessarily examples of theories that were in fact falsified eventually. In the case of theories that have survived for a long time in spite of anomalies, either (a) they have already been recognized as incomplete or partly incoherent, as with Ptolemy's universe, or (b) the anomalies have been resolved. That is why the theory has survived. Resistance to anomalies has significance only in the case of theories that later have been shown to be wrong. The history of theories turning out to be wrong, however, is a history that contrary evidence does finally count against theories. Science is a long-term process.

52. Nor is it the place to discuss the other major relatively recent work along Kuhnian lines, Shapin and Schaffer, *Leviathan and the Air-Pump*. The authors treat Boyle's attempts to educate others in how to build their own

air pumps and how to duplicate his experiments as rhetorical devices to make Boyle seem honest and noble. They pass over in silence the function of this education: to help others test Boyle's claims for themselves by first-hand evidence (59–60). Rose-Mary Sargent, *The Diffident Naturalist: Robert Boyle and the Philosophy of Experiment* (Chicago: University of Chicago Press, 1995), in a careful, thorough, knowledgeable analysis of Boyle's work and rhetoric, says their description of Boyle is distorted. I agree. Feyerabend's major work, *Against Method*, is weaker than either Kuhn's or Shapin and Schaffer's, except in rhetorical dazzlement.

53. Rorty, *Philosophy and the Mirror of Nature*, 322–327.

54. Thomas Kuhn, *The Essential Tension* (Chicago: University of Chicago, 1977 [1962]), 321–322.

55. A charge of vagueness against the criterion of fit matches the charge of a general "linguistic unreliability" by Steve Fuller in his *Philosophy of Science and Its Discontents* (Boulder, CO: Westview Press, 1989), 4–5. He relishes the potential ambiguity of language even as he ignores the effectiveness of science in producing vaccines, ICBMs, and CDs in China the same as in the United States. Three- and four-year-old children spend a great deal of time "disambiguating" the natural fuzziness of language and learn to use it quite well. Fuller, like contemporary deconstructionists, seems to believe that this natural fuzziness prevents us from being clear and consistent in talking across cultures. The factual success of science cross-culturally seems to conflict with this theoretical possibility.

56. For Kantian reasons, we may not be able to avoid the general method of "fit." It is as innate as any other Kantian category. This is also Hume's point about how we arrive at conclusions through constant association of ideas. We learn what fits the patterns of events.

57. Ian G. Barbour, *Issues in Science and Religion* (New York: Harper Torchbook, 1966), 177.

58. David Tracy, "The Religious Dimension of Science," in *The Persistence of Religion*, eds. Andrew Greeley and Gregory Baum (New York: Herder and Herder, 1973), 128–135.

Chapter 10

1. John Whitmore argues that to the abductees, it is a strongly religious experience, a visitation from beings from on high, portending apocalypse or possibly a future redemption. "Religious Dimensions of the UFO Abductee's Experience," in James R. Lewis, ed., *The Gods Have Landed: New Religions from Other Worlds* (Albany: SUNY Press, 1995), 65–84.

2. Of the many titles on this topic see, for example, Michael D. Yapko, *Suggestions of Abuse: True and False Memories of Childhood Sexual Trauma* (New York: Simon and Schuster, 1994); or Richard Ofshe and Ethan Watters, *Making Monsters: False Memories, Psychotherapy, and Sexual Hysteria* (New York: Scribner's, 1994); or Claudette Wassil-Grimm, *Diagnosis for Disaster: The Devastating Truth About False Memory Syndrome and Its Impact on Accusers and Families* (New York: Overlook Press, 1995).

3. Mikael Stenmark, *Rationality in Science, Religion, and Everyday Life: A Critical Evaluation of Four Models of Reality* (Notre Dame, IN: University of Notre Dame Press, 1995), argues that a believer is rationally justified in committing firmly to a religious tradition, on the grounds it is irrational to de-

mand we all give full rational warrants for all beliefs. There are too many such beliefs; few can be expert on them. A well-functioning tradition provides a coherent way of life, which we need. Stenmark makes an exception for Fundamentalist theologians, who, he says, have accepted a responsibility to give full rational warrants for their beliefs. He seems to imply every theologian must likewise be open to challenges to community tradition and is obliged to give the kind of publicly available evidence that science requires as warrants for truth-claims.

4. Rudolph Otto, *The Idea of the Holy* (New York: Oxford University Press, 1958), 8–11.

5. Peter Berger, *The Sacred Canopy* (New York: Macmillan, 1967), is a major statement of the theory that religion protects people from feelings of anomy by ascribing the social order, the "nomos," to a sacred order. People can thus build a secure identity on that social order.

6. "When the feeling of pleasure or pain in the soul is most intense, all of us naturally suppose that the object of this intense feeling is then plainest and truest: but this is not the case," says Socrates in the *Phaedo*, in Charles W. Eliot, ed., *The Apology, Phaedo and Crito of Plato*, Benjamin Jowett, trans. (New York: Grolier, 1980), 75–76. R. D. Laing gives his own spin by proposing that religious experience is a kind of insanity. For Laing this is not insulting to religion; he favors a degree of madness in life. But it suggests again that experience of the sacred may be a purely subjective state. Laing, *The Politics of Experience* (New York: Pantheon, 1967).

7. Some parts of the following section appeared in Michael Barnes, "Having Faith, Being Critical, and Seeking Truth," *Method and Theory in the Study of Religion* 6:1 (1994): 63–79.

8. See Wayne Proudfoot, *Religious Experience* (Berkeley: University of California Press, 1985), 98–118.

9. See also, for example, Alexander F. Skutch, *The Golden Core of Religion* (New York: Holt, Rinehart, and Winston, 1970), a title many refer to in order to label this theme of a single religiousness within the many forms of religion.

10. Edward E. Evans-Pritchard, whose work on the Azande people of the upper Nile has provided a frequent example of the use of magic, complains of those "reductionist" explanations which start out with disbelief in souls, spirits, and gods. *Theories of Primitive Religion* (New York: Oxford University Press, 1965), 119–121. He says that these beings are considered natural by primitive people, rather than supernatural, but in any case he acknowledges that he wants to defend belief in such things (Ibid., 109–110). Other historians of religion may want to do so, too, but rarely say so.

11. Ian Barbour, *Religion in an Age of Science* (San Francisco: Harper & Row, 1990), 36–38.

12. I believe that there is indeed potentially available to everyone an experience which raises the most basic religious *question*, the metaphysical question of whether reality ultimately is aimless and meaningless or not. Otto in particular is not far from this. But those who defend the *sacred* as a unique category of reality may have much else in mind. A little more on this topic will appear later in this chapter.

13. For example, the Catholic theologian Avery Dulles explicitly uses this kind of argument, following the lead of Bernard Lonergan. Dulles, "Fundamental Theology and Conversion," *The Thomist* 45:2 (April 1981): 181–182.

14. Stephen Jay Gould, *Wonderful Life* (New York: Norton, 1986); and Richard Dawkins, *The Blind Watchmaker* (New York: Oxford University Press, 1989).

15. A Roman Catholic practice confirms this. A panel of medical experts reviews claims of miraculous cures at Lourdes. They weigh the evidence to determine (1) whether a startling change in health occurred, and (2) whether the panel cannot attribute it to any natural cause of which they are aware. Similarly, Norman Geisler, *Miracles and the Modern Mind: A Defense of Biblical Miracles* (Grand Rapids, MI: Baker Book House, 1992), 138–139, argues that miracles themselves are evidence, of the truth of Christianity.

16. R. Douglas Geivett, "The Evidential Value of Miracles," explores this from the viewpoint of an Evangelical Protestant who believes in miracles. In *In Defense of Miracles: A Comprehensive Case for God's Action in History*, eds. R. Douglas Geivett and Gary Habermas (Downers Grove, IL: InterVarsity Press, 1997), 178–195. This entire volume consists of articles defending some specific miracles, such as Jesus' resurrection, or the possibility and reality of miracles in general. It is a good collection of formal operational-style arguments, using rational criteria of logical coherence and fit with the evidence.

17. Langdon Gilkey, "Nature, Reality, and the Sacred: A Meditation in Science and Religion," *Zygon* 24:3 (September 1989): 282–298. He repeats this in his *Nature, Reality, and the Sacred: The Nexus of Science and Religion* (Minneapolis: Fortress Press, 1993).

18. Barbour, *Religion in an Age of Science*, is a summary of contemporary religious approaches to science by someone who has been at the forefront of the field of religion and science since the 1960s. See also, for example, Arthur Peacocke, *God and the New Biology* (London: J. M. Dent and Sons, 1986), esp. chs. 5 and 6, on various approaches taken on religion and science in the last century.

19. Two whose views on this have some influence today are Phillip Johnson, *Darwin on Trial* (Downers Grove, IL: InterVarsity Press, 1991) and *Reason in the Balance: The Case Against Naturalism in Science* (Downers Grove, IL: InterVarsity Press, 1995); and Michael J. Behe, *Darwin's Black Box: The Bio-Chemical Challenge to Evolution* (New York: Free Press, 1996). Both argue that the process of evolution gives strong evidence that it could not have happened without intelligent design, or without divine interventions.

20. See David Ray Griffith, *God, Power, and Evil: A Process Theodicy* (Philadelphia: Westminster, 1976); and John Hick, *Evil and the God of Love* (London: Collins, 1970), for religious interpretations. Also see the philosophical analysis by Richard Taylor, *Good and Evil: A New Direction* (New York: Macmillan, 1970). Terrence W. Tilley, *The Evils of Theodicy* (Washington, DC: Georgetown University Press, 1991), argues that it is a mistake for religious people to try to make metaphysical and moral sense out of evil.

21. Lindbeck distinguishes between cognitive, cultural-linguistic, and experiential-expressive interpretations of the nature of religion in *The Nature of Doctrine* (Philadelphia: Westmister, 1984), 31–32. According to Lindbeck, the experiential-expressive notion of religion supposes that religion is fundamentally the same everywhere because religion expresses an underlying, universally available experience of the sacred. The cultural-linguistic notion of religion does not claim any universal underlying experience of the sacred.

22. Keith Thomas *Religion and the Decline of Magic: Studies in Popular Belief in Sixteenth and Seventeenth Century England* (London: Weidenfeld and Nicolson, 1971), 638–639.

23. See Hugh R. Trevor-Roper, *The European Witch-Craze of the Sixteenth and Seventeenth Centuries and Other Essays* (New York: Harper Torchbooks, 1969); and Norman Cohn, *Europe's Inner Demons: An Inquiry Inspired by the Great Witch-Hunt* (New York: New American Library, 1975), which includes a response to Trevor-Roper.

24. Owen C. Thomas, ed., *God's Activity in the World* (Chico, CA: Scholars Press, 1983), is a collection of articles by leading American and a few European theologians and philosophers, all of them trying to interpret traditional belief that God acts in history and nature in such a way as to preserve this belief without, however, asserting that miracles (in the sense of supernatural interventions to cause what natural causes would or could not have done) do happen.

25. Friedrich Schleiermacher, *On Religion: Speeches to its Cultured Despisers* (New York: Harper & Row, 1958 [1893]), see 35–36.

26. Commentators still try to analyze whether Schleiermacher should be called a pantheist, treating Nature as the divine Unity or Whole. In his later works he carefully argued that he was a theist. See his argument in *The Christian Faith* (Edinburgh: T. & T. Clark, 1928), 38–39, that pantheism is an empty charge, without clear meaning.

27. Ibid., 179.

28. Ibid., 374, 385–390.

29. Ibid., 703–707.

30. Karl Barth, *Dogmatics in Outline* (New York: Harper & Row, 1959), 154.

31. Langdon Gilkey, "The Idea of God Since 1800," 354–366 in *The Dictionary of the History of Ideas* (New York: Scribner's, 1973), vol. 2, 361.

32. As in Rudolph Bultmann, *Jesus Christ and Mythology* (New York: Scribner's, 1958), 18, 32–44. The debate between Karl Jaspers and Bultmann on the need to mythologize even without miracles illustrates the difficulty of this issue for believers. In Rudolph Bultmann and Karl Jaspers, *Myth and Christianity: An Inquiry into the Possibility of Religion Without Myth* (Noonday Press, 1958).

33. Rudolph Bultmann, *Jesus and the Word*, Erminie Huntress Lantero and Louise Pettibone Smith, trans. (New York: Scribner's, 1958), 172–179.

34. Not all defenders of miracles are Fundamentalists. See Robert C. Newman, "Fulfilled Prophecy as Miracle," in *In Defense of Miracles: A Comprehensive Case for God's Action in History*, eds. R. Douglas Geivett and Gary R. Habermas (Downers Grove, IL: InterVarsity Press, 1997), 214–225.

35. Followers of creation science attempt an evaluation of evolution by logical (classical) analysis of flaws in the theory, and by finding empirical evidence against the theory (modern). But they do a poor job of this. Their efforts are ersatz analysis and empiricism, the appearance of scientific rationality without the reality of it.

36. See, for example, Laurie R. Godfrey, ed., *Scientists Confront Creationism* (New York: W. W. Norton, 1983), for an excellent selection of articles on aspects of science related to the creationists' claims.

37. Mark A. Noll, *The Scandal of the Evangelical Mind* (Grand Rapids, MI: Eerdmans, 1994), esp 137–145, wishes fellow Evangelicals would be even

more rational, even while remaining Evangelical and supportive of miracles.

38. John Polkinghorne, *Science and Providence: God's Interaction with the World* (Boston: Shambhala, 1989), 32; and *Reason and Reality: The Relationship Between Science and Theology* (London: SPCK Press, 1991), 45. Drees, however, claims this is theoretically possible only if the input is infinitely slow. Willem Drees, "Gaps for God?" in *Chaos and Complexity: Scientific Perspectives on Divine Action*, eds. Robert John Russell, Nancey Murphy, and Arthur R. Peacocke (Vatican City: Vatican Observatory Publications, 1995), 223–237.

39. Terence C. Williams, *The Idea of the Miraculous: The Challenge to Science and Religion* (New York: St. Martin's Press, 1990), proposes that God works on the same levels as telepathic and other psychic forces, which he calls the "Super-Normal."

40. Harold Nebelsick, *Theology and Science in Mutual Modification* (New York: Oxford University Press, 1981), has a fair amount of respect for science, but still tries to carve out some rule for miracles by calling failure to believe in miracles a remnant of the Newtonian closed-system style of thought, as though it were only the closed-system classical style and not modern science that called miracles into question (161).

41. Adam Ford, *Universe* (Mystic, CT: Twenty-Third Publications, 1987), 39.

42. There has been an ongoing discussion among theologians about the meaning of the belief that God somehow acts in history. A collection of positions on this can be found in Owen C. Thomas, ed., *God's Activity in the World*. The selection from Gilson is not on miracles but on the question of secondary causality and human freedom. The other selections either manage to talk around the issue of miracles or demythologize belief in them.

43. His organic philosophy of nature is presented in Alfred North Whitehead, *Process and Reality* (New York: Harper & Row, Torchbook 1957).

44. See Karl Rahner, *Theological Investigations*, vol. 21, *Science and Christian Faith*, trans. Hugh M. Riley (New York: Crossroads, 1988), 28–29, 33–34, 42–46. Or see D. R. G. Owen, "The Sacramental View of Reality: The Spirit-Matter Problem, in F. Kenneth Hare, ed., *The Experiment of Life* (Toronto: University of Toronto Press, 1983), 24.

45. Wolfhart Pannenberg, *Theology and the Philosophy of Science*, trans. Francis McDonagh (Philadelphia: Westminster, 1976), 334–339.

46. See Michael J. Buckley's warning to this effect, for example, in his *At the Origins of Modern Atheism* (New Haven, CT: Yale University Press, 1986), 359–363.

47. An excellent exception is Warren S. Brown, Nancey Murphy, and H. Newton Maloney, eds., *Whatever Happened to the Soul? Scientific and Theological Portraits of Human Nature* (Minneapolis: Fortress Press, 1999). The authors of the book's articles all agree on a "nonreductive physicalism" to explain "soul."

48. See Terrence W. Tilley et al., *Postmodern Theologies* (Maryknoll, NY: Orbis Books, 1995). The chapters describe a variety of different kinds of postmodern thought in religion.

49. Mircea Eliade, *The Sacred and the Profane* (New York: Harper Torchbooks, 1961), 11. A place to begin to sort out possible types of experiences of the sacred is Kirk Elifson and Robert Margolis, "A Typology of Religious Experience," *Journal of the Scientific Study of Religion* 18:1 (March 1979): 61–

67. Factor analysis exposed four different of experiences of the sacred. The authors agree with other investigators on general qualities found in all of them: "ineffability, noetic quality, transience, and passivity." But, as described in this article, the religious experiences seem to be simply psychological experiences, without evidence for some sacred reality other than the state of mind of the subjects.

50. See the review of arguments about religion as sui generis by Daniel L. Pals, "Is Religion a *Sui Generis* Phenomenon?" *Journal of the American Academy of Religion* 50:2 (Summer 1987), 259–282, and, in the same issue, Axel D. Steuer, "The Epistemic Status of Theistic Belief," 235–256.

51. Invoking Wittgenstein, Phillips argues this in "The Devil's Disguises: Philosophy of Religion, 'Objectivity' and 'Cultural Divergence,'" in *Objectivity and Cultural Divergence*, ed. Stuart C. Brown (New York: Cambridge University Press, 1984), 61–77. See also Phillips's *Religion Without Explanation* (Oxford: Basil Blackwell, 1976). Norman Malcolm, "The Groundlessness of Belief," in *Reason and Religion*, ed. Stuart C. Brown (Ithaca, NY: Cornell University Press, 1977), 143–157, argues not so much that religion has no beliefs as that religious beliefs do not have to have any rational grounds.

52. I find Penner's comment apropos: It is precisely what the anthropologist finds to be false, according to scientific standards of true and false, that the anthropologist then categorizes as symbolic or emotionally expressive rather than as truth-claims. In this indirect way Phillips is probably accepting the standards of science as to what is true or false. Hans Penner, "Rationality and Religion: Problems in the Comparison of Modes of Thought," *Journal of the American Academy of Religion* 54:4 (Winter 1986): 645–671.

53. For criticism of Phillips (and a challenge to the way Kuhn is used in similar arguments by others), see Edward L. Schoen, *Religious Explanations: A Model from the Sciences* (Durham, NC: Duke University Press, 1985), 15–21.

54. Lindbeck, *The Nature of Doctrine*, 32–35 for the various phrases and sentences quoted in this paragraph; 67, 80 for his dealing with beliefs in the resurrection of Jesus; and 80 for his assertion that doctrines "affirm nothing about extra-linguistic or extra-human reality."

55. See ibid., 66–68, for a discussion of affirmations about God and about Jesus' resurrection; and 23 for the Christian claim that it is "true, universally valid, and supernaturally revealed."

56. Lindbeck's wording is often in the negative: Doctrines are not merely rules but are real propositions, yet "These are, however, second-order rather than first-order propositions and affirm nothing about extra-linguistic or extra-human reality" (80). At least not from the postliberal perspective. The believer who does not use this reflexive approach will blithely affirm these propositions as true about "extra-linguistic" reality.

57. For a comparable analysis, see Thomas Nagel, *The Last Word* (New York: Oxford University Press, 1997).

58. David Tracy places correlational theologies in relation to liberal, neo-orthodox, and other theologies, as well as his own "revisionist" form of correlation in his *Blessed Rage for Order* (New York: Seabury Press, 1975), 22–34.

59. Tillich has a brief but good statement of this in his *Dynamics of Faith*, 41–54.

60. See Michael H. Barnes, "Demythologization in the Theology of Karl Rahner," *Theological Studies* 55:1 (March 1994): 24–45. Maurice Wiles, *God's*

Action in the World (London: SCM Press, 1986), esp. 93, 107, similarly makes the entire universe a single act by God.

61. The approach is widespread among science-minded theologians. A survey of recent textbooks in science and religion, almost all of them written partly in defense of religious belief, shows that few of them give serious consideration to miraculous interventions and many of them deny the reasonableness of such belief. These texts usually emphasize ways in which religion and science are compatible. The exceptions to this are books published by the more traditionalist Christian presses, such as Baker Book House and InterVarsity Press.

62. See David Tracy, "The Religious Dimension of Science," cited at the end of chapter 9. He adopts the phrase "knower in the world" and the idea of implicit (or "anonymous" faith) from Karl Rahner, though a major source of inspiration for his argument is Bernard Lonergan.

BIBLIOGRAPHY

Abelard, Peter. 1977. *Sic et non: a Critical Edition* ed. Blanche B. Boyer and Richard McKeon. Chicago: University of Chicago Press.

Adkins, Arthur W. H. 1972. *Moral Values and Political Behaviour in Ancient Greece: From Homer to the End of the Fifth Century.* New York: W. W. Norton.

Agassiz, Louis. 1962 (repr. of 1857). *Essay on Classification.* Cambridge, MA: Belknap Press.

Aldridge, A. Owen. 1973. "Primitivism in the Eighteenth Century." In *Dictionary of the History of Ideas,* vol. 3. Philip P. Warner, ed. New York: Scribner's. Pp. 598–605.

Alves, Ruben A. 1981. "What Does It Mean to Say the Truth?" In *The Sciences and Theology in the Twentieth Century.* Arthur R. Peacocke, ed. Notre Dame, IN: Notre Dame University Press. Pp. 163–181.

Andersson, Theodore M. 1964. *The Problem of Icelandic Saga Origins: A Historical Survey.* New Haven, CT: Yale University Press.

Annas, Julia, and Jonathan Barnes. 1985. *The Modes of Scepticism: Ancient Texts and Modern Interpretations.* New York: Cambridge University Press.

Anselm of Canterbury. 1962. *Basic Writings.* S. N. Deane, trans. La Salle, IL: Open Court.

Anthony, David W. 1996. "Shards of Speech." *The Sciences* 36(1):34–39.

Appleman, Philip, ed. 1979. *Darwin.* New York: W. W. Norton.

Aquinas, Thomas. 1947. *Summa Theologiae.* New York: Benziger Brothers.

Aquinas, Thomas. 1956. *Summa Contra Gentiles.* Notre Dame, IN: University of Notre Dame Press.

Aristotle. 1966. *Metaphysics.* Hippocrates G. Apostle, trans. Bloomington: Indiana University Press.

Augustine. 1952. "The Writings of Saint Augustine." In *The City of God.* The Fathers of the Church, vol 14. Stephen McKenna, ed. Washington, D.C.: Catholic University Press of America.

Augustine. 1963. *On the Trinity*, vol. 3. The Fathers of the Church, Vol. 45. Stephen McKenna, ed. Washington, D.C.: Catholic University of America Press.

Augustine. 1982. *The Literal Meaning of Genesis*. The Ancient Christian Writers, vols. 41 and 42. John Hammond Taylor, S.J., trans. and annotator. New York: Newman Press.

Bacon, Francis. 1857. *The Works of Francis Bacon*, vol. 3. Robert Leslie Ellis, Douglas Denon Heath, and James Spedding, eds. London: Longman.

Bacon, Francis. 1937. *Essays, Advancement of Learning, New Atlantis, and Other Pieces*. Richard Foster Jones, ed. New York: Odyssey Press.

Bacon, Francis. 1960. *The New Organon and Related Writings*. Fulton H. Anderson, ed. New York: Liberal Arts Press.

Bailey, Cyril, trans. 1970 (reprint of 1926). *Epicurus: The Extant Remains*. Hildesheim: Georg Olms.

Bainbridge, William. 1988. "Is Belief in the Supernatural Inevitable?" *Free Enquiry* 8(2):21–26.

Baird, Robert D., and Alfred Bloom. 1972. *Indian and Far Eastern Religious Traditions*. New York: Harper & Row.

Barbour, Ian G. Barbour. 1966. *Issues in Science and Religion*. New York: Harper Torchbook.

Barbour, Ian. 1990. *Religion in an Age of Science*. San Francisco: Harper & Row.

Barnes, Barry. 1982. *T. S. Kuhn and Social Science*. New York: Columbia University Press.

Barnes, Michael. 1993. "Primitive Religious Thought and the Evolution of Religion." *Religion* 22:21–46.

Barnes, Michael. 1994. "Demythologization in the Theology of Karl Rahner." *Theological Studies* 55(1):24–45.

Barnes, Michael. 1994. "Having Faith, Being Critical, and Seeking Truth." *Method and Theory in the Study of Religion* 6(1):63–79.

Barnes, A. A. 1963. "The Survival of the Magical Arts." In *The Conflict Between Paganism and Christianity in the Fourth Century*. Arnaldo Momigliano, ed. Oxford: Clarendon Press. Pp. 100–123.

Barstow, Ann Llewellyn. 1982. *Married Priests and the Reforming Papacy: The Eleventh Century Debates*. New York: Mellen.

Barth, Karl. 1959. *Dogmatics in Outline*. New York: Harper & Row.

Batson, C. Daniel, and W. Larry Ventis. 1982. *Religious Experience: A Social-Psychological Perspective*. New York: Oxford University Press.

Behe, Michael J. 1996. *Darwin's Black Box: The Bio-Chemical Challenge to Evolution*. New York: Free Press.

Beidelman, Thomas O. 1981. "Review of Hallpike's *The Foundations of Primitive Thought*." *American Ethnologist* 8:812–813.

Bellah, Robert. 1970. *Beyond Belief*. San Francisco: Harper & Row.

Bender, Barbara, and Brian Morris. 1988. "Twenty Years of History, Evolution, and Social Change in Gatherer-Hunter Studies." In *Hunters and Gatherers*. Vol. 1, *History, Evolution, and Social Change*. Tim Ingold, David Riches, and James Woodburn, eds. New York: St. Martin's Press. Pp. 4–14.

Benedict, Ruth. 1946. *The Chrysanthemum and the Sword*. Boston: Houghton Mifflin.

Berger, Peter. 1967. *The Sacred Canopy*. New York: Macmillan.

Berger, Peter, and Thomas Luckman. 1966. *The Social Construction of Reality*. New York: Doubleday.

Berlin, Isaiah. 1973. "The Counter-Enlightenment." In *The Dictionary of the History of Ideas*, vol. 2. Philip P. Warner, ed. New York: Scribners. Pp. 100–112.

Berry, John W. 1976. *Human Ecology and Cognitive Style*. New York: John Wiley and Sons.

Berry, John W., Pierre Dasen, Ype H. Poortinga, and Marshall H. Segall. 1990. *Human Behavior in Global Perspective: An Introduction to Cross-Cultural Psychology*. Oxford: Pergamon Press.

Bhattacharya, Ram Shankar, and Gerald J. Larson, eds. 1987. *Samkhya: A Dualist Tradition in Indian Philosophy*. Vol. 4 of *Encyclopedia of Indian Philosophies*. Princeton, NJ: Princeton University Press.

Bidell, Thomas R., and Kurt W. Fischer. 1992. "Cognitive Development in Educational Contexts: Implications of Skill Theory." In *Neo-Piagetian Theories of Cognitive Development*. Andreas Demetriou, Michael Shayer, and Anastasia Efklides, eds. New York: Routledge. Pp. 11–30.

Biggs, John B., "Modes of Learning, Forms of Knowing, and Ways of Schooling." In *Neo-Piagetian Theories of Cognitive Development*. Andreas Demetriou, Anastasia Efklides, and Michael Shayers, eds. New York: Routledge. Pp. 31-51.

Bierhorst, John. 1985. *The Mythology of North America*. New York: William Morrow.

Biersack, Aletta. 1982. "The Logic of Misplaced Concreteness: Paiela Body Counting and the Nature of the Primitive Mind." *American Anthropologist* 84(4):811–829.

Birrell, Anne. 1993. *Chinese Mythology: An Introduction*. Baltimore: John Hopkins University Press.

Blank, Jonah. 1992. *Arrow of the Blue-Skinned God: Retracing the Ramayana Through India*. New York: Doubleday Image.

Bloomfield, Morton W. 1952. *The Seven Deadly Sins: An Introduction to the History of a Religious Concept, with Special Reference to Medieval English Literature*. East Lansing: Michigan State University Press.

Boas, Franz. 1991 (reprint of 1938). *The Mind of Primitive Man*. New York: Macmillan.

Bochenski, Joseph M. 1970 (reprint of 1961). *A History of Formal Logic*. Ivo Thomas, trans. New York: Chelsea Publishing.

Bossey, John. 1973. "Blood and Baptism." In *Sanctity and Secularity: The Church and the World*. Derek Baker, ed. New York: Barnes and Noble. Pp. 129-143.

Boswell, John. 1994. *Same-Sex Unions in Premodern Europe*. New York: Villard Books.

Bourne, Edmund J., and Richard Shweder. 1984. "Does the Concept of the Person Vary Cross-Culturally?" In *Culture Theory: Essays on Mind, Self, and Emotion*. Robert A. LeVine and Richard A. Shweder, eds. New York: Cambridge University Press. Pp. 158–199.

Boyce, Mary, ed. and trans. 1984. *Textual Sources for the Study of Zoroastrianism*. Totowa, NJ: Barnes and Noble.

Boyd, Robert, and Peter J. Richerson. 1985. *Culture and the Evolutionary Process*. Chicago: University of Chicago Press.

Boyer, Pascal. 1994. *The Naturalness of Religious Ideas: A Cognitive Theory of Religion*. Berkeley: University of California Press.

Boyle, Robert. 1966 (reprint of 1772). "A Free Inquiry." In *The Works of the Honourable Robert Boyle in Six Volumes*, vol. 5. Hildesheim: Georg Olms.

Brady, Jules M., S.J. 1964. "St. Augustine's Theory of Seminal Reasons." *The New Scholasticism* 38:141–158.

Bringuier, Jean-Claude. 1980. *Conversations with Jean Piaget*. Chicago: University of Chicago Press.

Brinton, Crane, John B. Christopher, and Robert Lee Wolff. 1984 (6th ed.). *A History of Civilization*, vol. 1. Englewood Cliffs, NJ: Prentice-Hall.

Brooke, Christopher, and Rosalind Brooke. 1984. *Popular Religion in the Middle Ages*. London: Thames and Hudson.

Brooke, John Hedley. 1991. *Science and Religion: Some Historical Perspectives*. New York: Cambridge University Press.

Brown, Donald E. 1991. *Human Universals*. Philadelphia: Temple University Press.

Brown, Peter. 1967. *Augustine of Hippo*. New York: Dorset Press.

Brown, Peter. 1975. "Society and the Supernatural: A Medieval Change." *Daedalus* 104(2):131–151.

Brown, Peter. 1981. *The Cult of the Saints*. Chicago: University of Chicago Press.

Brown, Stuart. 1984. *Leibniz*. Minneapolis: University of Minnesota Press.

Brown, Warren S., Nancey Murphy, and H. Newton Maloney, eds. 1999. *Whatever Happened to the Soul? Scientific and Theological Portraits of Human Nature*. Minneapolis: Fortress Press.

Bruner, Jerome. 1986. *Actual Minds, Possible Worlds*. Cambridge, MA: Harvard University Press.

Brush, Stephen G. 1988. *The History of Modern Science*. Ames: Iowa State University Press.

Buckley, Michael J., S.J. 1978. "Transcendence, Truth, and Faith: The Ascending Experience of God in All Human Inquiry." *Theological Studies* 39(4):633–655.

Buckley, Michael J., S.J. 1986. *At the Origins of Modern Atheism*. New Haven, CT: Yale University Press.

Bultmann, Rudolph. 1958. *Jesus and the Word*. Erminie Huntress Lantero and Louise Pettibone Smith, trans. New York: Scribner's.

Bultmann, Rudolph. 1958. *Jesus Christ and Mythology*. New York: Scribner's.

Bultmann, Rudolph, and Karl Jaspers. 1958. *Myth and Christianity: An Inquiry into the Possibility of Religion Without Myth*. New York: Noonday Press.

Burkhardt, Richard, Jr. 1977. *The Spirit of System: Lamarck and Evolutionary Biology*. Cambridge, MA: Harvard University Press.

Burns, Norman T., and Christopher J. Reagan. 1975. *Concepts of the Hero in the Middle Ages and the Renaissance*. New York: SUNY Press.

Burnyeat, Myles, ed. 1983. *The Skeptical Tradition*. Berkeley: University of California Press.

Bynum, Caroline W. 1973. "The Spirituality of Regular Canons in the Twelfth Century: A New Approach." In *Medieval and Renaissance Spirituality*. Paul Maurice Clogan, ed. Denton: North Texas State University Press. Pp. 3–24.

Carey, Susan. 1988. "Are Children Fundamentally Different Kinds of Thinkers and Learners Than Adults?" In *Cognitive Development to Adolescence*.

Ken Richardson and Sue Sheldon, eds. Hove, East Sussex: Lawrence Erlbaum Associates. Pp. 105–138.

Case, Robbie. 1985. *Intellectual Development: Birth to Adulthood.* New York: Academic Press.

Case, Robbie, and Wolfgang Edelstein, eds. 1993. *The New Structuralism in Cognitive Development: Theory and Research on Individual Pathways.* New York: Karger.

Celsus. 1987. *On the True Doctrine: A Discourse Against Christians.* R. Joseph Hoffman, trans. and reconstructor. New York: Oxford University Press.

Chadwick, Henry. 1966. *Early Christian Thought and the Classical Tradition: Studies in Justin, Clement, and Origen.* New York: Oxford University Press.

Chagnon, Napoleon. 1992 (3rd ed.). *Yanomamö: The Fierce People.* New York: Harcourt Brace Jovanovich.

Chan, Wing-Tsit. 1963. *A Source Book in Chinese Philosophy.* Princeton, NJ: Princeton University Press.

Chatwin, Bruce. 1987. *The Songlines.* New York: Viking Penguin.

Chen, Robert Shannu. 1992. *A Comparative Study of Chinese and Western Cyclic Myths.* New York: Peter Lang.

Chenu, Marie-Dominique. 1969. *Nature, Man, and Society in the Twelfth Century.* Chicago: University of Chicago Press.

Child, Alice B., and Irvin L. Child. 1993. *Religion and Magic in the Life of Traditional Peoples.* Englewood Cliffs, NJ: Prentice-Hall.

Cicero, Marcus Tullius. 1950. *Brutus; On the Nature of the Gods; On Divination; On Duties.* Hubert M. Poteat, trans. Chicago: University of Chicago Press.

Cicero, Marcus Tullius. 1967. *De Officiis.* John Higgenbotham, trans. Berkeley: University of California Press.

Claggett, Marshall. 1971 (reprint of 1955). *Greek Science in Antiquity.* Freeport, NY: Books for Libraries Press.

Clark, Stuart. 1984. "The Scientific Status of Demonology." In *Occult and Scientific Mentalities in the Renaissance.* Brian Vickers, ed. New York: Cambridge University Press. Pp. 351–369.

Clement of Alexandria. 1926. *Stromata.* The Ante-Nicene Fathers, vol. 2. New York: Scribner's.

Cohn, Norman. 1975. *Europe's Inner Demons: An Inquiry Inspired by the Great Witch-Hunt.* New York: New American Library.

Cole, Michael, John Gay, Joseph A. Glide, and Donald A. Sharp. 1971. *The Cultural Context of Learning and Thinking.* New York: Basic Books.

Cole, Michael. 1996. *Cultural Psychology: A Once and Future Discipline.* Cambridge, MA: The Belknap Press of Harvard University Press.

Colish, Marcia. 1985. *The Stoic Tradition from Antiquity to the Early Middle Ages.* Vol. 1, *Stoicism in Classical Latin Literature.* Leiden: E. J. Brill.

Commons, Michael L., Jan D. Sinnott, Francis A. Richards, and Cheryl Armon, eds., 1989. *Adult Development.* Vol. 1, *Comparisons and Applications of Developmental Models.* New York: Praeger.

Comstock, Richard W. 1972. *The Study of Religion and Primitive Religion.* New York: Harper & Row.

Comte, Auguste. 1853. *The Positive Philosophy of Auguste Comte.* Harriet Martinau, trans. 2 vols. London: Chapman.

Comte, Auguste. 1975. *Auguste Comte and Positivism: The Essential Writings,* Gertrude Lenzer, ed. Chicago: University of Chicago Press.

Conan, James Bryant, et al., eds. 1964 (reprint of 1948). *Harvard Case Histories in Experimental Science*, vol. 1. Cambridge, MA: Harvard University Press.

Conn, Walter E. 1977. "Piaget as a Critical Realist." *Angelicum* 54(1):67–88.

Cook, William R., and Ronald B. Herzman. 1983. *The Medieval World View: An Introduction*. New York: Oxford University Press.

Coon, Carleton S. 1971. *The Hunting Peoples*. Boston: Little, Brown.

Coulmas, Flourian. 1989. *The Writing Systems of the World*. Oxford: Basil Blackwell.

Crombie, A. C. 1953. *Robert Grosseteste and the Origins of Experimental Science, 1100–1700*. Oxford: Clarendon Press.

Crombie, A. C. 1959 (rev. ed.). *Medieval and Early Modern Science*, vol. 2. Garden City, NY: Doubleday Anchor.

Curley, Michael J., trans. 1979. *Physiologus*. Austin: University of Texas Press.

Dasen, Pierre R., and Alastair Heron. 1981. "Cross-Cultural Tests of Piaget's Theory." In *The Handbook of Cross-Cultural Psychology*. Vol. 4, *Developing Psychology*. Harry C. Triandis and Alistair Heron, eds. Boston: Allyn and Bacon. Pp. 295–341.

Dawkins, Richard. 1989. *The Blind Watchmaker*. New York: Oxford University Press.

Deason, Gary B. 1986. "Reformation, Theology, and the Mechanistic Conception of Nature." In *God and Nature*. David Lindberg and Ronald Numbers, eds. Berkeley: University of California Press. Pp. 167–191.

Dentan, Robert K. 1968. *The Semai*. New York: Holt, Rinehart, and Winston.

Descartes, René. 1984. "Principles of Philosophy." In *The Philosophical Writings of Descartes*, vol. 1. John Cottingham, Dugald Murdoch, and Robert Stoothoff, trans. New York: Cambridge University Press. Pp. 177–291.

Descartes, René. 1984. "The World or Treatise on Light." In *The Philosophical Writings of Descartes*, vol. 1. John Cottingham, Dugald Murdoch, and Robert Stoothoff, trans. New York: Cambridge University Press. Pp. 81–98.

DeVore, Irven, and Richard B. Lee, eds. 1968. *Man the Hunter*. Chicago: Aldine.

Diamond, Jared. 1993. *The Third Chimpanzee: The Evolution and Future of the Human Animal*. New York: HarperPerennial.

Dick, Steven J. 1982. *Plurality of the Worlds: The Origins of the Extraterrestrial Life Debate from Democritus to Kant*. New York: Cambridge University Press.

Diener, Paul. 1980. "Quantum Adjustment, Macroevolution, and the Social Field: Some Comments on Evolution and Culture." *Current Anthropology* 21(4):423–431.

Dietz, T., Burns, T. R., and F. H. Buttel. 1990. "Evolutionary Theory in Sociology: An Examination of Current Thinking." *Sociological Forum* 5(2):155–171.

Dijksterhuis, Eduard R. 1961. *The Mechanization of the World Picture*. C. Dikshoorn, tran. Oxford: Clarendon Press.

Dodds, Eric Robertson. 1959. *The Greeks and the Irrational*. Berkeley: University of California Press.

Donald, Merlin. 1991. *The Origins of the Modern Mind: Three Stages in the Evolution of Culture and Cognition.* Cambridge, MA: Harvard University Press.

Donovan, Arthur, Larry Laudan, and Rachel Laudan, eds. 1988. *Scrutinizing Science: Empirical Studies of Scientific Change.* Boston: Kluwer Academic Publishers.

Doran, Robert M. 1990. *Theology and the Dialectics of History.* Toronto: University of Toronto Press.

Drees, Willem. 1995. "Gaps for God?" In *Chaos and Complexity: Scientific Perspectives on Divine Action.* Robert John Russell, Nancey Murphy, and Arthur R. Peacocke, eds. Vatican City: Vatican Observatory Publications. Pp. 223–237.

Driesch, Hans. 1914. *History and Theory of Vitalism.* C. K. Ogden, trans. London: Macmillan.

Dulles, Avery. 1971. *A History of Apologetics.* Philadelphia: Westminster Press.

Dulles, Avery. 1981. "Fundamental Theology and Conversion." *The Thomist* 45(2):175–193.

Dunbar, Robin. 1995. *The Trouble with Science.* Cambridge, MA: Harvard University Press.

Durant, John. 1985. "Darwinsim and Divinity: A Century of Debate." In *Darwinism and Divinity: Essays on Evolution and Religious Belief.* John Durant, ed. New York: Basil Blackwell. Pp. 9–39.

Durham, William H. 1990. "Advances in Evolutionary Culture Theory." *Annual Review of Anthropology* 19:187–210.

Durham, William H. 1992. "Applications of Evolutionary Culture Theory." *Annual Review of Anthropology* 21:331–355.

Durkheim, Emile. 1965 (reprint of 1915). *The Elementary Forms of the Religious Life.* New York: Free Press.

Eamon, William. 1994. *Science and the Secrets of Nature: Books of Secrets in Medieval and Modern Culture.* Princeton, NJ: Princeton University Press.

Earle, Timothy K. 1987. "Chiefdoms in Archeological and Ethnological Perspective." *Annual Review of Anthropology* 16:279–308.

Easlea, Brian. 1980. *Witch Hunting, Magic, and the New Philosophy.* Atlantic Highlands, NJ: Humanities Press.

Egan, Kieran. 1997. *The Educated Mind: How Cognitive Tools Shape Our Understanding.* Chicago: University of Chicago Press.

Eisenstadt, Shmuel Noah, ed. 1986. *The Origins and Diversity of Axial Age Civilizations.* Albany: SUNY Press.

Eliade, Mircea. 1967. *Myths, Dreams, and Mysteries: The Encounter between Contemporary Faiths and Archaic Realities.* New York: Harper Torchbook.

Eliade, Mircea. 1961. *The Sacred and the Profane.* New York: Harper Torchbook.

Eliade, Mircea. 1963. *Patterns in Comparative Religion.* Rosemary Eliade, trans. New York: New American Library.

Elifson, Kirk, and Robert Margolis. 1979. "A Typology of Religious Experience." *Journal of the Scientific Study of Religion* 18(1):61–67.

Eliot, Charles, W., ed. 1980. *The Apology, Phaedo and Crito of Plato.* Benjamin Jowett, trans. New York: Grolier.

English, Edward D. 1995. *Reading the Wisdom: The* De Doctrina Christiana *of Augustine in the Middle Ages*. Notre Dame, IN: University of Notre Dame Press.

Epictetus. 1940. The *Discourses of Epictetus*. P. E. Matheson, trans. In *The Stoic and Epicurean Philosophers*. Whitney J. Oates, ed. New York: Modern Library.

Evans, Robert D., and Bimal Krishna Matilal, eds. 1982. *Buddhist Logic and Epistemology: Studies in the Buddhist Analysis of Inference and Language*. Boston: D. Reidel.

Evans-Pritchard, Edward E. 1937. *Witchcraft, Oracles, and Magic Among the Azande*. Oxford: Clarendon Press.

Evans-Pritchard, Edward E. 1965. *Theories of Primitive Religion*. New York: Oxford University Press.

Finley, John H., Jr. 1966. *Four Stages of Greek Thought*. Stanford, CA: Stanford University Press.

Finnegan, Ruth. 1970. *Oral Literature in Africa*. Oxford: Oxford University Press.

Fischer, Kurt W., and Louise Silvern. 1985. "Stages and Individual Differences in Cognitive Development." *Annual Review of Psychology* 36:613–648.

Fleming, N., and Alexander Sesonske. 1956. *Meno: Text and Criticism*. Belmont, CA: Wadsworth.

Fodor, Jerry A. 1983. *The Modularity of Mind: an Essay on Faculty Psychology*. Cambridge, MA: MIT Press.

Ford, Adam. 1987. *Universe*. Mystic, CT: Twenty-Third Publications.

Fowler, James W. 1981. *Stages of Faith: The Psychology of Human Development and the Quest for Meaning*. San Francisco: Harper & Row.

Fowler, James W. 1996. *Faithful Change: The Personal and Public Challenges of Postmodern Life*. Nashville, TN: Abingdon Press.

Frankfort, Henri, et al. 1949. *Before Philosophy*. New York: Penguin.

French, Peter. 1972. *John Dee: The World of an Elizabethan Magus*. New York: Dorset Press.

Fuller, Steve. 1989. *Philosophy of Science and Its Discontents*. Boulder, CO: Westview Press.

Funkenstein, Amos. 1986. *Theology and the Scientific Imagination from the Middle Ages to the Seventeenth Century*. Princeton, NJ: Princeton University Press.

Gale, George. 1979. *Theory of Science: An Introduction to the History, Logic, and Philosophy of Science*. New York: McGraw-Hill.

Garcia, Rolando, and Jean Piaget. 1989. *Psychogenesis and the History of Science*. New York: Columbia University Press.

Gassendi, Pierre. 1984. "Fifth Set of Objections." In *The Philosophical Writings of Descartes* vol. 2., John Cottingham, Dugald Murdock, and Robert Stoothoff, trans. New York: Cambridge University Press. Pp. 179–240.

Geary, Patrick J. 1978. *Furta Sacra: Thefts of Relics in the Central Middle Ages*. Princeton, NJ: Princeton University Press.

Geivett, R. Douglas, and Gary Habermas, eds. 1997. *In Defense of Miracles: A Comprehensive Case for God's Action in History*. Downers Grove, IL: InterVarsity Press.

Gelfand, Michael. 1966. *An African's Religion: The Spirit of Nyajena*. Cape Town: Juta and Company.

Gellner, Ernest. 1988. *Plough, Sword, and Book: The Structure of Human History*. London: Collins Harvill.

Gellner, Ernest. 1992. *Reason and Culture: The Historic Role of Rationality and Rationalism*. Oxford: Blackwell.

Gilbert, William. 1952. *On the Lodestone and Magnetic Bodies*. Chicago: William Benton. Pp. 1–126.

Gilkey, Langdon. 1973. "The Idea of God Since 1800." In *The Dictionary of the History of Ideas*, vol. 2. Philip P. Warner, ed. New York: Scribner's. Pp. 354–366.

Gilkey, Langdon. 1989. "Nature, Reality, and the Sacred: A Meditation in Science and Religion." *Zygon* 24(3):282–298.

Gilkey, Langdon. 1993. *Nature, Reality, and the Sacred: The Nexus of Science and Religion*. Minneapolis: Fortress Press.

Gilligan, Carol, and John Michael Murphy. 1979. "Development from Adolescence to Adulthood." In *Intellectual Development Beyond Childhood*. Deanna Kuhn, ed. San Francisco: Jossey-Bass. Pp. 85–99.

Girandot, Norman J. 1985. "Behaving Cosmogonically in Early Taoism." In *Cosmogony and Ethical Order: New Studies in Comparative Ethics*. Robin Lovin and Frank Reynolds, eds. Chicago: University of Chicago Press. Pp. 67–97.

Gjersten, Derek. 1984. *The Classics of Science*. New York: Lilian Barber Press.

Gladwin, Thomas. 1964. "Culture and Logical Process." In *Explorations in Cultural Anthropology: Essays in Honor of George Peter Murdock*. Ward H. Goodenough, ed. New York: McGraw-Hill. Pp. 167–177.

Gnuse, Robert. 1989. *Heilsgeschichte as a Model for Biblical Theology*. Lanham, MD: University Press of America.

Godfrey, Laurie R., ed. 1983. *Scientists Confront Creationism*. New York: W. W. Norton.

Godlove, Terry. 1984. "In What Sense Are Religions Conceptual Frameworks?" *Journal of the American Academy of Religion* 52(2):289–305.

Golinski, Jan V. 1989. "A Noble Spectacle: Phosphorus and the Public Cultures of Science in the Early Royal Society." *Isis* 80(301):11–39.

Goodspeed, Edgar J., trans. and ed. 1955. *The Letter of Barnabus*. In *The Apostolic Fathers*. London: Independent Press. Pp. 23–45.

Goody, Jack. 1977. *The Domestication of the Savage Mind*. New York: Cambridge University Press.

Goody, Jack. 1987. *The Interface Between the Written and the Oral*. New York: Cambridge University Press.

Goody, Jack, and Ian Watt. 1962–1963. "The Consequences of Literacy." *Comparative Studies in Society and History* 5:304–345.

Gopnik, Alison, and Andrew N. Meltzoff. 1997. *Words, Thoughts, and Theories*. Cambridge, MA: MIT Press.

Gould, Stephen Jay. 1983. *Hens' Teeth and Horses' Toes*. New York: W. W. Norton.

Gould, Stephen Jay. 1986. *Wonderful Life*. New York: W. W. Norton.

Graham, Angus Charles. 1989. *Disputers of the Tao: Philosophical Argument in Ancient China*. LaSalle, IL: Open Court.

Graham, Angus Charles. 1992. *Unreason Within Reason: Essays on the Outskirts of Rationality*. LaSalle, IL: Open Court.

Grant, Edward. 1971. *Physical Sciences in the Middle Ages.* New York: John Wiley and Sons.

Grant, Edward. 1986. "Science and Theology in the Middle Ages." In *God and Nature: Historical Essays in the Encounter Between Christianity and Science.* David Lindberg and Ronald Numbers, eds. Berkeley: University of California Press. Pp. 49–75.

Grant, Robert M. 1952. *Miracle and Natural Law: In Greco-Roman and Early ChristianThought.* Amsterdam: North-Holland.

Green, Miranda. 1986. *The God of the Celts.* Totowa, NJ: Barnes and Noble.

Gregor, Thomas. 1977. *Mehinaku.* Chicago: University of Chicago Press.

Griffith, David Ray. 1976. *God, Power, and Evil: A Process Theodicy.* Philadelphia: Westminster.

Guddemi, Phillip. 1992. "When Horticulturalists Are like Hunter-Gatherers: The Sawiyano of Papua New Guinea." *Ethnology* 31(4):303–314.

Guerlac, Henry. 1973. "Newton and the Method of Analysis." In *Dictionary of the History of Ideas*, Vol. 3. Philip P. Warner, ed. New York: Scribner's. Pp. 378–391.

Guidice, S., R. W. Thatcher, and R. A. Walker. 1986. "Human Cerebral Hemispheres Develop at Different Rates and Ages." *Science* 236:1110–1113.

Guthrie, Stewart Elliott. 1993. *Faces in the Clouds.* New York: Oxford University Press.

Haan, N. S., L. Kohlberg, D. Kuhn, and J. Langer. 1977. "The Development of Formal Operations in Logical and Moral Judgement." *Genetic Psychology Monographs* 95:97–188.

Hahn, Roger. 1986. "LaPlace and the Mechanistic Universe." In *God and Nature.* David C. Lindberg and Ronald L. Numbers, eds. Berkeley: University of California Press. Pp. 256–276.

Hallpike, Christopher R. 1972. *The Konso of Ethiopia: A Study of the Values of a Cushitic People.* Oxford: Clarendon Press.

Hallpike, Christopher R. 1977. *Bloodshed and Vengeance in the Papuan Mountains: The Generation of Conflict in the Tauade Society.* Oxford: Clarendon Press.

Hallpike, Christopher R. 1979. *The Foundations of Primitive Thought.* New York: Oxford University Press.

Hallpike, Christopher R. 1983. "Reply to Shweder's 'On Savages and Other Children.'" *American Anthropologist* 85:656–660.

Hallpike, Christopher R. 1984. "Anthropology's Romantic Rebellion Against the Enlightenment." In *Culture Theory.* Robert A. LeVine and Richard Shweder, eds. New York: Cambridge University Press. Pp. 49–51.

Hallpike, Christopher R. 1986. *The Principles of Social Evolution.* Oxford: Clarendon Press.

Hankins, Thomas L. 1985. *Science and the Enlightenment.* New York: Cambridge University Press.

Hardy, Jean. 1987. *A Psychology with a Soul: Psychosynthesis in Evolutionary Context.* New York: Routledge and Kegan Paul.

Harris, Roy. 1986. *The Origins of Writing.* LaSalle, IL: Open Court.

Harrison, Jane. 1955 (3rd ed.). *Prolegomena to the Study of Greek Religion.* New York: Meridian Books.

Harvey, William. 1965. *On Animal Generation.* In *The Works of William Harvey.* Robert Willis, trans. New York: Johnson Reprint. Pp. 169–518.

Hawking, Stephen. 1988. *A Brief History of Time: From The Big Bang to Black Holes*. New York: Bantam Books.

Hayden, Hiram. 1950. *The Counter-Renaissance*. New York: Harcourt, Brace, and World.

Heath, Shirley Brice. 1983. *Ways with Words: Language, Life, and Work in Communities and Classrooms*. New York: Cambridge University Press.

Henderson, John B. 1984. *The Development and Decline of Chinese Cosmology*. New York: Columbia University Press.

Herman, A. L. 1976. *An Introduction to Indian Thought*. Englewood Cliffs, NJ: Prentice-Hall.

Heron, Alastair, and Harry C. Triandis, eds. 1981. *Handbook of Cross-Cultural Psychology*, vol. 4. Boston: Allyn and Bacon.

Hick, John. 1970. *Evil and the God of Love*. London: Collins.

Hobbes, Thomas. 1962. *Leviathan*. New York: Collier/Macmillan.

Hobhouse, Leonard T. 1951 (reprint of 1906). *Morals in Evolution: A Study in Comparative Ethics*. London: Chapman and Hall.

Hooker J. T., et al. 1990. *Reading the Past: Ancient Writing from Cuneiform to the Alphabet*. Berkeley: University of California Press.

Horton, Robin. 1967. "African Traditional Thought and Western Science." *Africa* 37(1):50–71, 37(2):155–187.

Horton, Robin. 1970. "African Traditional Thought and Western Science." In *Rationality*. Bryan R. Wilson, ed. Evanston, IL: Harper & Row. Pp. 131–171.

Horton, Robin. 1982. "Tradition and Modernity Revisited." In *Rationality and Relativism*. Martin Hollis and Steven Lukes, eds. Cambridge, MA: MIT Press. Pp. 201–260.

Hoy, David. 1991. "Is Hermeneutics Ethnocentric?" In *The Interpretive Turn: Philosophy, Science, and Culture*. David Hiley et al., eds. Ithaca, NY: Cornell University Press. Pp. 155–175.

Hsü, Cho-yun. 1986. "The Unfolding of Early Confucianism: The Evolution from Confucius to Hsün-Tzu." In *Confucianism: The Dynamics of Tradition*. Irene Ebert, ed. New York: Macmillan. Pp. 22–38.

Hultkranz, Äka. 1983. "The Concept of the Supernatural in Primal Religion." *History of Religions* 22(3):231–251.

Hume, David. 1962. *On Human Nature and the Understanding*. Crane Brinton and Paul Edwards, eds. New York: Collier.

Hussey, Edward. 1986. "Matter Theory in Ancient Greece." In *The Physical Sciences Since Antiquity*. Rom Harré, ed. New York: St. Martin's Press. Pp. 10–28.

Hutchins, Edwin. 1980. *Culture and Inference*. Cambridge, MA: Harvard University Press.

Hyman, Ray. 1985. "A Critical Overview of Parapsychology." In *A Skeptic's Handbook of Parapsychology*. Paul Kurz, ed. Buffalo, NY: Prometheus. Pp. 3–96.

Ingold, Tim. 1986. *Evolution and Social Life*. New York: Cambridge University Press.

Irenaeus. 1868. *Against Heresies*, book II, ch. 28.2–3. In *The Writing of Irenaeus*, vol. 1; Vol. 5 of Ante-Nicene Christian Library. Edinburgh: T. & T. Clark. Pp. 220–221.

Izutsu, Toshihiko. 1983. *Sufism and Taoism: A Comparative Study of Key Philosophical Concepts*. Berkeley: University of California Press.

Jahoda, Gustav. 1982. *Psychology and Anthropology: A Psychological Perspective*. New York: Academic Press.

Jaspers, Karl. 1953. *The Origin and Goal of History*. New Haven, CT: Yale University Press.

Jaynes, Julian. 1976. *The Origin of Consciousness in the Breakdown of the Bicameral Mind*. Boston: Houghton Mifflin.

John of Salisbury. 1955. *The Metalogicon*. Daniel D. McGarry, trans. Berkeley: University of California Press.

Johnson, Phillip. 1991. *Darwin on Trial*. Downers Grove, IL: InterVarsity Press.

Johnson, Phillip. 1995. *Reason in the Balance: The Case Against Naturalism in Science*. Downers Grove, IL: InterVarsity Press.

Jones, A. H. M. 1963. "The Social Background of the Struggle Between Paganism and Christianity in the Fourth Century." In *The Conflict Between Paganism and Christianity in the Fourth Century*. Arnoldo Momigliano, ed. Oxford: Clarendon Press. Pp. 17–37.

Justin, Martyr. 1953. "The First Apology of Justin Martyr." In *The Early Christian Fathers*, vol. 1. Philadelphia: Westminster Press. Pp. 242–276.

Kamstra, Jacques. 1972. "Changes in the Idea of God in Non-Western Religions and Culture." In *New Questions on God*. Johannes B. Metz, ed. New York: Herder and Herder. Pp. 123–133.

Kegan, Robert. 1994. *In over Our Heads: The Mental Demands of Modern Life*. Cambridge, MA: Harvard University Press.

Keightley, David N. 1989. "The Origins of Writing in China: Scripts and Cultural Contexts." In *The Origins of Writing*. Wayne M. Senner, ed. Lincoln: University of Nebraska Press. Pp. 171–202.

Kemp, Eric Waldram. 1948. *Canonization and Authority in the Western Church*. London: Oxford University Press.

Kitchener, Karen Strohn. 1983. "Cognition, Metacognition, and Epistemic Cognition: A Three-Level Model of Cognitive Processing." *Human Development* 26(4):222–232.

Knight, David. 1986. *The Age of Science: The Scientific Worldview in the Nineteenth Century*. Oxford: Basil Blackwell.

Koertge, Noretta, ed. 1998. *A House Built on Sand: Exposing Postmodernist Myths About Science*. New York: Oxford University Press.

Kohlberg, Lawrence. 1981. *The Philosophy of Moral Development: Moral Stages and the Idea of Justice*. San Francisco: Harper & Row.

Kohlberg, Lawrence. 1984. *The Psychology of Moral Development: The Nature and Validity of Moral Stages*. New York: Harper & Row.

Kramer, Deirdre A., and Diana S. Woodruff. 1986. "Relativistic and Dialectical Thought in Three Adult Age-Groups." *Human Development* 29(5): 280–290.

Kramer, Samuel Noah. 1981. *History Begins at Sumer*. Philadelphia: University of Pennsylvania Press.

Kramer, Samuel Noah, and Diane Wolkstein. 1983. *Inanna, Queen of Heaven and Earth*. New York: Harper & Row.

Kuhn, D., J. Langer, L. Kohlberg, and N. S. Haan, "The Development of Formal Operations in Logical and Moral Judgments." *Genetic Psychology Monographs* 95 (1977):97–188.

Kuhn, Thomas. 1957. *The Copernican Revolution*. Cambridge, MA: Harvard University Press.

Kuhn, Thomas. 1970 (2nd ed.). *The Structure of Scientific Revolutions*. Chicago: University of Chicago Press.

Kuhn, Thomas. 1977 (reprint of 1962). *The Essential Tension*. Chicago: University of Chicago Press.

Lactantius. 1964. *The Divine Institutes*, book IV, ch. 12. The Fathers of the Church, vol. 49. Washington, DC: Catholic University of America Press.

Laing, Ronald David. 1967. *The Politics of Experience*. New York: Pantheon.

Laudan, Larry. 1984. "Explaining the Success of Science: Beyond Epistemic Realism and Relativism." In *Science and Reality: Recent Work in the Philosophy of Science*. James T. Cushing, C. F. Delany, and Gary M. Gutting, eds. Notre Dame, IN: Notre Dame University Press. Pp. 83–105.

Laudan, Larry. 1984. *Science and Values*. Berkeley: University of California Press.

Laudan, Rachel. 1987. *From Mineralogy to Geology: The Foundations of a Science*. Chicago: University of Chicago Press.

Lawrence, Bruce D. 1989. *Defenders of God: The Fundamentalist Revolt Against the Modern Age*. San Francisco: Harper & Row.

Leadbeater, B. 1986. "The Resolution of Relativism in Adult Thinking: Subjective, Objective, or Conceptual?" *Human Development* 29(5):291–300.

Lee, Richard B. 1992. "Art, Science, or Politics? The Crisis in Hunter-Gatherer Studies." *American Anthropologist* 94:31–54.

Leff, Gordon. 1976. *The Dissolution of the Medieval Outlook*. San Francisco: Harper & Row.

Le Goff, Jacques. 1981. *The Birth of Purgatory*. Chicago: University of Chicago Press.

Lenzer, Gertrude, ed. 1975. *Auguste Comte and Positivism: The Essential Writings*. Chicago: University of Chicago Press.

LePan, Don. 1989. *The Cognitive Revolution in Western Culture*. Vol. I. London: Macmillan.

Lesser, Ronnie, and Marilyn Paisner. 1985. "Magical Thinking in Formal Operational Adults." *Human Development* 28(2):57–70.

LeVine, Robert A. 1984. "Properties of Culture." In *Culture Theory: Essays on Mind, Self, and Society*. Robert A. LeVine and Richard A. Shweder, eds. New York: Cambridge University Press. Pp. 67–85.

Levinson, David, and Martin J. Malone. 1980. *Toward Explaining Human Culture: A Critical Review of the Findings of Cross-Cultural Research*. New Haven, CT: HRAF Press.

Lévi-Strauss, Claude. 1966. *The Savage Mind*. Chicago: University of Chicago Press.

Lévy-Bruhl, Lucien. 1923. *Primitive Mentality*. Lilian A. Clare, trans. New York: Macmillan.

Lévy-Bruhl, Lucien. 1975. *The Notebooks on Primitive Mentality*. Peter Riviere, trans. New York: Harper & Row.

Lévy-Bruhl, Lucien. 1983. *Primitive Mythology: The Mythic World of Australian and Papuan Natives*. Brian Elliott, trans. New York: University of Queensland Press. Originally published as *La Mythologique Primitive*, 1935.

Lévy-Bruhl, Lucien. 1985 (reprint of 1926). *How Natives Think*. Lilian A. Clare, trans. Princeton, NJ: Princeton University Press.

Lieberman, Philip. 1989. "The Origins of Some Aspects of Human Language and Cognition." Paul Mellar and Chris Stringer, eds. *The Human Revolu-*

tion: Behavioral and Biological Perspectives on the Origin of Modern Humans. Princeton: Princeton University Press. Pp. 391–414.

Lienhardt, Douglas. 1961. *Divinity and Experience: The Religion of the Dinka.* Oxford: Clarendon Press.

Lightman, Bernard. 1987. *The Origins of Agnosticism.* Baltimore: John Hopkins University Press.

Lincoln, Bruce. 1981. *Priests, Warriors, and Cattle: A Study in the Ecology of Religions.* Berkeley: University of California Press.

Lindbeck, George. 1984. *The Nature of Doctrine: Religion and Theology in a Postliberal Age.* Philadelphia: Westminster.

Little, Lester K. 1978. *Religious Poverty and the Profit Economy in Medieval Europe.* Ithaca, NY: Cornell University Press.

Liu, Wu-Chi. 1966. *An Introduction to Chinese Literature.* Bloomington: Indiana University Press.

Lloyd, Geoffrey Ernest Richard. 1979. *Magic, Reason, and Experience: Studies in the Origin and Development of Greek Science.* New York: Cambridge University Press.

Lloyd, Geoffrey Ernest Richard. 1990. *Demystifying Mentalities.* New York: Cambridge University Press.

Lloyd-Jones, Hugh. 1992. "Becoming Homer." *New York Review of Books.* March 5:52–57

Lonergan, Bernard. 1972. *Method in Theology.* New York: Herder and Herder.

Lonergan, Bernard. 1973. *Philosophy of God and Theology.* Philadelphia: Westminster.

Lonergan, Bernard. 1978. "Aquinas Today: Tradition and Innovation." In *Celebrating the Medieval Heritage: A Colloquy on the Thought of Aquinas and Bonaventure.* Journal of Religion Supplement. 58:S4. Pp. S1–S17.

Lonergan, Bernard. 1994. "Philosophy and the Religious Phenomenon." *Method: Journal of Lonergan Studies* 12(2):127–147.

Lopreato, Joseph. 1990. "From Social Evolutionism to Biocultural Evolutionism." *Sociological Forum* 5(2):187–212.

Lord, Albert B. 1964. *The Singer of Tales.* Cambridge, MA: Harvard University Press.

Losee, John. 1972. *A Historical Introduction to the Philosophy of Science.* London: Oxford University Press.

Losee, John. 1987. *Philosophy of Science and Historical Inquiry.* Oxford: Clarendon Press.

Louth, Andrew. 1981. *The Origins of the Christian Mystical Tradition: From Plato to Denys.* Oxford: Clarendon Press.

Lovejoy, Arthur O. 1936. *The Great Chain of Being.* Cambridge, MA: Harvard University Press.

Lucretius. 1975. *De Rerum Natura.* W. H. D. Rouse, trans. Cambridge: Harvard University Press.

Luhmann, Niklas. 1984. *Religious Dogmatics and the Evolution of Societies.* Peter Beyer, trans. New York: E. Mellen Press.

Lukes, Steven. 1972. *Emile Durkheim: His Life and Work.* New York: Harper & Row.

Lumsden, Charles J., and Edward O. Wilson. 1981. *Genes, Mind, and Culture: The Coevolutionary Process.* Cambridge, MA: Harvard University Press.

Lumsden, Charles J., and Edward O. Wilson. 1983. *Promethean Fires: Reflections on the Origin of Mind.* Cambridge, MA: Harvard University Press.

Luria, Alexander R. 1976. *Cognitive Development: Its Cultural and Social Foundations.* Martin Lopez-Morillas and Lynn Solotaroff, trans. Cambridge, MA: Harvard University Press.

Lynch, Joseph H. 1986. *Godparents and Kinship in Early Medieval Europe.* Princeton, NJ: Princeton University Press.

Macy, Gary. 1984. *The Theologies of the Eucharist in the Early Scholastic Period.* Oxford: Clarendon Press.

Malandra, William W., trans. and ed. 1983. *An Introduction to Ancient Iranian Religion: Readings from the Avesta and Achaemenid Inscriptions.* Minneapolis: University of Minnesota Press.

Malcolm, Norman. 1977. "The Groundlessness of Belief." In *Reason and Religion.* Stuart C. Brown, ed. Ithaca, NY: Cornell University Press. Pp. 143–157.

Malinowski, Bronislaw. 1954. *Magic, Science, and Religion.* New York: Doubleday Anchor.

Marrou, Henri. 1957. *St. Augustine and His Influence Through the Ages.* Patrick Hepburne-Scott, trans. New York: Harper and Brothers.

Martin, Henri-Jean. 1994. *The History and Power of Writing.* Lydia G. Cochrane, trans. Chicago: University of Chicago Press.

Martin, Luther. 1987. *Hellenistic Religions.* New York: Oxford University Press.

Martinau, Harriet, ed. 1853. *The Positive Philosophy of Auguste Comte.* London: John Chapman.

Mason, Stephen F. 1962. *A History of the Sciences.* New York: Macmillan.

Matsumoto, David. 1994. *People: Psychology from a Cultural Perspective.* Pacific Grove, CA: Brooks/Cole.

Mayr, Ernst. 1988. *Toward a New Philosophy of Biology: Observations of an Evolutionist.* Cambridge, MA: Belknap Press.

McEvedy, Colin. 1967. *The Penguin Atlas of Ancient History.* New York: Penguin.

McGinn, Bernard. 1979. *Visions of the End: Apocalyptic Traditions in the Middle Ages.* New York: Columbia University Press.

McGrath, Alister. 1987. *The Intellectual Origins of the European Reformation.* Oxford: Basil Blackwell.

McKnight, Stephen A. 1989. *Sacralizing the Secular: The Renaissance Origins of Modernity.* Baton Rouge: Louisiana State University Press.

McMullin, Ernan. 1988. *Newton on Matter and Activity.* Notre Dame, IN: University of Notre Dame Press.

McMullin, Ernan. 1988. "The Shaping of Scientific Rationality: Construction and Constraint." In *Construction and Constraint: The Shaping of Scientific Rationality.* Ernan McMullin, ed. Notre Dame, IN: University of Notre Dame Press. Pp. 1–47.

McNally, Robert E. 1986 (reprint of 1959). *The Bible in the Early Middle Ages.* Atlanta: Scholars Press.

McNeill, William H. 1976. *Plagues and Peoples.* New York: Doubleday.

Meadows, Sara. 1988. "Piaget's Contribution to Understanding Cognitive Development: An Assessment for the Late 1980's." In *Cognitive Development to Adolescence.* Ken Richardson and Sue Sheldon, eds. Hove, East Sussex: Lawrence Erlbaum Associates. Pp. 19–31.

Meek, Ronald L. 1976. *Social Science and the Ignoble Savage*. New York: Cambridge University Press.

Mellars, Paul, and Chris Stringer, eds. 1989. *The Human Revolution: Behavioral and Biological Perspectives on the Origin of Modern Humans*. Princeton, NJ: Princeton University Press.

Middleton, John. 1960. *Lugbara Religion: Ritual and Authority Among an East African People*. London: Oxford University Press.

Miller, Barbara Stoler. 1986. *The Bhagavad Gita: Krishna's Counsel in Time of War*. New York: Bantam.

Miller, Jeanine. 1985. *The Vision of Cosmic Order in the Vedas*. Boston: Routledge and Kegan Paul.

Minucius Felix, Marcus. 1974. *The Octavius of Marcius Minucius Felix*. G. W. Clarke, trans. New York: Newman Press.

Mithen, Steven. 1996. *The Prehistory of the Mind: The Cognitive Origin of Art, Religion, and Science*. London: Thames and Hudson.

Morris, Brian. 1987. *Anthropological Studies of Religion: An Introductory Text*. New York: Cambridge University Press.

Morris, Colin. 1972. *The Discovery of the Individual: 1050–1200*. New York: Harper & Row.

Murphy, Nancey, Arthur R. Peacocke, and Robert J. Russell, eds. 1995. *Chaos and Complexity: Scientific Perspectives on Divine Action*. Vatican City: Vatican Observatory Publications.

Murray, Alexander. 1978. *Reason and Society in the Middle Ages*. Oxford: Clarendon Press.

Nagel, Thomas. 1997. *The Last Word*. New York: Oxford University Press.

Nakamura, Hajime. 1983. *A History of Early Vedanta Philosophy*. Delhi: Motilal Banarsidass.

Naroll, Raoul. 1973. "Holocultural Theory Tests." In *Main Currents in Cultural Anthropology*. Frada Naroll and Raoul Naroll, eds. New York: Appleton-Century-Crofts. Pp. 309–384.

Nebelsick, Harold. 1981. *Theology and Science in Mutual Modification*. New York: Oxford University Press.

Needham, Joseph. 1955. "Mechanistic Biology and Religious Consciousness." In *Science, Religion, and Reality*. Joseph Needham, ed. New York: George Braziller. Pp. 225–264.

Needham, Joseph. 1956. *Science and Civilization in China. History of Scientific Thought*, vol. 2. New York: Cambridge University Press.

Newman, Robert C. 1997. "Fulfilled Prophecy as Miracle." In *In Defense of Miracles: A Comprenesive Case for God's Action in History*. R. D. Geivett and Gary Habermas, eds. Downers Grove, IL: InterVarsity Press. Pp. 214–225.

Newton, Isaac. 1950. *Theological Manuscripts*. H. McLachlan, ed. Liverpool: Liverpool University Press.

Newton, Isaac. 1952 (4th ed.). *Optics*. New York: Dover Publications.

Newton, Isaac. 1960. *Principia*. Florian Cajori, ed. Berkeley: University of California Press.

Nielsen, Kai. 1967. "Wittgensteinian Fideism." *Philosophy* 42:191–199.

Nigosian, S. A. 1993. *The Zoroastrian Faith: Tradition and Modern Research*. Montreal: McGill-Queen's University Press.

Noll, Mark A. 1994. *The Scandal of the Evangelical Mind*. Grand Rapids, MI: Eerdmans.

Novotny, Helga. 1979. "Science and Its Critics: Reflections on Anti-Science." In *Counter-Movements in the Sciences*. Helga Novotny and Hilary Rose, eds. Dordrecht: D. Reidel. Pp. 1–26.

Oakley, Francis. 1984. *Omnipotence, Covenant, and Order: An Excursion in the History of Ideas from Abelard to Leibniz*. Ithaca, NY: Cornell University Press.

O'Flaherty, Wendy Doniger. 1988. *Textual Sources for the Study of Hinduism*. Totowa, NJ: Barnes and Noble.

Ofshe, Richard, and Ethan Watters. 1994. *Making Monsters: False Memories, Psychotherapy, and Sexual Hysteria*. New York: Scribner's.

Oldroyd, David R. 1986. *The Arch of Knowledge: An Introductory Study of the History of the Philosophy and Methodology of Science*. New York: Methuen.

O'Meara, Dominic. 1985. "Plotinus on How Soul Acts on Body." In *Platonic Investigations*. Dominic O'Meara, ed. Washington, DC: Catholic University of America Press. Pp. 247–262.

Ong, Walter. 1967. *The Presence of the Word*. New Haven, CT: Yale University Press.

Ong, Walter. 1977. *Interfaces of the Word: Studies in the Evolution of Consciousness and Culture*. Ithaca, NY: Cornell University Press.

Ong, Walter. 1978. "Technology Outside Us and Inside Us." *Communio* 2(Summer):1–21.

Ong, Walter. 1982. *Orality and Literacy: The Technologizing of the World*. New York: Methuen.

Opler, Morris Edward. 1994 (reprint of 1938). *Myths and Tales of the Jicarilla Apache Indians*. New York: Dover.

Oser, Fritz K., and Paul Gmunder. 1991. *Religious Judgment: A Developmental Perspective*. Birmingham: Religious Education Press.

Otto, Rudolph. 1958. *The Idea of the Holy*. New York: Oxford University Press.

Owen, D. R. G. 1983. "The Sacramental View of Reality: The Spirit-Matter Problem." In *The Experiment of Life: Science and Religion*. F. Kenneth Hare, ed. Toronto: University of Toronto Press. Pp. 17–26.

Owens, Joseph. 1981. "The Aristotelian Conception of the Sciences." In *Aristotle: The Collected Papers of Joseph Owens*. John A. Catan, ed. Albany: SUNY Press. Pp. 23–34.

Overmyer, Daniel L. 1986. *Religions of China*. San Francisco: Harper & Row.

Pals, Daniel L. 1987. "Is Religion a *Sui Generis* Phenomenon?" *Journal of the American Academy of Religion* 55(2):259–282.

Pannenberg, Wolfhart. 1976. *Theology and the Philosophy of Science*. Francis McDonagh, trans. Philadelphia: Westminster.

Paper, Jordon. 1995. *The Spirits Are Drunk: Comparative Approaches to Chinese Religion*. Albany: SUNY Press.

Parkinson, Claire L. 1985. *Breakthroughs: A Chronology of Great Achievements in Science and Mathematics, 1200–1930*. Boston: G. K. Hall.

Parsons, Talcott. 1977. *The Evolution of Societies*. Englewood Cliffs, NJ: Prentice-Hall.

Passmore, John. 1970. *The Perfectibility of Man*. New York: Scribner's Sons.

Peacock, James L., and Thomas A. Kirsch. 1970. *The Human Direction: An Evolutionary Approach to Social and Cultural Anthropology*. New York: Appleton-Century-Crofts. 3rd ed. Englewood Cliffs, NJ: Prentice-Hall, 1980.

Peacocke, Arthur. 1986. *God and the New Biology*. London: J. M. Dent and Sons.

Pearson, Lionel. 1962. *Popular Ethics in Ancient Greece*. Stanford, CA: Stanford University Press.

Peckham, Morse. 1986. *The Birth of Romanticism, 1790–1815*. Greenwood, FL: Penkevill Publishing.

Peel, John David Yeadon. 1987. "History, Culture, and the Comparative Method: An African Puzzle." In *Comparative Anthropology*. Ladislav Holy, ed. Oxford: Basil Blackwell. Pp. 88–118.

Pellegrin, Pierre. 1986. *Aristotle's Classification of Animals: Biology and the Conceptual Unity of the Aristotelian Corpus*. Anthony Preus, trans. Berkeley: University of California Press.

Penner, Hans. 1968. "Rationality and Religion: Problems in the Comparison of Modes of Thought." *Journal of the American Academy of Religion* 54(4): 645–671.

Perry, William. 1970. *The Forms of Intellectual and Ethical Development in College Years*. New York: Holt, Rinehart, and Winston.

Peters, Francis E. 1968. *Aristotle and the Arabs: The Aristotelian Tradition in Islam*. New York: New York University Press.

Phillips, Dewi Zephaniah. 1971. *Faith and Philosophical Enquiry*. New York: Schocken Books.

Phillips, Dewi Zephaniah. 1976. *Religion Without Explanation*. Oxford: Blackwell Press.

Phillips, Dewi Zephaniah. 1984. "The Devil's Disguises: Philosophy of Religion, 'Objectivity,' and 'Cultural Divergence.'" In *Objectivity and Cultural Divergence*. S. C. Brown, ed. New York: Cambridge University Press. Pp. 61–77.

Piaget, Jean, and Barbel, Inhelder. 1958. *The Growth of Logical Thinking: From Childhood to Adolescence*. New York: Basic Books.

Piaget, Jean. 1970. *Structuralism*. Chaninah Maschler, trans. New York: Basic Books.

Piaget, Jean. 1973. *The Child and Reality: Problems of Genetic Psychology*. Arnold Rosin, trans. New York: Grossman.

Pickman, Edward Motley. 1962. *The Sequence of Belief: A Consideration of Religious Thought from Homer to Ockham*. New York: St. Martin's Press.

Pinker, Steven. 1994. *The Language Instinct: How the Mind Creates Language*. New York: Harper Perennial.

Plotinus. 1952. *The Six Enneads*. Chicago: Encyclopedia Britannica.

Polkinghorne, John. 1989. *Science and Providence: God's Interaction with the World*. Boston: Shambhala.

Polkinghorne, John. 1991. *Reason and Reality: The Relationship Between Science and Theology*. London: SPCK Press.

Popper, Karl. 1963. *Conjectures and Refutations*. London: Routledge and Kegan Paul.

Popper, Karl. 1972. *Objective Knowledge: An Evolutionary Approach*. Oxford: Clarendon Press.

Pritchard, James B. 1955. *Ancient Near Eastern Texts Relating to the Old Testament*. Princeton, NJ: Princeton University Press.

Proudfoot, Wayne. 1985. *Religious Experience*. Berkeley: University of California Press.

Puhvel, Jaan. 1987. *Comparative Mythology*. Baltimore: John Hopkins University Press.

Quine, Willard Van Orman. 1963. *From a Logical Point of View*. New York: Harper Torchbook.

Radding, Charles M. 1985. *A World Made by Men: Cognition and Society, 400–1200*. Chapel Hill: University of North Carolina Press.

Radetsky, Peter. 1995. "Gut Thinking." *Discover* May:76–81.

Radin, Paul. 1937. *Primitive Religion: Its Nature and Origin*. New York: Dover.

Radin, Paul. 1952. *African Folktales and Sculpture*. New York: Pantheon.

Radin, Paul, ed. 1983 (reprint of 1952). *African Folktales*. New York: Schocken Books.

Rahner, Karl. 1988. *Theological Investigations*. Vol. 21. Hugh M. Riley, trans. New York: Crossroads.

Rawson, Elizabeth. 1985. *Intellectual Life in the Late Roman Republic*. Baltimore: John Hopkins University Press.

Reale, Giovanni. 1985. *The Systems of the Hellenistic Age*. Vol. 3. of *A History of Ancient Philosophy*. Albany: SUNY Press.

Reardon, Bernard M. G. 1985. *Religion in the Age of Romanticism*. New York: Cambridge University Press.

Reif, Wolf-Ernst. 1983. "Evolutionary Theory in German Paleontology." In *Dimensions of Darwinism*. Marjorie Grene, ed. New York: Cambridge University Press. Pp. 173–203.

Reiss, Timothy J. 1982. *The Discourse of Modernism*. Ithaca, NY: Cornell University Press.

Renou, Louis. 1962. *Hinduism*. New York: George Braziller.

Rhadakrishnan, Sarvepalli, and Charles Moore, eds. 1957. *A Sourcebook in Indian Philosophy*. Princeton, NJ: Princeton University Press.

Richards, Robert J. 1987. *Darwinism and the Emergence of Evolutionary Theories of Mind and Behavior*. Chicago: University of Chicago Press.

Richardson, Ken, and Sue Sheldon, eds. 1988. *The New Structuralism in Cognitive Development: Theory and Research on Individual Pathways*. New York: Karger.

Roberts, John M., and Brian Sutton-Smith. 1981. "Play, Games, and Sports." In *Handbook of Cross-Cultural Psychology*, vol. 4. Harry C. Triandis and Alastair Heron, eds. Boston: Allyn and Bacon. Pp. 425–471.

Roche, John. 1986. "The Transition from the Ancient World Picture." In *The Physical Sciences Since Antiquity*. Rom Harré, ed. New York: St. Martin's Press. Pp. 29–40.

Roe, Shirley A. 1981. *Matter, Life, and Generation: Eighteenth Century Embryology and the Haller-Wolffe Debate*. New York: Cambridge University Press.

Rogoff, Barbara. 1981. "Schooling and the Development of Cognitive Skills." In *Handbook of Cross-Cultural Psychology*, vol. 4. Alastair Heron and Harry C. Triandis, eds. Boston: Allyn and Bacon.

Roosevelt, Anna Curtenius. 1922. "Secrets of the Forest." *The Sciences* November/December:22–28.

Rorty, Richard. 1979. *Philosophy and the Mirror of Nature*. Princeton, NJ: Princeton University Press.

Rorty, Richard, 1982. *Consequences of Pragmatism*. Minneapolis: University of Minnesota Press.

Russell, Colin A. 1985. *Cross Currents: Interactions Between Science and Faith*. Downers Grove, IL: InterVarsity Press.

Russo, Joseph A. 1992. "Oral Theory: Its Development in Homeric Studies and Applicability to Other Literature." In *Mesopotamian Epic Literature: Oral or Aural?* Herman L. Vanstiphout and Marianna E. Vogelzang, eds. Lewiston, NY: Edwin Mellen. Pp. 7–21.

Rutter, Marjorie, and Michael Rutter. 1993. *Developing Minds: Challenge and Continuity Across the Life Span.* New York: Basic Books.

Sabatier, Auguste. 1902. *Outlines of a Philosophy of Religion Based on Psychology and History.* New York: George H. Doran. Reprinted New York: Harper Torchbook, 1957.

Sagan, Carl. 1980. *Cosmos.* New York: Random House.

Saggs, Henry William Frederick. 1962. *The Greatness That Was Babylon: A Sketch of the Ancient Civilization of the Tigris-Euphrates Valley.* New York: New American Library.

Sanderson, Stephen K. 1990. *Social Evolutionism: A Critical History.* New York: Cambridge University Press.

Sandmel, Samuel. 1979. *Philo of Alexandria: An Introduction.* New York: Oxford University Press.

Sargent, Rose-Mary. 1995. *The Diffident Naturalist: Robert Boyle and the Philosophy of Experiment.* Chicago: University of Chicago Press.

Sarton, George. 1952. *A History of Science: Ancient Science Through the Golden Age of Greece.* New York: W. W. Norton.

Schlegel, Richard. 1982. "Is Science the Only Way to Truth?" *Zygon* 17(4): 343–359.

Schlagel, Richard H. 1995. *From Myth to Modern Mind: A Study of the Origins and Growth of Scientific Thought.* Vol. I, *Theogony through Ptolemy.* New York: Peter Lang.

Schleiermacher, Friedrich. 1958. *On Religion: Speeches to Its Cultured Despisers.* New York: Harper & Row.

Schleiermacher, Friedrich. 1928. *The Christian Faith.* Edinburgh: T. & T. Clark.

Schmandt-Besserat, Denise. 1988. "From Accounting to Written Language: The Role of Abstract Counting in the Invention of Writing." In *The Social Construction of Written Communication.* Bennet A. Raforth and Donald L. Rubin, eds. Norwood, NJ: Ablex. Pp. 119–130.

Schmidt, Wilhelm. 1972 (reprint of 1931). *The Origin and Growth of Religion: Facts and Theories.* New York: Cooper Square.

Schoen, Edward L. 1985. *Religious Explanations: A Model from the Sciences.* Durham, NC: Duke University Press.

Schrenk, Lawrence P., ed. 1994. *Aristotle in Late Antiquity.* Washington, DC: Catholic University of America Press.

Schubert-Soldern, Rainer. 1962. *Mechanism and Vitalism: Philosophical Aspects of Biology.* Notre Dame, IN: University of Notre Dame Press.

Schuster, John A. 1995. "Descartes Agonistes: New Tales of a Cartesian Natural Philosophy." *Perspectives on Science* 3(1):99–145.

Schwartz, Benjamin I. 1975. "Transcendence in Ancient China." *Daedalus* 104(2):57–68.

Schwartz, Benjamin I. 1985. *The World of Thought in Ancient China.* Cambridge, MA: Harvard University Press.

Scott, Eugenie C., and Robert M. West. 1995. "Again, Johnson Gets It Wrong." *Creation/Evolution* 37:26–27.

Seagrim, Gavin, and Robin Lendon. 1980. *Furnishing the Mind: A Comparative Study of Cognitive Development in Central Australian Aborigines.* Sydney and New York: Academic Press.

Seagrim, Gavin. 1977. "Caveat Interventor." In *Piagetian Psychology: Cross Cultural Contributions.* Pierre Dasen, ed. New York: Gardner Press.

Sears, Elizabeth. 1986. *The Ages of Man: Medieval Interpretations.* Princeton, NJ: Princeton University Press.

Segal, Robert. 1994. "Mythopoeic Versus Religious Thought: A Reply to Michael Barnes." *Religion* 24(1):77–80.

Sellars, Wilfred. 1956. "Empiricism and the Philosophy of Mind." In *The Foundations of Science and the Concepts of Psychology and Psychoanalysis.* Herbert Feigl and Michael Scriven, eds. Minneapolis: University of Minnesota Press. Pp. 253–329.

Sextus Empiricus. 1994. *Outlines of Scepticism.* Julia Annas and Jonathan Barnes, trans. New York: Cambridge University Press.

Sextus Empiricus. 1994. *Adversus Mathematicos.* In Annas and Barnes, trans., *Outlines of Scepticism.* Pp. 166–189.

Shannon, Richard S. III, and Benjamin A. Stolz. 1976. *Oral Literature and the Formula.* Ann Arbor: Center for the Coordination of Ancient and Modern Studies, University of Michigan.

Shapin, Steven, and Simon Schaffer. 1985. *Leviathan and the Air-Pump: Hobbes, Boyle, and the Experimental Life.* Princeton, NJ: Princeton University Press.

Sheils, Dean. 1974. "An Evolutionary Theory of Supportive Monotheism: A Comparative Study." *International Journal of Comparative Sociology* 15(1–2):47–56.

Shore, Bradd. 1996. *Culture in Mind: Cognition, Culture, and the Problem of Meaning.* New York: Oxford University Press.

Shoumatoff, Alex. 1986. *The Rivers Amazon.* San Francisco: Sierra Club.

Shutte, Augustine. 1976. "A Theory of Religion." *International Philosophical Quarterly* 16(3):289–300.

Shweder, Richard A. 1977. "Likeness and Likelihood in Everyday Thought: Magical Thinking in Judgements About Personality." *Current Anthropology* 18(4). Pp. 637–658.

Shweder, Richard A. 1981. "Rationality 'Goes Without Saying.'" *Culture, Medicine, and Psychiatry* 5(4):348–358.

Shweder, Richard A. 1982. "On Savages and Other Children." *American Anthropologist* 84:354–366.

Shweder, Richard A. 1985. "Has Piaget Been Upstaged? A Reply to Hallpike." *American Anthropologist* 87:138–144.

Shweder, Richard A. 1991. *Thinking Through Cultures: Expeditions in Cultural Psychology.* Cambridge, MA: Harvard University Press.

Singer, Dorothy G., and Jerome L. Singer. 1990. *The House of Make-Believe: Children's Play and the Developing Imagination.* Cambridge, MA: Harvard University Press.

Skutch, Alexander F. 1970. *The Golden Core of Religion.* New York: Holt, Rinehart, and Winston.

Smith, Jonathan Z. 1982. *Imagining Religion: From Babylon to Jonestown.* Chicago: University of Chicago Press.

Smuts, Barbara, et al., eds. 1986. *Primate Societies.* Chicago: University of Chicago Press.

Snarey, John R. 1985. "Cross-Cultural University of Social-Moral Development: A Critical Review of Kohlbergian Research." *Psychological Bulletin* 97(2):202–232.

Snell, Bruno. 1953. *The Discovery of the Mind*. Cambridge, MA: Harvard University Press.

Sokal, Alan, and Jean Bricmont. 1998. *Fashionable Nonsense: Postmodern Intellectuals' Abuse of Science*. New York: Picador USA.

Spear, Percival. 1961. *India: A Modern History*. Ann Arbor: University of Michigan Press.

Spencer, Herbert. 1880 (4th ed.). *First Principles*. London: A. L. Burt Home Library.

Sperber, Dan. 1996. *Explaining Culture: A Naturalistic Approach*. New York: Blackwell.

Stead, Christopher. 1994. *Philosophy in Christian Antiquity*. New York: Cambridge University Press.

Steadman, Lyle B. "Neighbours and Killers: Residence and Dominance Among the Hewa of New Guinea." Ph.D. dissertation, Australian National University.

Stenmark, Mikael. 1995. *Rationality in Science, Religion, and Everyday Life: A Critical Evaluation of Four Models of Reality*. Notre Dame, IN: Notre Dame University Press.

Steuer, Axel D. 1987. "The Epistemic Status of Theistic Belief." *Journal of the American Academy of Religion* 55(2):235–256.

Stiefel, Tiina. 1985. *The Intellectual Revolution in Twelfth Century Europe*. New York: St. Martin's Press.

Stock, Brian. 1972. *Myth and Science in the Twelfth Century: A Study of Bernard Silvester*. Princeton, NJ: Princeton University Press.

Stone, I. F. 1988. "Was There a Witch Hunt in Ancient Athens?" *New York Review of Books* January 21:37–41.

Stone, Jon R. 1993. "The Medieval Mappaemundi: Toward an Archeology of Sacred Cartography." *Religion* 23(3):197–216.

Stout, Jeffrey. 1981. *The Flight from Authority*. Notre Dame, IN: Notre Dame University Press.

Street, Brian V. 1984. *Literacy in Theory and Practice*. New York: Cambridge University Press.

Strodach, George K. 1963. *The Philosophy of Epicurus*. Evanston, IL: Northwestern University Press.

Swanson, Guy E. 1964. *The Birth of Gods: The Origins of Primitive Beliefs*. Ann Arbor: University of Michigan Press.

Talbot, Percy Amaury. 1967. *Tribes of the Niger Delta: Their Religions and Customs*. New York: Barnes and Noble.

Taylor, Richard. 1970. *Good and Evil: A New Direction*. New York: Macmillan.

Thomas, Keith. 1971. *Religion and the Decline of Magic: Studies in Popular Belief in Sixteenth and Seventeenth Century England*. London: Weidenfeld and Nicolson.

Thomas, Nicholas. 1989. *Out of Time: History and Evolutionism in Anthropological Discourse*. New York: Cambridge University Press.

Thomas, Owen C., ed. 1983. *God's Activity in the World: The Contemporary Problem*. Chico, CA: Scholars Press.

Thompson, Lawrence G. 1973. *The Chinese Way in Religion*. Belmont, CA: Wadsworth.

Thompson, William Irwin. 1981. *The Time Falling Bodies Take to Light: Mythology, Sexuality, and the Origins of Culture*. New York: St. Martin's Press.

Thompson, William M. 1977. *Christ and Consciousness: Exploring Christ's Contribution to Human Consciousness: The Origins and Development of Christian Consciousness*. New York: Paulist Press.

Thrower, James. 1980. *The Alternative Tradition: Religion and the Rejection of Religion in the Ancient World.* The Hague and New York: Mouton.

Tigay, Jeffrey H. 1982. *The Evolution of the Gilgamesh Epic*. Philadelphia: University of Pennsylvania Press.

Tilley, Terrence W. 1991. *The Evils of Theodicy*. Washington, DC: Georgetown University Press.

Tilley, Terrence W., et al. 1995. *Postmodern Theologies*. Maryknoll, NY: Orbis Books.

Tillich, Paul. 1957. *Dynamics of Faith.* New York: Harper & Row.

Time-Life Editors. 1987. *The Age of God-Kings*. Alexandria, VA: Time-Life Books.

Toland, John. 1967. "Christianity Not Mysterious." In *Deism and Natural Religion: A Source Book.* E. Graham Waring, ed. New York: Frederick Ungar.

Topping, Donald M. 1987. "Literacy in the Pacific Islands." *Interchange* 18(1/2):48–59.

Toulmin, Stephen, and Jane Goodfield. 1965. *The Discovery of Time.* Chicago: University of Chicago Press.

Tracy, David. 1973. "The Religious Dimension of Science." In *The Persistence of Religion.* Andrew Greeley and Gregory Baum, eds. New York: Herder and Herder. Pp. 128–135.

Tracy, David. 1975. *Blessed Rage for Order*. New York: Seabury Press.

Trevor-Roper, Hugh Redwald. 1969. *The European Witch-Craze of the Sixteenth and Seventeenth Centuries and Other Essays*. New York: Harper Torchbooks.

Turgot, Anne R. J. 1973. *Turgot on Progress, Sociology, and Economics.* Ronald L. Meek, ed. and trans. New York: Cambridge University Press.

Turnbull, Colin M. 1962. *The Forest People: A Study of the Pygmies of the Congo.* New York: Simon and Schuster.

Turner, Mark. 1996. *The Literary Mind.* New York: Oxford University Press.

Tylor, Edward Burnett. 1898. *Anthropology: An Introduction to the Study of Man and Civilization.* New York: D. Appleton.

Tylor, Edward Burnett. 1958 (reprint of 1871). *Religion in Primitive Culture*, vol. 2. New York: Harper & Row.

Ullmann, Walter. 1966. *The Individual and Society in the Middle Ages*. Baltimore: Johns Hopkins University Press.

Ullmann, Walter. 1975. *Law and Politics in the Middle Ages: An Introduction to the Sources of Medieval Political Ideas.* Ithaca, NY: Cornell University Press.

Urbach, Peter. 1987. *Francis Bacon's Philosophy of Science: An Account and a Reappraisal.* LaSalle, IL: Open Court.

van den Berghe, P. L. 1990. "Why Most Sociologists Don't (and Won't) Think Evolutionarily." *Sociological Forum* 5(2):173–185.

Vecsey, Christopher. 1986. "The Story and Structure of the Iroquois Confederacy." *Journal of the American Academy of Religion* 54(1):79–98.

Wach, Joachim. 1951. *Types of Religious Experience, Christian and Non-Christian.* Chicago: University of Chicago Press.

Wagner, Daniel A., and Harold W. Stevenson. 1982. *Cultural Perspectives on Child Development.* San Francisco: W. H. Freeman.

Ward, Benedicta. 1982. *Miracles and the Medieval Mind: Theory, Record, and Event, 1000–1215.* Philadelphia: University of Pennsylvania Press.

Wassil-Grimm, Claudette. 1995. *Diagnosis for Disaster: The Devastating Truth About False Memory Syndrome and Its Impact on Accusers and Families.* New York: Overlook Press.

Watson, Alan. 1970. *The Law of the Ancient Romans.* Dallas: Southern Methodist University Press.

Wertsch, James B. 1991. *Voices of the Mind: A Sociocultural Approach to Mediated Action.* Cambridge, MA: Harvard University Press.

Westfall, Richard. 1971. *The Construction of Modern Science: Mechanisms and Mechanics.* New York: John Wiley and Sons.

Westfall, Richard. 1986. "The Rise of Science and the Decline of Orthodox Christianity: A Study of Kepler, Descartes, and Newton." In *God and Nature.* David C. Lindberg and Ronald L. Numbers, eds. Berkeley: University of California Press. Pp. 218–237.

White, Haydn. 1978. *Tropics of Discourse: Essays in Cultural Criticism.* Baltimore: Johns Hopkins University Press.

White, Leslie. 1959. *The Evolution of Culture.* New York: McGraw-Hill.

White, Lynn, Jr. 1962. *Medieval Technology and Social Change.* London: Oxford University Press.

Whitehead, Alfred North. 1957. *Process and Reality.* New York: Harper & Row.

Whitmore, John. 1995. "Religious Dimensions of the UFO Abductee's Experience." In *The Gods Have Landed: New Religions from Other Worlds.* James R. Lewis, ed. Albany: SUNY Press. Pp. 65–84.

Wians, William, ed. 1996. *Aristotle's Philosophical Development: Problems and Prospects.* Lanham, MD: Rowman and Littlefield.

Wiebe, Donald. 1991. *The Irony of Theology and the Nature of Religion.* Montreal: McGill-Queens University Press.

Wightman, William P. D. 1951. *The Growth of Scientific Ideas.* New Haven, CT: Yale University Press.

Wilcox, Margaret Mary. 1979. *A Developmental Journey.* Nashville, TN: Abingdon Press.

Wiles, Maurice. 1986. *God's Action in the World.* London: SCM Press.

Wilken, Robert L. 1984. *The Christians as the Romans Saw Them.* New Haven, CT: Yale University Press.

Williams, Terence Charles. 1990. *The Idea of the Miraculous: The Challenge to Science and Religion.* New York: St. Martin's Press.

Wilson, Bryan, ed. 1970. *Rationality.* Evanston, IL: Harper & Row.

Winch, Peter. 1977. "Understanding Primitive Society." In *Understanding and Social Inquiry.* Fred Dallmayr and Thomas McCarthy, eds. Notre Dame, IN: Notre Dame University Press. Pp. 159–188.

Wiredu, Kwasi. 1984. "How Not to Compare African Thought with Western Thought." In *African Philosophy: An Introduction.* Richard A. Wright, ed. Lanham, MD: University Press of America. Pp. 149–162.

Wittfogel, Karl A. 1957. *Oriental Despotism; A Comparative Study of Total Power.* New Haven, CT: Yale University Press.

Wolfson, Harry Austryn. 1962 (reprint of 1926). *Philo: Foundations of Religious Philosophy in Judaism, Christianity, and Islam.* Cambridge, MA: Harvard University Press.

Worsley, Peter. 1968. *The Trumpet Shall Sound.* New York: Schocken Books.

Wuthnow, Robert. 1987. *Meaning and Moral Order: Explorations in Cultural Analysis.* Berkeley: University of California Press.

Yapko, Michael D. 1994. *Suggestions of Abuse: True and False Memories of Childhood Sexual Trauma.* New York: Simon and Schuster.

Yates, Frances A. 1964. *Giordano Bruno and the Hermetic Tradition.* Chicago: University of Chicago Press.

Yolton, John W. 1983. *Thinking Matter: Materialism in Eighteenth-Century Britain.* Minneapolis: University of Minnesota Press.

INDEX

Abelard, 140–142, 146
Aborigines, 40, 56, 89, 90
  Songlines, 37–38
abstraction
  in preliterate thought, 83–85
  promoted by literacy, 88
  unappealing to people, 101
Academy, ancient Greek, 122–123
accuracy in science, 190, 195
Advaita Vedanta, of Shankara, 116
Agassiz, Louis, on multiple extinctions, 284n62
agriculture, 20, 78–79
Akhenaton, and early monotheism,
  91
Albert the Great, and empirical
  method, 146
allegory
  replaces rational analysis, 131
  in early middle ages, 137
Alves, Reuben, on dangers of science, 179–180, 189
Amazon delta culture, 55
ancestors
  in ancient China, 103
  as spirits in Taoism, 116, 138
  and status in middle ages, 138
animism, 30, 112, 202
anomalies in science, 185, 194

Anselm of Canterbury, 145
  and God's honor, 138
  and proofs of God's existence, 142
anthropic principle, 212, 219
anthropology, 8, 37, 46, 85, 86, 190
  and cultural relativism, 35
  and exaggerated primitive cognition, 37–40
anti-foundationalism, 122–123. *See
  also* foundationalism
apocalyptic thought, 111, 136–137
saving the appearances, 150
Aquinas, St. Thomas, 167, 205–
  206, 211–212
  and God's power, 146
  and formal operational thought,
  143
  on materiality, 159
  and miracles, 145
archaic
  culture, 25, 78–79
  and gods, 79–80
  and literacy, 81–85
  in religion in middle ages, 124–
  125, 130, 136–139
  religion and intolerance,
  203–204
  thought style in religion, 115–116
  thought style today, 30–32

Chenu, M.-D., on late medieval culture, 139, 148
chiefs, in archaic cultures, 60, 64, 66, 82
Childs, Alice and Irvin, on aborigines, 60–61
children, stages of development, 20–22
    compared to adults, 48–49
China
    and classical culture, 102–107
    early literacy, 81, 255n13
Christian thought
    and deism, 161–163
    and Hellenic philosophy, 128–131
    stages of, 20
    and traditionalism, 204
Chuang Tzu, 105
Cicero, on Stoic thought, 118
classical culture, 93–97. See also axial age
classical thought, medieval rebirth of, 139–141
classless, primitive cultures as, 64, 69
Clement of Alexandria, 130–131, 217
cognitive elites, 17, 26, 112, 144, 176
cognitive styles, 7–9, 47–49. See also Piagetian stages; Kitchener; Lonergan
cognitive skills
    in contemporary culture, 30–33
    studies of post-adolescent, 238n30
    evaluated, 50–52
cognitive tools. See also literacy
    to aid reasoning, 49, 72, 96
    and formal schooling, 9–10
coherence
    as criterion in science
    as method in religion, 205–206
Cole, Michael, 78, 82, 88, 252n73
colonialist attitudes, 6, 8
collective representations, 73, 74, 77, 81
commonsense
    as concrete operational thought, 21
    forms of skepticism, 177
community, 203–204, 214, 224–226
Compte, 11–12, 113, 116
concrete operational thought, 21
    in contemporary society, 31
    and cultural stages, 30

dangers of, 203–204
    value of, 50, 51
conditional thought. See late formal operational thought
Confucianism, 10, 102, 103–104, 105, 262n45, 263n55
conjecture, and refutation, 183, 185–186, 200, 288n28
constructivism
    as an interpretation of science, 191, 195–196
    as postmodern, 187–189
    uses classical standards, 288n29
Copernicanism, 133, 150, 191–197, 210, 220
Corpus Hermeticum (see Hermeticism)
corpuscularist philosophy, 157
correlational theologies, 227–230
cosmology, 211–212, 218–220
Creator, God as, 27, 129, 142, 145, 212, 220
credulity, 127, 131, 142, 201–202
critical. See empirical-critical
cultural development, 17
    Comtean theories of, 11–12, 113, 116
    as social progress? 10–11, 34–37
    forms of, 15–16
    not a recapitulation theory, 235n1
    objection to theories of, 6, 8, 34–40
    parallel to individual development, 18
    Piagetian theory of, 3–5
    stages of, 23–28
    various kinds as evolution, 15–16, 241n7
cuneiform, 81

Damian, Peter, and God's power, 146, 147
Darwin, Charles, 168–172, 173
Dawkins, Richard, 21, 172, 210
deconstructionism, 86, 106, 206, 221–222
deism, 161–163, 212, 214–215
Democritus, 108, 116
demons, 156, 209, 214, 224
demythologization, 190
    of ancient gods, 96
    in correlational theology, 216, 219
    as intrinsic to theism, 229
    in late middle ages, 142

God
  and Greek philosophy, 128–130
  as infinite, ultimate, 93–94, 116
  as mystery, 116, 228–229
  and necessity, 143–144
  power of, 145–147
  as Sustainer of universe, 145, 220
  theologies of today, 219, 227–229
  and types of beliefs about,
    210–214
  See also monotheism; Creator; mir-
    acles
God-consciousness, 215
gods
  in ancient China, 103
  in ancient Greece, 115, 117
  in ancient India, 97–98
  and archaic culture, 25–27
    79–80
  and epic myths, 89, 94
  first appearance of, 5, 6, 78–80
  high gods, theory of, 60–62
  polytheism, 30
Gonja of Northern Ghana, stories of
  the, 82
Goody, Jack, 16, 81–85, 89
Gould, Stephen J., 210, 219
Grant, Edward, 125, 127, 131
Gratian, decrees of, 141
Greece. *See* axial age; God and
  Greek philosophy
Grosseteste, Robert, and medieval
  experimentalism, 149
Guddemi, Phillip, on Sawiyano, 62
Guthrie, Stewart, as Comtean, 11,
  113, 116

Haller, Albrecht von, 166, 173
Hallpike, Christopher, 48, 64, 76–
  83, 107
  on primitive thought, 69–73
  challenges to, 73–76
Han dynasty in China, 102, 106
Hardy, Jean, 178–180, 182
Harrapan culture, 79
Harvey, William, 159–160, 164–
  166, 173
Haydn, Hiram, on early anti-intellec-
  tualism, 278n99
Heath, Shirley Brice, on cognition,
  257n46
heaven, 94, 102–105, 129, 137, 230
Hebrew, monotheism 111, 128, 130,
  203
Hegel, 70, 165
heliocentric theory, 150, 191, 193

heresies, 209, 222
Hermeticism
  in 16th century, 127, 136, 155–
    157, 159–160
  in Copernicus, 191–192
  echoes of in recent times, 165
Hippocrates, and ancient science,
  125, 160
Hobbes, Thomas, 158
Hobhouse, Leonard, on moral evolution, 19
holy, 29, 70, 144
Holy Spirit, 116, 216
Homeric culture, 107–108
honor, 105, 108, 125, 138
Horton, Robin, 39–40, 68–69
  responds to critics, 239n43
Hui Shih, 26, 106
Hultkrantz, Äka, on the sacred, 63
Hume, David, 86, 162–163, 211
human universals, 7–8, 13, 190–
  191
hunter-gatherer. *See* primitive culture
Hussey, Edward, on ancient
  thought, 125, 127
Hutchins, Edwin, on preliterate
  thought, 38, 79
Hyman, Ray, on current ESP beliefs,
  280n5

idealism, in formal operational
  thought, 111, 120, 171
identity. *See* honor; individuality
ideology, and formal operational
  thought, 85–87
ignorance, 124, 130, 135, 211
imagination
  and credulity, 201–202
  imaginal thought, 179
  and pre-operational thought, 20,
    31
  in primitive culture, 74
indeterminacy, in quantum physics,
  174, 217
individualism
  in ancient Egypt, 91
  in axial age China, 105
  in axial age Greece, 108, 110
  in axial age India, 100–101
  late medieval renewal of,
    140–141
  in science, 198
Indo-Aryan culture, 79, 81, 90, 97,
  260n9
inference, 99, 100, 121, 202

inner feelings, 50, 214
instruments, in science, 162, 194
intellectualist, interpretations of religion, 73–75
intelligence, common human, 8–10, 17, 26, 33, 45, 96
intelligibility of universe, 113–116, 124, 144, 174
   early Christian views of, 130
   lack of evidence for, 120–121
   and miracles, 114, 115, 132, 163
   science's faith in? 199
intrasystematic, criteria of truth, 224
intuition, 12, 171, 180, 215
Io, Maori high god? 67
Isidore of Seville, 136
Irenaeus, 130
Iroquois, Christopher Vecsey on, 38
irrationality, 114, 205
Islam, 34, 46, 68, 112, 204
Islamic medieval philosophy, 139, 143, 205
Isvarakrshna, of samkhya school, 99, 105

Jahoda, Gustav, on Hallpike, 80, 83
Jaspers, Karl, 25, 93
Jayarasi, of carvaka school, 100
Jaynes, Julian, 97, on bicameral mind, 259n62
Jesus, 202, 215, 217, 228, 230
John of Salisbury, 142–143
jinns, in Arabic tradition, 46
Justin Martyr, and prophecies, 128

kami, Japanese spirits, 70
Kant, 177, 196–197, 212
   and constructivism, 196–197
Karma, 46, 96–97, 99–101, 116
Karmiloff-Smith, Annette, 44
Kegan, Robert, on cognition, 19
Kepler, Johannes, 192, 193
Khomeini, Ayatollah, 209
Kirsch, A. Thomas, on cultural evolution, 4
Kitchener, Karen, 20, 48, 95, 100, 224
Kohlberg, Lawrence, 19, 108
Kpelle, of Liberia, 71
Kuhn, Thomas, 87, 177, 188
   on values in science, 195
   overlooks evidence, 191–195
   evaluated, 290n50
Kwoth, as high god? 69

Labov, W, 88
Lafitau, Fr. Joseph, on high gods, 247n14
Lamarck, as mechanist, 283n53
language-game, religion as, 222–224
Language, first appearance of 238–239n37
LaPlace, Pierre, 118, 163, 214
late formal operational thought
   described, 22–23
   in empirical-critical culture, 27–28
   as postformal thought, 285n1
   as reflexive thought, 30
   in science, 175–177
   similar to ancient skepticism, 123
Lavoisier, Antoine, 163, 167, 173
law, early medieval, 268n33
laws of nature
   in deism, 161
   in early medieval thought, 137
   Epicurean view, 117
   in fundamentalism, 217
   in Hermeticism, 156
   and intelligibility, 115
   in liberal theology, 216
   in models of the universe, 154
   and nominalism, 147
   See also intelligibility; miracles
LePan, Donald, on medieval renewal, 16
Leukippus, 108, 109, 116
Levi-Strauss, Claude, 38–39
Levy-Bruhl, Lucien, 65–68, 78
liberal theology, 29, 215–217, 224, 227, 228
Lienhardt, Douglas, on supernatural, 63
Lincoln, Bruce, on the Dinka, 62
Lindbeck, George, 12, 223–225
   postliberal theology, 293n21
linguistic stage of culture, 12, 23, 80, 81, 84, 179
literacy
   autonomous model of, 85
   effects of, 81–85
   great divide, theory of, 85–89
   origins of, 80–81, 255n13
literate-mythical mode of thought, 30
Lloyd, Geoffrey, 125–126, 259n1
logic
   absence among primitives, 71, 90
   alternative logic, 38

in axial age, 22, 99–100, 106
challenges tradition, 96
and coherence of universe,
114–115
in current culture, 31–32
and empirical testing, 185
and fit with evidence, 182, 196
formalized, 10, 26, 81, vs. informal, 95
and late formal operational
thought, 176
in late medieval thought, 143, 148
as method in religious thought,
205, 207, 224–225
Logicians, in China, 102, 106
Logos, 27, 93, 110, 113, 117–121
Lonergan, Bernard, 4, 21, 23, 71,
95, 124, 198
and intellectual conversion, 198
Lord, Albert, on epics, 90, 140
Lovejoy, Arthur, and the great
chain of being, 136
loyalty, as social and moral standard, 51, 140, 204
Lucretius, 23, 105, on evolution of
culture, 238n32
Luhmann, Niklas, on cultural evolution, 4
Lukes, Stephen, on religion as cognitive, 250n54
Luria, Alexander, on cognition and
culture, 4, 5, 71, 107

machines, organisms as, 158, 163
macrocosmic-microcosmic connection, 153–154, 156
Macy, Gary, on medieval theology,
144
magi or magus, 128, 155–156, 157
magic
Christian belief in, 128
in current society, 30–31
natural magic, 119–120
and pre-operational thought, 20–
21, 73
See also Hermeticism; Neoplatonism
magnetism, 156, 158–160, 164
Mahabharata, Hindu epic, 90
Maimonides, Moses, on miracles,
277n89
Malcolm, Norman, religion as noncognitive, 250n58
Malebranche, 86, 166
Malinowski, Bronislaw, 38

Malpighi, Marcello, on fertility, 166
Maori, of New Zealand, 60
Martin, Luther, on ancient syncretism, 268n31
Martin, Henri-Jean, on Gregory of
Tours, 273n17
materialism
in ancient India, 100
dynamic vs. inert, 159, 164, 165,
168
early modern, 154, 158
Epicurean, 110, 116–118
Stoic, 117–118
mathematics, medieval, 275n52
Mayr, Ernst, on evolution, 168
Mbuti, pygmies, 64
McLachlin, H., on Newton's theology, 282n25
McNeill, William, on plagues,
269n44, 271n67
meaninglessness, threat of, 227
mechanistic philosophy, 157–161,
163–165, 168, 170
medicine, 94, 136, 155, 184
Mekranoti, of Amazon, 20
Meno, 110, 118
Mesopotamia, and early science, 25,
79, 81, 84
metacognition, 20, 22, 56, 95, 100
Metalogicon, of John of Salisbury,
142
metaphysics
and existential questions, 227,
229
imputed to primitive thought, 38
and religious beliefs, 212–214,
220–221
See also axial age thought
method, scientific, and values, 195,
197–198. See also Aristotle, carvaka, Epicurus, Mohism, Logicians, Lonergan
Middleton, John, 61, on Lugbara
high god, 248n18
Minucius, Felix, 129, 211
miracles
in Augustine, 133–136
and current religious thought,
214–218
and deism, 161–163
and demons, 134–135, 211
and God's power, 278n95
and intelligibility of the universe,
132
at Lourdes, 293n15

vs. high gods. *See also* gods
material spirits, 158–160
in primitive thought, 59, 65, 80, 96
See also animism, vitalism
spiritualism, 118, 171
Stenmark, Mikael, on rational standards in religion, 291n3
Stevenson, Harold, on primitive culture, 56
Stiefel, Tiina, on 12th Century Thought, 276n71
Street, Brian, 85–89
sui generis, the sacred as, 215, 222
Sumerians and Writing, 5, 80–81
summae, theologiae, 143
supernatural. *See* power, God's; miracles
superstition, 24, 28, 74
supra–systematic, criteria of truth, 224, 225, 231
Swanson, Guy, on religious evolution, 61
systematic thought
in Aristotle, 119
in axial age, 95, 108
in current culture, 30–33
in current theology, 205–206
formal operational thought as, 22–23
hard to sustain, 39, 139
late formal operational thought as, 176–177
medieval renewal of, 142–143, 148

Talbot, Amaury, on Niger delta tribes, 61
Taoism, 102–105, 116
Tao Te Ching, 5, 27, 99, 104
Tauade, and Hallpike, 72–73
Teilhard de Chardin, Pierre, 219
testing in science, open–ended, 182–187, 197–198
theism. *See* monotheism
theology
axial age origins of, 25, 94
correlational theologies, 227–230
as formal operational thought, 205–206
modern theologies, 213–219
natural theology, 211–212
theoretical thought among pre-literate people? 39
Thomas, Nicholas, on cultural evolution, 242n11

Thrower, James, on Yin Yang school, 105
Tierra del Fuegans, and high god, 67
Tillich and correlational theory, 70, 116, 227–229
Topping, Donald, and Pacific island schooling, 84
tradition
as authority in religion, 203–204
and postliberal thought, 223
in primitive and archaic cultures, 24–25
challenged, 26–27, 82, 95–96, 224–225
at end of antiquity, 124
truth
classical criteria of, 95–96
in China, 105–106, Greece, 109–110, India, 99–100
functional equivalence of, 177–178, 183–184, 199
as only local? 198, 226
standards of truthfulness, 231
truth-seeking vs. relativism, 13
Turgot, Anne R. J., and cultural evolution, 23
Turnbull, Colin, on Mbuti pygmies, 64
Tylor, Edward, early anthropologist, 64–67

UFO, 11, 20, 31, 186
Ullmann, Walter, on medieval law, 138
ultimate reality
and metaphysical questions, 212–213, 220–221
in classical thought, 94. *See also* axial age thought
universalism, 16, 103
classical universalism, 94
and intelligibility, 181–182
unitary, in science, 180–182, 184, 197, 220
universe, models of, 153–155, 157–161
Upanishads, 10, 98–99, 101, 102, 111, 113

values
as criteria of progress, 10–11
in science, 195–198
See also morality
Vedas, 10, 82, 97–98, 100, 111–112
verifiability, 123

DATE DUE

GAYLORD No. 2333   PRINTED IN U.S.A.